D0843211

DATE DUE

FEB 2 6 2000	

1898

Prelude To A Century

1898

Prelude To
A Century

John A. Corry

Published in 1998 by
John A. Corry
450 Lexington Avenue,
New York, NY 10017

THE TEXT OF THIS EDITION
WAS SET IN MONOTYPE WALBAUM
WITH CLOISTER OPEN FACE
FOR DISPLAY.
PRINTED ON MOHAWK OPAQUE PAPER
BY THE STUDLEY PRESS,
DALTON, MASSACHUSETTS.
BOUND IN KENNET CLOTH
BY NEW HAMPSHIRE BINDERY

Distributed to the trade by
Fordham University Press
2546 Belmont Avenue
Bronx, NY 10458

ISBN: 0-9661570-0-1

Design and Production by
Charles Davey *design*
165 West 95th Street, B-N
New York, NY 10025

To Emily

Contents

Illustrations

President William McKinley
(Courtesy of the Corbis-Bettman Archives)
facing page 20

Sir Robert Cecil, Marquess of Salisbury
(Courtesy of the New York Public Library)
facing page 35

The Sudan and the Upper Nile (map)
facing page 46

Marchand's Trek Across Africa (map)
following page 46

Captain Jean-Baptiste Marchand
facing page 50

Emile Zola
(Courtesy of the Corbis-Bettman Archives)
facing page 62

Dropping The Pilot
(Courtesy of the New York Public Library)
facing page 77

Admiral George Dewey on the *Olympia*
(Courtesy of the Corbis-Bettman Archives)
facing page 118

The Western Pacific and Manila Bay (maps)
facing page 124

The Right Honourable Joseph Chamberlain, M.P.
(Courtesy of the Corbis-Bettman Archives)
facing page 134

Admiral Pascual Cervera Topete
(Courtesy of the New York Public Library)
facing page 164

Preface

I n history, the calendar year is an artificial construct. Events move at their own pace, uninfluenced by yearly beginnings and endings. Once in a while, however, a year delineates a series of important events, some crucial in their own right and others for their effect on the future. Thus, Bernard De Voto's 1942 classic *The Year of Decision: 1846* was aptly named, for, as its preface states, it was a story of "the Far West at the moment it became nationally important."

1846 was the year in which the United States became a transcontinental nation. In 1898 it became a world power and positioned itself so that the twentieth century became to many "The American Century."

This was not the only way that 1898 set the course for the century that is now closing. It marked the denouement of the long-standing colonial rivalry between England and France, which in a short time permitted these two long-term adversaries to join in an entente that vitally affected world affairs during the first part of the twentieth century. The year also saw the first flowering of what became the "special relationship" between Britain and the United States that so strongly influenced the history of the next hundred years. At the same time, in 1898, Germany's indifference to England's initiative to develop closer relations, together with the former's first step to become a major naval power, were major influences in creating the antagonism that brought the two countries to war sixteen years later. Finally, the turmoil created by France's "l'Affaire Dreyfus" gave evidence of the strong anti-Semitism in supposedly enlightened Western Europe that foreshadowed the Holocaust.

If any year set the stage for the twentieth century, it was 1898.

Dramatis Personae

ABDULLAHI. Dervish leader and Khalifa of the Sudan.

ADAMS, HENRY. American historian. Great-grandson of President John Adams and grandson of President John Quincy Adams.

AGUINALDO, EMILIO. Filipino revolutionary leader.

ALGER, RUSSELL A. United States Secretary of War.

BALFOUR, ARTHUR JAMES. Leader of the House of Commons. Nephew of Lord Salisbury (qv).

BERMEJO, SEGISMUNDO. Spanish Minister of Marine.

BARATIER, LIEUTENANT ALBERT ERNEST. Second in command under Captain Jean-Baptiste Marchand (qv) of the expedition to seize the headwaters of the White Nile for France.

BEVERIDGE, ALBERT J. American politician and spokesman for imperialism.

BILLOT, GENERAL JEAN-BAPTISTE. French Minister of War.

BLACK, FRANK S. Governor of New York State.

BLANCO, GENERAL RAMÓN. Commander of Spanish forces in Cuba.

BLUM, LÉON. French Socialist leader.

BOISDEFFRE, GENERAL RAOUL DE. French Army Chief of Staff.

BONCHAMPS, MARQUIS CHRISTIAN DE Leader of the unsuccessful 1897 French effort to reach the Nile from Ethiopia.

BRISSON, HENRI. French politician and Premier, succeeding Jules Méline (qv).

BRYAN, WILLIAM JENNINGS. Unsuccessful 1896 Democratic Presidential candidate.

BÜLOW, BERNHARD VON. German Foreign Minister.

CÁMARA, ADMIRAL MANUEL DE LA. Commander of the Spanish naval force sent to reconquer the Philippine Islands in Spanish-American War.

CAMBON, JULES. French Ambassador to the United States.

CAMBON, PAUL. Older brother of Jules Cambon. French Ambassador to Great Britain, succeeding Baron de Courcel (qv).

CARNEGIE, ANDREW. American industrialist and anti-imperialist.

CAVAIGNAC, GODEFROY. French Minister of War succeeding Jean-Baptiste Billot (qv).

CERVERA Y TOPETE, ADMIRAL PASCUAL. Commander of squadron sent to defend Spanish Caribbean colonies in Spanish-American War.

CHAPMAN, JOHN JAY. Leader of New York State Independent Party.

CHANOINE, GENERAL CHARLES. French Minister of War, succeeding General Emile Zurlinden(qv).

CHICHESTER, CAPTAIN EDWARD. Commander of British squadron in Manila Bay.

CHURCHILL, LADY RANDOLPH.

Widow of British politician Lord Randolph Churchill. Mother of Winston Churchill and active in furthering his career.

CHURCHILL, WINSTON SPENCER. Twenty-four-year-old British army lieutenant, writer, and would-be politician.

CLEMENCEAU, GEORGES. French Radical Party politician and journalist.

COURCEL, BARON DE. French Ambassador to Great Britain.

CROKER, RICHARD. Democratic politician and head of New York's Tammany Hall.

CROMER, EVELYN BARING, LORD. British Consul General and administrator in Egypt.

DAY, WILLIAM RUFUS. Assistant United States Secretary of State and later Secretary of State following the resignation of John Sherman (qv).

DELCASSÉ, THEOPHILE. French Foreign Minister, succeeding Gabriel Hanotaux (qv).

DEWEY, GEORGE, COMMODORE AND LATER ADMIRAL. Commander of United States Asiatic Squadron.

DIEDRICHS, ADMIRAL OTTO VON. Commander of German Asiatic Squadron.

DREYFUS, ALFRED. French Army captain imprisoned on Devil's Island following conviction of treason.

DREYFUS, LUCIE. Wife of Alfred Dreyfus.

DREYFUS, MATHIEU. Brother of Alfred Dreyfus.

DU PATY DE CLAM, MAJOR MERCIER. French army officer involved in the intrigues against Captain Dreyfus.

DUPUY, CHARLES. French politician and Premier, succeeding Henri Brisson (qv).

DUPUY DE LÔME, ENRIQUE. Spanish Ambassador to the United States.

ECKARDSTEIN, BARON HERMANN VON. German diplomat serving in London.

ELIZABETH, EMPRESS OF AUSTRIA. Wife of Emperor Franz Joseph (qv).

ESTERHAZY, MAJOR FERDINAND WALSIN. French army officer involved in the sale of military documents to Germany for which Alfred Dreyfus (qv) was convicted.

FAURE, FÉLIX. President of France.

FRANZ JOSEPH, Emperor of Austria.

GONSE, GENERAL CHARLES ARTHUR. Deputy French Army Chief of Staff.

GORDON, GENERAL CHARLES "CHINESE." British officer defeated and killed at Khartoum in 1885.

GREY, SIR EDWARD. Foreign policy spokesman for British Liberal Party.

GULLÓN, PIO. Spanish Foreign Minister.

HANNA, MARCUS ALONZO "MARK." Ohio industrialist and Senator. Close friend and advisor of President William McKinley (qv).

HANOTAUX, GABRIEL. French Foreign Minister.

HATZFELDT, COUNT PAUL VON. German Ambassador to Great Britain.

HAY, JOHN. United States Ambassador to Great Britain. Succeeded William Rufus Day (qv) as Secretary of State.

HEARST, WILLIAM RANDOLPH. American newspaper publisher.

HENRY, LIEUTENANT COLONEL HUBERT. French counterintelligence officer and document forger.

HICKS-BEACH, SIR MICHAEL. British Chancellor of the Exchequer.

HOAR, GEORGE F. Republican Senator from Massachusetts.

HOBSON, RICHMOND P. American naval officer.

HOHENLOHE, PRINCE CHLODWIG ZU. German Chancellor.

HOLLEBEN, THEODOR VON. German Ambassador to the United States.

HOLSTEIN, FRIEDRICH VON. First Consular of the German Foreign Ministry.

JAURÈS, JEAN. French Socialist leader.

KIPLING, RUDYARD. English writer and apostle of imperialism.

KITCHENER, HERBERT HORATIO. British general and commander-in-chief, or Sirdar, of Anglo-Egyptian army in the Sudan.

LABORI, FERNAND. French Dreyfusard lawyer.

LASCELLES, SIR FRANK. British Ambassador to Germany.

LAWTON, HENRY W. American general active in the Cuban campaign.

LEE, FITZHUGH. United States Consul General at Havana, Cuba.

LINARES, GENERAL ARSENIO. Commander of Spanish troops at Santiago de Cuba.

LODGE, HENRY CABOT. Republican Senator from Massachusetts and close friend of Theodore Roosevelt (qv).

LONG, JOHN D. United States Secretary of the Navy.

MAHAN, ADMIRAL ALFRED THAYER. American naval officer and historian.

MARCHAND, CAPTAIN JEAN-BAPTISTE. French army officer and commander of expedition to seize the headwaters of the White Nile for France.

MARIA CRISTINA. Queen Regent of Spain.

McKINLEY, WILLIAM. President of the United States.

MÉLINE, JULES. French Premier.

MENILEK II. Emperor of Ethiopia.

MERCIER, GENERAL AUGUSTE. Former French Minister of War and important figure in Dreyfus Affair.

MERRITT, GENERAL WESLEY A.. Commander of United States expedition to the Philippines.

MILES, GENERAL NELSON A. Commanding officer of United States Army.

MONSON, SIR EDMUND. British Ambassador to France.

MUN, COUNT ALBERT DE. Anti-Dreyfusard French political leader.

MURAVIÈV, COUNT MIKHAIL. Russian Foreign Minister.

NICHOLAS II. Tsar of Russia.

ODELL, BENJAMIN B. New York Republican Party State Chairman.

O'CONOR, SIR NICOLAS. British Ambassador to Russia.

PAUNCEFOTE, SIR JULIAN. British Ambassador to the United States.

PAYN, LOUIS F. New York State Superintendent of Insurance.

PELLIEUX, GENERAL GEORGES DE. French army officer involved in Dreyfus Affair.

PLATT, ORVILLE H. Republican Senator from Connecticut.

PLATT, THOMAS COLLIER. New York Senator and Republican Party "boss."

PICQUART, LIEUTENANT COLONEL GEORGES. French army officer who played important role in defense of Dreyfus.

POLO DE BERNABE, LUIS. Spanish Ambassador to the United States, succeeding Enrique Dupuy de Lôme (qv).

PROCTOR, REDFIELD. Republican Senator from Vermont.

QUIGG, LEMUEL ELY. New York City Republican Party Chairman.

REED, THOMAS B. Republican Congressman from Maine and Speaker of the House of Representatives.

REID, WHITELAW. American journalist and diplomat.

ROOSEVELT, THEODORE. Assistant Secretary of the Navy, lieutenant colonel and colonel of the Rough Riders, and successful Republican candidate for Governor of New York.

ROOT, ELIHU. Prominent New York lawyer.

ROSEBERY, ARCHIBALD PHILIP, 5TH EARL OF. Former British Prime Minister and leader of the Liberal Party.

SAGASTA, PRÁCEDAS MATEO. Spanish Prime Minister.

SALISBURY, ROBERT ALBERT TALBOT GASCOYNE-CECIL, 3RD MARQUESS OF. British Prime Minister and Foreign Secretary.

SAMPSON, REAR ADMIRAL WILLIAM T. Commander of United States North Atlantic Squadron.

SCHEURER-KESTNER, CHARLES AUGUSTE. French Senator and early Dreyfus supporter.

SCHLEY, COMMODORE WINFIELD SCOTT. Commander of United States Flying Squadron.

SCHWARZKOPPEN, COLONEL MAXIMILIEN VON. German military officer in France.

SHAFTER, GENERAL WILLIAM R. Commander of United States Cuban expeditionary force.

SHERMAN, JOHN. United States Secretary of State.

SIGSBEE, CAPTAIN CHARLES D. Commanding officer of U.S.S. *Maine*.

SPRING-RICE, CECIL ARTHUR. British diplomat and friend of John Hay and Theodore Roosevelt (qv).

TELLER, HENRY M. Democratic Senator from Colorado.

TIRPITZ, ADMIRAL ALFRED VON. German Naval Minister.

VAN WYCK, AUGUSTUS. New York judge and unsuccessful Democratic candidate for Governor of New York.

VICTORIA. Queen of the United Kingdom of Great Britain and Ireland and Empress of India.

WALES, Albert Edward, Prince of. (Later Edward VII of Great Britain).

WEYLER Y NICOLAU, GENERAL VALERIANO. Former commander of Spanish forces in Cuba.

WHEELER, JOSEPH. Democratic Congressman from Alabama and American general active in the Cuban campaign.

WHITE, ANDREW D. United States Ambassador to Germany.

WILLIAM II. Kaiser of Germany.

WILLIAMS, OSCAR F. United States Consul General at Manila, Philippine Islands.

WITTE, COUNT SERGEI. Russian Finance Minister.

WOOD, COLONEL LEONARD. Commanding officer of the Rough Riders.

WOODFORD, STEWART L. United States Ambassador to Spain.

ZOLA, EMILE. French novelist and Dreyfus supporter.

ZURLINDEN, GENERAL EMILE. French Minister of War, succeeding Godefroy Cavaignac (qv).

ONE

"This Means War"

In 1898, as the new century approached, the United States stood at a major crossroads. The American West had been "won." As the scholar Frederick Jackson Turner had observed five years earlier in his seminal address at the 1893 Chicago Worlds Fair, *The Significance of the Frontier in American History*, the United States had reached the limits of its continental expansion. The obvious but unanswered question was whether, in an imperialistic age, the country's frontiers should be extended beyond its shores.

With the Civil War more than thirty years past, the sense of the United States as a single nation had grown. Furthering this, the Chicago Fair awakened a sense of national pride in its many visitors. Henry Adams, not easily overawed, later wrote, "Chicago was the first expression of American thought as a unity."[1] There was no reason why such a country could not become a world power like any major European state.[2]

To most of its business and financial leaders, however, the nation's major concerns were domestic. The economy was still recovering from the 1893 depression, and the primary goal of the less than one year old McKinley Administration was to encourage business expansion and not rock the boat. In 1896 the voters had rejected the "free silver" populism of Democratic candidate William Jennings Bryan. The next year, responding to the industrial and financial interests that had made possible his election, the new President had pushed through Congress the high tariff legislation that was their major goal and was taking steps to establish a single gold standard.[3] With increased business confidence, the economy was prospering.

William McKinley was the third of the Ohio dynasty that produced five Republican presidents between 1876 and 1923.[4] Born in the northeastern part of the state, he had distinguished himself in Civil War fighting at Antietam and in the Shenandoah Valley. Mustered out as a brevet major, he returned to Canton, Ohio, where he became a lawyer.[5] In 1876, when his commanding officer, Rutherford B. Hayes, was elected President, he ran successfully for the House of Representatives. Except for one term he remained there until 1890, when he was defeated largely because of the high tariff legislation that bore his name. His political career quickly recovered, and he was elected Governor of Ohio, where he twice served two-year terms. Then, with the aid of Ohio industrialist Mark Hanna's highly effective organizing skill, he gained the 1896 Republican presidential nomination. That fall, after a bitterly contested campaign, he won a close but nevertheless clear mandate to take over the White House from retiring Democrat Grover Cleveland. McKinley's role in the 1896 campaign had been largely passive, spent on his "front porch" where he was visited daily by large and enthusiastic delegations. Theodore Roosevelt commented later that Hanna had "marketed McKinley as if he were a patent medicine." But, together with the effective anti-Bryan "scare campaign," it had worked, and McKinley went to the White House.

The President was affable and outgoing. He made friends easily, mostly with politicians and businessmen, foremost among whom was Hanna. In appearance McKinley was impressive—handsome with a large massive head. He was deeply religious, and viewed from today's perspective could be described as priggish. But in the late Victorian era in which he lived, such a habit as refusing to be pictured with an otherwise habitual cigar so as not to set a "bad example" to young men was deemed commendable.[6]

However McKinley was far from forceful when it came to most public matters. Although Mark Hanna referred to his tact as "that never failing remedy of yours"[7], others were less kind. They regarded him as essentially pliant and excessively influenced by the opinion of the moment.[8] A mid-twentieth century historian called him "a kindly soul in a spineless body".[9]

The new President had little experience in foreign policy and national security matters. His cabinet was hardly better in that regard. Secretary of State John Sherman was a renowned statesman who, to put it kindly, had seen better days. A founder in the 1850s of the Ohio Republican Party and Secretary of the Treasury from 1877 to 1881, he was best known to history as sponsor of the Sherman Anti-Trust Act. Although he sat for ten years on the Senate Foreign Relations Committee, he had shown little interest in foreign policy. He had been appointed Secretary of State primarily to provide a Senate vacancy that could be filled by fellow Ohioan Mark Hanna.[10] Seen largely as an impressive figurehead, by year end 1897 he was showing progressive enfeeblement and loss of memory.[11]

If anyone was running the State Department it was Assistant Secretary

William Rufus Day. Forty-eight years old, a Canton neighbor of the President, his only prior government service had been as a federal district
judge. But to his old friend McKinley, who relied heavily on him, he had a
"genius for common sense."[12] Unassuming and retiring, he was McKinley's real foreign policy advisor.

At least Secretary of War Russell A. Alger had had military experience—more than thirty years earlier in the Civil War, where he rose from
the ranks to leave as a brevet major general. His service record, plus political skills, had made him at different times a one-term governor of
Michigan and head of the Grand Army of the Republic, a Civil War veterans' organization that was a powerful force in the Republican Party. A
former lumber magnate, he was "smooth as silk"[13] and, as described by a
subordinate, was "the most egotistical man with whom I have ever come
into contact."[14]

Secretary of the Navy John D. Long had been a popular three-term
governor of Massachusetts in the early 1880s and then had served with
McKinley in the House of Representatives. Fifty-eight years old, he was
in poor health—or, as a hypochondriac, thought that he was.[15] A kindly
and lovable person,[16] he fancied himself a poet, having written such
books as *At the Fireside* and *Bites of a Cherry*.[17] Indolent by nature, he
had no prior experience in naval matters.

Thus, when Assistant Secretary Day expressed agreement with "the
newspaper talk about the diplomacy of this administration as 'amateur-
ish,'"[18] he could have said the same of the background of the civilians
who would direct any war efforts the United States might have to conduct. An exception, at least in his own eyes, was Assistant Secretary of the
Navy Theodore Roosevelt. Thirty-nine years old, a New York patrician
who had hardened himself in the Dakotas in the 1880s, he had run
unsuccessfully for mayor of New York and was a member from 1893 to
1895 of the United States Civil Service Commission. Later, as president of
the New York City Police Board, his policies antagonized many politicians, including the powerful New York Republican boss Thomas Collier
Platt.

Roosevelt had been interested in naval matters ever since, at the preco-
cious age of twenty-two, he had written *The Naval War of 1812*, which at
once became a definitive work on the subject.[19] In 1890, when the naval
officer and historian Alfred Thayer Mahan wrote his seminal work *The
Influence of Sea Power in History*, Roosevelt wrote an admiring *Atlantic
Monthly* review.[20] He had worked hard for McKinley's election, and des-
perately sought the assistant secretaryship.[21] McKinley initially had

resisted the supportive efforts of Roosevelt's close friend Henry Cabot Lodge and others, saying to the wife of an old Ohio colleague:

"I want peace and I am told that your friend Theodore—whom I know only slightly—is always getting into rows with everybody. I'm afraid he is too pugnacious."[22]

However the President eventually relented, partly because Secretary Long welcomed an assistant who would brave the heat of a Washington summer while the Secretary could take refuge at his Massachusetts home. Also, Boss Platt and his aides decided that their nemesis would be less troublesome to them in Washington than in New York.

McKinley's suspicions were well founded. Roosevelt was a member of a circle of influential Washingtonians that included Lodge, John Hay, whom McKinley named Ambassador to Great Britain, and Henry and Brooks Adams, whose ancestors included Presidents John and John Quincy Adams. They strongly believed that America should take its place in the ranks of the major world powers, Lodge more than the others except for Roosevelt, who was the most chauvinistic of them all.[23] In Roosevelt's first public address as Assistant Secretary, before the Naval War College at Newport, Rhode Island on June 2, 1897, he used as his theme "To be prepared for war is the most effective means to promote peace." However, his speech, which used the word "war" sixty-two times, seemed to go further:

"No triumph of peace is quite so great as the triumphs of war... It may be that at some time in the dim future of the race the need for war will vanish, but that time is yet ages distant. As yet no nation can hold its place in the world, or can do any work worth doing, unless it stands ready to guard its rights with armed hand."[24]

Then, in a peroration that reminded a later-day biographer of Winston Churchill's 1940 "blood, sweat and tears," he proclaimed that:

"there are other things in life than the soft and easy enjoyment of material comfort. It is through strife, or the readiness for strife, that a nation must win greatness. We ask for a great navy partly because we feel that no national life is worth living if the nation is not willing, when the need shall arise, to stake everything on the supreme arbitrament of war, and to pour out of its blood, its treasure and its taxes like water, rather than submit to the loss of honor and renown."[25]

President William McKinley

Roosevelt's speech was widely printed, and won him nationwide praise. As a person, he made an equally overwhelming impression. After their first brief encounter, the young Kansas journalist William Allen White "was afire with the splendor of the personality I had met." Describing their luncheon the next day, White wrote many years later:

"...he poured into my heart such visions, such ideas, such hopes, such a new attitude toward life and patriotism and the meaning of things, as I never dreamed men had. . . . So strong was the young Roosevelt—hard muscled, hard voiced even when the voice cracked in falsetto, with hard wriggling jaw muscles, and snapping teeth, even when he cackled in raucous glee, so completely did the personality of the man overcome me that I made no protest and accepted his dictum as my creed."[26]

To Roosevelt and his fellow believers the testing time was at hand. In nearby Cuba an insurrection had expanded into a revolutionary war with Spain. The "Pearl of the Antilles" had been discovered by Columbus during his first voyage in 1492. Its capital, Havana, possessed one of the world's finest ports, and its crops of tobacco and, later, sugar made it Spain's wealthiest colony. Except for a year's interval during the Seven Years War in the mid-eighteenth century, it had remained under Spanish rule.

From the earliest days of the American Republic, its northern neighbor had recognized Cuba's strategic importance to the Caribbean and the Gulf of Mexico. In 1848 President Polk offered to purchase the island but was abruptly rebuffed. Twenty years later an insurrection called the "Ten Years War" was largely financed from private sources in the United States. In 1873 a Spanish ship captured an American blockade runner, and more than fifty of her crew, mostly United States citizens, were summarily sentenced to death and executed. The not surprising United States reaction was a spontaneous public outcry and, when the Spanish government initially rejected the Grant Administration's demand for an apology, the threat of war was real. Wisely, after a few days Madrid backed down. The revolution ended in 1878, with a limited grant of the rebels' demands for abolition of slavery and representation in the Spanish Cortes, but no independence.

Affairs remained in this state until 1895, when a new revolt broke out under the leadership of the eloquent poet Jose Marti and a seventy-two-year-old professional soldier, Maximo Gomez. The revolution was largely initiated by Cuban emigres living in the United States, and it is possible that the island could have worked out its own destiny under Spanish rule were it not for this outside incitement.[27] Be that as it may, the initial Spanish efforts to defeat the insurgents failed and Gomez led his forces west across Cuba, burning the most profitable sugar plantations on the island.*

Madrid's response was to send as a new governor general the ruthless General Valeriano Weyler, an admirer of U.S. Civil War General William Tecumseh Sherman, known for his destructive march through Georgia. In October 1896, Weyler commenced a program of "reconcentration" of peasants into fortified towns.[28] There they could no longer feed and shelter the rebels and could themselves be held as hostages. Food supplies in the towns were inadequate, and during the next twenty-four months between 200,000 and 400,000 Cubans reportedly died from disease and starvation.[29]

When these conditions were reported in the United States, sympathy for the rebels turned into indignation. The rebels seized the opportunity to lobby the administration of President Grover Cleveland and Congress for recognition of their belligerency, which would publicly identify them as something more than outlaws. On April 6, 1896, Congress passed a resolution to that effect, but Cleveland and his advisors refused to act on it. As a less extreme alternative, Secretary of State Richard Olney proposed mediation, but Madrid rejected that proposal. Outgoing President Cleveland's last message to Congress in December 1896 warned of "a limit to our patient waiting for Spain to end the conflict."[30]

Thus, as William McKinley took office in March, 1897, the war continued and the suffering in the "reconcentrados" worsened even further. The "yellow press," with William Randolph Heart's New York *Journal* in the lead, lost no opportunity to dramatize the war in all its lurid details. Much of what the press reported was overdrawn, and some of it was untrue, but the public and the politicians generally accepted it without question.[31] The *Journal* sent the renowned correspondent Richard Harding Davis to Cuba, where he movingly described the destruction of the countryside and the firing squad execution of at least one insurgent. Davis was accompanied by artist Frederick Remington to whom, in response to his report that there was nothing worth painting, Hearst reportedly replied, "Please remain. You furnish the picture and I'll furnish the war."[32]

---

* With the Spanish army was twenty-one-year-old Winston Churchill, a second lieutenant in Her Majesty's Fourth Hussars, who was in Cuba not only as an official observer but also under contract to send letters to the British *Daily Graphic* at five guineas each.

Like Cleveland, McKinley wanted to avoid war over Cuba. The goal of his Administration was to further business prosperity—not to embark on a foreign adventure whose end was uncertain. Moreover, McKinley was inherently a peaceful person, who, unlike Roosevelt and most other "hawks," had seen war's horrors at firsthand during his Civil War service. But, as hostilities continued, American patience grew thin.

Nevertheless, Weyler's program seemed to be succeeding. Then, on August 8, 1897, an Italian anarchist assassinated Spanish Prime Minister Canovas. He was replaced by Liberal Práxedas Mateo Sagasta, who with his ministers had previously condemned the "barbarity" and "futility" of his predecessors' policy.[33] This was the altered situation in September, when the new United States Ambassador to Spain, Stewart L. Woodford, presented the Spanish Government with a note asking that before November 1, it provide "such assurances as would satisfy the United States that early and certain peace can be promptly secured..." Otherwise, 'the United States must consider itself free to take such steps as its government should deem necessary to procure that result. . . . .'[34]

On October 6, Madrid indirectly responded by replacing Weyler with the more moderate General Ramón Blanco. Prime Minister Sagasta also announced that on January 1 Cuba would be granted political autonomy. In an October 29 note to the United States, he pledged that Cuba would have full self-government under Spain, excepting only "foreign relations, the army, the navy and the administration of justice."[35] The new Spanish policy included a decree announcing an easing of reconcentration.[36]

Like many compromises, these actions satisfied neither side. They annoyed Spanish hard-liners, and, more significantly, intensified revolutionary feeling in Cuba. They seemed to confirm Spanish weakness and encouraged the rebels in their policy of laying waste the countryside, thus further intensifying food shortages and the resulting death rate.[37] McKinley's annual message to Congress in December urged "a righteous peace," but to objective observers that seemed less possible than before.

Thus, as the new year opened, Roosevelt ordered seven warships, including the new battleship *Iowa*, to participate in the upcoming exercises of the North Atlantic Squadron. It was no accident that these would take place in the Gulf of Mexico. The fleet was the most powerful the United States had assembled since the Civil War.[38]

In January 1898 the future King Alfonso XIII was only thirteen years old, so Spain was ruled by his mother, Maria Cristina, acting as Queen Regent.

A former Austrian archduchess, she was a strong-minded woman who was exerting all her abilities to avoid war with the United States. On January 13, when Ambassador Woodford attended a reception at the palace, she drew him aside for a confidential conversation. Woodford reported to McKinley that once she confirmed that he was the President's personal friend:

"She drew herself up and looked every inch a queen as she said:
'I will crush any conspiracy in Spain. Upon this you may rely. I believe that my government will keep peace in Havana and reduce Army officers to obedience. I want your President to keep America from helping the rebellion until the new plan of autonomy has had a fair chance.'"[39]

Woodford added that if autonomy did not succeed, "the Queen will have to choose between losing her throne or losing Cuba at the risk of war with us."[40]

The general consensus in both the United States and Europe was that, without allies, Spain would lose such a war. The unanswered question was whether any kind of pro-Spanish coalition could be developed, especially among the European monarchies that sympathized with the potentially hapless Spanish Queen. The American Ambassador to Germany, Andrew D. White, believed they could not.[*] On January 7, he reported on the subject of possible European involvement in a United States war with Spain:

"On the Continent there has never been a time, probably, when ill will towards the United States has been so strong as at present. Nevertheless, I do not believe that a coalition will be formed against us. The interests of European nations are so diverse, and in many respects so mutually hostile, that it would be very difficult to organize a coalition of them against us. This is the more true, because feeling is more intense about the questions dividing Europe, than it is about those between America and Europe."[41]

During the first few days of January, the new Spanish autonomy policy toward Cuba seemed to be working successfully. On the morning of

---

[*] White was a respected educator and diplomat who had been the first president of Cornell University.

January 12, however, riots broke out in Havana. The demonstrators apparently were led, or at least actively encouraged, by Spanish army officers who opposed autonomy. Shouting "Long Live Weyler" and "Death to Blanco", the mob concentrated its efforts on the offices of newspapers that had attacked the army.[42]

The United States Consul-General in Havana was Fitzhugh Lee, a Confederate cavalry general in the Civil War and a nephew of Robert E. Lee. Easily excited, as soon as he learned of the disturbances he cabled the State Department:

"Mobs, led by Spanish officers, attacked today the offices of the four newspapers here advocating autonomy. Rioting at this hour, 1 P.M., continues."

That evening, Lee sent off a second dispatch, stating that there was no rioting at present, but that "rumors of it are abundant" and "serious disturbances" could develop.[43] He also sent Captain Charles D. Sigsbee of the *U.S.S. Maine* in Key West, Florida the two-word message "Two Dollars." This was the prearranged code ordering the *Maine* to stand on alert to steam to Havana to protect American lives and property.[44]

The *Maine* was one of the first two modern steel battleships built by the Navy. Although she was less than ten years old, her rating already had been downgraded to a second-class battleship by the addition of four larger and more powerful vessels during the prior two years.[45] She had been detached from the Atlantic Fleet to Key West so as to be closer to Cuba in case of trouble there. Her captain was a fifty-two-year old Civil War veteran with a background in science and engineering and the author of a work on *Deep Sea Sounding and Dredging*.[46]

Lee's fears proved unjustified, as calm returned to Havana. He therefore did not send the anticipated second telegram that would summon the *Maine* to Cuba. She continued to stand by in the event of future trouble, however.

Even more aroused over the Havana riots than the Consul-General was the Assistant Secretary of the Navy. The morning of January 13, as Secretary Long was sitting quietly in his second floor office overlooking the White House, he was interrupted by an excited Roosevelt, who announced that if war came with Spain, he planned "to abandon everything and go to the front." The startled Secretary tried to calm Roosevelt down by joking with him, but to no avail. As Long wrote in his diary, "The funny part of it all is, that he actually takes the thing seriously," and that "By tomorrow he will have got a half dozen heads of bureaus together and have spoiled twenty pages of good writing paper, and lain awake half the night..."[47]

Thus, the Secretary was probably not taken aback by the several thousand word letter that Roosevelt gave him the next day. It argued that the Navy must be in a position "to strike" should there be war with Spain during the next few months and that "the disposition of the fleet on foreign stations should be radically altered, and altered without delay." The letter then detailed a vessel-by-vessel deployment plan that emphasized concentration of scattered units. In closing, Roosevelt warned that "(w)hen the war comes it should come finally on our initiative, and after we had had time to prepare."[48]

Perhaps the letter was what the lethargic Long needed. Shortly thereafter the Navy ordered a small force to Lisbon, where it could observe Spanish waters, and sent the powerful North Atlantic Squadron to join the *Maine* at Key West.[49]

Meanwhile, Roosevelt was making plans for his own future. On January 13 he wrote to a friend who was Adjutant General of New York:

"If there is a war I, of course, intend to go."

and, trying to establish his credentials for a post of major or lieutenant colonel:

"I have served three years as captain in the State Militia (not to speak of having acted as sheriff in the cow country!)."[50]

Since it was unable to justify sending the *Maine* to Havana because of a likely danger to United States lives and property, the McKinley Administration was seeking another excuse for doing so. The ingenious solution, as Secretary Long wrote in his diary the night of January 24, was a visit "...to exchange courtesies and civilities with the Spanish authorities there, and thus to emphasize the change and the improved condition of things which have resulted from the new Spanish policy."[51]

Assistant Secretary Day broached the plan to Spanish Ambassador Dupuy de Lôme earlier in the day in a State Department meeting. When the Ambassador was unable to object to a mission with such ostensibly peaceful purposes, Day and Long met with McKinley, who approved the proposal.[52] Day cabled Ambassador Woodford in Madrid and Consul-

General Lee in Havana that the *Maine* would be sent in "a day or two." Lee, who had not been consulted in advance, immediately urged a week's postponement out of concern that the visit might hamper the autonomy program and even spark demonstrations.[53]

Lee might just as well have kept silent. The United States Government was as uncoordinated in 1898 as it sometimes is today. According to *The New York Times*, the Navy Department had already announced that

"the *Maine* was to go to Havana, not at once, but as soon as she could be made ready to leave Key West and after the announcement of her intended visit could be made at Madrid."[54]

In fact, the *Maine* had been ready to sail since January 13, and left Key West for Havana the afternoon of the 24th. When she steamed under the batteries of the Morro into Havana harbor at eleven the next morning, she was welcomed by the salutes of the forces and the warships in the harbor.[55] The friendly reception was due to the good judgment of those on the scene, since the local authorities had received no instructions from Madrid and Captain Sigsbee's orders did not cover the possibility that the *Maine* might be refused admission. In that event, he would have been faced with the alternatives of trying to force his way into port or returning to Key West with his mission an embarrassing failure.[56] As he spent the day making the appropriate calls on Spanish officials, who were all politeness, an increasingly relieved Consul-General Lee was sending almost hourly messages to the State Department, each ending: "No demonstrations so far."[57]

Official Washington breathed a collective sigh of relief. At the Administration's first diplomatic dinner at the White House on January 26, McKinley asked Ambassador Dupuy to sit at his table. Dupuy was a reactionary diplomat who had been appointed by the previous Canovas ministry. He was strongly opposed to the moderate Cuban policy of the new Sagasta Government and had no use for McKinley. But he knew that by sitting at the presidential table with the ambassadors of Britain, France, and Germany, he had been leapfrogged over nine other diplomats. So when McKinley immediately came up to him, saying, "I see that we have only good news" and that "you have no occasion to be other than satisfied and confident," he was suitably impressed.[58]

In two weeks Dupuy's flattered equanimity would be cruelly shattered. On February 9, Assistant Secretary of State Day had just settled himself in his office when he received an unexpected visit from a legal advisor to the Cuban revolutionaries and a prominent New York lawyer who strongly sympathized with the rebels. They handed Day the original of a letter from Dupuy to the editor of a Madrid newspaper.[59] At about the same time, the Assistant Secretary was shown a copy of that morning's edition of William Randolph Hearst's New York *Journal*, which had just arrived in Washington and carried the blazing headline: "The Worst Insult to the United States in Its History."[60]

The letter was a personal communication to an editor in Madrid. In it the Ambassador commented on McKinley's December 1897 annual message to Congress, and gave vent to his personal animosity toward the President:

"[b]esides the ingrained and inevitable bluntness with which is repeated all that the press and public opinion in Spain has said about Weyler, it shows once more what McKinley is, weak and a popularity hunter, besides being a would-be politician who tries to keep a door open behind him while remaining on good terms with the jingoes of his party."[61]

The Cuban junta had obtained the letter from a Cuban friend of its intended recipient, who had removed it from its envelope before the editor had opened it. Representatives of the junta had also given it to the *Journal*.[62] When Day read the letter, he immediately called on the Ambassador and asked whether he had written it. Dupuy had learned the previous day that the letter was in the hands of the press. Realizing that his usefulness in Washington was at an end, he had cabled his resignation to Madrid before Day's arrival. Therefore, it was unnecessary for the United States to demand his departure.[63]

To the American war party, the letter was not only an insult to the United States and its President, but also tangible evidence of the insincerity of Spanish promises of Cuban reform. McKinley tried to stop the outcry by requesting an official apology. Reluctantly, because the letter was a private one, the Spanish Government on February 14 advised Ambassador Woodford that it "with entire sincerity lamented the incident."[64] That seemingly closed the matter, but it would not be forgotten should another confrontation occur.

Roosevelt had no doubts as to what should be done. At a reception on the night of the ninth, a guest of Senator Mark Hanna who had recently arrived from Paris found herself backing away

"...from the active elbow of a burly gentleman until she was against a wall and could not escape his flailing sleeve. His teeth flashed and his eyeglasses sparkled. He was alarming in the force of his objection to Mr. McKinley's uncertainty."

When Hanna came over to see what was going on, Roosevelt was saying:

"I hope to see the Spanish flag and the English flag gone from the map of North America before I'm sixty."

On the way home after the party, Hanna muttered to his wife and their friend that it was a good thing Roosevelt wasn't in the State Department, for in that event, "We'd be fighting half the world."[65]

In trying to converse with Roosevelt, Hanna's guest reported that she had heard in Paris that France and Germany were likely to object to an American attack on Cuba. On February 9, the Spanish Government asked both German Foreign Secretary Bernhard von Bülow and the German Ambassador to Spain whether Germany would head a group of European monarchies protesting "against American republican encroachments." In reply, Bülow advised Ambassador Radowitz to tell the Spanish that while the Kaiser was a strong supporter of the monarchical principle, republican France could hardly be expected to join a coalition formed on that basis. However, Bülow continued, if France, with her longstanding financial and political ties to Spain, were to take the lead, Germany likely would follow. But the Spanish should "observe proper discretion" since "(A) suggestion of this kind from France would cease to exist as soon as the suspicion was aroused in France that it was in accordance with German wishes and would serve German needs."[66]

Three weeks had elapsed since the *Maine*'s arrival in Havana and Consul-General Lee's fears still had not materialized. There had been no violence, and there were no signs of impending trouble. Instead, the Spanish had provided the Americans with a lavish reception. Lee and Captain Sigsbee favored their "hosts" with attendance at two bullfights.[67]

The evening of February 15 was clear, warm, and humid, a beautiful night in the tropics. At 9:40, Sigsbee had just completed and was sealing a letter to his wife when the calm was shattered by a violent explosion. By the time he had made his way through the suddenly darkened ship to the deck, the *Maine* was listing to port. It was clear that she was rapidly sinking. In fact she already was partially under water.[68]

The explosion shook downtown Havana. It damaged buildings near the harbor and put out all the lights in the city. Initially some observers feared that the palace had blown up, but the cloud of smoke over the spot where the *Maine* had been riding at anchor quickly indicated what had happened. New York *World* correspondent Sylvester Scovel, who was in a boat with Havana's police chief, described the scene:

"The superstructure alone loomed up, partly colored by the red glare of the flames glancing upon the black water. At first it appeared as if her bow was totally demolished. Then the mass of beams and braces was seen that was blown forward by the awful rending."[69]

Boats from nearby ships and the Havana police department were quickly in the water rescuing survivors. The wounded were removed to nearby hospitals. American Red Cross founder and president Clara Barton, still indefatigable at age 76, had arrived in Havana a few days earlier to help supervise a Cuban relief program for American charities. She quickly went to one of the hospitals to lend at least moral support. She later described the wounded men she had seen:

"They had been crushed by timbers, cut by iron, scorched by fire, and blown sometimes high in the air, sometimes driven down through the red hot furnace room and out into the water, senseless, to be picked up by some boat and gotten ashore. Their wounds were all over them—heads and faces terribly cut, internal wounds, arms, legs, feet and hands burned to the live flesh."[70]

Sigsbee remained on the *Maine* until he could be assured that everyone who could be found had been rescued. He was then rowed to the *City of Washington*, a nearby passenger ship to which some of the wounded had been taken. After visiting them, he went to the captain's cabin, where he penned his report of the disaster:

"Secnav, Washington, D.C.

Maine blown up in Havana harbor at nine forty to-night and destroyed. Many wounded and many more killed or drowned. Wounded and others aboard Spanish man-of-war and Ward Line steamer.

Send Light House Tenders from Key West for crew and the few pieces of equipment above water. No one has clothing other than that upon him. Public opinion should be suspended until further report. All officers believed saved, Jenkins and Merritt not yet accounted for. Many Spanish officers, including representatives of General Blanco, now with us to express sympathy." [71]

Sigsbee handed the dispatch to New York *World* correspondent George Bronson Rea, who had come aboard the *City of Washington*, and asked him to send it immediately. [72]

Early the next morning in Washington, Secretary Long's daughter Helen had just returned home from a ball. At two o'clock, still up, she was summoned to the door by an insistent knocking and found a messenger from the Navy Department with an urgent telegram for Long. It was Sigsbee's report. She immediately took it to her father, whose stunned reaction was that "(i)t was almost impossible to believe that it could be true, or that it was not a wild and vivid dream." [73] Clearly, however, the news was real, and Long dispatched a naval officer to the White House to rouse the President. The night watchman who awoke McKinley remembered him pacing the floor, repeating in shocked tones, "The *Maine* blown up! The *Maine* blown up!" [74]

The editors of the morning newspapers had received the news even before the Secretary and the President. When William Randolph Hearst arrived home from the theater, he was handed a message to call his office for important news. When the editor suggested that other stories might also prominently appear on the *Journal's* front page, Hearst sharply replied:

"There is not any other big news. Please spread the story all over the page. This means war." [75]

TWO

Splendid Isolation

In 1898 Europe was at peace, and largely had been since Napoleon's defeat at Waterloo in 1815. The only major wars had been localized in the Crimea, the Balkans, and on the borders of the newly powerful Germany.

Instead of fighting each other, the major powers were devoting their energies to industrial expansion and the gaining of colonial possessions, where they could acquire inexpensive raw materials and sell finished products. The British Empire was the example to which other nations looked with a mixture of admiration and envy. It was only natural that, with varying degrees of success, they would try to emulate England. South America, protected by the Monroe Doctrine, was generally off limits, but Africa, Eastern Asia, and the Western Pacific were all fair game. By 1898, however, the supply of potential overseas possessions was limited, and differing views as to acquisition right and spheres of influence were leading to increasing tensions.

At least two other forces were driving the imperialist urge. With the advent of Darwinism in the mid-nineteenth century, the view developed that survival, and thus acquisition by the "fittest," was a natural law that justified colonialism. The wishes of the inhabitants of these less fortunate lands could be ignored for they were "lesser breeds without the Law."[1] This aggressive doctrine was reinforced by a perceived duty to bring the benefits of western civilization and Christianity to far-flung parts of the globe. As Rudyard Kipling proclaimed in late 1898, it was "the White Man's burden"

> To serve your captives' need;
> To wait in heavy harness
> On fluttered folk and wild;...
> Fill full the mouth of famine
> And bid the sickness cease...[2]

If the century to come was to be "the American century," the imperialistic century that was about to end was "the British century," and the year

32

just ended was probably its apogee. As 1897 closed, England, and indeed the entire British Empire, was coming off an unprecedented "high." The year had marked Queen Victoria's Diamond Jubilee, and her subjects around the world had rejoiced in the sixty-year reign of a monarch who was the symbol of the power and unity of Britain's globe-spanning dominions and colonies. Although probably few of her subjects sensed it, the coming century would be one of steady decline for Britain as a world power.

The old Queen was more than the symbol of the strict morality that later generations associated with the "Victorian Age." Although a constitutional monarch, she kept closely in touch with public affairs, and her ministers paid careful attention to her usually cautious advice. Perhaps because her tastes were somewhat middle class, it was possible for her last Prime Minister, Lord Salisbury, to say, "I always thought that when I knew what the Queen thought, I knew pretty well what her subjects would take, and especially the middle class of her subjects."[3]

Robert Albert Talbot Gascoyne-Cecil, third Marquess of Salisbury, had a pedigree that stretched back almost as far as that of his Queen. One of his forbears, Lord Burghley, had been Chief Minister to the first Queen Elizabeth, and Burghley's son Robert Cecil held the same post for her successor, James I. Cecil became the first Earl of Salisbury, and later converted the old Palace of Hatfield, where the first Elizabeth had lived prior to assuming the throne, into a magnificent Jacobean edifice. The third Marquess lived there all his life, and its aura of the past must have reinforced his innate conservatism.

Salisbury was sixty-seven and somewhat sickly as 1898 commenced. His illustrious public career had included service as Benjamin Disraeli's Foreign Secretary from 1878 to 1880, when he played an important role at the Congress of Berlin. After a short term as Prime Minister from 1885 to 1886 and, although in the House of Lords, he returned to power later in 1886 in a second ministry that lasted until 1892. He again became Prime Minister after the Conservative victory of 1895, serving in the dual role of Foreign Secretary as he had in his prior ministry. Salisbury's experience in foreign affairs was vast, and his reputation was legendary. The British people correctly recognized him as a man of principle. A biographer commented on the "startling paradox that though Disraeli showed the greater trust in the British people, the people came to trust Salisbury in a way they never trusted Disraeli."[4]

Salisbury was a true conservative in foreign as well as in domestic affairs. His foreign policy had been described as "splendid isolation," in which Britain stayed free of alliances with any other major powers, thus preserving maximum freedom of action.[5] He once stated that the aim of British foreign policy "is to drift lazily downstream, occasionally putting out a boat hook to avoid a collision."[6] His careful conduct of foreign affairs was far from lazy, however. He kept a close watch for potential trouble, and was willing to compromise non-vital British interests to avoid major conflicts. Thus, in 1895, when United States concern under the Monroe Doctrine regarding a dispute over the boundary between Venezuela and British Guiana threatened war, Salisbury backed off, commenting, "War between the two nations would be an absurdity as well as a crime."[7] With prescience, he added:

"...the two nations are allied and more closely allied in sentiment and in interest than any other nations on the face of the earth. While I should look with horror upon anything in the nature of a fratricidal strife, I should look forward with pleasure to the possibility of the Stars and Stripes and the Union Jack floating together in defense of a common cause sanctified by humanity and justice."[8]

Shortly after the crisis had been resolved, in answer to a question from an American embassy official, Salisbury responded that the possible United States annexation of Cuba would be "no affair of ours."[9]

Physically, Salisbury was a big man, six feet, four inches tall, large of head and body, and burdened with excessive weight.[10] While his great joys were his wife and ten children,[11] he generally preferred solitude, when he could think and relax undisturbed.[12] His great outside interest was science, especially chemistry; one of his experiments ended in an explosion that shook the house. Hatfield was one of the first houses in England to have a telephone system, albeit a primitive one.[13]

Salisbury did most of his own paperwork,[14] and this undoubtedly exacerbated his extreme myopia. He also could be extremely absent-minded, once not recognizing one of his own sons, and at another time asking the name of a man sitting close to him at a meal, only to be told that the supposed stranger was an old friend who at the time was Chancellor of the Exchequer.[15] But these were only superficial weaknesses, for Salisbury was clearly the dominant force in British public life. As Winston Churchill wrote, "there was a tremendous air about this wise old Statesman."[16] He was the unquestioned leader of the Conservative Party, and his nephew, Arthur Balfour, led the Tories in the House of Commons, where he implemented his uncle's policies.

Sir Robert Cecil, Marquess of Salisbury

By 1898 Salisbury's policy of splendid isolation was in question. Some feared that, as other countries formed alliances, Britain's ability to influence world affairs would wane. The 1894 alliance between Russia, with which Britain was at odds along the Indian border, and France, was disturbing. Like Britain, France had colonial ambitions in Africa, and, as will be seen, a collision there was likely. As the new century approached, there was increasing concern that England needed friends.

Colonial Secretary Joseph Chamberlain shared this view and wanted to act on it. Chamberlain was totally different from Salisbury in both background and temperament. Born in 1832 into a middle class family, he never attended college, but at age eighteen began to work in a family owned screw manufacturing factory in Birmingham. When he retired eighteen years later as head of the business, the plant produced two-thirds of all the metal screws made in England.[17] The newly wealthy Chamberlain plunged into politics. Within a year he was elected Birmingham's mayor, and kept political control of that city for the rest of his life. In 1876 he went to Parliament as a Radical Liberal. As a younger minister he had the temerity to attack the concept of a House of Lords— "the divine right of peers is a ridiculous figment"[18]—and challenged Salisbury as one of those who "toil not, neither do they spin."[19] Salisbury, in return, dubbed Chamberlain "a Sicilian bandit."[20]

But in England as in the United States, politics can make strange bedfellows. In 1886 Chamberlain opposed Liberal Prime Minister Gladstone on Home Rule for Ireland. A powerful orator and, indeed, something of a rabble rouser, he vigorously attacked his former colleagues, who responded in kind, comparing him unfavorably to Judas Iscariot, who at least became "contrite...was ashamed" and "went out and hanged himself."[21] He and his Irish Unionist followers remained Liberals for the time being, but more often than not voted with the Conservatives. In return, they received Tory support for social legislation such as universal public education, which was a long time Chamberlain goal.

Although Chamberlain was not in the Government, in 1887 Salisbury sent him to Washington, where he headed a British delegation whose mission was to settle a fishing dispute with the United States. During his three months there he not only concluded a treaty but met and married thirty-three-year-old Mary Endicott, the daughter of President Cleveland's Secretary of War. Perhaps influenced by that impending alliance, on a visit to Toronto, he said to a Canadian audience:

"I refuse to speak or think of the United States as a foreign nation. They are our flesh and blood. Our past is theirs...Their forefathers sleep in our churchyards."[22]*

In 1895, Lord Rosebery's Liberal Government lost a snap vote in the House of Commons and resigned. Queen Victoria asked Lord Salisbury to form a new government. He had no choice but to ask Chamberlain to take an important post. Although to late twentieth century eyes, Chamberlain, with his daily fresh orchid and gold monocle in his right eye, might be considered a fop, to his Birmingham constituents he was a "swell."[23] The support of Chamberlain's middle-class followers and of his block of Liberal Unionists was necessary if Salisbury was to form a viable government. Accordingly, he offered this potential "bull in a china shop" a choice of Cabinet positions. Rather than a more prestigious post such as Chancellor of the Exchequer he opted to become Colonial Secretary. As Winston Churchill later commented:

"His instinct was a sure one. Interest in home affairs had languished... The excitement of politics lay in the clash of Imperial forces in the continents of Africa and Asia, and it was there that Chamberlain resolved to make his mark. . . . The Municipal Socialist and Republican of his Birmingham years was now the architect of Empire. 'It is not enough,' he declared, "to occupy certain great spaces of the world's surface unless you can make the best of them—unless you are willing to develop them. We are landlords of a great estate; it is the duty of a landlord to develop his estate.'"[24]

In 1898, these two leaders would have to face major foreign policy issues which, as Chamberlain's biographer observed "were advancing by forced marches."[25] Britain's first major foreign policy concern appeared to be in the Far East. When Russia agreed with Germany to let the latter occupy Kiau-chow on China's Yellow Sea coast, it decided that it also needed a warm water Pacific port and occupied Port Arthur in southern Manchuria.† This caused an outcry in Britain, which, because of the long Russian border with India, was concerned over any Russian expansion in

---

* Chamberlain had married twice as a young man, but both wives had died in childbirth. Both sons survived. The first, Austen, served twice as Chancellor of the Exchequer and once as Foreign Secretary. His younger half brother, Neville, was Prime Minister from 1937 until, after failing to bring back "peace in our time" from Munich, he was replaced in 1940 by Winston Churchill.

† China, no match for the combination of Germany and Russia, had no choice but to yield.

Asia. Chamberlain wrote Salisbury on December 29, 1897, that "(p)ublic opinion has been expecting some sensational action on our part...and if we do absolutely nothing...I fear the effect of self effacement on both our own friends and on foreign governments."[26] In part because of Britain's extensive commercial interests in the Far East, the usually cautious Prime Minister agreed, responding the next day:

"I agree with you that the 'public' will require some territorial or carto-graphic consolation in China. It will not be useful and will be expensive; but as a matter of pure sentiment, we shall have to do it."[27]

The British Government wasted no time in taking a stronger public posi-tion on the role of foreign powers in China. On January 17, speaking at Swansea, Chancellor of the Exchequer Sir Michael Hicks-Beach seem-ingly escalated the controversy:

"We do not regard China as a place for conquest or acquisition by any European or other Power. We look upon it as the most hopeful place of the future for the commerce of our country and the commerce of the world at large, and the Government was absolutely determined, at whatever cost, even—and he wished to speak plainly—if necessary, at the cost of war, that the door should not be shut against us."[28]

Yet, the same day, Salisbury instructed the British Ambassador to Russia, Sir Nicholas O'Conor, to ask the influential Finance Minister Count Sergei Witte

"...whether it is possible that England and Russia could work together in China. ... We would go far to further Russian commercial objects in the north, if we could regard her as willing to work with us."[28]

Although very different in tone, the two statements were not inconsis-tent. Britain was willing to cooperate with Russia on commercial matters so long as Russia's role in northern China went no further. Salisbury knew that Britain's naval superiority could not keep Russia from playing a major role vis-a-vis her southern neighbor. His goal was an "open door" policy under which a non-partitioned China would retain her indepen-dence. These seemingly bellicose comments were intended to influence Russia to accept that position.[30]

A week later, the Russians replied. At 7:30 A.M., on January 25 the

Foreign Office received a private message to Lord Salisbury from Ambassador O'Conor, who had met the previous day with Witte. Witte

"...wanted to find out how far Her Majesty's Government would go with Russia, for he knew if we came to an understanding our rule would be law in the Far East.... He is in favour of an alliance as he termed it, and he is ready to support what he calls England's practical and commercial policy provided England will not impede Russian ambition in the North. He regards the Yangtze as England's proper sphere of influence and between us we could hold Germany in check."[31]

Unfortunately, O'Conor had neglected to report one important part of his January 24 conversation. On January 30, he wrote Salisbury that he had "omitted to refer to one point"—that Witte had taken "from a carefully locked desk a map of China," had "proceeded to draw his hand" over four provinces, and "said that sooner or later Russia would probably absorb all this territory."[32] Clearly, the Russians had more in mind than Britain was willing to concede.

Meanwhile, a wave of indignation greeted a report in the London *Times* that the British Government was trying to reach a Far Eastern accommodation with Russia. Members of the Liberal opposition called Salisbury's efforts "a national humiliation."[33] To some Conservatives as well, his efforts looked like dangerous appeasement. Among them was Joseph Chamberlain. In a letter written on February 3 from his country home at Highbury, he suggested to Arthur Balfour that if

"...you read all the papers just now...I think you would agree with me that grave trouble is impending upon the Government if we do not adopt a more decided attitude in regard to China..."[34]

Possibly thinking that his suggestions might better be received by the Prime Minister from his nephew than from him, the Colonial Secretary proposed that Britain officially approach both the United States and Germany and "ask an immediate reply...to the question, 'Will you stand in with us in our policy?'" He then urged:

"Our Chinese policy to be a declaration that any port occupied by a foreign nation shall be, ipso facto, a Treaty port, open to all on precisely similar conditions. That if Russia refuses these terms we should summon her fleet to leave Port Arthur and make her go if necessary."[35]

Although Salisbury did not follow this provocative advice, he was willing to assert the British position in a less forthright manner. Thus, the *China Gazette* reported from Shanghai that the British, Indian, Australian, and Pacific squadrons had been ordered to prepare to reinforce the Far Eastern fleet, thus providing a force able to face "any combination opposing British policy."[36]

Russia, however, refused to back down. On February 19, Count Vladimir Lamsdorff, an assistant to the Russian Foreign Minister, told British Ambassador O'Conor that his country's demands in China "were very simple, merely a lease for, say, twenty years of Talienwan and Port Arthur, or some other port in the North which may ultimately be considered more desirable as a terminal railway station." He added that Russia "intended to hold to these ports at any cost." O'Conor replied that these demands were "of a totally different nature to those preferred by Her Majesty's Government."[37]

By late March Salisbury had concluded that "the only thing to be done is to object to the military occupation of Port Arthur in language sufficiently measured to allow Russia to find a way out." The trouble with such a policy was that Russia was not looking for an excuse to leave.[38] Further, although Salisbury wrote Ambassador O'Conor that the British "must retain their entire liberty of action to take what steps they think best to protect their own interests and to diminish the evil consequences which they anticipate,"[39] he had already convinced his Cabinet that there was little that Britain could or should do in China. British efforts to secure American and Japanese support had not even met with initial interest.[40] Russian occupation of Port Arthur was a *fait accompli*.

Moreover, Salisbury's primary concern related to a potential conflict with France that was brewing in Africa. His daughter Lady Gwendolen Cecil described how a group of ministers, irate over Russia's Far East activities, had called on the seriously ill Prime Minister at his home in early April to urge strong British action:

"His temperature was high and the doctor absolutely forbade an interview. His colleagues therefore wrote a short draft of the message which they suggested sending to Russia, and I was asked to take it up to him for approval or rejection. He read it over, observed that its transmission would probably mean war, and then, after a short pause, said with the peculiar inflection in his voice and glint in his eyes which warned his intimates against taking his words in any pedantically matter-of-fact sense: 'Of course the Russians have behaved abominably and if it would be any satisfaction to my colleagues I should have no objection to fighting them. But I don't think we carry enough guns to fight them and the French together." [41]

When Lady Gwendolen "expressed somehow my incomprehension of what the French had to do with the matter," her father replied:

"What the French had to do with it? Did I forget that Kitchener was actually on the march to Khartoum? In six month's time we shall be on the verge of war with France; I can't afford to quarrel with Russia now." [42]

Accordingly, the message sent to St. Petersburg was very different from the original draft. To Britain, Africa was more important than China.

THREE

"France Is Going To Fire Her Pistol"

On the west bank of the White Nile in the southern Sudan 469 miles due south of Khartoum was the site of a former trading post and fort named Fashoda. It was an insignificant elevation less than six feet above high water, and yet was the only spot in a hundred miles where boats could be landed. To the north, as described by twenty-four-year-old Winston Churchill:

"At times the river flowed past miles of long grey grass and swamp-land, inhabited and habitable only by hippopotami. At times a vast expanse of dreary mud-flats stretched as far as the eye could see. At others the forest, dense with an impenetrable undergrowth of thorn-bushes, approached the water, and the active forms of monkeys and even of leopards darted among the trees. But the country—whether forest, mud-flat or prairie—was always damp and feverish: a wet land steaming under a burning sun and humming with mosquitoes and all kinds of insect life."[1]

Not far to the southwest, the Nile emanates from a long shallow lagoon of dead water surrounded by an immense and dismal labyrinth of pools, islands, and false channels named Lake No. Into Lake No the White Nile flows from the south through fields of reeds and water grasses. From the west flows the Bahr al-Ghazal, the river of the gazelles, out of the province of the same name, and, like the country surrounding the Nile to the north, a desolate land of blazing hot humidity, decaying vegetation, and mud. Yet it was Fashoda and its surroundings that were the focal points for a rivalry that in 1898 was to bring England and France to the verge of war.[2]

The potential crisis had long-standing origins. Since Napoleon's aborted expedition of 1798, France had maintained a strong interest in Egypt. It was whetted by the fact that Ferdinand de Lesseps, the builder of the

Suez Canal, was a Frenchman. England's purchase of the Canal in 1875, however, made Egyptian stability a matter of paramount British national interest. Thus, an anti-European uprising in 1882 led a reluctant British Prime Minister Gladstone to intervene, and a British army took possession of Egypt, including the Canal. The French could have joined in the occupation, but chose not to do so—a decision that they soon came to regret and that led to future controversy with Britain.[3]

As yet, the British had not seized the Sudan. By 1883, however, the Khedive of Egypt had attempted to quash a rebellion against his country's interests in the northern Sudan that was led by a self-proclaimed Mahdi, or "messiah," who announced that he was the man who would fulfill Mohammed's prophecy that one of his descendants would arise and rekindle the fires of Islam.[4] After his forces soundly defeated the Khedive's army, Prime Minister Gladstone sent General Charles "Chinese" Gordon to supervise the evacuation of the Sudanese capital of Khartoum. Instead, Gordon, who opposed Gladstone's policy of withdrawal, remained in Khartoum. After a siege of 320 days, in January 1885 he was defeated and killed by the Mahdists, only ten days before the arrival of a relieving army.[5] The British public, including Queen Victoria, was enraged, and Gladstone's government fell.[6] Although the defeat rankled, there was no attempt to avenge it and conquer the Sudan until the mid 1890s.

Meanwhile France had made clear to England that it did not regard the Egyptian question as settled.[7] French Foreign Minister Gabriel Hanotoux attempted to reach an agreement with England, but the two countries had irreconcilable goals: the French for the British to leave Egypt and the British for France to acknowledge England's presence there— perhaps permanently,[8] even though some years earlier Gladstone had stated that for England to remain in Egypt "would be absolutely at variance with all of the principles and views of Her Majesty's Government and the pledges they have given to Europe."[9] As a later-day historian has described the impasse:

"Egypt, 'discovered' and 'awakened' by Bonaparte's legions and made part of the modern world by the French-built canal at Suez some twenty years before, had, as the French saw it, been stolen by the unprincipled British. As the British saw it, however, Egypt had been saved from anarchy by Her Majesty's redcoats and its waterway to India magnanimously secured for the benefit of international commerce, only to be menaced by the imperial plottings of the insatiable French."[10]

By early 1895 the potential battle lines had been drawn. On February 28, a leading French colonialist told the Chamber of Deputies that if Britain would not keep what the French considered to be Gladstone's promise to stay out of Egypt, France would "take Britain in the rear" by moving across Africa from the west into the Sudan. Thirty days later, Sir Edward Grey, Under Secretary for Foreign Affairs in the Gladstone Government, told the House of Commons that the entire Nile was British, and that to send "a French expedition under secret instructions, right from the other side of Africa, into a territory over which our claims have been known for so long...would be an unfriendly act and would be so viewed by England." Grey emphasized the words "unfriendly act."[11]

The next year began what came to be known as "the race to Fashoda." The British started first. This was only fitting, since the stakes for them were greater. It was not only French control of the Upper Nile that motivated them. There was the effect that this would have on Cecil Rhodes' dream of a Capetown to Cairo railway, as well as the fears of their Egyptian allies of incursions by the forces of the deceased Mahdi's successor Khalifa Abdullahi, who was growing increasingly bellicose. Finally, as Winston Churchill wrote after the race to Fashoda became history, although Britain's motives for conquering the Sudan were numerous, "the man in the street—and there are many men in many streets—said, it is to avenge General Gordon."[12]

Churchill's observation notwithstanding, it was concern over the French that was the immediate cause of the Salisbury Government's abrupt decision in March 1896 to move troops south at least as far as Dongola, below the Third Cataract of the Nile.[13] In late March a force of 10,000 Egyptian soldiers led by British officers and supported by a flotilla of steamers started up the Nile.[14] They were commanded by General Sir Herbert Horatio Kitchener. Forty-eight years old, he had served at one time as an aide to Gordon, and since 1892 had been commander-in-chief, or Sirdar, of the Egyptian army. Like Gordon, he was a lifelong bachelor who had no interest in women and refused to select married officers to serve under him on the basis that marriage would distract them from more important, military matters.[15]

Extremely and obviously ambitious, and for that reason unpopular, Kitchener was unbending, ruthless, and apparently unfeeling towards his men.[16] Yet they admired him just as much as they feared him. Years later he was described as having "towered above his men in a way that few field commanders ever have done."[17] Especially important, Salisbury thought highly of him.[18]

Kitchener did not stop at Dongola. Instead, his army pushed south to Abu Hamed, where the Nile turns south after a temporary northern loop, and built a 230 mile railroad shortcut across the desert with the aid of a thousand natives, Mahdist prisoners, and Sudanese troops.[19] Below the Fifth Cataract, he stopped at Berber while Lord Cromer, the British consul general in Egypt, argued to the Salisbury Government in London that a further advance could have dire consequences.[20] These warnings were to no avail. Not only did the Khalifa announce a *jihad*, or religious war, against the Anglo-Egyptian infidels, but the British attitude towards the French hardened. As far as England was concerned, Kitchener had a green light to seize Fashoda in 1898.

A year earlier there had been a third contender for the Sudan. King Leopold of Belgium, flush with funds from newly developed rubber production in the Belgian Congo and expectant of much more to come, decided to make his own attempt to seize the Upper Nile.[21] In December 1895 he suggested to Lord Salisbury that if Britain were to leave Egypt (and in the process obtain a concession to Belgium of the Nile south of Khartoum), the French would be so overjoyed that they would give England a free hand in Asia to "annex China to the Indian Empire."[22] Needless to say, the British rejected this harebrained scheme. But Leopold was not deterred. He commissioned Baron François Dhanis, a hero of earlier African wars, to lead an expedition eastward from the Congo and seize and annex the Sudan.[23] In late 1896 the Baron set out with a few Belgian officers and 2,500 tribesmen eastward through the deadly, primeval Ituri Forest, populated by hostile pygmies and replete with other dangers.[24] After 150 days they emerged just a few days march from Lake Albert and the head of the White Nile.[25] But then, plagued by attacks by local natives and pushed by their officers almost beyond endurance, the Congolese troops mutinied in mid-February 1897, killing most of their Belgian officers.[26] Dhanis escaped by hiding in the forest and eventually made his way back to Stanleyville, which barely held out as the mutinous army took temporary control of most of the Congo.[27] For Belgium, the race to Fashoda had ignominiously ended.

This left the French to challenge England. They mounted separate expeditions that would converge on Fashoda from French Somaliland on the Red Sea and from the French Congo on the Atlantic. Initially, the eastern prong of this pincers movement seemed the more promising. The French plan was to secure the active assistance of Ethiopian Emperor Menelik II, across whose land they must cross, and his powerful army, which in 1896 had soundly defeated an Italian invading force. Menelik had signed a treaty with France, promising Ethiopia the east bank of the

Upper Nile.[28] He was also talking with the British, however, and saw no reason to go out of his way to help the gullible French, who seemed willing to proceed on the basis of informal promises of military support.[29]

There were two French Ethiopian expeditions, the first under a Captain Clochette, and a second commanded by Marquis Christian de Bonchamps. The initial plan was for them to unite before attacking the Sudan. Before Bonchamps arrived in the Ethiopian capital of Addis Ababa, however, the French ambassador Leonce Lagarde, perhaps out of concern that the British would beat the French to Fashoda, ordered Clochette to make haste for the Nile.[30] Clochette, seriously ill with a sick liver caused by a kick from a mule, did his best, and with a force of 200 Ethiopians struggled west through icy rains to Gore, about a week's march from Fashoda. At that point he became too ill to go any further and eventually died.[31]

Meanwhile, Bonchamps left Addis Ababa to catch up with Clochette, only to be sent by the devious Menelik on a roundabout route three times longer than Clochette's.[32] After a tortuous forty-two-day march in heavy rains, he arrived at Gore to find Clochette dying.[33] Continuing west for another fifty miles, his force was suddenly confronted, close to the Sudanese border, by 2,000 Ethiopian warriors whose chief ordered Bonchamps to stop "in the name of the Emperor."[34] The emissaries that Bonchamps sent the 200 miles back to Addis Ababa were told by Menelik there had been a mistake and that the French were free to continue their expedition. But now, Ambassador Lagarde, who had promised them men, supplies, and a collapsible boat, produced only two camels and ten Senegalese soldiers.[35] If these disappointments were not enough, Menelik instructed the French to approach the Nile seventy-five miles south of Fashoda.[36] This involved traveling through the most difficult part of the Sudan—swamps where elephants charged them through high grass and where the heat and polluted water sickened both men and animals.[37] By December 31, 1897, faced by grass four feet high and deserting porters, Bonchamps turned back, still ninety miles from Fashoda.[38]

The French thrust from the east had failed, at least temporarily. That from the west, however, was very much alive. It was headed by a remarkable thirty-four-year-old career officer, Jean-Baptiste Marchand, whose exploits under fire in Mali in 1889 and 1890 had won him membership in the Legion of Honor.[39] After further successes in Western Africa, and now a captain, he returned to France in 1895. That September he presented Hanotaux with a detailed plan to march eastward from the Atlantic to Fashoda and eventually extend the French Congo to the Red Sea by way of Ethiopia, which somehow would agree to protectorate status.[40] Not surprisingly, in some quarters it was asked how "could Marchand and his men occupy a crumbling fort at the end of a 3,000-mile communication line when France had only 230 soldiers in the entire Upper Ubangi?"[41] But Marchand was insistent, arguing that he would strike an alliance with the Mahdists. When word came in March 1896 that Britain intended to occupy the Upper Sudan, final approval of his plan was secured. Preceded by supplies and handpicked subordinates, Marchand left France on June 25, with Hanotaux's parting words in his ears: "Go to Fashoda. France is going to fire her pistol."[42]

Marchand had planned his expedition carefully—plenty of supplies and only 150 men, all of whom were solid, dependable, and none from the cavalry—"they no longer have any value for us over there."[43] Portage of his men and 17,000 cases of supplies to the Congo from the port of Loango to Brazzaville was almost stopped by a revolt of the native Basundis, but the rebellion was finally quelled in December.[44] In January 1897, with King Leopold's approval, the French borrowed from the Belgians a 125-foot-long steamboat, *Ville de Bruges*. With it and dugout canoes, Marchand transported his men and supplies 800 miles northeast up the Congo and Ubangi. They traveled through territory that Joseph Conrad described six years later in *Heart of Darkness* as

"...like travelling back to the earliest beginnings of the world, where vegetation rioted on the earth and the big trees were kings. An empty stream, a great silence, an impenetrable forest. The air was warm, thick, heavy, sluggish. There was no joy in the brilliance of the sunshine."[45]

From Bangui, where Marchand had halted, the most direct route to Fashoda was 450 more miles upstream to Ouango, just below the rapids of the Mbomu, and then northeast through the level Deim Zubeir area to the tributaries of the White Nile.[46] Marchand was hopeful that with hard marching and good luck this itinerary would get him to Fashoda by year end 1897.[47] He had received word from Paris that Kitchener would be unable to seize Khartoum before then. The authorities in Paris, however, feared that if Marchand took this route, his expedition would frighten and antagonize the natives of the Deim Zubeir, with whom France had only recently concluded tenuous alliances.[48] Thus, Marchand received instructions to proceed instead due east and then reach the Bahr al-Ghazal from the south via the Sué River. Since that part of the Bahr was a huge swamp, Marchand needed a boat, which he managed to locate and seize

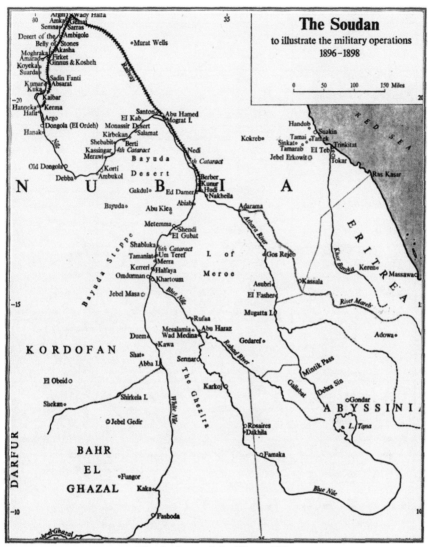

The Sudan and the Upper Nile

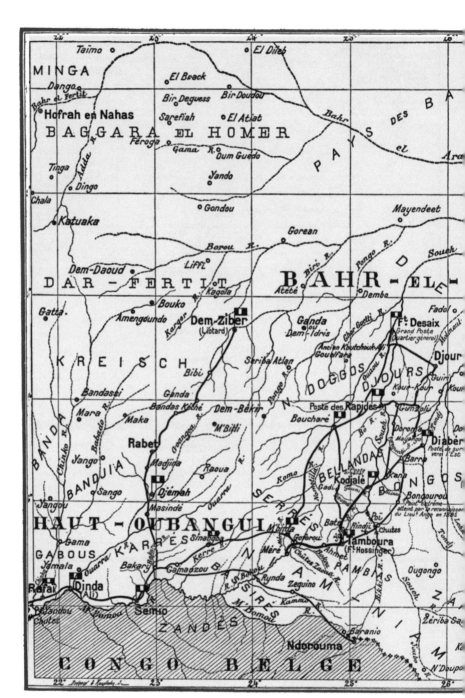

Marchand's Trek Across Africa

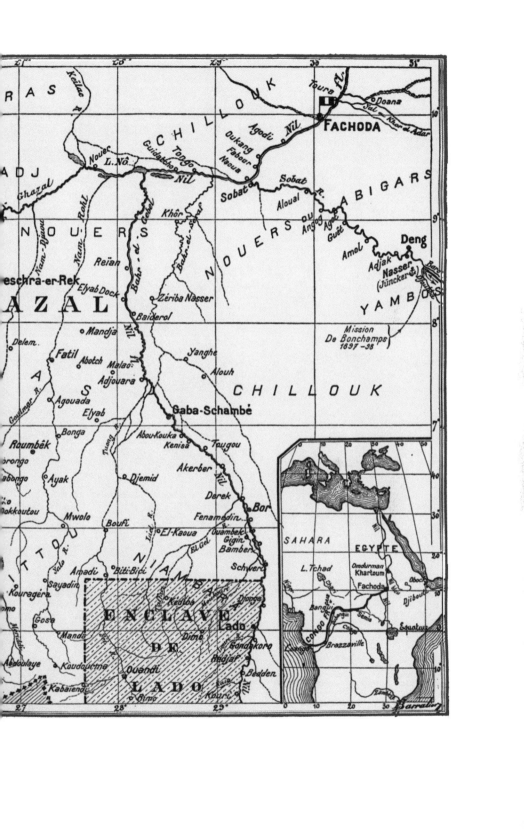

below the Mbomu.[49] It was mid-June, however, before the *Faidherbe*, which had to be disassembled and portaged around the rapids, arrived further up the Mbomu at a place called Zemio.[50]

The 150 miles from Zemio to Tambura, at the head of the Sué, was particularly hard going, in rain, through very high grass where many cases of supplies were lost.[51] Marchand's chief aide, Lieutenant Albert Ernest Baratier, found a river which permitted the French to steam the *Faidherbe* to a point fifty miles from Tambura,[52] but from there it had to be disassembled again and its parts carried in forty-five packloads to Tambura by 2,000 locally recruited porters.[53] Progress was frustratingly slow—only three miles a day due to the bulk of the ship's boiler. Supplies ran out and had to be replaced from the south.[54] Marchand built a fort at Tambura, and fifty miles northeast, at a point on the Sué where he planned to embark on his northern journey, he built slips for boat repair and a road sixteen feet wide and ninety miles long back to the upper Mboke. He then proceeded further down the Sué to Wau, an old trading center, where he built an encampment that he named Fort Desaix.[55]

At this point Marchand had come nearly 3,000 miles, but there were 500 more to Fashoda. The dry season had set in, perhaps prematurely, and the water level of the Sué and the Bahr al-Ghazal fell to a level that made impossible any progress by the two gunboats and ten barges of steel and aluminum that Marchand had just launched on the Sué. It was clear to Marchand that until the onset of the rainy season, he could not move his men and boats down the Sué and through the Bahr al-Ghazal to Fashoda. A small flying column might succeed, but the risks were too great. The nearby Dinkas, although not overly friendly, were unlikely to attack such an expedition, but other more distant tribes might do so. So also, as they neared Fashoda, might the Khalifa's troops. If these risks could be avoided, the French likely would be unable to defend themselves against the larger British force that was moving up the Nile toward Khartoum and that would advance on Fashoda if it defeated the Mahdists.[56]

At least the French would sit out the dry season in comfort. At Desaix they had planted fast growing fruits and vegetables, ducks and fresh fish were plentiful, and their many hardships had not kept them from transporting from the Atlantic wine that had been bought at the fashionable Fauchon in Paris's Place de la Madeleine.[57] Nevertheless, they were chafing at the prospect of a long period of inactivity, especially since they were relatively close to their goal. Thus, when Lieutenant Baratier proposed a more limited venture, Marchand approved it. The plan was for Baratier to take a boat down the Sué and then across the Bahr al-Ghazal to an old Egyptian port called Meshra'er Rek. From there, it was hoped, there might be clear water all the way to the Nile. En route, he was to do his best to placate the Dinkas. Thus, on January 15, 1898, Baratier set out, accompanied by an interpreter, twenty four Senegalese soldiers and ten native boatmen in the same portable red steel whaleboat that he had dismantled and carried across the watershed the previous year.[58]

Back in Europe, the diplomatic pot continued to simmer. On December 10, 1897, in the context of negotiations between England and France regarding the Niger Valley and Lake Chad, the British Ambassador to France, Sir Edmund Monson, wrote Hanotaux that this attempt at agreement "must not be understood to admit that any other European Power than Great Britain has any claim to any part of the Valley of the Nile," referring to Sir Edward Grey's 1895 statement in Parliament.[59] On December 24 Hanotaux replied that "the French Government cannot, under present circumstances, refrain from repeating the reservations which it has never failed to express every time that questions relating to the Valley of the Nile have been brought forward," pointing out that Grey's "declarations...gave rise to an immediate protest by our Representative in London," which had been repeated every time the issue was subsequently raised.[60] Although the Foreign Minister closed his letter by referring to the "same spirit of conciliation and harmony to which you appealed in your communication," these diplomatic niceties could not disguise the fact that the two countries were on a potential collision course that could result in military conflict. As *The New York Times* reported on January 13 from London, "the movements of the French were again becoming unpleasantly prominent to those who imagined that Great Britain had undisputed claims upon those regions." The report continued:

"Thus far, M. Hanotaux seems to have the advantage, but the game is dangerous. Fear of war with France will not stop Great Britain from recovering the whole of the Egyptian Sudan and driving out any French expeditions which may be found there, when, in the opinion of the Marquis of Salisbury, the proper time has arrived."[61]

By the end of January 1898 Kitchener's forces held a strong position along the Nile from Abu Hamed south to the mouth of the Atbara, less than 200 miles north of Khartoum. The Sirdar's pleas to the War Office for help following reports of a likely attack by the Khalifa had brought an immediate response. Egyptian and British units scattered north along the Nile were concentrated with the rest of Kitchener's forces. To them were added three British battalions from Cairo, with a fourth on the way. They were equipped with the most lethal modern weapons—both rapid-firing rifles and powerful artillery.[62]

If, as the British feared, the Dervish forces had attacked in late December, they might have stood a chance against Kitchener's strung-out command. They did not because, as Churchill explained:

"The burning question of the command had arisen. A dispute that was never settled ensued. When the whole army was regularly assembled, the Khalifa announced publicly that he would lead the faithful in person, but at the same time he arranged privately that many Emirs and notables should beg him not to expose his sacred person. After proper solicitation, therefore, he yielded to their appeals."[63]

There followed what to Western eyes was a comedy of errors involving officers whose personal ambition and dislike for each other seemed even greater than their enmity for the British and Egyptians. Thus it was that the Dervishes marched back to Khartoum "in vexation and disgust."[64]

Following this ignominious retreat, it appeared to Kitchener and his army that there would be no military action until midsummer, when the rising Nile would permit a major southern advance. To their surprise, they received word on February 15 that the Emir Mahmud, perhaps the Khalifa's most aggressive general, was crossing the Nile to its east bank, apparently intending to move north and attack Berber.[65] It was unclear why Mahmud had proposed this madcap plan and why the Khalifa had approved it. The British-Egyptian force against which the Dervishes were about to advance was now a powerful army, and its position was solidly entrenched. As Churchill surmised:

"Perhaps Mahmud did not realize the amazing power of movement that the railway had given his foes; perhaps he still believed, with the Khalifa, that Berber was held only by 2,000 Egyptians, or else—and this is the most probable—he was reckless of danger and strong in his own conceit."[66]

As for the Khalifa:

"What he had not dared with 60,000 men he now attempted with 20,000. The course of action which for three months offered a good hope of success he resolved to pursue only when it led to ruin. He forbade the advance when it was advisable. When it was already become mad and fatal he commanded it. And this was a man whose reputation for intelligence and military skill had been bloodily demonstrated."[67]

Be that as it may, by February 28 Mahmud's entire force was concentrated on the east side of the Nile at Shendi, about halfway between Khartoum and Berber. From there it was ready to move north.[68]

Since Meshra'er Rek was less than one hundred miles from Fort Desaix as the crow flies, the Baratier expedition had expected to get there and back within three weeks. But they had failed to reckon with the never ending reeds, the stinking vegetation, and the mud and shallow water that constantly confronted them. At most, progress was two or three kilometers a day. The constantly watching Dinkas were of no assistance until, with food almost gone and completely lost, the French were able, with generous offers of beads, to obtain Dinka guides and some dried fish and millet.[69]

Baratier's problems were exacerbated by the lack of animals such as bush-pigs and elephants to shoot and eat. The only source of meat was the Marabou storks. His Dinka guides, however, made clear that they regarded the storks as some form of relation not to be killed under any circumstances.[70]

It was a tremendous relief when, in the first week of February, signs of papyrus indicated to the French that clear water was nearby. This was followed by encounters with hippopotami and elephants that they could shoot and smoke for future consumption. Although the expedition had missed the channel opening to Meshra er Rek, by late February it was approaching Lake No and the Nile. Baratier, however, was becoming increasingly concerned that his failure to return to Fort Desaix would result in an expedition to find him or some other action that could imperil the goal of reaching Fashoda. Reluctantly, therefore, on February 25, he ordered a return to Fort Desaix.[71]

The return trip took more than a month. As Baratier had feared, a worried Marchand had sent Lieutenant Emmanuel Largeau and a few men to look for his expedition when it had not returned on schedule. The Largeau party, however, had gotten stuck in the reeds and was trying with

Captain Jean-Baptiste Marchand

difficulty to make its way back to the fort when a rifle shot from Baratier's group was heard. The "rescuers" were thus rescued. Their combined force returned to Fort Desaix on March 26. There would be no more expeditions until the rainy season came. In the meantime, with plentiful food supplies, competent military cooks and good wine, the French led a reasonably comfortable life.[72]

The French Government was displeased over Bonchamps's failure to reach the Nile from Ethiopia. If and when Marchand seized Fashoda, he would need supplies if he were to remain there. His experience in the Bahr al-Ghazal demonstrated that they could come from the west only during the rainy season. For the rest of the year, he would need access from the east, by way of Ethiopia.[73]

Bonchamps therefore was ordered to try again to join Marchand. The Ethiopians were promised inducements to help him, including trading profits from the anticipated new French Central African Empire. The wily Emperor Menelik, however, well aware that British success would make these promises illusory, decided that he had as much right to this territory as the two European rivals. He sent a message to the Khalifa that his projected expedition was not directed against the Mahdists, but only the Europeans who "intended to enter my country and yours and try and separate us and divide us."[74]

The army which Menelik was assembling was formidable, at least on paper, reportedly numbering a quarter of a million men. It was divided into three parts. One was sent north into the area between the Blue and White Niles, which Menelik coveted most. The second went south toward Lake Rudolf, while the third was to go west to the valley of the Sobat and then the White Nile in the area of Fashoda. When it left Gore on March 10, it was accompanied by a Monsieur Faivre from the French Department of Native Affairs and the artist Maurice Potter, who had accompanied Bonchamps the previous year. Including women and boys, who acted as cooks, orderlies, and servants, this colorful procession numbered more than 10,000. Bonchamps did not go with them, but instead returned to Addis Ababa for fresh instructions, funds, and the portable boat that he believed was necessary if he was to reach Fashoda.[75]

Twenty days after it had left Gore, the central Ethiopian army reached the head of the Sobat River, which eventually flowed into the Nile less than one hundred miles south of Fashoda. Potter persuaded the Ethiopian leader, Rus Tassama, that by now Marchand had reached Fashoda and

was probably looking for Clochette and Bonchamps. Rus Tassama obliged by ordering a force of 800 men to accompany Potter and Faivre down
the Sobat to the Nile.[76]

In early March Mahmud halted his advance up the east bank of the Nile
at a place called El Aliab, where a council was held. One of the older
Dervish leaders, Osman Digna, argued that a direct attack on Kitchener's
position would be foolhardy. He urged a flanking movement northeast
across the desert, which would put them in the rear of the British-Egyptian forces. Mahmud reluctantly agreed, and on March 18 the Dervish
army left El Aliab and struck out for the village and ford of Hudi on the
Atbara. From there a long desert march would return it to the Nile at
Berber.[77]

The Dervish army, some 12,000 men strong, moved fast, but not speedily enough. On the nineteenth, British gunboats on the Nile reported
Mahmud's departure. Kitchener's army, not deterred by what Churchill
described as a "fearful dust-storm," quickly moved the ten miles to Hudi
in time to construct fortifications before nightfall.[78] Since Mahmud did
not feel strong enough to attack this position, the next day he turned in a
more easterly direction, and reached the Atbara at Nakheila, more than
twenty miles upstream from Hudi. From there Berber was too far distant
to reach with the Dervishes' limited supply of water. They would have to
sit and wait.[79]

This put Kitchener in a quandary. Should he continue to await an
attack by Mahmud, which seemed increasingly unlikely, or should he
order a British-Egyptian movement against the Dervishes? One of his
chief subordinates recommended an assault, while the other, General
Archibald Hunter, advocated a further wait.[80] The Sirdar telegraphed
Cromer in Cairo for his "views on the subject," but the latter, not having
any military experience, referred the matter to London, meanwhile
counseling delay.[81] When General Garnet Wolseley, the British Army's
Commander-in-Chief read it, he promptly wrote Kitchener: "You should
not have asked such a question. You must know best. Men and Governments at a distance are prone to panic and weak measures, and are not to
be trusted—no, not the best of them."[82]

Before Kitchener had received this reply, Hunter changed his mind,
so that the Sirdar's chief lieutenants were now unanimous in recommending offensive operations.[83] Although Kitchener was generally

superstitious of Fridays, he decided to launch his attack on the next Friday, April 8. Because it was Good Friday, he reasoned that the Dervishes might not expect the British to commence battle on such a holy day. Indeed, Good Friday would be an appropriate occasion to avenge the defeat and death of Gordon thirteen years ago.[84]

Accordingly, after a successful reconnaissance on April 5, Kitchener moved his army the next day to Umdabia, only seven miles as the crow flies from the Dervish encampment on the east bank of the Atbara, which was almost entirely a dry bed at this time of year.[85] Before sunset on the seventh, the entire British-Egyptian army commenced a difficult night march in order to attack and hopefully surprise the Dervishes at daybreak on the eighth. The need to avoid bushes, and the bends of the river, added another five miles to the journey, and progress through the desert, with sand kicked up by a night breeze, was slow—barely two miles an hour. From nine to one the army rested. Then, under a full moon, the advance recommenced and continued another two hours until the Dervish fires were sighted to the south. At this point the ranks were formed for battle, with the British on the left and the Egyptians on the right.[86]

At six, still in darkness, the line halted. Then, as Churchill later wrote:

"...after what seemed to many an interminable period, the uniform blackness was broken by the first glimmer of the dawn. Gradually, the light grew stronger until, as a theater curtain is pulled up, the darkness rolled away, the vague outlines in the haze became definite, and the whole scene became revealed.

"Half a mile away, at the foot of the ridge, a long irregular black line of thorn bushes enclosed the Dervish defenses. Behind the zeriba low palisades and entrenchments bent back to the scrub by the river. Odd shapeless mounds indicated the positions of the gun-emplacements, and various casements could be seen in the middle of the enclosure.... Within, were crowds of little straw huts and scattered bushes, growing thither to the southward. From among this rose the palm trees, between whose stems the dry bed of the Atbara was exposed, and a single pool of water gleamed in the early sunlight."[87]

By now, the Dervishes were aware of the approaching army, but made no attempt to be the first to attack. At six-thirty, the British artillery opened fire with a barrage that continued for nearly an hour. Kitchener then ordered a general advance on the Dervish position. As Churchill, always intoxicated by the spectacle of war, described the scene:

"The whole mass of the infantry, numbering nearly eleven thousand men, immediately began to move forward upon the zeriba. The scene as this great force crested the ridge and advanced down the slope was magnificent and tremendous. Large solid columns of men, preceded by a long double line, with the sunlight flashing on their bayonets and displaying their ensigns, marked to the assault. The array was regular and precise. The pipes of the Highlanders, the bands of the Sudanese, and the drums and fifes of the English regiments added a wild and thrilling accompaniment."[88]

By the time that the advancing forces were 250 yards from the zeriba, the Dervish fusillade had become furious and effective. But still the British and Egyptians relentlessly came on, broke into the enclosure and swept it with musket fire of their own.[89] As the advance continued, the romance of the charge was replaced, in Churchill's words, by what

"...seemed to those who took part in it more like a horrible nightmare than a waking reality....Jibba-clad figures sprung out of the ground, fired or charged, and were destroyed at every step. And onwards over their bodies—over pits choked with dead and dying, among heaps of mangled camels and donkeys, among decapitated and eviscerated trunks, the ghastly results of the shell fire; women and little children killed by the bombardment or praying in wild terror for mercy; blacks chained in their trenches, slaughtered in their chains—always onward marched the conquerors, with bayonets running blood, clothes, hands and faces all besmeared; the foul stench of a month's accumulated filth in their nostrils, and the savage whistle of random bullets in their ears."[90]

Kitchener's victory was costly. More than 500 of his men were killed and wounded, of whom more than 100 were British. The Dervish casualties were frightful, with more than 3,000 killed and 4,000 wounded or captured.[91] Among the latter was Mahmud, whom Kitchener disgracefully had put in chains and led in triumph, lashed and reviled like a Roman slave, in a victory parade several days later.[92] The Sirdar, who always regarded the victory as the turning point in his career, was roundly applauded by his officers and was warmly congratulated by the Queen and by Salisbury.[93]

The victory made Kitchener and his officers increasingly confident that they would eventually complete their triumph and thereafter raise the Union Jack at Fashoda. After the battle, their army went into summer quarters between Berber and the Atbara, waiting until the seasonal rise of the Nile in August would make possible a final advance on Khartoum by water.[94]

———⊰◦⊱———

As 1897 closed, an important participant in the affairs of the first half of the next century was about to enter the public arena. Future Nobel Laureate for Literature Winston Spencer Churchill, twenty-three years old and an army lieutenant in Hyderabad, India, had just completed his first book. On December 31 he sent off *The Story of the Malakand Field Force*, an account of a recent campaign in Northwestern India, to his mother, Lady Randolph Churchill, in London. She was to arrange for its publication. His instructions could have been those of an experienced author:

"Now dearest Mamma I don't want anything modified or toned down in any way. I will stand or fall by what I have written. I only want bad sentences polished & any repetitions of phrase or fact weeded out...

As to the price, I have no idea what the book is worth but don't throw it away. A little money is always worth having..."

and

"My last words, like the bishop's are 'verify my quotations.'"[95]

Lady Randolph was successful. On January 20, A. P. Watt, a literary agent to whom she had entrusted the manuscript, wrote her that Longmans had agreed to publish it on terms which "are such as you may with entire confidence accept." Royalties would range from ten percent to twenty percent on copies of the English edition sold above 3,000. There also would be an American edition.[96]

The Story of the Malakand Field Force appeared in British booksellers at a price of six shillings. It was an instant success. The *Pioneer* found in it "a wisdom and comprehension far beyond" its author's years. The *Athenaeum* praised Churchill's style as reminiscent of Burke and Disraeli, and called the book "a literary phenomenon." Sadly, his uncle Moreton Frewes, to whom correction of the proofs had been entrusted, had made a series of misspellings and errors in punctuation that led to adverse comment that partly offset the reviewers' otherwise fulsome praise.[97]

On balance, however, the young author had every reason to feel proud of his accomplishment. Among others, the Prince of Wales wrote him "to congratulate you on the success of your book." The Prince had read *The Story of the Malakand Field Force* "with the greatest interest and I think the descriptions and the language generally excellent." He advised Churchill not to run for Parliament for the time being: "You have plenty of time before you, and you should certainly stick to the Army before adding M.P. to your name." Four days later, he sent a copy of the book to his mother, the Queen, commenting that it was "by Mr. Winston Churchill the late Ld Randolph's eldest son—& written by so young a man shows remarkable ability...."[98]

To its author, the book was to be a stepping stone to other, more important things. On January 26 he wrote his mother that its publication "will be certainly the most noteworthy act of my life" but added:

"Up to date (of course). By its reception—I shall measure the chances of my future success in the world."

and then, with the confidence he was to demonstrate throughout his long life:

"Although on a larger subject and with more time I am capable of a purer and more easy style and of more deeply considered views—yet it is a sample of my mental cast."[99]

Churchill was actively looking for "new worlds to conquer." He had just returned from a trip to Calcutta, where his name gave him entree to the Viceroy, with whom he stayed, and the commander-in-chief of the British forces, with whom he dined. He had written his mother on January 19:

"All were unanimous in advising me to use every effort to go to Egypt."[100]

As with the promotion of his book, Churchill was relying on his mother to pave the way. As it happened, Lady Randolph was already planning to spend part of the winter in Cairo. Her son was hoping to take his three months leave on the Nile, starting in late June, when Kitchener's campaign should have reached a crucial phase. On February 25 he wrote Lady Randolph:

"You should make certain of my being employed there. This will be an easier matter than official attachment to the Egyptian army and is more likely to be allowed as it involves the Egyptian Govt in no extra expense. But you probably know that it all rests with the Sirdar who does as he likes."[101]

Word of Kitchener's Atbara victory even further whetted Churchill's interest in getting to the Sudan before the war was over. On April 13 he wrote Lady Randolph, "I need not tell you how bitter my own feelings were to think I had not been there." But he had not given up hope:

"I do not think this will alter the prospects of an autumn campaign, tho it may diminish the resistance to be encountered. The Nile will not rise before it is ready, and I am quite easy in my mind that even July would be time enough. We shall see. If I am too late and all is over I can only conclude that perhaps Fate intervened because Chance would have been malicious had I gone.

"Meanwhile relax not a volt of your energy. 'The Importunate Widow' and the appropriate scriptural instances occur to me."[102]

FOUR

"Truth Is On The March"

rance had made a remarkable recovery from her 1870 defeat by Prussia and her German allies. The required indemnity to Germany was rapidly paid, and the economy, aided by France's natural resources, grew by leaps and bounds. The 1889 Paris Worlds Fair, with the Eiffel Tower as its central attraction, showed off to multitudes of visitors both France's material accomplishments and the pride that the country took in them. In the early 1890s, Monet's "series paintings" reflected the same feelings. Paris was the center of the world of art, fashion, and gastronomy, and the "City of Light" became a focal point for foreign travelers, including the Prince of Wales, who returned home full of enthusiasm over what they had seen and done.[1]

France had also acquired overseas possessions. To Algeria, taken earlier in the century, in 1878 France added Tunisia, partly with the assistance of Bismarck, who thought that if France sought a colonial empire, it would become embroiled in conflict with England, all to Germany's benefit. There followed Senegal and other parts of Western Africa, Madagascar, the balance of Indo-China and islands in the Pacific Ocean.[2]

France's national obsession was the provinces of Alsace and Lorraine, ceded to Germany in 1871. That defeat, symbolized by the surrender of Napoleon III and his army the previous year, rankled throughout the country, but especially in the army. Time had not cured it. The words of the hero Léon Gambetta, "N'en parlez jamais; pensez-y toujours (Never speak of it; think of it always)" were firmly embedded in the national consciousness.[3] Thus, when Germany decided in 1890 not to renew its Reinsurance Treaty with Russia, France was more than willing to seek a Russian relationship. In less than four months, officers of a visiting French naval flotilla were honored, in the presence of the Tsar, by a playing of the "Marseillaise," which as a revolutionary song had been banned in Russia until that time.[4] The next year the two countries reached an "entente." Politically it was an odd alliance, between the only major European power that was not a monarchy and probably the most despotic country on the continent. But for both countries, fear of the German-Austrian combination and the ill feeling both had toward England made it viable.

In contrast to this record of economic and foreign policy successes stood the domestic political scene. France had not been kind to its republican governments. The Third Republic, established in 1875, still survived, but there was constant concern that it might be replaced by a monarchy or a military cabal. In 1889 the government almost fell to a coup headed by General Georges Boulanger, who was supported by the collective Right, including royalists and the Catholic Church.[5] But for his own hesitation, he likely would have succeeded. On July 27, 1889, however, when his supporters were ready to march with him to the presidential palace, he chose instead to go home to spend the night with his mistress.[6] The Government took heart and several weeks later the General fled to Brussels. The Right was seriously weakened, but when, in 1893, a financial scandal resulted from an unsuccessful attempt to dig a canal across Panama and compromised a number of Radical Party officials, the conservatives took a new lease on life.[7] As 1897 drew to a close, moderate conservatives had been in power for several years.[8]

Into this relatively tranquil scene, the Dreyfus case, known as l'Affaire, was about to erupt with full force. On December 22, 1894, Captain Alfred Dreyfus, a Jewish general staff officer, had been convicted of turning important military secrets over to the German military attache in Paris, Colonel Maximilien von Schwarzkoppen. The French counterintelligence service had obtained evidence that the secrets, relating to French artillery, had been provided by someone whose last name started with "D." Because Dreyfus's handwriting was similar to that on the leaked material and since to some in the military his Jewish origin made him suspect, he had been arrested. At his trial, Major Hubert Henry, a counterintelligence officer, had testified under oath that certain unnamed "unimpeachable sources" had identified Dreyfus as the traitor. This, together with a "secret file" concocted by Minister of War Auguste Mercier and anti-Semitic general staff officer Major Mercier Du Paty de Clam, led to his conviction. Dreyfus was dishonorably discharged from the army and was sentenced to life imprisonment on Devil's Island, a penal settlement for hardened criminals located off the Guiana coast in northern South America.[9]

In 1896, Major Georges Picquart, who had recently been named head of counter-espionage of the Deuxième Bureau, was shown an intercepted letter from the German military attache to French Major Ferdinand Walsin-Esterhazy, a friend of Henry. At the same time Picquart came across an application for transfer signed by Esterhazy, and on a hunch compared the handwriting with the *bordereau* or memorandum supposedly written by Dreyfus that transmitted the military documents to von Schwarzkoppen. The two were unmistakenly the same.[10] When confronted with this evidence, however, Picquart's superior officer was concerned with the reputation of the Army and refused to reopen the case. Instead Picquart was sent overseas to duty on the Tunisian frontier. In November 1896 Henry's superiors, concerned that more evidence might be needed to sustain Dreyfus's conviction, encouraged the Major to doctor a number of otherwise non-incriminating documents which could be used if necessary to support the Army's case against Dreyfus.

Picquart would not be silenced. In mid-1897 he allowed his lawyer to tell his story to certain members of Parliament, among them the long-time vice president of the Senate Charles Auguste Scheurer-Kestner.[11] The Radical politician and editor Georges Clemenceau, who had previously condemned Dreyfus, now took up the cause in his daily journal *L'Aurore*.[12]

On November 16, 1897, Alfred Dreyfus's brother Mathieu publicly denounced Esterhazy as a traitor. This led to an investigation by General Georges de Pellieux, who was temporarily in charge of military operations in Paris. After speaking with General de Boisdeffre, the Chief of the General Staff, he reported to the Council of Ministers that Esterhazy was innocent, but they asked him to investigate further.[13] He did this and apparently was about to dismiss the charges against Esterhazy, when the plot took a new turn. Mme de Boulancy, Esterhazy's former mistress, whom he had swindled and who decided to take revenge, had her lawyer show a set of old letters to Scheurer-Kestner, allowing him to keep the most violent. In one of them Esterhazy wrote:

"If someone were to come tell me this evening that I would be killed tomorrow as a Uhlan captain running through Frenchmen with my saber, I would certainly be perfectly happy," and

"I would not hurt a puppy, but I would have a hundred thousand Frenchmen killed with pleasure."[14]

Scheurer-Kestner took the "Uhlan" letter to Pellieux, and another copy found its way to *Le Figaro*, which published it on November 28. Events now escalated. Esterhazy denied the letter's authenticity, and much of the press backed him. However, in *L'Aurore*, Clemenceau asked, "Who is protecting Commandant Esterhazy?" and

"What secret power, what unstable reasons are countering the action of justice? Who is obstructing its path?"[15]

The General Staff suggested that Esterhazy ask for a court martial, at which his innocence would be established, and Dreyfus indirectly convicted a second time. On December 2 Esterhazy did so and Pellieux's report the next day exonerated him. Then, in the Chamber of Deputies on December 4, the celebrated right-wing orator and deputy Count Albert de Mun denounced a Jewish syndicate "which had been working for German wages...to cast suspicion at will on those who command our Army..." As emotions rose in the Chamber, he called on the Minister of War, Jean Baptiste Billot, who announced to loud acclaim:

"The Dreyfus Affair was adjudicated justly and without irregularity. For my part, in my soul and conscience, as Chief of the Army, I consider the verdict to have been fairly rendered and Dreyfus to be guilty."

The Chamber of Deputies by a large majority then approved a motion approving Dreyfus' conviction. A few days later the Senate concurred.[16]

The French Government hoped that only Esterhazy's expected court martial acquittal remained to bring a final end to the Affair. Others were less sure. Among them was Russian Finance Minister Witte who said to a visiting French diplomat in August, 1897:

"I can see only one thing that could cause great trouble in your country. It is this business of a captain condemned three years ago who is innocent."[17]

Emile Zola was probably the best known and most financially successful French author of his day. At fifty-seven, he had completed his twenty volume masterpiece *Les Rougon-Macquart*, describing in stark naturalistic detail the decay of a family plagued by alcoholism, disease, and degeneracy. His novels were read in translation outside France, and his renown was worldwide.

Zola's success had not lessened his sympathy and advocacy for the workers and others whose impoverishment and suffering he believed were the result of the industrialization that had brought great prosperity to so many others. The feelings bred by his own youthful poverty, when he broiled rats for nourishment, were sustained by the enmity toward him that his attacks on the rich and powerful and the brutal realism of his novels engendered in the political and artistic establishment. Thus, Zola was well recognized as a champion of humanitarian causes.[18]

Zola's involvement in the Dreyfus case began on November 16, 1897, at a lunch at Scheurer-Kestner's home, when he was riveted by an account of the proceedings by Picquart's lawyer, Louis Leblois. Zola was a public opponent of anti-Semitism, but it was the drama of the case that especially gripped him. As he listened to the lawyer's amazing narrative, he exclaimed: "It's thrilling! It's horrible! It's a frightful drama! But it's also drama on the grand scale!" This, coupled with his outrage over Dreyfus's plight, made him an immediate and fervent advocate for the prisoner. He must have known that this course was likely to antagonize many of his largely middle-class readers, who were largely anti-Dreyfus, and deny him forever any chance of membership in the Académie Française. But he quickly pushed aside any such concerns and launched a campaign to have Dreyfus's conviction annulled.[19]

Zola's plan was to publish a series of articles on different aspects of the case to arouse public indignation. His first, on November 25 in *Le Figaro*, was a response to those attacking Scheurer-Kestner, but was remembered for his first use of the Dreyfusard rallying cry: "La verité est en marche, et rien ne l'arretera (Truth is on the march, and nothing will stop it.)."[20] There followed articles on December 1, attacking the claims and claimants of a Jewish conspiracy, and on December 13, urging the youth of France to show concern for their country's future and to "go to combat for Humanity, for Justice, and for Truth."[21] Then on January 6, in a brochure entitled *A Letter to France*, he emotionally urged his fellow countrymen "to remain in the eyes of a watchful Europe, the nation of honor, the nation of humanity, truth, and justice."[22] In the course of his long plea, he warned them of the dangers of military dictatorship:

"At bottom, yours is not yet the real republican blood; the sight of a plumed helmet still makes your heart beat quicker, no king can come amongst us but you fall in love with him. Your Army—ah, yes indeed! It is not of your Army that you are thinking, but of the General who happens to have caught your fancy. And the Dreyfus case has nothing to do with this. While General Billot was getting the Chamber to applaud him,

Emile Zola

I saw the shadow of the sword drawn upon the wall. France, if you do not take care, you are walking straight to a dictatorship."[23]

In closing, he entreated his nation to "delay no longer but come back to your true self" and so "have triumphant reawakenings to Justice and to Truth."

A week later, the two-day court martial of Major Esterhazy ended, as expected, in a unanimous acquittal. Most of the leading players in the drama were there as witnesses—Picquart, Scheurer-Kestner, Henry, and Du Paty de Clam. The audience was strongly pro-Esterhazy. Thus, when Mathieu Dreyfus stated, "I defend my brother in every respect," his answer was greeted by hoots and jeers. When Scheurer-Kestner explained his strong belief that the *bordereau* had not been written by Dreyfus, several of the military officers in the audience audibly sneered, to which the dignified old man scornfully answered, "You find that funny?" On the other hand, when the "defendant," testifying as a hero unjustly slandered, stepped down, the audience applauded him.[24]

Because of alleged security concerns, Picquart was forced to testify in secret, thus depriving the public of the facts of the detailed case against Esterhazy. He was so roughly handled that one of the magistrates intervened: "I see that Colonel Picquart is the true defendant. I request that he be permitted to present all the explanations necessary to his defense." Henry and others accused Picquart of lying. The court's acquittal verdict, reached after only three minutes, was greeted with shouts of "Death to the Jews!" and "Death to the syndicate!" Esterhazy was carried from the courtroom on the shoulders of his admirers.[25]

Some of the foreign press who covered the proceedings stated, as did the *New York Tribune*, that "the day's proceedings have revealed the utter hollowness of the Dreyfusians charge against Esterhazy." Others were not fooled. A Vienna newspaper commented that what had occur-red "was without precedent and well-nigh incredible." Prophetically, Budapest's leading newspaper wrote, "The Esterhazy trial is finished, but the real investigation of the Dreyfus Affair has yet to begin."[26]

Until the Esterhazy court martial, Zola had felt himself constrained from presenting the facts of the Dreyfus case in all their sordid details. Its trumped-up verdict freed him from that self-imposed limitation and also fueled his resolve that he must do something to turn the case around.[27] He wanted to be the man who would accomplish this, admitting to a friend his "prima donna's fear that someone would have his idea at the same time...and take away his part."[28]

So sure was Zola of Esterhazy's acquittal that he spent the night of January 10–11, as well as the following evening, composing at a feverish pace a long letter addressed "Monsieur le Président" to the President of the Third Republic, Fèlix Faure.[29] Initially, his idea was to publish it as a brochure, but at the last minute he decided that it would reach a wider public if it appeared in a newspaper.[30] Since *Le Figaro* had left the Dreyfusard camp, on January 12 he took the letter to *l'Aurore*, where Clemenceau was not only enthusiastic but from the letter's close took the words that gave it the title *J'Accuse* that has ever since identified this classic polemic. With those arresting words appearing as a banner headline, on the morning of January 13 a special edition of 300,000 copies was hawked throughout the streets of Paris by hundreds of news vendors hired for the occasion. More than 200,000 copies were sold.[31]

At the outset, Zola observed, "A council of war has just dared to acquit an Esterhazy in obedience to orders, a fatal blow at all truth, at all justice."

"Since they have dared, I too will dare, for I have promised to tell it, if the courts, once regularly appealed to, did not bring it out fully and entirely. It is my duty to speak. I will not be an accomplice.[32]

There followed a long and detailed discussion of "the truth as to the trial and conviction of Dreyfus,"[33] and then of the Esterhazy case. The letter's close has resounded down the years:

"But this letter is long, Monsieur le Président, and it is time to finish.

"I accuse Lieutenant-Colonel Du Paty de Clam of having been the diabolical workman of judicial error—unconsciously, I am willing to believe—and of having then defended his calamitous work, for three years, by the most guilty machinations.

"I accuse General Mercier of having made himself an accomplice, at least through weakness of mind, in one of the greatest iniquities of the century.

"I accuse General Billot of having had in his hands certain proofs of the innocence of Dreyfus, and of having stifled them; of having rendered himself guilty of his crime of *lèse-humanité* and *lèse-justice* for a political purpose, and to save the compromised staff.

"I accuse General de Boisdeffre and General Gonse of having made themselves accomplices in the same crime, one undoubtedly through clerical passion, the other perhaps through that *esprit de corps* which makes the war offices the Holy Ark, unassailable.

"I accuse General de Pellieux and Major Ravary of having conducted a rascally inquiry—I mean by that a monstrously partial inquiry, of which we have, in the report of the latter, an imperishable monument of naïve audacity.

"I accuse the three experts in handwriting, Belhomme, Varinard, and Couard, of having made lying and fraudulent reports, unless a medical examination should declare them afflicted with diseases of the eye and of the mind.

"I accuse the war offices of having carried on in the press, particularly in *L'Éclair* and in *L'Écho de Paris,* an abominable campaign, to mislead opinion and cover up their faults.

"I accuse, finally, the first council of war of having violated the law by condemning an accused person on the strength of a secret document, and I accuse the second council of war of having covered this illegality, in obedience to orders, in committing in its turn the judicial crime of knowingly acquitting a guilty man.

"In preferring these charges, I am not unaware that I lay myself liable under Articles 30 and 31 of the press law of July 29, 1881, which punishes defamation. And it is wilfully that I expose myself thereto.

"As for the people whom I accuse, I do not know them, I have never seen them, I entertain against them no feeling of revenge or hatred. They are to me simple entities, spirits of social ill-doing. And the act that I perform here is nothing but a revolutional measure to hasten the explosion of truth and justice

"I have but one passion, the passion for the light, in the name of humanity which has suffered so much, and which is entitled to happiness. My fiery protest is simply the cry of my soul. Let them dare, then, to bring me into the Assize Court, and let the investigation take place in the open day.

"I await it."[34]

The reaction to *J'Accuse* was intense. Very rarely in history has a single writing had such a powerful and immediate effect. Overnight, Zola had brought together and unified the disparate elements of Dreyfusard sentiment. As the politician Léon Blum wrote, "Dreyfusism was reinvigorated...we could feel the confidence well up and rise within us."[35]

Indeed, Zola had touched sentiments that were much deeper and more widespread than concern for the prisoner on Devils Island. Writer Anatole France spoke of "a moment in the conscience of mankind."[36] As copies of *J'Accuse* were published outside France, Zola received piles of supporting letters and telegrams from around the world."[37] Indicative of the reaction was Mark Twain's comment in the *New York Herald*:

"Such cowards, hypocrites, and flatterers as the members of the military and ecclesiastical courts the world could produce by the millions every year. But it takes five centuries to produce a Joan of Arc or a Zola."[38]

The government's initial reaction was to make no official response to *J'Accuse*, on the basis that in that event the excitement would blow over.[39] This was also Esterhazy's opinion. However, just as Zola coalesced support for Dreyfus, so also his article inflamed those who believed that the Captain was guilty.[40] Count de Mun charged that it was "a bloody outrage to the leaders of the Army," and he and other deputies demanded action against Zola—a response that the latter seemed to be courting in his article.[41]

Thus, on January 18, the Council of Ministers drafted a complaint against Zola, to be presented by the Minister of War. Cleverly, the draftsmen made no reference to the Dreyfus case, in order that the document would provide no basis for reopening that proceeding. Instead, the complaint was based on a single sentence in the article, in which Zola accused Esterhazy's court martial of acquiring the Major "on command" and of committing "the juridical crime of knowingly acquitting a guilty man."[42] The trial was scheduled to begin on February 7.[43]

Meanwhile, anti-Semitic riots broke out in Paris and other French cities. Demonstrations lasted six days in Rouen and five days in Marseilles. Segments of the Catholic clergy and press were particularly critical of the Jews. The anti-Semitic campaign was also fueled by economic discontent, nourished "as much in Rothschild as in Judas," and by a nationalist fervor that viewed the Dreyfus camp as subverters of French national interests exemplified by the Army.[44] A *New York Times* correspondent warned from Paris that "the anti-Jewish crusade is assuming most alarming proportions."[45]

Zola was vilified to an extent almost unimaginable. He was burned in effigy, there were demonstrations against him on the Paris boulevards, and his mail included packages of excrement. The world watched in amazement at these attacks on the man who was probably France's best known author and also at the implications of the army's alleged crimes.[46]

⸻⸻

On January 22 the debate in the Chamber of Deputies erupted into physical violence. When the assembly gave Premier Jules Méline a standing ovation for an attack on Zola, it precipitated an impassioned response from socialist Jean Jaurès. The danger to the republic, he warned, was not from

"those who warn us in time of our errors, but those who commit them, yesterday court generals protected by the Empire, today Jesuit-spawned generals protected by the Republic."

By now, said one observer,

"...he was thundering, his face gone purple, his arms stretched out toward the ministers he was protesting and the right all aroar."

When he called one deputy "a scoundrel and a coward," the latter attacked him, other deputies also came to blows, and the military was called in to restore order.[47]

On February 7 Zola's trial commenced in a frenzy that the staid old Palais de Justice never had seen. The courtroom was jammed, with onlookers sitting on windowsills, stoves, and even on other persons' knees. The crowd was infiltrated by army officers, who were primed to demonstrate in support of the prosecution whenever it became necessary or appropriate. Zola could take solace from the more than 400 supporting telegrams he received from all over the world, including one signed by 1,000 Belgian lawyers and literary celebrities.[48]

The judge, Jules Delegorgue, was a portly and amiable man, whose *amour propre* at presiding at such an important event was equaled only by his evident desire not to antagonize the government, to which he was beholden for his job.[49] The prosecution was headed by Advocate General Edmond Van Cassel, described as "surly and brutal." Zola was represented by the giant and loud-voiced Fernand Labori, and co-defendant and *L'Aurore* managing editor Perrenx's lawyer was Georges Clemenceau's brother Albert. The twelve-man jury was largely lower middle class.[50] Their names had been published in advance, so that, according to the Dreyfusards, they could be more easily intimidated.[51]

Labori had assembled a strong defense team, including Léon Blum, who was also an outstanding lawyer. They planned to call nearly 200 witnesses, including Esterhazy and Ministers of War Mercier and Billot.[52] When Van Cassel learned of the large number of prospective witnesses, however, he correctly surmised that Labori's goal was to use the case as a vehicle to prove Dreyfus innocent. At the trial's outset he therefore moved successfully to limit discussion to the charge based on Zola's claim that Esterhazy's judges had been biased.[53]

On February 11, as his trial moved into its fifth day, Zola insisted on replying to Pellieux's charge of the prior day that his conduct had been a disservice to France:

"I would ask General de Pellieux if he does not think that there are many ways to serve France. One can serve it with the sword and with the pen."

However favorable an impression these words may have made on the jury, they were more than offset when Zola's ego then got the better of him as he proclaimed that he would be remembered long after the General had been forgotten.[54]

The following day Picquart took the witness stand. His testimony, like the man himself, was restrained and unemotional. However, perhaps for this reason, it was especially well received, and the previously subdued Dreyfusards in the courtroom gave him an ovation.[55]

After the recess, Picquart was confronted by a series of officers ready to contradict his testimony. When recently promoted Lieutenant Colonel Henry testified that, when he had seen Picquart and his lawyer Louis Leblois perusing the General Staff's secret dossier, an important photocopy protruded from the envelope containing it, Leblois interrupted. He reminded the court that in other testimony, Henry had said, "The photocopy never left the envelope."[56] Henry tried to recover by saying that if he had seen Leblois and Picquart reviewing the secret dossier it was in a "figurative sense."[57] Then, suddenly excited and striking the stand with his hand, he shouted, "And I, I stand by everything that I said and I will add that Colonel Picquart has lied." He offered his cheek as if daring Picquart to strike it, and the latter raised his arm, only to lower it. Judge Delegorgue tried to ease the tension that filled the courtroom by mildly commenting, "You two are in disagreement."[58]

Henry's charge temporarily broke Picquart's reserve. For an hour, through clenched teeth, he described the facts of the Dreyfus case as he knew them to be. Emotionally, he concluded:

"Gentlemen of the jury, it has now been I don't know how much time, months that I have been heaped with insults by newspapers that are paid to spread such slander and untruth.... For months, I remained in the situation most horrible for an officer, since my honor was attacked and I was unable to defend myself. Tomorrow, perhaps, I will be expelled from the Army that I love and to which I have given twenty-five years of my life. That did not stop me, when I thought it my duty to pursue truth and justice. I did so, and in so doing I believed I was doing a greater service to my country and to the Army."[59]

By February 16 the prosecution had become worried. On the previous evening the War Ministry had received police reports that the jurors "are weary of interminable squabbles" and, because "they feel uncertain of where the truth lies...are inclined to acquit Zola."[60] On February 17 the prosecution brought General de Pellieux to the stand in order to turn the tide by a call for the vindication of the army:

"What do you want the army to become on the day of danger, which may be closer than you think? What do you want the poor soldiers to do, who will be led into battle by leaders discredited in their eyes? It is to the slaughterhouse that your sons would be led, gentlemen of the jury! But Zola would have won a new battle, he would write a new Debacle, he would carry the French language everywhere to a Europe from which France would have been expunged."[61]

A contemporary observer described Pellieux as "(a) superb swordsman deploying in the service of his conviction the ardor, eloquence, and fearlessness of a believer attesting to his faith."[62] He was all of that as he held the courtroom, including the jury, emotionally spellbound with his peroration:

"We would have been happy had the court-martial of 1894 acquitted Dreyfus; it would have proven that there was not a traitor in the army, and we are still in mourning over that fact. But what the court-martial of 1898 would not countenance, the abysmal deed it would not commit, is this: it would not put an innocent man in the place of Dreyfus, be he guilty or not."[63]

After the midday recess, Picquart returned to the stand to explain how Dreyfus could not have written the fateful *bordereau* and Esterhazy easily could have done so. Pellieux dramatically interrupted, demanding to be heard on the basis that the "pact of silence" about the Dreyfus court-martial had just been broken and that he was now free to tell the truth.[64] He went on to quote from a letter that "came to the Ministry of

War...whose origin cannot be contested." What Pellieux apparently did not know or even suspect was that the sentences he had read had been added in 1896 by Major Henry to an otherwise unimportant letter in order to further establish Dreyfus's guilt in the face of Picquart's efforts to prove the Captain's innocence.[65]

Zola's lawyer Labori immediately intervened, urging that the letter be made part of the proceedings. Probably aware of doubts as to its authenticity, he argued:

"So long as we do not recognize it, so long as we have not discussed it, so long as it will not have been made publicly known, it will not count...."[66]

Deputy Chief of Staff, General Gonse, fully aware of Henry's forgery, tried to retrieve the situation:

"The Army...does not at all fear saying where the truth is in order to save its honor. But prudence is needed; and I do not at all see how one can publicly bring here evidence of that nature, which exists, which is real, which is absolute."[67]

The excitement in the court then rose to a fever pitch as Pellieux, carried away by his own eloquence and apparent success, asked for General de Boisdeffre, the Army Chief of Staff, to be summoned for immediate testimony. Not only would his word dispose of the issue, but "there are other documents, which General de Boisdeffre will describe."[68]

De Boisdeffre was not immediately available, and his testimony was postponed until the next day. A frightened Henry later commented: "What Pellieux did was absurd. Documents as secret as that should not be discussed in public."[69] His concern was more than justified, for as one astute chronicler of the Affair observed, Pellieux had made an "enormous blunder" which in the end would "deliver up the key to Henry's machinations."[70]

The next day General de Boisdeffre was a striking figure as he stood before the jury in his impressive dress uniform covered with medals.[71] He had been primed overnight, and supported Pellieux on every count. His position as Army Chief of Staff made his short and clearly memorized statement especially convincing:

"I will be brief. I confirm on all points General Pellieux's deposition as being exact and authentic. I have not a single word more to say; I don't have the right to, gentlemen, I repeat, I don't have the right to."[72]*

This, however, was not de Boisdeffre's closing word. There remained an appeal to French patriotism and military honor:

"Permit me, in closing, to tell you something. You are the jury, you are the nation. If the nation does not have confidence in the chiefs of the Army, in those who have the responsibility for national defense, they are prepared to leave to others this heavy task. You have only to speak. I shall not say another word."[73]

When Labori rose to cross-examine the General, Judge Delegorgue stopped him: "You do not have the floor. The incident is closed."[74]

Emotions were running high outside as well as inside the courtroom. *The New York Times*'s Paris correspondent reported that Pellieux "was so overcome by his reception on leaving that his tears flowed freely while shaking hands with the crowd, which applauded him as though he had driven the Germans back across the Rhine." At the same time, Zola was attacked by a crowd on his way home and was saved by the police from a probable lynching.[75]

Although the trial would continue for five more days, the rest would be anticlimax. The jury had no real choice but to convict Zola. The cost to the reputation of the Army and of France would be significant, however. Thus, an English newspaper, the *Westminster Gazette*, commented that "[T]he Third Republic no longer exists...General de Boisdeffre's coup d'état differs from Napoleon's only in the degree of brutality of the attendant circumstances."[76]

On February 21, reading from a prepared text in a tremulous voice frequently drowned out by jeers and insults, Zola made a plea to the jury not so much for himself as for Dreyfus:

"You are the heart and reason of Paris, of my great Paris, where I was born and of whom I have been singing for almost forty years...In striking me, you will only make me greater.

Dreyfus is innocent, I swear it. I pledge my life that that is so, I pledge my honor. At this solemn hour,...before all of France, before the entire world, I swear that Dreyfus is innocent...And by all that I have conquered, by the name I have made for myself, by my works, which have advanced

---

* The implication was that his silence was required for national security reasons.

the cause of French letters abroad, I swear that Dreyfus is innocent. May it all crumble, may my works perish if Dreyfus is not innocent. He is innocent."[77]

The Zola jury had made up its mind several days earlier. Thus on February 23 it took it only thirty-five minutes to return guilty verdicts. Zola was sentenced to a year in prison, the maximum penalty, and editor Perrenx to four months. Each was fined 3,000 francs. Undaunted by the verdict, Zola turned to a figure of Christ hanging over the bench and exclaimed: "Today, associated with Christ, I, too, am a victim of mob violence, official cowardice, and a grand miscarriage of justice."[78]

Both inside and outside the Palais de Justice there were cheers of "Long live the Army!" and "Long live France!," but also shouts of satisfied vengeance: "Death to Zola!" and "Death to the Jews!" As Zola left the building, he muttered to a group of protecting friends, "They are cannibals." Clemenceau later commented, "Had Zola been acquitted, not one of us would have come out alive." Throughout the night and into the next day, demonstrators ran through the streets of Paris, yelling insults to the Jews and praise for the Army.[79]

Next day, in the Chamber of Deputies, Premier Méline announced that the jury verdict should put an end to further controversy over Dreyfus and threatened:

"As of tomorrow, all those who would continue the struggle would no longer be arguing in good faith....We will apply to them the full severity of the laws, and if the arms at our disposal are insufficient, we will ask you for others."[80]

However, even in the unlikely event that the Government could quell further internal discord, it could do nothing to stop the avalanche of criticism from abroad. The London *Times* wrote that "Zola's true crime has been in daring to rise to defend the truth and civil liberty...for that courageous defense of the primordial rights of the citizens, he will be honored wherever men have souls that are free..."[81] A Budapest newspaper asked rhetorically, "To what depths must the nation have sunk which casts Zola into prison?"[82]

Across the Atlantic, the Dreyfus case had become front page news. Excitement over the *Maine* did not displace an almost equal interest in Zola's trial and outrage at the verdict. That pillar of midwest Republicanism, the Chicago *Tribune*, protested: "Such a farcical perversion of the methods of justice could not be conceived as occurring in England or America..." *The New York Times*, after making a comparison to "our yellow journals," charged that

"...the sensational press of Paris...has turned a public trial into a farce, played by the mob as chorus and Generals in uniform as principals, making speeches directing the jury what to do and producing incredible statements upon which they declined to face cross-examination. Such a mockery of justice has not been seen in modern times in a civilized country."[83]

The British Ambassador to France, Sir Edmond Monson, was becoming worried over the effect of the Dreyfus case on Anglo-French relations. By February 26, he had completed extended conversations regarding the case's disruptive nature with his counterparts from Germany, Austria, and Italy. He immediately sent Lord Salisbury a disturbing dispatch:

"...my three colleagues are of opinion that the present temper of France is a standing danger and menace to Europe: that she is recurring to the frame of mind of one hundred years ago, when she looked upon the rest of Europe as banded against her, and when she had but the one thought with which she is now possessed, that between herself and destruction there stands only her army.

There are other intelligent observers, Frenchmen as well as foreigners, who are losing all hope that France can escape an internal convulsion; a convulsion in which the Army will take a prominent part, and which will equally be followed by a foreign war."

Monson then penned this warning:

"What I do agree with is the opinion that the public temper is dangerously irritable, and especially against foreign countries; and none the less so that the new ally Russia is suspected of already regretting having entered into a mesalliance. In the flurry of excitement and under the influence of the irritability of the Army it might be a relief to France to pick a quarrel with the one Great European Power who cannot invade her, personal jealousy of whom supplies almost as much ample ground for vindictiveness as is furnished by Germany by the memory of the last international struggle."[84]

FIVE

"For Germany The Most Dangerous Enemy Is England"

Less than thirty-years old, the German empire was the strongest power in Europe. By its defeat of Austria in 1866 and France in 1870, the Prussia of Kaiser William I and his Chancellor Otto von Bismarck had demonstrated an awe-inspiring military superiority that was enhanced by the German unification of 1871.

For the next nineteen years Bismarck utilized this powerful position to acquire possessions in Africa while at the same time seeking friendly relations with Germany's European neighbors. Recognizing that the rapprochement with Austria established after 1866 offered neither a strong ally nor protection on Germany's major flanks, he joined Russia to that alliance in 1873 in a League of Three Emperors. This relationship was imperiled when Germany and Britain warded off a conflict between Austria and Russia at the 1878 Congress of Berlin by forcing the latter to surrender some of the Balkan possessions she had just seized from Turkey. But Bismarck persisted in seeking a positive relationship with his eastern neighbor by renewing the Three Emperors League in 1884 and following up in 1887 with a Reinsurance Treaty with each country. At the same time he cultivated friendly relations with Britain.

By 1898 much of what Bismarck had created was gone. In 1888 the old Kaiser, who had consistently supported his chancellor, died at age eighty-nine. His son Frederick was already dying of cancer and ruled less than three-and-a-half months. Frederick's son, William, age only twenty-nine, succeeded to the throne. Unlike Bismarck, he was emotional, impulsive, and self-confident. He was especially prone to flattery and, unfortunately for one so easily influenced, liked to practice his own diplomacy.

These traits, plus their forty-four-year age difference, inevitably led to a collision between the two men. On March 18, 1890, feeling unable to function properly, Bismarck resigned. The Kaiser accepted, not unhappily. As a famous *Punch* cartoon of the time observed, the nautically minded William had "dropped the pilot."[1] Although he remained a potent political force, Bismarck never returned to power. By late 1897 he was a dying man. Consistently at odds with the Kaiser, he attributed the purpose of William's last visit, in December, as "to see how long the old man will last."[2]

The effects of Bismarck's resignation were immediate and far reaching. The three-year Reinsurance Treaty with Russia had only three months to run. The Kaiser and his new Chancellor, George Leo von Caprivi, were concerned that this secret agreement was inconsistent with Germany's treaty with Austria, which was unaware of the Russian agreement. Despite warnings from the Russians that failure to resume the arrangement would force them to seek a French alliance, the Germans decided not to do so. Shortly thereafter Franco-Russian discussions commenced and led the following year to a formal understanding between Germany's eastern and western neighbors.

During the 1890s German industrial production and trade grew at an accelerated pace. By 1897 the country's ruling classes had agreed that both national pride and continuing prosperity demanded the acquisition of new colonies, trading ports, coaling stations, and naval bases.[3] Germany, like England, must be a world power—"Weltmacht"—with all its trappings. The Kaiser believed that he should lead the implementation of this policy. Unable to cope with his ruler, Caprivi had resigned in 1894, and was replaced by an increasingly infirm septuagenarian, Prince Chlodwig zu Hohenlohe, who had little influence on the increasingly confident and assertive Kaiser.

In 1897, the Kaiser named the forty-eight-year-old diplomat Bernhard von Bülow as his new Foreign Secretary. Bülow's guiding principle was not to antagonize William. By nature a flatterer, he easily complied with the suggestion of the Kaiser's close friend Philip von Eulenberg at the time of his appointment:

"Only if you take the Kaiser in the right way can you be of use to your country…. He wants to teach others, but learns unwillingly himself…. He loves glory and is ambitious and jealous. In order to get him to accept an idea, you must act as though the idea was his. You must make everything easy for him. He readily encourages others to take bold steps but throws them overboard if they fail. Never forget that His Majesty needs praise…. He is as grateful for it as a good and clever child."[4]

Witty and cultivated, but contemptuous of others, Bülow reportedly had so little character that his long-time associate Admiral Alfred von Tirpitz remarked that compared to Bülow an eel was like a leech.[5]

Friedrich von Holstein, the well-established First Consular of the Foreign Ministry, was no better. Hard working, clever, and seemingly all-knowing, he was also cantankerous and furtive. A master of "machiavellian intrigue,"[6] he was known as the "Monster of the Labyrinth."[7] Completely amoral, he kept "secret dossiers with the evidence of young sailors and bath attendants" that he would be able to use on Bülow and Eulenberg. Bismarck once observed that "if the fear of good is demoniacal, then Holstein is a real demon."[8]

The Kaiser's mother was Queen Victoria's oldest daughter, so William regarded himself as half British. He was extremely fond of his "Grandmama," who had been kind to him as a boy. But his relationship with his mother was poor, and with her brother and his uncle, the Prince of Wales, was increasingly antagonistic.[9] He was often enraged that, as the German envoy to London said to Lord Salisbury, the Prince "treated him as an uncle treats a nephew instead of recognizing that he was an emperor who, though young, had been of age for some time."[10] The Kaiser also believed that democratic England was morally lax and overly interested in material wealth.[11] Like many of his countrymen, he objected to a perceived British air of international superiority and to the ability that England's control of the seas gave it to extend its empire seemingly at will.

At the end of 1895 a Dr. Jameson made an unauthorized and unsuccessful raid from South Africa into the Boer republic of the Transvaal. William took pleasure in sending a telegram to Boer President Kruger, congratulating him for repelling the invasion. The British public exploded, but Salisbury refused to be stampeded into a conflict. Hohenlohe for once was able to exert himself and persuade William to write his grandmother Queen that the telegram was not "intended as a step against England or your Government."[12] Tensions ebbed, but the episode left in England a residue of ill feeling toward Germany.[13] It also caused the latter to realize that its naval weakness would have precluded it from sending armed support to the Boers even had it wished to do so.[14] This, plus surprise over the strength of the British reaction to the telegram, gave strong support to the German advocates of a powerful navy.[15]

Their policy won official approval with the appointment of von Tirpitz as Navy Minister. At his first audience with the Kaiser on June 15, 1897, the new minister made clear his opinion that a battleship fleet would be necessary to fight England:

Dropping The Pilot

"For Germany the most dangerous enemy at the present time is England. It is also the enemy against which we most urgently require a certain measure of naval force as a political power factor....Our fleet must be so constructed that it can unfold its greatest military potential between Heligoland and the Thames.... The military situation against England demands battleships in as great a number as possible"[16]

The Kaiser, always interested in naval matters, quickly approved Tirpitz's memorandum.[17] Bülow, the new Foreign Secretary, also supported a large fleet since it would further his goal of Weltpolitik. He recognized that while the fleet was being authorized and constructed, the task of German foreign policy was to provide "cover" until the German navy would be a match for England's.[18] To that end, he believed that what he thought would be an inevitable Anglo-Russian war in Asia should be secretly encouraged.[19] Such a conflict would weaken both countries, and make it easier for Germany to become the predominant world power.[20]

By year end 1897 legislation that would enact Tirpitz' program had been drafted and initially debated in the Reichstag.[21] Previously, the Admiral had obtained endorsements from leading personages, including Bismarck. Before visiting the former Chancellor to gain his support, Tirpitz had persuaded William to name the next big warship to be launched "First Bismarck" (Prince Bismarck).[22] After a day-long visit during which the ex-Chancellor consumed two large bottles of beer as he took Tirpitz on a lengthy carriage ride over his estate, he gave the Admiral a letter in which he supported a modest increase in the navy's size.[23] In the Reichstag, the need for a stronger navy was carefully explained as defensive. Thus, in his Speech from the Throne, the Kaiser denied that "it can be our aim to compete with the sea powers of the first rank."[24] The need for a larger fleet was to "assert German prestige in the eyes of the people of the world."[25]

Despite these efforts, the outcome was in doubt, and Tirpitz redoubled his efforts to drum up support for the naval bill.[26] An example was a mass meeting of businessmen in Berlin on January 13 in response to an invitation signed by 251 individuals and groups including the heads of 78 chambers of commerce. The loud outcries of support these activities engendered had a force of their own. As one journal, the *Neu Zurcher Zeitung*, ruefully observed on January 19:

"On all sides interest groups are being called upon to participate in political life. Their votes are beginning to achieve a significance in support of the government which parallels the real, legal parliaments equipped with proper constitutional rights by the Prussian and German constitutions."

A 1960s commentator referred to this as the first German use of what was "later to be a favorite device" of the Nazis:

"By creating a deafening uproar outside, the parliamentarians inside could be frightened and baffled into approving anything."[27]

=⏻❂⏻=

The proposed German naval buildup had not gone unnoticed in England. British colonial policy, and, indeed, British foreign policy in general were based on a powerful navy. Since 1889 it had been accepted by both political parties that the British fleet must be at least twice the size and strength of the naval forces of any other two countries. This fundamental policy goal was fueled by commercial interests, who knew that Britain's prosperity depended on overseas trade, by the doctrines of Admiral Mahan, and by tradition going back to the days of Drake and, more recently, Nelson.[28]

There was, therefore, increasing British concern that, when combined with the Austrian Mediterranean fleet, the Kaiser's navy might be more than half the strength of the British forces, thus vitiating the two-power principle. On February 4, First Sea Lord Admiral Sir Frederick Richards wrote George Goschen, First Lord of the Admiralty:

"We all know that the present accepted basis of mere equality with two Powers is not a sufficient margin for the Navy which occupies the inferior strategical position.... For a nation which claims for herself supremacy upon the high seas, the margin which England allows herself for securing her dominion is decidedly small."[29]

The British press had already taken up the issue. Two months earlier, the London *Times* had warned that the expansion that the Reichstag was considering "cannot in the nature of the things be final, and is probably not seriously intended to be final by its authors." Not surprisingly, this outcry played into the hands of Tirpitz and his allies, who used the British reaction as proof of the need to build up the Reich's sea power as a defense against England.[30]

=⏻❂⏻=

The Reichstag's Budget Committee began its considerations of Tirpitz's Navy Bill on February 24. The pressure on the committee to approve the legislation was intense. The committee's reporter, Dr. Lieber, proposed that the legislation be considered in three steps: its content, its form and its financial basis. After this proposal was promptly agreed to, he put the question as how and why the Navy had arrived "at this clear plan," and could "the Navy assert that this Bill was not developed in three months but is the result of many years of experience?" Tirpitz evaded the question by justifying a larger fleet on the basis of the needs of German shipping, trade, and national defense. Lieber overruled objections by the opposition members to the secret nature of the proceedings and then closed debate by concluding that Tirpitz had given a satisfactory answer. The meeting then adjourned.[31]

On February 26, the Budget Committee commenced discussion of the second stage of its agenda—the form the navy legislation would take. Since the program would extend beyond the life of the current Reichstag, Lieber stated that it was important that the Government "must for its part agree to an understanding that it will not demand higher sums of money than the law provides within the next seven years."[32] As he did two days earlier, Tirpitz evaded the question. Instead, he responded:

"...in my opinion the Navy Law would be unacceptable to the Associated Governments if it were not to provide legal certainty that (1) the fleet will be completed within the time specified by the Associated Governments within the proportions which those governments regard as necessary; and (2) the fleet held to be necessary can be maintained in combat readiness."[33]

Tirpitz had chosen not to name a monetary limit on expenditures so that no one could later accuse him of breaking a promise. As Lieber knew, he would expect there to be some limit, but wished to make it appear as if it had been forced on the Government. With this tacit understanding, the committee quickly finished its work on the second phase of the legislation.[34]

To date, the bill had seen smooth sailing in the Reichstag, but passage still depended on the support of the ninety-six deputies of the Centre Party. At a March 8 party caucus, some of the deputies complained that they had been duped. Their objection related to a provision in the bill that approval of the Government as well as the Reichstag was required for any alteration in the terms originally agreed on as to the replacement of obsolete vessels. To Tirpitz, this Government veto was vital, since it would prevent Reichstag tampering with what otherwise would be an automatic modernization of the fleet. He wrote the leader of the Centre Party that he would resign if the Reichstag were given this power unilaterally.[35]

Tirpitz's threat may have been a bluff, but it succeeded. The Admiral was the Centre Party's only ally in the administration; if he left, the party faced a future of the same lonely opposition that had previously been its lot. The proposal that had incensed Tirpitz was withdrawn, and the Budget Committee's deliberations continued on a positive note.[36]

Its final discussion took place on the evening of March 16. Earlier that day Tirpitz had made another threat: either a minimum of fifty Centre Party deputies voted for the bill, or the Government would be forced to dissolve the Reichstag and call for a general election. Lieber and his allies also must abandon their proposal to finance the naval expansion by progressive income taxes levied by the German states in favor of a substitute that spoke of "taxes which burden mass consumption," e.g., the tariff. With no other practical choice, a weary Lieber backed down, and the following morning the committee approved the bill by a nineteen-to-eight vote.[37]

On March 23 the Reichstag began its final consideration of the Navy bill. By now approval was assured, and speeches by the bill's opponents recognized the outcome. Among them, however, was a prophetic warning by the antimilitarist Socialist party leader August Bebel:

"There is, especially on the right side of this house, a large group of fanatical anglophobes made up of men who want to pick a fight with England and who would rather fight today than tomorrow. But to believe that with our fleet, yes, even if it is finished to the very last ship demanded in this law, we could take up the cudgels against England, is to approach the realm of insanity. Those who demand it belong not in the Reichstag but in the madhouse...."[38]

Bebel's statement was greeted with laughter. A post-World-War-II historian of the period has speculated that this derision stemmed from the very madness that Bebel described, which reflected an anti-British attitude that had become prevalent in the Reichstag even though Tirpitz had decided that his anti-English plan had to be clothed in more circumspect raiment if it were to be approved.[39]

Following Bebel's speech, the voting commenced on the afternoon of March 24 and resumed on March 26. Each paragraph of the bill was the subject of a separate vote, but discipline was such that on each provision there were at least 198 "yea" votes and the "nays" never exceeded thirty. At 5:10 P.M. March 26, Tirpitz telegraphed the Kaiser that all paragraphs of the legislation had been approved. Bülow sent a similar message a few minutes later, adding the postscript "Long Live the Kaiser." There was great rejoicing in Government and military circles.[40]

British reaction to its enactment was surprisingly restrained. The London *Times*'s March 28 comment reflected the general feeling:

"Every reasonable man must admit that in these circumstances she does well to consider her naval position."[41]

The *Times* believed that the major effect of the German action would be that France and Russia would feel obligated to expand their fleets, and that this rather than the German buildup would require Britain to add to her navy in order to maintain the two-power standard. A major British concern was that Germany would ally itself with Russia and France and, like Napoleon, threaten to invade England with a much more powerful fleet than Napoleon's.[42] But, as the *Times* concluded:

"In these circumstances, whatever we may think of the policy involved, there is not much than can profitably be said..."[43]

In the short run, Tirpitz had been completely successful: he could effect the German naval buildup immune from concern over the British reaction. The long-range consequences were to be far different. As a noted American historian observed:

"...as we look back we cannot fail to note that this fundamental change was one of the most important factors making for the later alignment of the powers. It was one of the most dangerous of innovations. It helped tremendously to embitter Anglo-German relations, and thereby to set the stage for the ultimate conflict."[44]

SIX

A Futile Search For Peace

The headline on Hearst's February 16 *Journal*'s first report of the disaster "Cruiser *Maine* Blown Up In Havana Harbor" was circumspect enough. So was the almost identical "U.S.S. *Maine* Blown Up in Havana Harbor" in Joseph Pulitzer's competing New York *World*. By afternoon, however, the *Journal* had abandoned all restraint with one of editor Arthur Brisbane's unique split headlines:

CRISIS AT HAND
Cabinet in Session, Growing Belief In
SPANISH TREACHERY[1]

The initial reaction in Washington and throughout the country was a numbing shock at the unbelievable news. Quickly, however, to the stunned "How?" was added an increasingly insistent "Who?" and much of the press pointed an accusatory finger at Spain. But McKinley would not be stampeded into judgment, even though a large number of Senators and Congressmen spoke of an immediate declaration of war. The deeply worried President told a friend whom he invited to the White House the evening of the sixteenth:

"I don't propose to be swept off my feet by the catastrophe. My duty is plain. We must learn the truth and endeavor, if possible, to fix the responsibility. The country can afford to withhold its judgment and not strike an avenging blow until the truth is known. The Administration will go on preparing for war, but still hoping to avert it. It will not be plunged into war until it is ready for it."[2]

To Theodore Roosevelt, there was no doubt where responsibility for the disaster lay. Officially, in a memorandum to Secretary Long, to whom he expressed "the greatest regard and respect for you personally," he appeared noncommittal:

"It may be impossible to ever settle definitively whether or not the *Maine*

82

was destroyed through some treachery on the part of the Spaniards."[3]

To an old friend and fellow Harvard Porcellian Club member, however, he was more open:

"Being a Jingo, as I am writing confidentially from one porc man to another, I will say, to relieve my feelings, that I would give anything if President McKinley would order the fleet to Havana tomorrow. This Cuban business ought to stop. The *Maine* was sunk by an act of dirty treachery on the part of the Spaniards I believe, though we shall never find out definitely, and it will go down an accident."[4]

At dawn on February 16, Captain Sigsbee arose from a brief and fitful sleep in a cabin on the *City of Washington* and went on deck. He later described the awful sight of his former ship that greeted him:

"The forward part of the central superstructure had been blown upward and somewhat to starboard, and had folded back on its afterpart, carrying the bridge, pilothouse, and six-inch gun and conning tower with it, and completely capsizing them. The broad surface that was uppermost was the ceiling of the berth deck, where many men had swung from beam to beam in their hammocks the night before. On the white paint of the ceiling was the impression of two human bodies—mere dusting."[5]

Later that day Sigsbee received the grim news that of the 350 men and officers aboard the *Maine* at the time of the explosion, more than 250 were either killed or missing and thus presumed dead. Another eight would later die of their injuries.[6]

Havana had gone into deep mourning, with flags everywhere at half mast and theaters and many shops closed. The hospitals could not have been more caring, and, as Sigsbee wrote, the Spaniards did for the wounded "all they habitually did for their own people and even more."[7] Meanwhile, a worried Spanish government instructed Governor General Blanco "to gather every fact you can to prove the *Maine* catastrophe cannot be attributed to us."[8]

Two days after the *Maine* disaster, speculation was rising as to its cause.

The New York *World*'s story, written by its Havana correspondent Sylvester Scovel, was reasonably impartial, stating that the cause would be determined by whether the "indentation in the hull is inward." In that event "the conclusion that the magazine was exploded by a bomb or torpedo placed beneath the vessel is inevitable." On the other hand, "If the indentation is outward, it will be indicated that the first explosion was in the magazine."[9]

The *World*'s headline was less balanced. It read: "Maine Explosion Caused by Bomb or Torpedo?" and the continuation of Scovel's story on page two carried a page-wide headline: "Growing Suspicion That a Torpedo Was Used."[10] To the readers of Hearst's *Journal* there could be no doubt, since their eyes were greeted with: "WAR! SURE!," followed by: "Maine Destroyed by Spanish: This Proved Absolutely by Discovery of the TORPEDO HOLE." Hearst also offered a "$50,000 Reward for Detection of the Maine Outrage," and the next day's *Journal* sales exceeded one million.[11]

It was little wonder that the Associated Press found it necessary to report from Washington:

"The cruiser New York has not been ordered to Havana; Consul-General Lee has not been assassinated; there is no conference of the Cabinet; Congress is not in session tonight, both Houses having adjourned at the usual hour until tomorrow; President McKinley did not go to the Capitol, and the situation is decidedly quiet."[12]

The *Maine* disaster was bringing forth an outpouring of British support for the United States. It ranged from messages from Queen Victoria and the Prince and Princess of Wales to a request by the owner of the *Morning Post* to open subscriptions in his newspapers for the relief of the families of the *Maine* casualties. The London *Times* commented that nowhere would sympathy for the United States "be so general or profound as amongst their British and Irish kinsfolk at home and in the colonies."[13]

In Havana harbor Spanish patrol boats were turning back American divers that were trying to examine the *Maine*'s wreck. On February 18 Captain Sigsbee and Consul-General Lee went to the palace to protest. General Blanco replied that there should be no difficulties, but then suggested a joint Spanish-American investigation of the disaster. Spanish honor was at stake, he said. Sigsbee and Lee promised to transmit his request to Washington. They believed that the United States would want to conduct its own investigation, but would not object if the Spanish chose to conduct a separate inquiry.[14]

Sigsbee and Lee were correct; the United States would investigate the disaster on its own.[15] The decision apparently was primarily made on political grounds. As Roosevelt wrote to Secretary Long after conferring with Assistant Secretary of State Day:

"I myself doubt whether it will be possible to tell definitely how the disaster occurred by an investigation; still it may be possible, and it may be that we could do it as well in conjunction with the Spaniards as alone. But I am sure we never could convince the people at large of this fact. There is of course a very large body of public opinion to the effect that we some time ago reached the limit of forbearance in our conduct toward the Spaniards, and this public opinion is already very restless, and might easily be persuaded to turn hostile to the administration."[16]

In fact, a naval court of inquiry had already been named and had been ordered to commence its proceedings two days later in Havana. It was to be headed by Captain William T. Sampson, commander of the battleship *Iowa*. Both the other two members of the panel had technical experience, and one of them, Captain French E. Chadwick, was a former chief of naval intelligence. The judge advocate was Lieutenant Commander Adolph Marix, a former executive officer of the *Maine*, who was chosen because of his familiarity with the ship.[17]

On February 21 the court convened on the U.S. lighthouse tender *Mangrove* in Havana harbor. Captain Sigsbee was the first witness at its secret proceedings. His most significant testimony was that he had been told by Captain Stevens of the *City of Washington* that on his frequent visits to the port he had never known a warship to be moored at the buoy at which the *Maine* had been placed when she arrived at Havana. His implication was that the spot might have been mined in anticipation of the *Maine*'s arrival.[18*] Judge Advocate Marix's remaining questions addressed possible causes of an internal explosion—the condition of the ship's coal and coal bunkers, the state of the electrical and fire alarm

---

* As it later developed, although Stevens's statement to Sigsbee about the mooring was literally accurate, merchant vessels had occupied the *Maine*'s buoy fairly frequently.

systems, and the temperature of the ammunition magazines. Sigsbee responded that he was unaware of any problems.[19]

The Spanish investigation had commenced two days earlier by interrogating Sigsbee in his Havana hotel room. To the obvious disappointment of his questioner, Spanish Admiral Manterola, Sigsbee's answers tended to refute the notion that the explosion had resulted from the ship's boiler, gunpowder, or some other internal cause. When Sigsbee was asked what he personally believed had caused the disaster, he cagily replied that the ship could have been blown up from the outside intentionally, and that any proper investigation must consider all possible causes. He could reach no conclusion until the Americans had completed their own inquiries.[20]

A major question in the minds of the members of the American court of inquiry was whether the explosion on the *Maine* could have been caused by internal combustion, probably originating in the ship's coal supply. On February 23, the *Maine*'s chief engineer, Charles T. Howell, fueled this suspicion by reporting that the coal in one of the ship's bunkers had been taken on board at Newport News, Virginia, three months before the explosion. Thus, there was plenty of time for internal combustion to have taken place. Sigsbee, who was present during Howell's testimony, questioned this hypothesis since internal combustion could only take place over a period of days through a gradual buildup of heat. Bunker A16, where the coal was stored, adjoined a narrow and frequently used passageway. Surely, said Sigsbee, sailors walking through the corridor would have noticed heat as they brushed against the plating. In fact, he had touched it the day before the explosion and it was cool.[21]

The next witness was Ensign Wilfred Powelson, a recent Naval Academy alumnus who had studied naval architecture in Scotland after his graduation. He had been working with the Navy divers for nearly a week, analyzing and organizing their reports. One of them had discovered a deep depression like a pit in the mud on the port side of the wreck, with the ship's hull bent upward at the same spot. This suggested to Powelson that the explosion had taken place outside the hull, probably from a submerged mine.[22]

〰️

On February 25 Ambassador Woodford met with Spanish Foreign Minister Gullón and Minister of the Colonies Moret. He reported to President McKinley:

"I think that I have now secured the practical adjustment of every important matter that has been committed to me up to date. Autonomy cannot go backward. It must go forward and its results must be worked out in Cuba... They cannot go further in open concessions to us without being overthrown by their own people here in Spain... They want peace if they can keep peace and save the dynasty. They prefer the changes of war, with the certain loss of Cuba, to the overthrow of the dynasty."[23]

Rear Admiral Pascual Cervera y Topete was Spain's foremost sailor and at age fifty-nine had been appointed to command a naval squadron stationed at Cadiz. Cervera had previously served as Minister of Marine in the Sagasta Government, but had resigned when his naval reform policies had not been adopted. He was skeptical as to the outcome of a war with the United States for, as he had written a cousin on January 30, "we are reduced, absolutely penniless, and they are very rich."[24] But, his letter continued:

"...my purpose is not to accuse, but to explain why we may and must expect a disaster. But as it is necessary to go to the bitter end, I hold my tongue, and go forth resignedly to face the trials which God may be pleased to send me."[25]

Four weeks later Cervera was no longer resigned to accepting the inevitable. On February 26, he wrote to the Minister of Marine, to remain silent would

"make myself an accomplice in adventures which will surely cause the total ruin of Spain. And for what purpose? To defend an island which was ours, but belongs to us no more, because even if we did not lose it by right in the war we have lost it in fact, and with it all our wealth and an enormous number of young men, victims of the climate and the bullets, in the defense of what is now no more than a romantic idea."

The Admiral asked the Minister to pass on his comments to the Queen and the Council of Ministers.[26]

Although the proceedings of the court of inquiry were supposed to be strictly secret, reports may have filtered out to Consul-General Lee. He suggested to officials in Washington that the mine might have been a makeshift device planted where the *Maine* would swing against it while lying at anchor, with the resulting explosion igniting the powder magazine, thus blowing up the ship. This could only have been the work of amateurs; the Spanish Army would have been much more professional.

This report intrigued McKinley, still hopeful that the crisis could be resolved short of war. On February 28 he called Secretary Long, Assistant Secretary of State Day, and the chief of the Navy's Ordinance Bureau to the White House to discuss Lee's report. Although there is no recorded evidence of what was said at the meeting, its tenor must have been optimistic, for Long wrote that evening in his diary: "I believe that war will be averted, for I am satisfied that the Spanish government is not responsible for the disaster." [27]

McKinley's confidantes saw the President as a pillar of quiet strength, restraining a growing body of war-hungry hawks until a peaceful solution could be found. But to Theodore Roosevelt, the President had "no more backbone than a chocolate eclair." [28]

In fact, both the United States and Spain faced grave and potentially insoluble dilemmas. For the McKinley Administration, apart from its potential cost in men and money and not entirely certain outcome, war would open up issues of national expansion that this conservative business-oriented government would prefer to avoid. On the other hand, the growing political pressure for action could cause a serious erosion of the President's political support if he was felt to be dragging his heels. For its part, the Spanish Government recognized that war would lead to almost certain defeat and the loss of Cuba and perhaps other overseas possessions. However, if Spain were to sell Cuba or otherwise grant the rebels major concessions, a domestic revolution might well erupt. [29]

On March 3 Assistant Secretary Day warned Ambassador Woodford of the difficulties ahead. Whatever the naval board might determine had caused the *Maine* disaster,

"The de Lôme incident, the destruction of the *Maine*, have added much to the popular feeling upon this subject, although the better sentiment seems to be to await the report of the facts, and to follow the action of the President after the naval board has made its report. Whatever that report may be, it by no means relieves the situation of its difficulties. The policy of starvation, the failure of Spain to take effective measures to suppress the insurrection, the loss of our commerce, the great expense of patrolling our coast—these things, intensified by the insulting and insincere character of the de Lôme letter, all combine to create a condition that is very grave, and which will require the highest wisdom and greatest prudence on both sides to avoid a crisis."[30]

For its part, the Spanish Government was attempting to address public concern that, in the event of war, the United States would attack the Philippines. A leading Madrid newspaper quoted "an unnamed high personage" as stating that "America has not so many warships as to warrant such bold action." He then threatened: "If the Yankees go to the Philippines, the Spaniards will go to New York."[31]

Spanish Minister of Marine Bermejo reflected this opinion in his reply to Cervera's pessimistic letter of February 27. The Admiral, he wrote, had overestimated American naval strength. The *Oregon*, one of four first-class battleships, was on the West Coast and never could reach the Caribbean on time to be effective there. The Spanish Pacific Squadron could harass American shipping in the Pacific and might even threaten West Coast ports, including San Francisco. Bermejo apparently had not conveyed Cervera's warning to either the Queen or the Spanish cabinet, and had no intention of doing so.[32]

It is unclear whether Bermejo was acquainted with the actual relative strengths of the two navies, or whether he was intentionally misleading Cervera. Against the four first-class American battleships, Spain had only one, and it was laid up and never saw service. None of her four armored cruisers was in good condition, and the most powerful had not yet received her main-battery guns. Cervera had accurately compared the ratio of Spanish to American strength as one to five, and the United States was about to embark on a further expansion of its fleet whereas the Spaniards would have to make do with the little they had.[33]

On Sunday evening March 16, House Appropriations Committee Chairman Joseph G. (Uncle Joe) Cannon was abruptly summoned to the White House. He was immediately ushered into the library, where he was greeted by McKinley. Without the usual preliminary courtesies, the President announced:

"Cannon, I must have money to get ready for war. I am doing everything possible to prevent war, but it must come and we are not prepared for war. Who knows where this war will lead us; it may be more than a war with Spain. How can I get this money for these extraordinary expenditures?"

In his twenty-year acquaintanceship with McKinley, Cannon "had never seen him in a more agitated frame of mind."[34]

The Congressman responded that he had already considered this possible need for funds, and that they could be raised without either a bond issue or additional taxes. He suggested that the President send a message to Congress asking for the appropriation. McKinley initially demurred because he was still negotiating with Spain, and such a message therefore "would be accepted by Europe as a declaration of war and he would be accused of double-dealing." Couldn't the regular appropriations be made available in advance? Cannon replied that this was impossible, but

"...I agreed to introduce a bill if he would prepare it...The President walked over to the table and wrote on a telegraph blank a single sentence: 'For national defense, fifty million dollars.' It wasn't a bill nor a message nor an estimate, but it was the President's memorandum as to what he wanted done, and I put the slip of paper in my pocket."[35]

Later in the evening, as he prepared the bill, Cannon grew enthusiastic over the proposal: "It might also impress Spain with the determination of this Government to induce her to give up Cuba, thus averting war."[36] The next day, when he introduced the "Fifty Million Bill" in the House of Representatives, it was greeted with "more unanimity, more harmony, and more real enthusiasm" than he had ever known. From the Democratic side of the aisle separating the two parties, Congressman and former Confederate cavalry general Joseph Wheeler let out a rebel yell.[37]

The same day, Secretary Long sent a telegram to the *U.S.S. Brooklyn*, which was off the Venezuelan coast: "The situation is getting worse. Proceed without delay to Hampton Roads."[38]

British Ambassador Sir Julian Pauncefote was an experienced diplomat who had represented England in Washington since 1889, first as minister and since 1893 as ambassador. He was a strong proponent of friendly relations between the two countries. On March 8 he called on the President at the White House. Although the subject of the meeting was not made public, *The New York Times* surmised that its purpose was to carry a message of good will relating to the Cuban crisis. The next day, the London *Times* declared, without disagreement: "America fully believes that she has England's moral support in the policy of which she accepts the President as exponent."[39]

On March 9 the Senate unanimously passed the Fifty Million Bill. The enthusiastic support on the floor and in the galleries had seldom been paralleled. So many members wished to address the chamber that each speech was limited to less than five minutes.[40]

If, as Cannon had surmised, one of McKinley's goals had been to shock the Spaniards, that purpose was achieved. Ambassador Woodford wrote the President that passage of the bill

"...has not excited the Spaniards—it has stunned them. To appropriate fifty millions out of money in the Treasury, without borrowing a cent, demonstrates wealth and power. Even Spain can see that. To put this money without restriction and by unanimous vote absolutely at your disposal demonstrates entire confidence in you by all parties. The ministry and the press are simply stunned."[41]

Queen Regent Maria Christina reflected this concern. A member of the Austrian royal family, she called in the Austrian ambassador to make a personal appeal to Emperor Franz Joseph and "his heart." If Austria took the lead for peace, she said, France and Germany likely would follow. In that event McKinley would "be able to point out to certain groups that [her] fate would not be a matter of indifference to the rest of the world."[42]

Maria Christina had not been relying only on hoped-for Austrian support. At the same time that she was meeting with the Austrian ambassador, she sent a secret message to Woodford in which she raised the possibility that Spain might sell Cuba to the United States. This otherwise unspeakable suggestion had recently been made by some Catholic clerics as a way of protecting the church in Cuba. The Queen Regent had proposed a meeting with Woodford, but, two days later on March 13, the Ambassador was advised that she no longer wished to see him. As Woodford advised McKinley, "The Queen evidently lost courage between Friday afternoon and Sunday noon."[43]

The Queen Regent's overnight change of mind may not have been caused by a loss of courage, but by news from Vienna. On receiving her plea, Franz Joseph and his Foreign Minister, Count Agenor Goluchowski, agreed to do their best for the Emperor's distant relative. As the French Ambassador to Austria reported, "His Majesty...cannot withhold his support from the Queen Regent in her distress." The Ambassador added that the Emperor "is very much moved, though he has little hope of inducing the powers to act."[44]

The Austrian proposal was that the major European powers join in some form of collective representation to the United States. To his German and Russian counterparts, Goluchowski sought support on the basis of monarchical solidarity, whereas to the English and French he stressed the joint interest of the colonial powers vis-a-vis the United States. Since Austria, however, was the weakest of the major European powers and had no large navy or important American trade, his words had little substance behind them. If there was to be outside support for Spain, some other great power would have to add its muscle to Austria's efforts.[45]

Great Britain would not be that country. Although the Salisbury Government was appropriately silent, rumors were spreading of some form of joint cooperation between England and the United States, not only regarding Spain but also in response to Russian expansion in the Far East. On March 14 government ministers were asked in the House of Commons whether Britain would loan warships to the Americans in a war with Spain, if Ambassador Pauncefote had suggested a Far Eastern alliance; and whether offers of mediation in the Cuban crisis had been made to President McKinley from "exalted quarters" in England. That all these questions received negative answers did little if anything to stop the rumors.[46]

Indeed, the McKinley Administration's restrained policy was making it difficult for Spain to organize a European coalition in support of its position. *The New York Times* reported "a diplomatist who probably is the recipient of more confidences than any man in London" as stating:

"If America had designed, with a set purpose, the events of the past week, she could not by any possibility, have developed anything which, in its impressive dignity, would have had such an effect upon Europe as the way in which the Executive, Congress, and the people have met the crisis and have risen to the responsibilities involved in dealing with the Cuban question."[47]

Redfield Proctor was a Republican senator from Vermont, a former Secretary of War and a friend of McKinley. He was a respected conservative businessman who had taken no strong public views on the Cuban question. Thus, when he spoke on the Senate floor on March 17 regarding his recent fact finding trip to Cuba, not only the Senate but also the country at large paid close attention.[48]

The purpose of Proctor's trip, he said, was not to investigate the *Maine* explosion. On that he had no opinion. Instead, he had visited Cuba to examine at first hand the condition of its people. Speaking dispassionately from a prepared text, he described how the country outside Havana "is desolation and distress, misery and starvation." He spoke of the *reconcentrados*

"torn from their homes, with foul earth, foul water and foul food or none, what wonder that one-half have died and one-quarter are so diseased that they cannot be saved?"

He described "hopeless" cases of small children

"walking about with arms and chest terribly emaciated, eyes swollen and abdomen bloated to three times the natural size."

To a stunned Senate, Proctor explained that he

"went to Cuba with a strong conviction that the picture had been overdrawn.... I could not believe that out of a population of one million six hundred thousand, two hundred thousand had died within these Spanish forts... My inquiries were entirely outside of sensational sources... Several of my informants were Spanish-born, but every time the answer was that the case had not been overstated."

As for United States intervention, Proctor concluded:

"To me, the strongest appeal is not the barbarity practiced by Weyler nor the loss of the *Maine*...but the spectacle of a million and a half of people, the entire native population of Cuba, struggling for freedom and deliverance from the worst misgovernment of which I ever had knowledge."[49]

Proctor's speech had a powerful effect. One senator explained, "It is just as if Proctor had held up his right hand and sworn to it."[50] House Speaker Thomas B. Reed could sneer at Proctor, Vermont's marble king: "A war will make a large market for gravestones,"[51] but he was almost alone in his criticism. As the *Wall Street Journal* commented two days later:

"Senator Proctor's speech converted a great many people in Wall Street who had heretofore taken the ground that the United States had no business to interfere in a revolution on Spanish soil."[52]

The new Spanish Ambassador, Luis Polo de Bernabe, cabled Madrid that Proctor's speech had "produced great effect because of his temperate stand." He added that, before making the speech, Proctor "had seen the President and Day, for which reason more importance is attached to his words."[53]

━━━◦)◦(◦━━━

In Berlin, Foreign Minister Bülow opposed any German initiative in support of Spain. On March 17 he wrote Ambassador Radowitz in Madrid that "if Spain was hoping for European action in her favour, she must first of all gain closer touch with Russia and look for support there." He also referred to a French government report of "Russian-American intimacy," which made it unlikely that Russia would intervene.[54]

Bülow enclosed a memorandum he had sent two days earlier to the German Ambassador in Vienna, which summarized the European situation as he saw it. France would not act without Russia, and England "looks on the maintenance of good relations with America as much more important than her relations with Spain." Then, after agreeing that

"...our gracious Master, His Majesty the Emperor, is justified in deploring that so remarkable a personality, and one so thoroughly sympathetic to himself as the Queen-Regent, should have to bear the consequences of hundreds of years' maladministration,"

he suggested that the Pope might mediate the Cuban conflict:

"The authority of the latter as arbitrator, which is recognized nowhere in the world more unquestionably than in Spain, would then cover the Regent's responsibility and minimize the dangers threatening the Monarchy...."[55]

Meanwhile, the Queen Regent was continuing to seek help wherever she might find it. On March 17 she addressed an emotional plea to Queen Victoria:

"...Full of trust in you, I am writing to explain my difficult position, convinced that you will support me with your powerful help and good advice.... We should long ago have brought the war in Cuba to an end, had America remained neutral, but she continually sent money, munitions, and weapons to the rebels; and now, when the insurrection is nearly over, the Americans intend to provoke us and bring about a war, and this I would avoid at all costs. But there are limits to everything, and I cannot let my country be humbled by America...

I have applied to the Emperor of Austria, who promised me to approach the other Powers in order that common action may be taken for the preservation of peace; but I wished to address myself to you at the same time to beg you not to deny me your powerful protection. I know how with the greatest kindness you always interest yourself in my poor fatherless son—for his sake I beg you to help me. It would so distress me if England were not at one with the other Great Powers in this matter!..."[56]

Ambassador Woodford had concluded, by speaking with the government officials in Madrid, that there was little hope that the Cuban rebellion could be suppressed before the rainy season began. They asked him for a definite statement of the American terms for settling the conflict.[57] Because there were none, Assistant Secretary Day could advise Woodford only in generalities. His March 18 response was that although the naval court was likely to find that the *Maine* had been blown up by a mine, "no doubt Congress will act wisely, ...particularly if there be certainty of prompt restoration of peace in Cuba."—by all odds an unlikely contingency. Then, after suggesting that "full reparation" might resolve the issue of the *Maine* loss, Day added:

"But there remain general conditions in Cuba which can no longer be endured, and which will demand action on our part, unless Spain restores honorable peace which will stop starvation of people and give them opportunity to take care of themselves, and restore commerce now wholly lost. April 15 is none too early [a] date for accomplishment of the purposes."[58]

Day's surmise was correct. On Sunday, March 20, the Navy Department had received confidential information that, as expected, the court of inquiry would report unanimously that the *Maine* had been blown up by an underwater mine. A careworn McKinley knew that when the report became public in the next few days, it would increase even further the efforts of the congressmen and senators who were calling for war and that he would be hard pressed to continue his policy of restraint.[59]

As the Spanish Minister of Marine had observed to Admiral Cervera, the powerful American battleship *Oregon* was in San Francisco Bay, far from the Caribbean. After De Lesseps's failed attempt, there was as yet no canal across the Isthmus of Panama. To reach Cuba the *Oregon* would have to steam around the southern tip of South America, a voyage of 16,000 miles. On March 19 she pulled up anchor, proceeded through the Golden Gate, and headed south. A 12,000 ton battleship with a crew of 30 officers and 438 men, she was the strongest United States warship and one of the most powerful in the world. Her captain and crew would strain to the utmost to reach the Caribbean to join in any fighting that lay ahead.[60]

On March 23 Ambassador Woodford met with Foreign Minister Gullón and Minister for the Colonies Moret. Gullón asked the United States to defer any action regarding Cuba until the rainy season began. By then, he asserted, the Spaniards and the insurgents would have reached a mutually acceptable accommodation. Partly because he knew that most Spanish Government officials other than Moret disagreed with this prognosis, Woodford replied that such a delay was impossible. Unless a "just and honorable peace" was reached "in a very few days," McKinley would have no recourse but to submit the Cuban question to Congress. The two ministers promised to report the conversation at a Cabinet meeting later that day.[61]

The next day Moret made an "unofficial" proposal to Woodford: an immediate truce would be ordered by Spain if the United States could assure its acceptance by the insurgents. The Cubans, both insurgents and Spanish colonials, would try to reach a permanent settlement at a congress which was to meet on May 4. If no agreement could be reached by the end of the rainy season in mid-September, the United States and Spain would enforce on both parties terms determined by the two Governments.[62]

Since March 20, the President had conferred frequently with Republican leaders of the House and Senate, who warned him of the political dangers of procrastination. He also met with leading Democrats and Populists to try to garner bipartisan support for his policy.[63]

On March 24 word had leaked that the naval officers bringing the naval court's *Maine* report would arrive from Key West that evening. Such a large crowd was at Pennsylvania Station to greet them that they had difficulty making their way to the street. If this throng hoped that the officers, including the "muscular" lieutenant carrying the white canvas pouch containing the report, would make an announcement of its contents, it was disappointed. The five cabloads of reporters who pursued them to their hotel watched in frustration as they left the lobby for their rooms with the statement that there would be no news that evening.[64]

The next morning McKinley and his Cabinet met at 10:30 A.M. and spent most of the day discussing the naval court's report, which already had been formally delivered to the President. It had concluded that the *Maine* had been blown up on the port side and that the resulting shock had caused the explosion of two of the ship's magazines. There was no solid evidence, however, that a mine had been intentionally laid in Havana harbor, whether by Spain or by anyone else. The group decided to delay until Monday transmitting the report to Congress. Their goal was still to find a peaceful solution, although Secretary of War Alger, with his well-tuned political antennae, suggested that in the end war probably would be necessary.[65]

Following up on the prior day's Cabinet meeting, Day cabled Ambassador Woodford on March 26 that, despite the naval board's finding on the *Maine* explosion, "*Peace* is the desired end."[66] After reiterating that the United States did not want Cuba, he wrote:

"For your own guidance the President suggests that if Spain will revoke the reconcentration order and maintain the people until they can support themselves and offer to the Cubans full self-government with reasonable indemnity, the President will gladly assist in its consummation. If Spain should invite the United States to mediate for peace and the insurgents would make like request, the President might undertake like offer of friendship."[67]

The Administration's emphasis on Cuban self-government reflected the increasingly intense political pressures for action that were coming from Congress and the press. Speaking at the annual Gridiron Club dinner that Saturday evening, the Assistant Secretary of the Navy publicly confronted Hanna, who was one of the most influential proponents of a peace policy. In his typically vigorous style, Roosevelt declared, "We will have this war for the freedom of Cuba." He then issued a clear public challenge as he turned to stare at the Senator, who was sitting nearby: Although "the interests of the business world and financiers might be paramount in the Senate," they were not with the people, and anyone who wanted to stand in their way "was welcome to try the experiment." As Roosevelt sat down to thunderous applause, he turned to Hanna, whose neck reportedly had turned purple, and said calmly, "Now, Senator, may we please have war?" [68]

Roosevelt was exploring all contingencies. The previous day he wrote Secretary Long that the Director of the Geological Survey had just shown him

"some interesting photographs of Professor Langley's flying machine. The machine has worked. It seems to me worth while for this government to try whether it will work on a large enough scale to be of use in the event of war."

Roosevelt recommended that a four-man committee be appointed

"to inform us whether or not they think it could be duplicated on a large scale, to make recommendations as to its practicality and prepare estimates as to its cost. I think this is well worth doing." [69]

Long eventually agreed and appointed a board headed by the Chief of Naval Intelligence. Thus, five and a half years before the Wright Brothers's successful flight at Kitty Hawk, Congress appropriated $50,000 for further experimentation by Langley, who was head of the Smithsonian Institution and a friend of Roosevelt. None of the flights were successful, and the matter was dropped. After air power became an indispensable element in twentieth century military strategy, Roosevelt was rightly recognized as the first official proponent of United States naval aviation. [70]

Roosevelt was also in a strangely pensive mood. Perhaps because his wife, Edith, with the aid of surgery, was only now recovering from a prolonged life-threatening illness, thoughts of his own possible death in the impending Spanish war were on his mind. [71] In a letter to a close friend, he revealed a man with very human feelings that existed side by side with his impassioned jingoism:

"I say quite sincerely that I shall not go for my own pleasure. On the contrary if I should consult purely my own feelings I should earnestly hope that we would have peace. I like life very much. I have always led a joyous life. I like thought, and I like action, and it will be very bitter to me to leave my wife and children, and while I think I could face death with dignity, I have no desire before my time has come to go out into the everlasting darkness..., so I shall not go into a war with any undue exhilaration of

spirits or in a frame of mind in any way approaching recklessness or levi-
ty; but my best work here is done.

"Moreover, a man's usefulness depends upon his living up to his ideals
in so far as he can.... One of the commonest taunts directed at men like
myself is that we are armchair and parlor jingoes who wish to see others do
what we only advocate doing. I care very little for such a taunt, except as it
affects my usefulness, but I cannot afford to disregard the fact that my
power for good, whatever it may be, would be gone if I didn't try to live up
to the doctrines I have tried to preach...it seems to me that it would be a
good deal more important from the standpoint of the nation as a whole
that men like myself should go to war than that we should stay comfortably in offices at home and let others carry on the war that we have
urged."[72]

In Madrid, Foreign Minister Gullón was increasingly concerned that
diplomatic efforts to obtain foreign support for Spain were not bearing
fruit. On March 25 he wrote Spain's diplomatic representatives that it was
important that the United States consider matters relating to Cuba and
the *Maine* "in a tranquil atmosphere, and outside of congress...." He
asked them to advise the foreign governments to which they were accredited as to where matters stood between Spain and the United States and to
ask their

" friendly offices in order that the President of the United States may retain under federal control all questions affecting the relations or differences with Spain in order to bring them to an honorable conclusion."[73]

One reason for Gullón's concern was that more than a week had passed
without a reply to the Queen Regent's letter to Queen Victoria. On March
26 he cabled the Spanish ambassador in London and asked him to inquire
"if Great Britain actually has made any agreement with the United
States in the event of war, or if Britain's silence is due solely to her wish to
keep her hands free, and not to be bound in advance by any commitment."[74] Meanwhile, German Foreign Minister Bülow asked his country's ambassador to the Vatican to explore the possibility that the Pope
might offer to mediate or otherwise help resolve the confrontation between Spain and the United States. He was not optimistic that Vatican
intervention would be successful, however, because "the Catholic element
is not very strong in the American Congress."[75]

On March 27, Assistant Secretary Day sent Ambassador Woodford another cable—this time with a concrete proposal from McKinley to present to the Spanish government:

"First. Armistice until October 1. Negotiations meantime looking to peace between Spain and insurgents, through friendly offices of the President of the United States.

Second. Immediate revocation of reconcentration order so as to permit people to return to their farms and the needy to be relieved with provisions and supplies from United States, cooperating with authorities, so as to afford full relief."[76]

Earlier, in response to the American message of the previous day, the Spanish asked Woodford for the meaning of "full self-government" for Cuba. Day cabled Woodford to reply that it meant "Cuban independence." It is unclear whether the McKinley Administration, apparently serious in wanting to avoid a military confrontation, understood that political conditions in Spain made that course unacceptable. Such an affront to Spanish pride would almost certainly mean the fall of the government and perhaps of the monarchy itself. Both governments had become prisoners of internal forces over which they had little control.[77]

SEVEN

America Remembers The Maine

D espite the extraordinary efforts that had been taken to prevent leaks of the contents of the *Maine* report, the March 20 morning newspapers carried an Associated Press dispatch that contained an accurate and detailed description of the naval board's findings.[1] Thus, when the report itself was delivered to Congress at noon, it was an anticlimax. Moreover, the President's transmittal message was a political disaster. It contained no statement of the Administration's purposes and no indication that a later message would be submitted recommending a course of action. McKinley merely asked "deliberate consideration" of the report, which was the last thing in the minds of most congressmen. They were infuriated by the words, and the ranks of the war party swelled as a result. The House and Senate leaders rushed to the White House to warn that they probably could not stop a "Cuban outbreak."[2]

The same day, Spanish Ambassador Polo delivered to the State Department the findings of the Spanish inquiry into the cause of the explosion. It concluded:

"The absence of all circumstances which necessarily accompany the explosion of a torpedo having been proved by witnesses and experts, it can only be honestly asserted that the catastrophe was due to internal causes."

The evidence that the report cited for its conclusion included the absence of dead fish, the fact that no water was thrown up, as would have occurred as a consequence of a mine explosion, and the danger that a mine would have presented to other shipping in the harbor.[3]

Not surprisingly, the Spanish report received little publicity in the American press. Even if it had, given the war hysteria that was beginning to grip the country, few would have believed it.

101

McKinley's restraint on Cuba infuriated Roosevelt and his fellow jingoes, but it was widely appreciated in England, and led to increasingly strong support for the United States. The generally pro-American attitude of the British press was illustrated by a London *Chronicle* article which, after suggesting that under similar circumstances Britain would already have intervened in Cuba, continued:

"Whatever may have been our differences with the United States, the heart of our people will go out to the great attempt to be made to liberate an American colony from a cruel joke."[4]

Commenting on American reaction to the naval board report that was released the previous day, the London *Times* referred to "our sympathy to the people of the United States in circumstances which would have made it difficult even for our own countrymen to preserve their boasted calm." The author then proposed closer commercial relations between the two countries, especially in the Far East.[5] On a more emotional level, on this same March 29, Poet Laureate Alfred Austin published in the *Times* a poem entitled "A Voice from the West," the last stanza of which read

> Yes, this is the voice of the bluff March gale;
>   We severed have been too long;
> But now we have done with a worn-out tale—
>   The tale of an ancient wrong—
> And our friendship shall last as love doth last
> And be stronger than death is strong."[6]

American Ambassador John Hay had just returned to London after a vacation trip on the Nile with Henry Adams and other friends. He quickly sensed the prevailing sentiment, writing McKinley, "The commonest phrase (from Liberals, Conservatives and Radicals) is 'We wish you would take Cuba and finish up the work.'"[7]

At first glance France seemed more favorably inclined than England towards the Spanish position on Cuba. On March 26 Foreign Minister Hanotaux had sent a telegram asking the Russian foreign minister if his country "could not consent to join in a demarche altogether amicable and in no way wounding to the United States by some or all of the powers." To the German ambassador in Paris he suggested that joint action by the European powers might prevent war between Spain and the United States. He also asked the French ambassador to England to press that country to join such a coalition.[8]

As Hanotaux had stated to his Russian counterpart, however, he had no intention to make demands on or threaten the McKinley Administration. Instead, his apparent aim was to lend support to the President in his avowed goal of resolving the crisis short of war. To that end, on March 29 he instructed Ambassador Jules Cambon in Washington to tell Secretary of State Sherman that France would not take any action on Cuba without American consent. France was not about to jump on any bandwagon that supported Spain against the United States.[9]

By the end of March the pressure on the Administration to intervene was becoming unbearable. On March 30 Day telegraphed Woodford:

"You should know and fully appreciate that there is profound feeling in Congress, and the gravest apprehension on the part of the most conservative members that a resolution for intervention may pass both branches in spite of any effort which can be made. Only assurances from the President that if he fails in peaceful negotiations he will submit all the facts to Congress at a very early date will prevent immediate action on the part of Congress."[10]

Congress, in turn, was feeling the heat of public opinion aroused by the "yellow press." A Maine representative later commented: "Every Congressman had two or three newspapers in his district—most of them printed in red ink...and shouting for blood." A historian later wrote:

"Newspaper editors and their assistants differed from those between 1850 and 1860, who made their appeals to the electorate by cogent editorials directed against the slave power. Now recourse was had to the news columns in which Spain was painted as perfidious and untrustworthy."[11]

"Remember the *Maine*" was the slogan of the day.

Roosevelt was almost beside himself with impatience. He wrote his brother-in-law William Sheffield Cowles:

"Of course I cannot speak in public, but I have advised the President in the presence of his Cabinet, as well as Judge Day and Senator Hanna, as strongly as I knew how, to settle this matter instantly by armed intervention, and I told the President in the plainest language that no other course was compatible with our national honor, or with the claims of humanity on behalf of the wretched women and children of Cuba. I am more grieved and indignant than I can say at there being any delay on our part in a matter like this. A great crisis is upon us, and if we do not rise level to it. we shall have spotted the pages of our history with a dark blot of shame." [12]

McKinley probably paid little attention to Roosevelt's frequent outbursts, but the calls for action from Capital Hill were another matter. The time for a diplomatic solution to the crisis was rapidly running out. [13]

On March 29 Woodford presented the non-negotiable American position: an armistice and the revocation of the reconcentration order. The Spanish ministers replied on March 31 that Spain was already satisfying the second of these requirements, and that it was willing to submit the *Maine* loss to arbitration. Beyond this, a saddened Woodford telegraphed, the discussion

"...has turned, as I feared, on a question of punctilio. Spanish pride will not permit the ministers to propose and offer an armistice, which they really desire, because they know that armistice now means certain peace next autumn. I am told confidentially that an offer of armistice by the Spanish Government would cause revolution here. Leading generals have been sounded within the last week, and ministers have gone as far as they dare to go to-day." [14]

Woodford was still unwilling to give up all hope. Spain, after all, had made two major concessions in repealing the reconcentration order and agreeing to arbitration regarding the *Maine*. Moreover, the populace as a whole was much less war-minded than the previous fall, and the pressure for war rather than capitulation was largely confined to the army. The ministries, he reported: "are ready to go as far and as fast as they can and still save the monarchy here in Spain." All they needed was time. [15]

Time, however, was something that McKinley did not have to give. It was no longer a case of restraining Lodge and the other Republican imperialists. Democratic populists and free silver Republicans saw a rare opportunity for political gain and now outdid the Republican jingoists in urging armed intervention. A member of one Congressional delegation accused McKinley to his face of trying to protect Wall Street investors in Spanish bonds. When the word "peace" was mentioned on the House floor, it was greeted with hisses from the galleries. Thus, when Woodford's dispatch reached the President and his advisors at the White House very late in the evening of March 31, their saddened reaction was that war was inevitable.[16] Perhaps a stronger man could have held the hawks at bay for the weeks or months it would take to achieve Cuban independence without war. William McKinley could not.

⸻◎⸻

For a short while, the efforts of the German government to secure Papal intervention in the Cuban crisis seemed to be bearing fruit. On March 30 the German minister to the Vatican wrote Bülow that although

"the Pope considers it impossible for the Spanish Government to relinquish Cuba,...His Holiness...will not fail to enquire in Madrid as to what is felt there on this question."[17]

Bülow's March 31 telegram to the Spanish ambassador in Madrid described the current state of play:

"...This initiative of the Curia, which is to be attributed to suggestions from here, will be a relief to the Spanish government, for public opinion in the country might easily take for cowardice a suggestion in this sense, if made by Spain. The Imperial government considers all else to be the affair of those interested, i.e., the parties and the eventual arbitrator. We ought to avoid mixing further in the affair, since, on the one hand, we have no wish to assume moral responsibility for the results of the loss of Cuba, whilst, on the other, it seems fairly improbable that America will accept the Pope's arbitration, without previous assurances regarding the concessions mentioned in the last part of your report of March 22nd."[18]

These hopes were quickly dashed. On April 1 Bülow telegraphed the Kaiser that the Papal Nuncio in Madrid "reports that, in answer to his inquiry, the Spanish Government declares it to be impossible to accept arbitration on the basis of cession of Cuba." The Kaiser, clearly annoyed, responded, "Then there is no way of helping them! They will lose Cuba all the same."[19]

Queen Victoria received similar advice from Lord Salisbury regarding the Queen Regent's appeal for help:

"The Spanish question is very grave, and Lord Salisbury would not like to advise your Majesty to give any understanding to assist the Queen of Spain without consulting his colleagues; for any communication from this country to the United States in the way of remonstrances might arouse their susceptible feelings and produce a condition of some danger, without any corresponding advantage. At the same time Lord Salisbury thinks that your Majesty would not refuse to join in any course taken by all the other Great Powers, but he doubts expediency of action by them. It is more likely to help the war party in the United States than to weaken them.

"The position of the Queen Regent of Spain is most lamentable and grievous. It is impossible not to feel the deepest sympathy for her."[20]

Following this advice, on April 4 Queen Victoria wrote the Queen Regent that she could provide no assistance to her fellow monarch in her travail.[21]

At the Vatican's request, on April 3 Archbishop John Ireland of St. Paul, Minnesota, paid a visit to McKinley to discuss the possibility of a papal call for an armistice in Cuban hostilities.[22] Apparently as the result of an overly optimistic account of the meeting, Spanish Foreign Minister Gullón called on Ambassador Woodford that evening to tell him that McKinley had requested papal intervention so as to permit Spain to grant an immediate ceasefire. He added that the possibility of Spain agreeing to such a course would be helped if the American North Atlantic squadron were withdrawn from Key West, only sixty miles from Havana. An optimistic Woodford immediately wired McKinley that

"...when armistice is once proclaimed, hostilities will never be resumed and ... permanent peace will be secured. If, under existing conditions in Washington, you can do this, I hope that you will."[23]

The Spanish Foreign Minister was mistaken, however. McKinley had not suggested intervention by the Pope. Indeed, any intimation that he had would have been a political disaster, given the prevailing war fever and the prejudice toward the Catholic Church that existed in many parts of the United States. Day thus immediately replied:

"The President has made no suggestions to Spain except through you. He made no suggestions other than those which you were instructed to make for an armistice to be offered to Spain and insurgents, and which Spain has already rejected…the disposition of our fleet must be left to us…the President cannot hold his message to Congress longer than Tuesday."[24]

The unanimous view in both the Administration and Congress was that war was inevitable. Only if Spain unconditionally accepted the American terms would peace be possible. A much relieved Theodore Roosevelt wrote New York lawyer Elihu Root:

"Thank Heaven, this morning it looks as if the administration had made its mind up to lead the movement instead of resisting it with the effect of shattering the party and of humiliating the nation."[25]

The *Oregon* was doing her utmost to take part in the impending conflict. On April 4, at Callao, Peru, she made her first coaling stop since she left San Francisco, having steamed 4,112 nautical miles in sixteen days.[26]

Notwithstanding his earlier message to Queen Victoria, Salisbury sympathized with Spain, and mistakenly thought that a joint European declaration in favor of peace might help McKinley hold off the war hawks in Congress. When Ambassador Pauncefote reported that Assistant Secretary of State Day had told him that such a statement would not be resented so long as it was addressed to both the United States and Spain, the British Cabinet agreed on April 4 to instruct Sir Julian to join the other ambassadors in Washington in preparing such an appeal. It was essential, however, that Pauncefote receive McKinley's personal assurance that this course would not offend the United States.[27] Indeed, the British Government had assured Ambassador Hay that Britain would take no action in the Cuban crisis which was not "acceptable" to the United States.[28]

This official British position in part reflected the strong support that the United States was receiving from the English public. On April 4, Hay wrote McKinley:

"There is certainly a very wonderful change in public sentiment since I came here, a year ago. All classes, from the throne to the man in the street, now wish us well. I hear evidence of this from the most unexpected sources. Earl Grey, for instance, said yesterday, 'Why do not the United States borrow our navy to make a quick job of Cuba? They could return the favor another time.'"[29]

During the morning of April 6, the representatives of Great Britain, Germany, France, Austria-Hungary, Russia, and Italy met with McKinley. They presented a statement, drafted by Pauncefote and already approved by the State Department, and possibly also McKinley, which set forth "a pressing appeal to the feelings of humanity and moderation of the President and the American people in their existing differences with Spain." It was hoped that "further negotiations will lead to an agreement..." The President read a prearranged reply which, after referring to America's desire for peace, spoke of the need "to fulfill a duty to humanity by ending a situation the indefinite prolongation of which has become insufferable."[30] For the moment there was nothing more to be said or done.

The President's war message was due to be delivered to Congress at noon the same day. Consul-General Lee, however, had urged several days delay in order for all Americans to be evacuated from Cuba. McKinley also may have seen Lee's plea as an excuse for more time in which peace might be secured.[31] The President had completed his message, and more than 10,000 spectators thronged in and around the Capitol to hear it or otherwise participate in the great event that was about to take place. Against the recommendation of his advisors, who warned of the political and legislative consequences of delay, McKinley opted for deferral, saying: "I will not send in that message today. I will not do such a thing if it will endanger the life of an American citizen in Cuba."[32]

The official Congressional delegation that was summoned to the White House to be told of the postponement accepted the decision without official protest, but there was no hiding the rage and bitterness that resulted from the delay. The Republicans were in complete disarray, while former Democratic doves like William Jennings Bryan were trumpeting the cause of Cuban independence.[33]

At 3:00 P.M. on April 9, Foreign Minister Gullón met with the Papal Nuncio and the ambassadors of the major European powers to announce, according to German Ambassador Radowitz,

"...that, in consequence of the repeated representations of the Holy Father, supported by the friendly advice of the representatives here of the six Powers, the Government had decided to inform the Holy Father that the General commanding in Cuba had been instructed to obtain an immediate cessation of hostilities for a period which he might consider suitable in order to prepare for a permanent peace, and to proceed with the work. The withdrawal of the American ships is no longer mentioned as a condition."[34]

Gullón immediately gave the news to Woodford, who reported it to Washington. Early the next morning, he followed up with a telegram to the President:

"I hope that nothing will now be done to humiliate Spain, as I am satisfied that the present government is going, and is loyally ready to go, as fast and as far as it can. With your power of action sufficiently free, you will win the fight on your own lines."[35]

A week or so earlier the Spanish announcement might have turned the tide towards peace. With Spain's declaration of an armistice, the United States had won nearly everything that it demanded. All that remained was Cuban independence, and Woodford believed that this was only a formality that would be achieved by August 1.[36] Under different circumstances, a stronger man than McKinley could have announced total victory and won the praise of a large popular majority.

Almost all the Cabinet personally favored a settlement, and Senator Mark Hanna and House Speaker Thomas B. Reed strongly opposed intervention.[37] But by now it was too late. Reed, and McKinley's other allies could not control Congress. As the Speaker sadly commented to reporters a few days earlier regarding a suggestion from former New York Governor Morton that he "dissuade" his fellow congressmen from intervention: "Dissuade them! The Governor might as well ask me to step out in the middle of a Kansas waste and dissuade a cyclone!"[38] And in this case, the cyclone, whipped up by the press, was also blowing in the country at large outside Washington.[39]

During Easter Sunday, April 10, the President met constantly with congressional leaders, and twice with the Cabinet.[40] Initially, he suggested revising the almost completed message he was to deliver to Congress the next day to propose deferring action until the effects of the armistice could be determined. His advisors unanimously disagreed: he must lead the country into war or run the serious risk of destroying the Republican Party.[41] The strains of never ending pressures, overwork, and sleepless nights were too much.[42] The President's message would go to Congress tomorrow as written, amended only to add a brief reference to the Spanish surrender.[43] Although McKinley continued to voice hope "that under the Providence of God some way may yet be found to bring about peace without the resort to arms," his final draft did not include that sentence.[44]

The next morning the President's message was delivered to Congress, and was read to the members. It emphasized the plight of the Cuban people and the damage the civil war was causing American business. There was only a mere mention of the *Maine*, and no implication that Spain was responsible for its destruction. The message was explicit, however, in rejecting recognition of the insurgent government. In conclusion, McKinley stated:

"In the name of humanity, in the name of civilization, in behalf of endangered American interests which give us the right and the duty to speak and to act, the war in Cuba must stop.

"In view of these facts and of these considerations, I ask the Congress to authorize and empower the President to take measures to secure a full and final termination of hostilities between the government of Spain and the people of Cuba, and to secure in the island the establishment of a stable government, capable of maintaining order and observing its international obligations, insuring peace and tranquility and the security of its citizens as well as our own, ...and to use the military and naval forces of the United States as may be necessary to secure these purposes.

"The issue is now with the Congress....I have exhausted every effort to relieve the intolerable condition of affairs which is at our doors."[45]

Only at this point did the President mention the Spanish Government's weekend announcement of a Cuban armistice. He did so as though it were an afterthought that Congress could consider as it pleased:

"This fact, with every other pertinent consideration, will, I am sure, have your just and careful attention in the solemn deliberations upon which you are about to enter. If this measure attracts a successful result, then our aspirations as a Christian, peace-loving people will be realized. If it fails, it will be only another justification for our contemplated action."[46]

McKinley must have realized, however, that by referring the issue of intervention to Congress, he was abandoning any possibility that United States action would be delayed for the days, and probably even weeks, that would be required to determine whether an armistice, as he suggested, "attracts a successful result." The intervention that he was recommending, and Spain's almost certain reaction to it, would make the armistice declaration irrelevant.

The Spanish response to McKinley's message was an upsurge of patriotism mixed with anger. The President's cavalier treatment of an armistice declared in good faith was an insult to Spain's national honor. The Government denounced the United States for meddling in Spain's internal affairs. What particularly incensed some Spaniards was that

"...while protesting a desire for peace, a desired disinclination to the annexation of any territory, the people of the United States had done everything in their power to foment the rebellion in Cuba and to make it impossible for Spain to overcome it, either by peaceable or forcible means."[47]

There was great dissatisfaction in Congress that McKinley had not gone far enough. Initially, party discipline held firm and, after a bitter battle over a proposal to recommend recognizing Cuban independence, the House Foreign Affairs Committee reported a resolution that was limited to supporting intervention in Cuba.[48] This led to a battle royal the same day on the House floor. The Democratic minority introduced a resolution that would recognize the insurgent government. There ensued a passionate partisan debate, during which a Democratic representative, who had been called a liar by a Republican member, hurled a bound copy of the Congressional Record at his accuser. When the missile fell short, the two members rushed at each other. Other congressmen also became involved, but order was restored before any blows were struck.[49] The Rules Committee then limited debate to forty minutes, after which the Democratic resolution was defeated by a vote of 190 to 150. The House then adopted the committee proposal, 325 to 19.[50]

Meanwhile a new European peace initiative had begun. The actual facts are not entirely clear, in part because of different interpretations a few years later by England and by Germany. What does appear reasonably certain is that the major European powers were displeased over the American response to Spain's declaration of a Cuban armistice. On April 11 the Austrian Ambassador to the United States was instructed by Vienna to sound out his colleagues as to the possibility of a second joint note urging continuing efforts for peace. They agreed to cable home for instructions. In response, British Ambassador Pauncefote was advised, "We must leave any action on this request to your discretion."[51]

On the fourteenth the diplomats met at the British Embassy to consider what action to take. Pauncefote, although a staunch friend of the United States, was deeply concerned that America was moving too rapidly towards war. French Ambassador Jules Cambon reports him as having exclaimed at the meeting, "One cannot, without protesting in the name of conscience, allow to be committed the act of brigandage which the United States are preparing at this moment." Pauncefote presented to his colleagues a draft of a new note, which he proposed they deliver to the Secretary of State.[52]

At this point the details become murky. Apparently Cambon suggested a number of revisions. Among them was the insertion of the phrase that American intervention in Cuba "ne sera pas justifié."[53] Although Pauncefote seemingly did not notice this change and approved the revised proposal, the German Ambassador questioned the proposed procedure.[54] What if this second note proved no more effective than the April 6 declaration? If the note was addressed, as proposed, to the Secretary of State, would the Americans regard it as less important than the earlier note, which was delivered personally to President McKinley? At his suggestion, instead of sending a collective note, the ambassadors decided to recommend that each of their governments would send an identical note to the United States envoy accredited to it. They prepared a dispatch which each of them would send to his foreign minister. It read:

"The time has come to dispel the erroneous impression which prevails that armed intervention of the United States in Cuba...commands, in the words of the Message, the support and approval of the civilized world. Under these circumstances, Representatives of the Great Powers at Washington consider that their respective Governments might usefully...make it known that their approval cannot be given to an armed intervention which does not appear to them to be justified."[55]

Thus, unlike the collective note of April 6, the proposed communication was critical of the United States.

With varying degrees of enthusiasm, the governments of Austria, France, Italy, and Russia agreed to protest United States intervention in Cuba.[56] The German reaction was different. When Bülow telegraphed a description of the proposal to the Kaiser, he told William that "I personally feel fairly indifferent about publication," The Kaiser disagreed, replying: "I think it perfectly mistaken, pointless, and therefore harmful. We should put ourselves wrong with the Americans...."[57] William doubted that, when put to the test, any of the European powers would really act against the United States. Thus, regarding the suggestion in another memorandum that French Foreign Minister Hanotaux had agreed to participate in the diplomatic effort, the Kaiser commented: "Ask Hanotaux how many cruisers he would send if the United States rejected a new appeal."[58]

In England Arthur Balfour was both acting Prime Minister and Foreign Secretary during Salisbury's absence. He was unclear how to respond to Pauncefote's telegram and wired the Foreign Office:

"If Pauncefote had not associated himself with this policy, I should have rejected it at once, but...he is on the spot, and he is a man of solid judgment. It seems a strong order to reject his advice."

Accordingly, Balfour, described by an historian as "a man of tentative resolution" with "slackness in his blood and no vital enthusiasm in his heart," equivocated.[59] On April 16 he directed the Foreign Office to cable Pauncefote that England would join the other powers in an appeal similar to that of earlier in the month, but that "it seems very doubtful whether we ought to commit ourselves to a judgment adverse to the United States, and whether in the interests of peace anything will be gained by doing so." Although expressing the opinion that the note should be less potentially offensive to the United States than what the ambassadors were proposing, he did not veto the plan.[60]

Later in the day Balfour started to worry over Pauncefote's proposal and his reply. After a restless night, the next morning he cabled Colonial Secretary Joseph Chamberlain for advice, noting that because he had had only a few minutes to reply to Pauncefote, "it was just possible I should have been more preemptory."[61] Chamberlain instantly replied:

"Am convinced Message will do no good and will be bitterly resented. Americans insist that Spain shall leave Cuba. Nothing less will satisfy them. Spain will rather fight. Message practically takes part with Spain at critical juncture and will be so understood in America and this country."[62]

Upon receiving this advice, Balfour instructed Pauncefote to drop the proposal. Since Bülow had given similar orders to the German ambassador, the plan had been effectively vetoed. Thus, Britain took no action that would alter Chamberlain's observation in a follow-up letter the next day to Balfour that "public opinion in the States has gratefully recognized that we have been more sympathetic than the other Great Powers...."[63]

A postscript four years later further reinforced that conclusion. In 1902, following a Government response to a question in the House of Commons, both the British and American press claimed that England alone prevented a European challenge to the United States at this crucial time. This produced a violent German reaction, and the Kaiser's Government, itself wooing the United States, produced evidence that Pauncefote initially had favored European intervention. According to historian Bradford Perkins: "The Kaiser himself invaded the British embassy one night to shake his finger at a sleepy ambassador and demand his share of the credit."[64] By 1902, however, Anglo-American relations had become so friendly that the German response was greeted with disbelief, described by Henry Adams as "very maladroit and blundering and German." Theodore Roosevelt, by now President, gave the London *Times* an interview in which he professed his confidence in Pauncefote's goodwill toward the United States.[65] When Pauncefote died shortly thereafter, Roosevelt lowered the White House flag to half-mast and arranged for the battleship *Brooklyn* to carry the Ambassador's body back to England for burial. Thus, as Perkins commented: "In death as in life, a rare indiscretion aside, Pauncefote served the cause of friendship" between Britain and the United States.[66]

The Senate Foreign Relations Committee acted on April 13. Unlike its House counterpart, however, in recommending American intervention in Cuba, its report also declared that Cuba should be "free and independent."[67] Of particular concern to the Administration was that four members voted in favor of a minority report offered by Democrat David Turpie of Indiana that would explicitly recognize the Cuban republic.[68]

A co-author of the amendment was Ohio Senator Joseph B. Foraker, a political enemy of Mark Hanna. A powerful orator, known as "Fire Alarm Joe," he led the Republican support for the amendment during the four-day debate on the Senate floor. In a strong indictment, he accused the Administration of refusing to recognize independence because "this intervention is to be deliberately turned from intervention on the grounds of humanity into an aggressive conquest of territory" which the American people would not tolerate.[69] The Administration pulled out all the stops, including the use of patronage, to defeat the amendment, but to no avail. On the sixteenth, with the support of twenty-five Republican senators, it was adopted by a 51 to 37 vote.[70]

The Senate then adopted another far more significant amendment.

Offered by Democratic Senator Henry M. Teller of Colorado, it read:

"That the United States hereby disclaims any disposition or intention to exercise sovereignty, jurisdiction, or control over said island, except for the pacification thereof, and asserts its determination when that is accomplished to leave the government and control of the island to its people."[71]

Unlike the Turpie amendment, the Teller amendment commanded almost universal legislative support. Some said that this was due to the pressure of the sugar interests, which preferred to do business with an "independent" country that could be more easily controlled than a territory under United States domination. Others were concerned that annexation would add to the population of the United States a body of persons alien in race and language, whose Roman Catholic religion and supposed loyalty to Rome were viewed suspiciously by large numbers of the prevailing Protestant majority in the United States.[72] The primary motive, however, stemmed from the widely held anticolonial sentiment that, as one senator put it, was causing America to "intervene for humanity's sake...to aid a people who have suffered every form of tyranny and who have made a desperate struggle to be free." As the respected Illinois Senator Shelby Cullom said to an attentive Senate:

"If the people of this country shall do nothing more in this century than drive the Spaniards from this hemisphere, we as a people shall earn the praises of every lover of freedom and humanity the world over."[73]

The Teller amendment thus was included in the resolution that Congress approved early the following week. Sixty-five years later, after a confrontation between the United States and Russia over missiles in Fidel Castro's Cuba had brought the world to the brink of nuclear war, some Americans may have questioned that action.

At 3:00 A.M. on April 19, both Houses of Congress finally passed a joint resolution:

"for the recognition of the independence of the people of Cuba, demanding that the government of Spain relinquish its authority and government in the island of Cuba and Cuban waters, and directing the President of the United States to use the land and naval forces of the United States to carry these resolutions into effect."[74]

The resolution did not refer to the possible recognition of the Cuban republic. The preceding weekend had witnessed intense Administration pressure to enforce Republican party discipline and accept a provision that did not contain such a clause, which McKinley believed was an infringement on his constitutional foreign policy prerogative. So strongly did he feel that on Sunday, the seventeenth, he had decided to veto any resolution that did so. The Senate conferees finally conceded the point, and the resolution was cleared for passage.[75] As the Senate and House conferees deliberated into Monday night, and as the impatient congressmen waited to vote, an observer wrote that

"A half hundred of the Representatives gathered in the lobby in the rear of the hall and awoke the echoes with patriotic songs. "The Battle Hymn of the Republic" was sung by General Henderson of Iowa. "Dixie" and other songs were sung by some of the ex-Confederates, and then in tremendous volume the corridors rang with an improvising "Hang General Weyler to a Sour Apple Tree as We Go Marching on."[76]

In a ceremony at the White House the next day, McKinley signed the war resolution. It was delivered to the Spanish Ambassador, who immediately requested his passport. Shortly thereafter, Ambassador Woodford was notified that diplomatic relations between the United States and Spain had terminated.[77]

EIGHT

"You May Fire When You Are Ready, Gridley"

On January 1, 1898 Commodore George Dewey arrived in Nagasaki, Japan to take command of the Asiatic Squadron of the United States Navy, a force consisting of three cruisers and three gunboats.[1] Dewey was sixty years old, but his age had not diminished his ardent spirit. He had served under Admiral Farragut in the Civil War, and had never forgotten that that doughty fighter's first moment of glory came when he was sixty-one at New Orleans. Proud and ambitious, he was not widely popular. But Roosevelt recalled how he had assumed responsibility in an 1891 crisis with Chile, and marked him for future command. His opinion of the Commodore was further enhanced when he learned that Dewey shared his expansionist views.[2]

In late 1897 the commander of the Asiatic Squadron announced his retirement. Roosevelt took prompt action. In September, with Secretary Long not yet returned from his long summer vacation in Massachusetts, Roosevelt effectively derailed the candidacy of another officer by suggesting that Dewey find a friendly senator to intervene with the President on his behalf. Fortunately, Dewey knew the influential Redfield Proctor, who in turn talked with McKinley. When Long returned to the Navy Department, he found on his desk a memorandum from the President requesting Dewey's appointment. He had no choice but to oblige.[3]

Dewey's orders, in the event of war with Spain, were to defeat the Spanish naval forces in the Pacific and attack Manila, the capital of the Philippine Islands, which had been a Spanish possession since 1564. By the end of 1896 the Navy Department had drafted a war plan, and it had been officially approved on June 30, 1897. Influenced by Mahan's doctrine of the importance of sea power, the Navy had improved in both quality and quantity, and considered itself ready to fight a two-ocean war. The plan thus called for both an attempt to capture Manila as well as a blockade of Cuba.[4]

117

By February 25 Secretary Long was feeling the strain of the *Maine* disaster. The Navy Department had been the focus of inquiries regarding the explosion's cause and demands for a buildup in preparation for war. From time to time, Long had found relief in an osteopathic "mechanical massage," so at midday he decided to have a treatment and take the rest of the afternoon off. He left the Assistant Secretary in charge, apparently without instructions.[5]

As soon as Long had left the building, Roosevelt sprang into action. During the next three or four hours he arranged for the availability of large stocks of coal and ammunition, designated points where naval units could rendezvous if war was declared, made plans for a possible auxiliary fleet, and asked Congress for legislation permitting the unlimited recruitment of seamen. In short, in a single afternoon, he had placed the Navy on a quasi-war footing.[6] Roosevelt's most important act that afternoon, however, and the one for which posterity would remember him, was the cablegram he sent to Commodore Dewey in Hong Kong:

"Order the squadron, except the *Monocany*, to Hong Kong. Keep full of coal. In the event of declaration of war Spain, your duty will be to see that the Spanish squadron does not leave the Asiatic Coast, and then offensive operations in Philippine Islands. Keep Olympia until further orders."[7]

Roosevelt knew his man. Dewey immediately sent orders for the *Boston, Concord*, and *Raleigh* to join him, and arranged for part of the crew of the *Monocany*, which was laid up in Shanghai, to transfer to Hong Kong. He also asked Oscar F. Williams, the United States Consul in Manila, to report to him all possible information relating to the general defenses of the city and its harbor and keep close watch on the movements of the Spanish Asiatic squadron.[8] If war came, Dewey would be ready. Roosevelt's action might have appeared spontaneous, but as a biographer has stated, it "was the logical result of ten months of strategic planning."[9] A mid-twentieth-century historian stressed its significance:

"The Assistant Secretary had seized the opportunity given by Long's absence to insure our grabbing the Philippines without a decision to do so by either Congress or the President, or at least of all the people. This was important history made not by economic forces or democratic decisions, but through the grasping of chance authority by a man with daring and a program."[10]

Admiral George Dewey on the *Olympia*

Later day historians and some of Roosevelt's contemporaries may have applauded his action, but Secretary Long was appalled. As he confided to his diary the next day,

"During my short absence I find that Roosevelt, in his precipitate way, has come very near causing more of an explosion than happened to the Maine...the very devil seemed to possess him yesterday afternoon."[11]

Despite his annoyance, the Secretary apparently revoked none of Roosevelt's orders. It would be some time, however, before Long would take another afternoon off if the Assistant Secretary was in town.

"Discovered" by Captain James Cook in 1798, the Hawaiian Islands had been a kingdom for most of the nineteenth century. Initially named the Sandwich Islands, for a number of years they were considered part of England's sphere of influence. They were saved from an attempted British takeover in 1843 by a strongly worded statement by President John Tyler and a repudiation of an English coup by Foreign Secretary Lord Aberdeen.[12] Thereafter, trade with the United States, stimulated by American expansion to the Pacific coast, together with the efforts of missionaries led to a steady increase of American influence.

Although Hawaii remained independent, successive United States administrations were fully aware of its strategic position in the mid-Pacific. Annexation was always reserved as a possibility, especially if England or some other country were to try to take over the islands. Cession to the United States of a naval station at Pearl Harbor in 1887 as part of a reciprocal trade agreement made them even more important to the Americans.[13] Thus, in the early 1890s, when Queen Liliuokalani repudiated the pro-American policies of her predecessor and asserted a "Hawaii for the Hawaiians" regime, a revolt broke out under the auspices of American Minister Frederick Stevens. The Queen was quickly deposed and an annexation treaty with the United States was signed and rushed to the Senate for ratification.[14]

Unfortunately for annexation proponents, the treaty had been the doing of the Administration of President Benjamin Harrison, who had just been defeated for reelection by Grover Cleveland. Cleveland's opinion of the matter was very different from that of his predecessor. Thus, when the Senate was unable to ratify the treaty during the short period of time before Harrison left office, the new Administration withdrew it in

March 1893 for "the purpose of reexamination."[15] The ultimate result of this process was the establishment of a Republic of Hawaii, with Sanford B. Dole, a son of American missionaries, being elected its first President.[16]

There matters rested until 1898. Although the 1896 Republican platform had called for United States "control" of the Islands, the McKinley Administration initially had more urgent matters to contend with.[17] But the increasing China trade and front-page accounts of the 1894-1895 Sino-Japanese war had whetted public interest in the Far East and in Hawaii as an important station on the way to the Orient. Concern that Japan, fresh from her victory in that conflict, might seek to seize the islands led the President to send a new annexation treaty to the Senate in June 1897.[18] The Senate Democrats, however, adhered to the skeptical approach of the Cleveland Administration. Without some support from their side of the aisle, the necessary two-thirds majority for ratification was unavailable.[19]

By the following March, with a war with Spain in the offing, the Administration decided to try again. This time, however, using as precedent the annexation of Texas, the vehicle would be a joint resolution, which required only a majority vote of both Houses for enactment.[20] Thus, on March 16, the Senate Foreign Relations Committee favorably reported the proposal on the basis that annexation was

"a duty that has its origin in the noblest sentiments that inspire the love of a father for his children...or our Great Republic to a younger sister that has established law, liberty, and justice in a beautiful land that a corrupt monarchy was defiling..."[21]

The measure was also reported favorably to the House.[22] There was no immediate legislative action, however.

By late March, while the diplomats were still seeking a peaceful solution to the Cuban issue, Dewey was ready for war. The intrepid Consul Williams and others supplied him with information which he believed gave him an accurate picture of Spanish strength in the Philippines. On March 31, he wrote Washington a detailed estimation, which concluded:

"I believe I am not over-confident in stating that with the squadron now under my command, the vessels could be taken and the defenses of Manila reduced in one day. There is every reason to believe that with Manila taken or even blockaded, the rest of the islands would fall either to the insurgents or ourselves, as they are only held now through the support of the Navy, and are dependent upon Manila for supplies." [23]

On April 24 the authorities in Hong Kong advised Dewey that, since Britain was a neutral in the war between the United States and Spain that had just commenced, his squadron must leave the British colony within twenty-four hours. [24] Dewey had received no instructions as to his course in this eventuality, and cabled the Navy Department in Washington for orders. The head of the Bureau of Navigation, Arent Crowninshield, happened to be at the Department this Sunday, read the cable, and walked across the street to the White House to urge an immediate reply. The President, who had been conferring with Day and several other officials, considered the matter with his advisors. He asked that an order be drafted sending Dewey to the Philippines, where he was to attack the Spanish naval forces that were reportedly there. [25] The message that was prepared read:

"Dewey, Hong Kong

War has commenced between the United States and Spain. Proceed at once to Philippine Islands. Commence operations at once, particularly against the Spanish fleet. You must capture vessels or destroy. Use utmost endeavors." [26]

When Secretary Long returned from a drive in the country later in the day, he approved the message. He took it to the White House, where the President gave him the final authority to send it to Dewey. [27] Thus, the conflict, which had originated over concerns regarding Spanish misrule in Cuba, was about to turn into a global confrontation that involved Spanish possessions halfway around the world. Dewey would have the opportunity to further the imperialistic designs that he shared with Roosevelt and Lodge. The immediate results of the order would significantly influence United States history down the next century through World War II and beyond.

After leaving Hong Kong, Dewey's squadron anchored at Mira Bay, thirty miles away on the Chinese coast, to await the arrival from Manila of United States Consul Williams. At 11:00 A.M. on the 27th, he boarded Dewey's flagship *Olympia*, where he gave the assembled officers the latest news. By 2:00 P.M., the fleet had left Mira Bay in two columns, 1,200 yards apart, with the six fighting ships in one and the three auxiliary vessels in the other. They were steaming southwest, with a smooth sea and under a clear sky, to the entrance to Manila Bay, some 600 miles away.[28]

Among the passengers on the boat that carried Counsel Williams to Dewey's flagship were two representatives of the Filipino liberation organization in Hong Kong. Although it had received little attention in the American press, the Philippines, like Cuba, contained an active body of insurgents, who, Dewey had been informed, "are ready to rise at our first gun." One of Dewey's two passengers was Emilio Aguinaldo, an intelligent and forceful Filipino, who in a Singapore press interview equated the position of his group with that of the Cuba rebels. As the Americans would shortly find out, Aguinaldo was a passionate proponent of total Philippine independence.[29]

During recent months the national conscience had been preoccupied with the issue of Cuba, with little public attention being paid to America's role in the world at large. A little-known thirty-six-year-old Indianapolis, Indiana lawyer named Albert J. Beveridge was about to change the focus of the national debate. On April 27, speaking at a Boston dinner honoring the memory of General Grant, he described his fellow countrymen as "a conquering race" and then in a single paragraph set forth a credo of United States imperialism:

"American factories are making more than the American people can use; American soil is producing more than they can consume. Fate has written our policy for us; the trade of the world can be and shall be ours. And we will get it as our mother [England] has told us how. We will establish trading posts throughout the world as distributing points for American products. We will cover the ocean with our merchant marine. We will build a navy to the measure of our greatness. Great colonies governing themselves, flying our flag and trading with us, will grow about our posts of trade. Our institutions will follow our flag on the wings of our commerce. And American law, American order, American civilization, and the American flag will plant themselves on shores hitherto bloody and benighted, but by those agencies of God henceforth to be made beautiful and bright."

From the vantage point of more than one hundred years, it may be difficult to appreciate the enthusiasm with which these words were received. As Beveridge's audience cheered, he spoke of "the Stars and Stripes over an Isthmian canal...over Hawaii...over Cuba and the southern seas," and as he concluded:

"...In the Pacific is the true field of our earliest operation. ...In the Pacific, the United States has a powerful squadron. The Philippines are logically our first target."

At the war's outset, and before a single shot had been fired, Beveridge had defined its real significance. His ideas were to be the focus of intense and impassioned debate in the coming months.[30]

The Philippines are a group of some 7,000 islands and rocks; the largest is the northernmost island of Luzon. Manila Bay is an excellent landlocked harbor on the southwest coast of Luzon, about thirty-five miles wide and extending inland for thirty miles. Manila is on its eastern shore.

The Spanish naval forces in the Philippines were commanded by Admiral Patricio Montojo y Pasarón. Although he had some forty vessels under his orders, most were gunboats. Of his two largest vessels, both cruisers, one was constructed of wood. Like Admiral Cervera, he was pessimistic over his chances of success in any battle with the United States navy. His greatest need was mines to protect the entrance to Manila Bay. Minister Bermejo had advised him that these were on the way, but by the time that hostilities had commenced they had not arrived. Montojo believed that they would be too late to stop Dewey's fleet.[31]

Montojo had been told that fourteen underwater mines already guarded the much smaller Subic Bay, some thirty miles up the coast. Since he hoped that these might protect at least some of his ships from destruction, on the evening of April 25 he moved his six largest vessels to Subic. To his dismay, he found that only five of the mines had been put in place and that the guns that were supposed to be guarding the bay were still lying on the beach. While he was considering whether he might have time to remedy these defects, he received a telegram from the Spanish consul at Hong Kong that Dewey had left Hong Kong for the Philippines, and that the Americans' first landfall was likely to be at Subic Bay and thereafter Manila. At a council on the twenty-eighth, Montojo and his officers decided to return to Manila, where there were at least some effective shore batteries. Also, the water was much shallower than at Subic, providing a better chance of rescuing the crews of the ships that the pessimistic Admiral expected would be sunk.[32]

At 2:45 A.M. on April 30, one of Dewey's lookouts sighted Cape Bolinao, on the northwest coast of Luzon. The two-and-a-half-day trip from Mira Bay had been spent in frequent drills and the stripping of the ships' unneeded woodwork to lessen the danger of fire. Consul Williams had brought with him a copy of a proclamation of the Spanish Governor General of the Philippines, which referred to the Americans as "all the social excrements" who, unless stopped, would "profane the tombs of your fathers" and "gratify their lustful passions at the cost of your wives' and daughters' honor." Dewey had it posted in each of the vessels, where the men greeted it with a mixture of amusement and angry resolve.[33]

Dewey had been disturbed because Williams had also brought word that the Spanish fleet had left Manila Bay bound for Subic Bay, which, because of its narrower entrance, would be harder for him to attack. The American commander sent the cruiser *Boston* and the gunboat *Concord* ahead to Subic to reconnoiter, and later dispatched the cruiser *Baltimore* to help them if necessary. He was greatly relieved when, at about 3:30 p.m., he rounded a headland to find all three ships lying peacefully off the bay's entrance. "Now we have them!" he exclaimed, and thereafter was confident of success.[34]

Dewey's plan was simple. As he had thirty-six years earlier as a young officer under Admiral Farragut at the battle of New Orleans, he would wait until nightfall and before dawn run past the batteries that guarded the entrance to Manila Bay.[35] At 6:24 P.M., the squadron commenced its trip south to the bay, thirty five miles away. It was a beautiful tropical night, generally moonlit except for passing clouds. As one of the officers, Lieutenant B.A. Fiske, later described the journey:

"As darkness slowly descended the scene took on a character at once soothing and disturbing; soothing because everything was so beautiful and so calm; disturbing because of the grim preparations evident. The guns were all ready; considerable ammunition was on deck, and the men lay or sat or stood by their guns. As few lamps as possible were lit, and all lights which would shine outward were screened, except one small light over the stern of each ship....There was nothing to do, for all preparations had been made; there was nothing to see, except the dim outlines of a few ships and the vague outline of the coast two or three miles distant; and there was nothing to hear, except the sound of the night and the swish of the water along the sides."[36]

Manila Bay opens to the sea at its southwest end in a broad mouth of ten

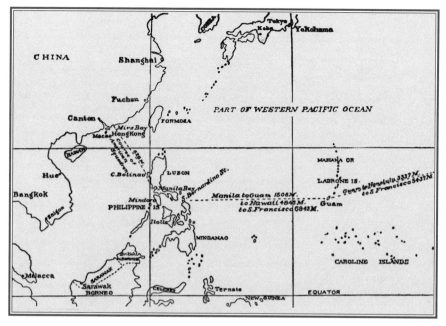

The Western Pacific

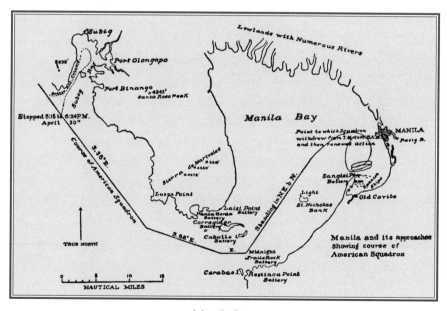

Manila Bay

nautical miles. The passage is divided by Corregidor Island, two miles off its northern shore and the smaller Caballe Island to its south, on both of which the Spaniards had stationed artillery batteries. It is another five-and-a-half nautical miles from Caballe to the bay's southern headland.[37]

It was into the broader southern passage, known as Boca Grande, that Dewey's ships steamed at about midnight. A few shots were fired by the shore batteries, but there were no hits and the squadron quickly moved into the bay. Manila was about twenty miles to the east. The ships made their way slowly toward the city, so as not to arrive before daylight. By 5:00 A.M. on May 1, they reached a point three miles from the shore. There, by the dawn's light they made out the shapes of a number of merchantmen, but there was no sign of Montojo's ships.[38]

By the evening of April 29, the Spanish forces had returned from Subic Bay. Strategically, their best course would probably have been to anchor and await battle off the bay's eastern shore opposite Manila, where their own guns would have been supported by the batteries that had been placed on the land for the defense of the city. But Montojo, although convinced that he must fight the Americans, was almost certain that Dewey's greater fire power would be too much for him. Further, as his official report stated:

"The idea of placing our ships near the city of Manila was rejected because, far from defending it, this would provoke the enemy to   bombard the plaza, which would infallibly have been demolished on account of its few defenses."[39]

Six-and-a-half miles southwest of Manila is the end of a peninsula running in a northeast and southwest direction. It forms a bay of its own, about three miles wide. Inside this bay, a smaller peninsula juts east out of the longer one. On it was the fortified navy yard of Cavite. It was in this small Bay of Canacao, under the guns of Cavite, that Montojo had formed his seven warships in line of battle. At about the same moment that the Americans saw that the Spanish warships were not at Manila, a lookout spotted them as they awaited Dewey several miles to the south. Led by the flagship *Olympia*, the Americans swung to starboard and steamed to the attack.[40]

Apart from the support that Montojo might receive from the land batteries, his force was seriously outclassed by Dewey's. The 19,098 tonnage of the Americans was more than fifty percent greater than the 11,589 of the Spaniards. The wooden *Castilla*, Montojo's second largest ship, had developed leaks that made her almost immobile. Some of the guns of three ships had been transferred ashore. The intense training that the Americans had undergone on the voyage from Mira Bay and earlier made the odds in Dewey's favor even greater.[41]

Since Dewey's ammunition supplies were limited, he planned to get as close as possible to the Spaniards to insure sinking their vessels. His goal was to strike first at their eastern flank and then turn west-northwest with Cavite and Montojo's fleet to port. At about 5:40 A.M, with his guns still silent notwithstanding enemy fire from the eastern shore of Manila Bay, the *Olympia* was within two-and-a-half miles of the Spaniards. At this point, Dewey turned to Captain Charles V. Gridley, the *Olympia*'s commander, and gave the laconic order that became famous in United States naval history:

"You may fire when you are ready, Gridley."[42]

The *Olympia* commenced firing from her forward turret guns. She continued south for another mile, and then turned west, opening with a general fire on the line of Spanish ships as she passed, only about 3,000 yards away. The line of American ships followed her, adding the fire of their port guns to that of the flagship. She then turned 180 degrees, and led the squadron east, pounding the Spanish vessels with her starboard guns. As Dewey's ships passed Montojo's forces, the Spaniards returned their fire, as did the batteries on Cavite. They scored a number of hits, but none were serious. The Americans, on the other hand, were inflicting severe damage on their foes. On Montojo's flagship, the *Reina Cristina*, exploding shells put several guns out of action and started fires that were so severe that it was found necessary to flood the magazine, where cartridges were beginning to explode.[43]

By now Dewey had closed to within 2,500 yards of the Spanish. This allowed their shorter-range guns to be used against the Americans and might have equalized matters somewhat but for the greater accuracy of Dewey's gunners. Through the smoke, the Americans were able to see the damage that their barrage had inflicted. Montojo's ships, however, continued firing, apparently still at close to full strength.[44]

Just as the Americans were turning east to make their fourth pass, the *Reina Cristina* left the Spanish line and moved out into the bay, apparently to attack the *Olympia*. This exposed her to several concentrated broadsides. By the time the two ships had closed to within 1,200 yards of each other, as an American officer later described the scene:

"Dark clouds of smoke poured up from the bow and stern and a plume of white smoke made clear another signal of distress. A shell had pierced the superheater, the ship was on fire in two places, the steering engine was shot away, and most of the guns were disabled."[45]

One of the *Olympia*'s eight-inch shells killed twenty Spanish seamen, another killed or wounded all the crew of the four rapid-fire forecastle guns, and a third carried away the mizzen mast. Montojo had no recourse but to order the flagship's crew to abandon ship before she sank. The total loss on the *Reina Cristina* was one hundred and fifty killed and ninety wounded.[46]

At 7:35 A.M., just as the squadron was about to begin its fifth pass, Captain Gridley informed Dewey that there remained only fifteen rounds of ammunition for each gun in the five inch battery. This supply could be used up in two minutes. Initially this gave Dewey great concern for, as he later wrote:

"So far as I could see, the Spanish squadron was as intact as ours. I had reason to believe that their supply of ammunition was as ample as ours was limited."[47]

Dewey had no recourse but to order his ships to abandon the battle for the moment, and steam to the middle of Manila Bay, where the total supply of ammunition could be determined and redistributed. As he turned north into the bay, however, and the smoke cleared away, his gloom was immediately dispelled as he and his officers were able to observe the destruction that their guns had inflicted.

At 8:40 A.M., Dewey held a council of war. His officers reported that damage was light, and, incredibly, only six seamen had been wounded and none had been killed. While the officers met, the men on deck watched the scene to the south, where the *Reina Cristina* blew up and the *Castilla* was in flames. At 11:16 the Americans returned to the fray and made short work of the remaining Spanish ships. By 12:30 the *Ulloa*, which had been the only remaining effective Spanish vessel, had been sunk and the naval station at Cavite had raised a white flag.[48]

Dewey then ordered his ships to turn north and anchor off Manila. At 3:00 P.M., the British consul asked to come aboard to request, on behalf of the foreign residents, that the city be spared from destruction. Dewey replied that he would be happy to comply, so long as the American warships were not fired upon, and he was provided with coal and permitted to use the cable to Hong Kong. When the Spanish commander agreed only to a cease-fire, Dewey ordered the cable cut. Manila was now cut off from the rest of the world.[49]

———❧———

The first word of the Manila battle that reached Madrid was a cable from the Governor General that both fleets had suffered heavy losses and that the Americans "took refuge behind the foreign merchant shipping on the east side of the bay." The resulting elation in the Spanish capital quickly turned to gloom on receipt of a later report, sent before the Manila cable was cut. Although it ascribed heavy losses to the Americans, it confirmed the complete destruction of Montojo's ships.[50]

The news of the Spanish disaster quickly spread. The London *Times* May 2 edition headlined "BATTLE OFF MANILA SPANISH DEFEAT," referring to news received by "private telegraph" and reporting "heavy damage" to both squadrons.[51] The next day, under the headline "DESTRUCTION OF THE SPANISH SQUADRON," the *Times* reported that the British government had advised the State Department that, according to dispatches it had received from Singapore, the battle had "resulted in the annihilation of the Spanish squadron."[52]

The American press at once passed on the good news to an excited public. The *New York Herald*'s May 2 headline, based on a correspondent's report wired from Manila just before the cable was cut, read: "SPAIN'S ASIATIC FLEET DESTROYED BY DEWEY." Hearst's *Journal*, not to be outdone, proclaimed "VICTORY, COMPLETE... GLORIOUS! ...THE MAINE IS AVENGED!"[53] But, with the Manila cable cut and no further news, the euphoria began to be tempered by concern over the heavy losses that reportedly had been sustained by the American victors.[54]

———❧———

The news from Manila, although fragmentary, caused a prompt reassessment of American military strategy. On May 2, at a White House meeting with McKinley attended by Secretaries Alger and Long; the Army's commanding officer General Nelson A. Miles; and the previous commander of the North Atlantic Squadron, Admiral Montgomery Sicard, the decision was reached to send 5,000 troops to support Dewey. It seemed likely, however, that this would be only the first installment. A much larger force probably would be required, especially if the entire archipelago were to be conquered. The total size of the invading army would depend on military and political decisions that would be taken only after further investigation and reflection.[55]

British diplomat Cecil Spring-Rice was a good friend of both Theodore Roosevelt, for whom he had acted as best man, and John Hay. A staunch supporter of closer Anglo-American ties and strongly anti-German, he had discussed with Hay in March and April the implications of a Spanish-American conflict, and continued to communicate with him on the subject. Based on Spring-Rice's reports from the British embassy in Berlin, Hay cabled the State Department on May 2 that "excellent authority in German matters suggests prompt annexation of Hawaii before war closes as otherwise Germany might seek to complicate the question with Samoa or Philippine Islands."[56]

McKinley did not need Hay's warning. In addition to concern over German intentions in the Central Pacific, there were fears that Britain or Japan might seek to annex Hawaii if the United States did not act. On May 4 he said to his secretary, George Cortelyou: "We need Hawaii just as much and a good deal more than we did California. It is Manifest Destiny." Speaker Reed would temporarily hold up a vote on the annexation question, but the handwriting was on the wall. Annexation was inevitable.[57]

By May 6, several days had passed since the earliest reports of Dewey's victory and there was no further news from the Philippines. The continuing delay exacerbated concerns created by the reports of heavy American as well as Spanish losses.[58]

Dewey was doing his best to get an official report to Washington. However, he could spare only the revenue cutter *McCulloch*, which had to refuel before she departed so that she could return from Hong Kong, since, as a neutral, Britain would not accord her that privilege there. Hence, she did not leave Manila Bay until May 5, and arrived in Hong Kong on May 7.[59]

The cipher experts at the Bureau of Navigation had been kept on a twenty-four watch. Early in the morning of May 7, they deciphered Dewey's five-sentence report announcing total victory with nominal loss. The press was alerted and Secretary Long, by now at his office, gave word that he would announce the contents of the message. Once again, he was upstaged by Roosevelt. The outgoing Assistant Secretary had leaned over the shoulders of the translators, and as soon as he had heard what they were saying, excitedly rushed out to report in detail the names of the destroyed Spanish warships and the fact that not a single American life had been lost. Thus, by the time that Long had made his official announcement, after perusing the translated message and telephoning the news to McKinley, the reporters had already sent its contents to the main telegraph office to be wired to their newspapers.[60]

A jubilant American public hailed Dewey's triumph as the greatest in United States naval history. McKinley promoted him to Acting Rear Admiral and Congress voted a resolution of thanks and appropriated $10,000 to purchase a handsome sword for the new hero and bronze medals for each of his officers and men.[61]

Dewey's victory immediately raised the issue of the long-term future of the Philippines. Once American troops had arrived to seize Manila and the surrounding area, what was to be done with the Islands? Certainly they should not be returned to Spain, but were they ready for independence? The only viable alternative, according to a growing body of press comment across the country, was that the United States must retain at least a naval base there.[62] Among the more prescient observations were those contained in a May 9 letter from *Atlantic Monthly* editor Walter Hines Page to the English historian and diplomat James Bryce:

"We see already the beginnings of an 'Imperial' party here. Indeed, I do not see, nor do I know anybody who has seen, how we are going to get rid of these islands, even if it were certain that we shall wish to get rid of them. The possession of the Philippines and the Hawaiian Islands will bring an overwhelming reason for as close an alliance as possible with Great Britain.

"How much of the present exultation and rapidly growing 'imperial' ambition is a mere passing joy of victory, it is hard to say; but there can be little doubt but a wider-looking policy has come into our political life to remain."[63]

Shortly following Dewey's victory, warships of several neutral countries arrived in Manila Bay to look out for their commercial interests and nationals in the Philippines. Among them were two British vessels commanded by Sir Edward Chichester, whose cousin Francis would gain fame in the next century when, alone, he circumnavigated the globe in the *Gypsy Moth*. Pursuant to international custom when a naval blockade was established, the British steamers, as well as those of France and Japan, immediately applied for and were granted the right to anchor in the bay so long as they carried on no intercourse with either the Filipino insurgents or the Spanish land forces.[64]

On May 6, however, the German cruiser *Irene*, on entering the bay, steamed past Dewey's flagship *Olympia* and dropped anchor without obtaining consent. Dewey overlooked this breach of the law of blockade, but when a second German cruiser, the *Cormoran*, arrived at 3:00 A.M. on May 8 and paid no attention to a steam launch sent by the Americans to identify her, the cruiser *Raleigh* fired a shot across her bow. She immediately stopped and assured the Americans that her intentions were purely neutral.[65]

Notwithstanding this statement of good will, Dewey paid close attention to the Germans. His small fleet was alone in the area, and could not expect immediate help from home. The British were of no concern, since from their actions when he had been in Hong Kong, and in general, they clearly sympathized with the United States as against Spain. On the other hand, it was well known that Germany was interested in acquiring colonies in the Far East to counterbalance those which England already possessed. The Americans believed, not without cause, that if the United States did not establish some form of control over the Philippines, Germany was likely to move in, using as a wedge the friendship toward Spain that the Kaiser's government had shown prior to the war.[66]

The American concern was well founded. Reports from the Far East had whetted the German Government's interest in the Philippines. Prince Henry of Prussia, who commanded the German Asiatic squadron, had cabled Foreign Minister Bülow from Hong Kong on May 11 that a Philippine rebellion was likely to be successful, and that in that event "the natives would gladly place themselves under the protection of a European power, especially Germany." Bülow received confirmatory advice from the German consul in Manila.[67]

In conveying this information to the Kaiser, Bülow stressed the importance of the Philippines: "...the control of the sea in the end may rest on the question of who rules the Philippines, directly or indirectly." England seemed to be the key. If she and the United States were to agree on the Islands' future, that probably would end the matter. On the other hand, if Britain withheld its consent to American annexation, the United States was unlikely to proceed on its own. Thus, for Germany to play any role in the Islands' future, there would have to be a prior understanding with "one or more first class naval powers." The Kaiser's marginal notes on Bülow's report expressed general agreement, but added that another power should not be permitted to take over the Philippines "without Germany's receiving an equivalent compensation."

On May 18 Bülow asked the German ambassador in London, Count Paul von Hatzfeldt, to try to determine the British position: would she support the United States, did she want a share of the spoils, or was her goal to neutralize the islands? After making appropriate inquiries, the Ambassador replied that all that was clear was that Salisbury believed that the McKinley Administration would not welcome any foreign proposals regarding the future of the archipelago.[69] That was yet to be decided.

NINE

"We Have Had No Allies—I Am Afraid We Have Had No Friends"

During his tour of duty in London, Ambassador Hatzfeldt had observed the increasing English frustration over that country's inability to thwart Russian policy towards China. He believed that the time might be propitious for an overture to the Salisbury Government that would lead to improved British-German relations, which had turned sour since the Jameson Raid and disagreements over colonial policies in Africa and China. He realized that this would be difficult, not only because of British reluctance to make any concessions to Germany, but also since Bülow and Holstein, who Hatzfeldt believed had an evil influence on Bülow, were very suspicious of British foreign policy. Nevertheless, to Hatzfeldt the effort was worthwhile making.[1]

Baron Hermann von Eckardstein, an official at the German London Embassy, was a familiar figure in the highest levels of British society. Six feet five inches tall, he was an impressive figure, especially when clad in his white uniform, helmet, and boots. He was a good friend of banker Alfred de Rothschild, whose hereditary bias was German and who disliked Russia because of its pogroms and other acts of oppression toward its Jewish population. Rothschild had good relations with leading figures in successive Liberal and Conservative Governments.[2]

Early in March, Eckardstein had been Rothschild's guest at a small dinner that was also attended by Chamberlain and the Duke of Devonshire, whose German wife's brother was a German general. Much of the discussion centered on British exasperation with Russian actions in the Far East.[3] When Eckardstein reported this conversation to Hatzfeldt, the latter decided to seize the opportunity, and asked Rothschild to organize a luncheon at which Hatzfeldt could meet informally with several Cabinet ministers. Somewhat disingenuously, Hatzfeldt telegraphed Berlin that it was his "impression that the initiative is not Rothschild's alone and that the main object is to make a confidential attempt at a rapprochement with Germany.[4]

Rothschild's only luncheon guests on March 25 were Hatzfeldt and Arthur Balfour, the leader of the House of Commons, who was acting as Foreign Secretary during Lord Salisbury's illness. Their host shortly excused himself, and his two guests conversed for about an hour and a half. The discussion was centered on different issues in Anglo-German relations and was probably intended as a general clearing of the air. Immediately after the luncheon Balfour called upon Salisbury, who was to leave to recuperate at his villa in the south of France the next morning. There followed a three-and-a-half-hour Cabinet meeting. Although Balfour reported to Queen Victoria that the discussion "was entirely confined" to Far Eastern matters, it can be surmised that he acquainted his fellow ministers of the particulars of his meeting with Hatzfeldt.[5]

The German reaction to the March 25 meeting was cautious. The view in Berlin was that the British were probably trying to gain German support against Russia in the Far East but that Britain would be unwilling to give Germany anything important in return. Nevertheless, neither Bülow nor Holstein was prepared to halt discussions at such a preliminary stage. Perhaps since he had hoped that Chamberlain would have joined Balfour on the twenty-fifth and because Chamberlain, unlike Balfour, was viewed as a power in his own right, Hatzfeldt asked the Colonial Secretary to join him for lunch at Rothschild's house on the twenty-ninth.[6]

If he expected Chamberlain to live up to his reputation as a hard headed negotiator, the German Ambassador could not have been more surprised by the openness that Chamberlain displayed at their meeting. The Colonial Secretary expressed his concern that Salisbury's "splendid isolation" would leave Britain friendless at a time when the other major European powers were establishing strong alliances. Since the British were embroiled in a major controversy with Russia in the Far East and faced a possible conflict with France over Central Africa, only Germany remained as a potential continental ally.[7] Further, in a conversation that Chamberlain later described as "in the nature of a skirmish," the Colonial Secretary stated, as a purely personal opinion on the "greater issues" involving Britain and Germany, "the interests of Germany were really identical with our own." Again on a personal basis, he suggested to a probably incredulous Hatzfeldt a formal alliance between their two countries, perhaps for a "term of years."[8] As Hatzfeldt described Chamberlain's statement in his report to Bülow later that same day:

The Right Honourable Joseph Chamberlain, M.P.

"In other words: if we would stand by England, England would stand by Germany if Germany were to be attacked. This would be equivalent to England joining the Triple Alliance, and would be confirmed by a treaty for which we would formulate our terms. [...] In this entire conversation Chamberlain expressed himself calmly and definitely, and he revealed with great frankness his desire for a treaty between Britain and the Triple Alliance. He repeated several times that there was no time to be lost on the matter because a decision had to be made within a very short time."[9]

The German Government was not interested in pursuing a formal alliance with England. Germany considered itself as having friendly relations with both England and Russia, and saw no reason to antagonize the latter by allying herself with the former. It no doubt was influenced by Russia's long boundary with Germany, which made it, if allied with France, a more potent enemy than England. More fundamentally, as Chamberlain's leading biographer observed, Germany saw no benefit in furthering British claims in the Far East, where the Imperial government also had colonial interests. Indeed, the more involved the Russians became in China, the less likely they were to create difficulties in the West for Germany and Austria.[10] For his part, Chamberlain had expressed no interest in joining forces against France.[11] The Colonial Secretary should have recognized "that time is telling against England" and have been "thankful for the offer of German neutrality as the only valuable advantage our harassed Empire could expect from any Power." He should have appreciated that German policy was

"...to await events, to strengthen the fleet, to encourage suitable antagonisms between other Powers, to keep free hands until the moment when a new trident might be thrown into wavering scales."[12]

Bülow instructed Hatzfeldt to discourage Chamberlain and to suggest that if Germany were in Britain's position she would try to reach an accommodation with Russia in order to free her hand in dealing with France over Africa.[13] On April 1, Hatzfeldt did so, but the Colonial Secretary did not accept this negative answer as final. He was perfectly willing to submit any treaty between the two countries to Parliament, with the expectation that, "subject to the details being satisfactory," Parliament likely would approve it. He made clear to the Ambassador that his primary concern was Russia's policy towards China and suggested that under the proposed alliance Germany would support Britain in the Far East and

Britain would reciprocate "if Germany were attacked by Russia." To this, Hatzfeldt responded that the Tsar "was an advocate of peace," and that although in ten years or so, after the Trans Siberian Railroad had been completed, the situation might change, "at this time neither he nor France desired war or was prepared for it." The skeptical Ambassador added that rumor had it Chamberlain and his colleagues "sometimes differed," and in his report to Bülow later that day, commented that Chamberlain had told him "with remarkable candor that the Cabinet even now did not know what to do, nor what to say in the House of Commons."[14]

Since Chamberlain was apparently so eager to reach an agreement with Germany, Bülow instructed Hatzfeldt on April 13 to continue their conversations. He should emphasize to the Colonial Secretary that it was a central tenet of German policy that Britain should continue to be a great power, and that this made an alliance between the two countries a likely eventuality at some future date. Meanwhile, the British should not jeopardize this result by creating difficulties on minor questions, i.e., Britain should be less truculent about colonial matters.[15] Holstein followed up these instructions in a private letter to the Ambassador referring to Chamberlain as "clever and unscrupulous," and ascribing to the Colonial Secretary a deliberate desire to "do us in" by "compromising Germany towards Russia irretrievably."[16]

Because of German suspicions as to Chamberlain's motives in suggesting an alliance, Hatzfeldt decided to present Berlin's position to Balfour. When he did so on April 5, the British minister told him that Chamberlain was trying to move too fast, and that it was doubtful whether an alliance would be approved by Parliament. He suggested that agreement on minor issues would help prepare public opinion in both countries for future cooperation on more important matters.[17]

The German diplomats were pleased with Balfour's attitude, so much closer to their own than Chamberlain's. They also must have appreciated his remarks regarding Germany that same day in the House of Commons, when, in a statement generally addressing the Chinese situation, he said:

"But fundamentally the interests of the two countries are the same and must be the same, and I certainly believe that we shall be able without difficulty to work hand in hand towards carrying out these general commercial objects, which I believe approve themselves in the sense of the House."[18]

On reflection, however, both governments realized even more clearly how difficult it would be to consummate a formal alliance on major matters. On April 7 the Kaiser wrote Chancellor Hohenlohe:

"Chamberlain must not forget that in East Prussia I have one Prussian army corps against three Russian armies and nine cavalry divisions, from which no Chinese wall divides me and which no English ironclads hold at arm's length."[19]

The next day he exulted in Chamberlain's confession of the failure of "splendid isolation": "The Jubilee swindle is already over," and, regarding the reports to him of Britain's eagerness to join the Triple Alliance, "The dead ride fast." As to England's reliability as a future ally he marginally scribbled, "Frederick the Great shamefully left in the lurch by George."[20]

On the English side, Salisbury, still recuperating in the south of France, wrote Balfour:

"The one object of the Emperor since he has been on the throne has been to get us into a war with France. I never can make up my mind whether this is part of Chamberlain's object or not. The indications differ from month to month."[21]

The English and German press voiced similar suspicions. On April 9 the London *Times* explained:

"It seems difficult for Germans to comprehend that an identity of commercial interests does not imply that this country should or would make political concessions, either to Germany or her allies, in order to purchase co-operation in the sphere of trade."[22]

On the same day a Hamburg newspaper editorialized:

"Our answer to the voice of the charmer should be dictated exclusively by our own practical political interests, and these interests point to the necessity for holding on to the course we are at present following....To give up for the sake of a few fine words, which every breeze may blow away, the principles of our east Asiatic policy, to let ourselves be elbowed out of our entente with Russia and France, these are things which are, of course, quite out of the question."[23]

Nevertheless, the idea of some form of Anglo-German cooperation would not die. Reporting on the apparently ended alliance discussions. Balfour wrote Salisbury that he "was very much entertained" by Hatzfeldt's suggestion that colonial concessions by Britain would make an entente easier to achieve

"but took care to express no dissent from it, as, although I am inclined to favor an Anglo-German agreement, it must, if possible, be made at the worst on equal terms. Of this loving couple I should wish to be the one that lent the cheek, not the one that imprinted the kiss. This, I take it, is not the German view; and they prefer, I imagine, reserving their efforts until they are sure of being well paid for them."[24]

Although disappointed over the breakdown of alliance talks, Hatzfeldt also continued to believe that it was possible to improve Anglo-German relations. In an April 20 letter to Bülow, he questioned the official government view that Chamberlain's proposal was based on a "secret plan of involving us in difficulties with Russia while he himself stood aloof." For the moment, he suggested that his goal should be to try to keep the British from making an alliance unfriendly to Germany by leaving open the possibility of a close relationship at some future date. To this end, he would try to persuade

"...Lord Salisbury and his colleagues of the necessity of paying more attention to relations with Austria and Italy on the one hand, and on the other of showing more consideration towards us in any minor question that might arise thereby preparing our public opinion as well for the establishment of amicable relations."[25]

Hatzfeldt stressed to Bülow that this policy could succeed only with the active support of the Berlin government. Salisbury must not be given the impression that Germany was trying to push England into war with France. The German press must tone down its anglophobia. Further, "I can probably press successfully for greater consideration for ourselves in any minor questions that might arise [,] only if, with the support of the imperial government, I can indicate the same friendly treatment of such questions for the English."[26]

Unfortunately, the press's enmity toward England reflected the views of important German government officials. On April 22 Dr. von Holleben, the German Ambassador to the United States, wrote to Chancellor

Hohenlohe, suggesting that "the European Powers should watch that their interests are not damaged by the Spanish-American war..." He then compared British Ambassador Pauncefote's role in urging European intervention in the Cuban crisis earlier in the month with the fact that he now "ridicules the whole affair," concluding: "There is a lot in Sir Julian's mouth when speaking of America."[27]

Apparently as a routine matter, Hohenlohe sent Holleben's message to the Kaiser. William's "minute" to it was indicative of the feelings he harbored towards Great Britain, which would continue to poison relations between those two countries:

"England wishes to play the same games as when, last year, she confessedly promoted the Greco-Turkish war. She suggests measures to be taken by all the Powers, and seems to be taking part in them, until the belligerent has been thoroughly compromised by them. Then she retires, beats her breast like a Pharisee, declares that she has had nothing to do with it, allies herself secretly with one of the contending parties—the strongest, of course—and excites him against the Continental Powers! And all the time she is begging for commercial favours at their expense."[28]

On the morning of April 22, just as the British, including Joseph Chamberlain, had become convinced that a German alliance was out of the question, Eckardstein reappeared on the scene. He called on Chamberlain to report that he had just returned from Germany where, according to a memorandum the Colonial Secretary wrote later that day, he had met with the Kaiser "who had fully discussed the question of a possible alliance between England and Germany." Eckardstein added:

"The Emperor viewed such a possibility with the greatest favour, and was most anxious that such an agreement should be come to. He was very desirous that the matter should be dealt with immediately, as he feared, if there was any delay, that the pourparlers would leak out and would come to the attention of Russia."

Chamberlain agreed that the matter should be treated as unofficial and confidential. The Baron said he would arrange a meeting between the two of them and Ambassador Hatzfeldt the following Monday.[29]

Chamberlain immediately reported this conversation to Balfour, who wrote Salisbury on the subject the same day. He commented that

Eckardstein's "story I can hardly disbelieve altogether." After noting that some observers would recommend that the British Government regard the matter "as a political comedy without any real significance," he stated:

"But I think this would be a mistake. The Emperor is a very odd man, and I really believe...he has now reverted to his original policy on an English alliance...I am seriously afraid that those irresponsible diplomatists have raised expectations in [his] mind which, if left unfulfilled will, acting on so impulsive a being, throw him violently into the opposite camp."[30]

On April 25, as previously planned with Eckardstein, Chamberlain lunched with Hatzfeldt and the Baron, who after lunch left his two guests alone to talk.[31] Although Chamberlain appeared at Eckardstein's invitation, the German Ambassador had advised Berlin that it was Chamberlain who wished to see him. Thus, both governments were proceeding on the basis of erroneous assumptions: Chamberlain in the belief that the Kaiser sought an agreement on almost any terms and the Germans thinking that the Colonial Secretary was so eager for an alliance that he was willing to overlook the German rebuff of earlier in the month.[32]

According to Chamberlain, Hatzfeldt continued to express objections to a direct alliance between their two countries, but suggested that "the question should be approached in a different way." This was for England to join herself with Austria and Italy, which, through the Triple Alliance, would bring about an indirect association with Germany. Chamberlain responded that an alliance with Austria might be inconsistent with the British policy of "preserving the integrity of the Turkish Empire," with which Austria was at odds in the Balkans. According to Chamberlain, Hatzfeldt "assented" to the Colonial Secretary's conclusion that "a direct defensive alliance between Germany and England was premature...but ...the opportunity might come later." In response, Chamberlain "reminded him of the French proverb, 'le bonheur qui passe.' "[33]

In his report to Berlin later in the day, Hatzfeldt emphasized his efforts to encourage Chamberlain to keep open the possibility of an alliance in the future.[34] He also recounted a prophecy that history would confirm:

"Mr. Chamberlain in reply developed in detail the view that if his idea of a natural alliance with Germany must be renounced, it would be no impossibility for England to arrive at an understanding with Russia or with France..."[35]

The German Ambassador accepted this prediction at face value, reporting that "if no political understanding can be reached with us, we must cease here to expect any concession in colonial matters from him."[36]

The next morning, a distraught Eckardstein called on Chamberlain to express "great regret" that the previous day's meeting with Hatzfeldt "had not led to more definite results." According to Chamberlain, he said, "I cannot understand it. I know that the Emperor was most anxious that the matter should be pressed.[37] Chamberlain responded that he did not

"...see that there was anything to be done. Either Count Hatzfeldt's language was that of the Emperor, in which case the matter was ended, or it was not, and in this case it was for the Emperor to make the next move."[38]

William would make no move toward an alliance. His marginal notes on Hatzfeldt's April 25 report demonstrated the degree to which Eckardstein had either misunderstood or intentionally misrepresented his position. His comment on Chamberlain's alliance proposals was "What's eating the man?" As for allying with England to halt further Russian Far East expansion, he wrote, "Certainly not! The deeper the Russians get involved in Asia, the quieter they will be in Europe." And, on reading Hatzfeldt's reference to a possible British agreement with Russia, he scribbled, "Impossible!"[39]

On April 30 Bülow passed on to Hatzfeldt the Kaiser's marginal comments and instructed him to go no further than promise the English that there were no insurmountable obstacles to an understanding. The same day, Holstein wrote privately to Hatzfeldt of his belief that France would never support Russia against England and of his suspicion of any arrangement with the British:

"If they really thought as Chamberlain talks, they could thus tackle Russia with complete peace of mind. But that is just it, they think differently; as always they are only thinking of how they can send the Triple Alliance into the fight and stay out themselves."[40]

This "Monster of the Labyrinth" foresaw an intricate scenario that would develop if Germany fell for Chamberlain's blandishments:

"...the Russians then would indeed offer a very high price to England to persuade her to stand by quietly while Russia and France settle accounts with us. Italy could probably also be bought; she would join the side which promised Albania. If Austria—on whom one cannot absolutely count in view of the Slavic movement—stood faithfully by us, we would then end with the alignment: Germany and Austria against Russia, France and Italy. [...] Perhaps you will think my mistrust is exaggerated, but at present I still do not believe that Chamberlain intends to make England participate in a war."[41]

These were prophetic words, but with one important exception: sixteen years later, England did "participate in a war," but not on Germany's side.

Meanwhile, Salisbury had returned to London from the south of France. On April 29 Chamberlain immediately passed him his notes of "some very curious conversations I have had with the German ambassador and Baron Eckardstein." Despite his discouraging discussion with Hatzfeldt, the Colonial Secretary had not changed his views on Britain's position:

"Recent experience seems to show that we are powerless to resist the ultimate control of China by Russia, and that we are at a great disadvantage in negotiating with France, so long as we retain our present isolation, and I think the country would support us in a Treaty with Germany providing for reciprocal defence.

"I think such a Treaty would make for peace and might be negotiated at the present time.

"But it is for you to say whether the matter should be pressed or allowed to drop..."[42]

Three days later, Hatzfeldt called on Salisbury, who immediately wrote Chamberlain that the German Ambassador

"...made a great many general reflections on the advantages of a better understanding between Germany and England; but was careful to add, at fixed intervals, that nothing could be hurried, and that until matters were ripe, no action could be taken."

Suggesting that Hatzfeldt's "business was evidently to throw cold water," Salisbury concluded:

"I quite agree with you that under the circumstances a closer relation with Germany would be very desirable, but can we get it?"[43]

Chamberlain's reply, written from the House of Commons the same afternoon, showed that the Colonial Secretary was not yet ready to give up his hopes for an alliance:

"I believe it would be quite possible to ascertain through Eckardstein whether the Emperor is determined to press the matter and if so to let him know that the initiative must come from him."[44]

This, however, was something that Salisbury was unwilling to do.

That evening, Salisbury made a major address at the Albert Hall at a gathering of the Primrose League, a Conservative organization whose purpose was to honor and further the policies of former Prime Minister Benjamin Disraeli.* After minimizing the importance of recent Russian expansion in Manchuria, he emphasized that in any future crisis

"we know that we shall maintain against all comers that which we possess, and we know, in spite of the jargon about isolation, that we are amply competent to do so."[45]

Following this obvious response to Chamberlain's concern about "splendid isolation," the Prime Minister, in a classic introduction of Darwinian principles into the field of foreign relations, stressed that while Britain would look out for its own interests, it would not be a world policeman:

"You may roughly divide the nations of the world as the living and the dying...the weak states are becoming weaker and the strong states are becoming stronger. For one reason or another—from the necessities of politics or under the pretext of philanthropy—the living nations will gradually encroach on the territory of the dying and the seeds and causes of conflict among the civilized nations will speedily appear. Of course, it is not to be supposed that any nation of the living nations will be allowed to have the monopoly of curing or cutting up these unfortunate patients and the controversy is as to who shall have the privilege of doing so, and in what measure he shall do it. These things may introduce causes of fatal difference between the great nations whose mighty armies stand opposed threatening each other... Undoubtedly we shall not allow England to be at a disadvantage in any rearrangement that may take place. On the other hand, we shall not be jealous if desolation and sterility are

---

* The League was so named because the primrose was Disraeli's favorite flower.

removed by the aggrandizement of a rival in regions to which our arms cannot extend."[46]

Salisbury could not foresee that forty years later one of these "civilized" nations, describing itself as a "master race," would cut up another while Chamberlain's son Neville, refusing to step in, described it as "a quarrel in a faraway country between people of whom we know nothing."[47]

Salisbury's speech provoked widespread comment. A London *Times* correspondent in Madrid reported concern that Salisbury was thinking of Spain when he referred in his May 4 speech to "weak nations...becoming weaker." The statement had produced in Madrid both "a profound impression and moral indignation." The article added that some Spanish observers had suggested that Salisbury intended "to convey, in somewhat brutal form, a piece of advice that Spain should recognize facts, however painful to patriotic sentiment."[48]

Other nations, including France, took offense at Salisbury's remarks, but were assured that he was not referring to them.[49] His speech was also criticized at home. On May 5, the *Times* welcomed Salisbury home from France, praising his past services and opining that there was no statesman whose future services "the people are more anxious to retain in a suitable sphere of endeavor." The editorial then attacked the Prime Minister, however, for his "temptation to succumb to listlessness, especially vis-a-vis China."[50]

On May 11 Hatzfeldt made his first call on Salisbury since the latter's "dying nations" speech. According to Salisbury, Hatzfeldt opened the discussion by complaining that Britain possessed so much of the globe that there was little left for the other major powers to occupy. As the Prime Minister described it:

"He intimated that the friendship or alliance of his Government could only be looked for if we could concede to the demands of Germany in the various parts of the world where our interests were at present apparently in collision."

Salisbury's reply could not have been clearer:

"I of course declined to admit that there was any ground for the assertion that we had obtained an excessive share of the advantages which might be derived from the less civilized portions of the world, and I could not recognize that Germany had any claim that we should purchase her support by concessions to which, except for the consideration of that support, we should be adverse."

Further, in view of the support of the Ottoman Empire which at the time was one of the foundations of British policy, how could Britain ally herself with Germany, and thus Austria, in view of the latter's design's on that Empire's Balkan possessions?[51]

In his report to Berlin, Hatzfeldt summed up Salisbury's remarks as: "You ask too much for your friendship." The prospect for an alliance between the two countries thus seemed as remote as ever.[52]

The furor over Salisbury's "dying nations" speech had not yet subsided on May 13 when Chamberlain made an address that raised even greater excitement. Speaking at a political gathering in his home city of Birmingham, the Colonial Secretary bluntly raised foreign policy issues that not only seemed to challenge Salisbury, but also proposed new and provocative initiatives. After referring to "a combined assault by the nations of the world upon the commercial supremacy of this country," he suggested that the crux of the situation was that:

"Since the Crimean War, nearly fifty years ago, the policy of this country had been a policy of strict isolation. We have had no allies—I am afraid we have had no friends... In this way we have avoided entangling alliances, we have escaped many dangers; but we must accept the disadvantages that go with such a policy...A new situation has arisen, and it is right the people of this country should have it under their consideration. All the powerful states of Europe have made such alliances, and as long as we keep outside these alliances, as long as we are envied by all, and as long as we have interests which at one time or another conflict with the interests of all, we are liable to be confronted at any moment with a combination of Great Powers so powerful that not even the most extreme, the most hotheaded politician would be able to contemplate it without a certain sense of uneasiness."[53]

In response to this potential crisis, Chamberlain proposed that Britain should first "draw all parts of the Empire closer together, to infuse into them a spirit of united and Imperial patriotism." It was the proposed next step that caused, perhaps, the most comment:

"...to establish and to maintain bonds of permanent unity with our kinsman across the Atlantic. They are a powerful and a generous nation. They speak our language, they are bred of our race. Their laws, their literature, their standpoint upon every question are the same as ours; their feeling, their interest in the cause of humanity and the peaceful development of the world are identical with ours. I do not know what the future has in store for us. I do not know what arrangements may be possible with us, but this I know and feel— that the closer, the more cordial, the fuller, and the more definite these arrangements are, with the consent of both peoples, the better it will be for both and for the world. And I even go so far as to say that, terrible as war may be...even war itself would be cheaply purchased if in a great and noble cause the Stars and Stripes and the Union Jack should wave together over an Anglo-Saxon Alliance."[54]

When Chamberlain turned to the Far East, his speech seemed to take on a particularly anti-Salisbury tone. After quoting, with regard to Russia, "a very wise proverb, 'Who sups with the Devil must have a long spoon,'" he observed that "unless we are allied to some great military power, as we were in the Crimean War...we cannot seriously injure Russia." He went on:

"It is impossible to over-rate the gravity of the issue...it is a question of the whole fate of the Chinese Empire, and our interests in China are so great...that I feel that no more vital question has been presented for the decision of a Government and the decision of a nation. If the policy of isolation, which has hitherto been the policy of this country, is to be maintained in the future, then the fate of the Chinese Empire may be, probably will be, hereafter decided without reference to our wishes and in defiance of our interests. If, on the other hand, we are determined to enforce the policy of the open door,...then we must not allow jingoes to drive us into a quarrel with all the world at the same time, and we must not reject the idea of an alliance with those Powers whose interests most nearly approximate to our own."[55]

If Chamberlain had intended to create shock waves, he surely succeeded. The May 16 London *Times* reported from Berlin "a sense of astonishment, almost amounting to a positive shock at the singularly clear, vigorous and unconventional language in which the English statesman chose to express his views." Other German commentators took pleasure in what they saw as an expression of British weakness. One French commentator called Chamberlain a "civilian Boulanger," and fears that the speech might have been directed at France almost caused a panic on the Paris Bourse.[56] Thus, three days later, *Le Gaulois* published a letter from a French rear admiral asking: "Is the French Navy ready for an eventual struggle with the English Navy?...Our inferiority is notable."[57]

Reaction on both sides of the Atlantic to Chamberlain's proposal of an Anglo-American understanding was generally favorable. The London *Times* commented:

"It is a foregone conclusion that the opportunity should be availed of establishing permanent relations of amity, and something more, with the United States, whose success in the operations that have lately taken place has been welcomed here, not only as justified by the goodness of her cause, but as a tribute to the practical capacity of the Anglo-Saxon race in the business of war, even when no adequate preparation for the struggle has been made."[58]

In the United States, the comments of many leading newspapers were even more enthusiastic. The *New York Tribune*, although recognizing that a formal alliance between the two countries was unlikely, expressed the hope that they "should live on terms of amity, so that if it is best at any time that they should act together there will be no existing bad feeling to make it more difficult for them to do so." *The New York Times*, which treated the speech as front-page news, commented that an Anglo-American alliance would couple the two countries "with the beneficent forces that guide the evolution of the human race throughout the world," and that "in all human probability it would make for peace, for it would be too powerful to be resisted successfully."[59] The Chicago *Tribune* opined:

"There may never be such an alliance in formal written terms. But what is unmistakable, not only inevitable, in the future but actual in the present, actual and potent, is this: that the two great branches of the Anglo-Saxon race are drawing nearer and nearer together for cooperation in peace, and in logical sequence, in war as well. Every move that promotes that movement is to be welcomed and applauded. Well to the fore among such words are those spoken by Mr. Chamberlain, directly to an English audience, but indirectly and no less meaningfully to all the world."[60]

The favorable response to Chamberlain's call for closer Anglo-American ties was tempered, however, by the recognition that, in part because America's large Irish population was strongly anti-British, any formal alliance lay far in the future. As a London *Times* New York correspondent wrote:

"Most members of Congress...are politicians bred in a school of distrust. Distrust of England is with many of them traditional. They distrust her no longer, but when the word "alliance" is pronounced, they ask for time."[61]

Sir Charles Dilke, one of the leaders of the opposition Liberal Party, echoed a similar view:

"Every man welcomes an alliance, if you like to call it, of hearts between the two countries, but none of us, and few Americans, think that it would be likely to produce what may be called a war alliance."[62]

There was even less support for Germany as a potential British ally. Liberal member of the House of Commons and future Prime Minister Herbert Henry Asquith expressed the view of many of his fellow countrymen when he indignantly asked:

"What have we done, what have the people of Great Britain done or suffered, that, after bearing, as we have done for nearly fifty years, the ever-growing weight of empire on our own unaided shoulders, without feeling the burden too heavy for the courage, the enterprise, the self-reliance of our people, what have we done or suffered that we are now to go touting for allies in the highways and byways of Europe?"[63]

Many Conservatives were not encouraged by Salisbury's reaction to Chamberlain's proposals. In reply to a question in the House of Lords as to whether Chamberlain was expressing the view of the Government and whether his position was contrary to Salisbury's, the Prime Minister lamely said that he had not yet read the full text of the speech, and then repeated his prior position:

"Our general policy is unchanged. We shall cultivate to the utmost of our ability the friendship of all the Powers with whom we come into contact."[64]

Meanwhile, the German Government was attempting to analyze Chamberlain's apparent renewed overture for a European alliance. As soon as the speech was reported, Ambassador Hatzfeldt relayed its contents to Holstein in Berlin and commented that the British may not have "*completely* given up hope in us here," but that once they did so, "we can in my opinion no longer either expect or ask for concessions or favours here." In other words, without an alliance Germany would be unable to acquire peacefully from England any of the latter's colonial territories that the former coveted.[65] Always skeptical about the English, Holstein replied on May 15: "As for Salisbury, he will apparently never change, i.e., he doesn't want to move at all. As long as he is in power England will never work with or against anyone." Hatzfeldt could tell the British that Germany had no agreement with Russia that would prevent her from reaching an understanding with England "so far as this would appear useful to us." But he could go no further.[66]

On May 17, the German Ambassador again tried to convince his superior that if Chamberlain were able to secure a defensive treaty with the Triple Alliance of Germany, Austria, and Italy, Salisbury would not oppose it. He reiterated his opinion that Chamberlain's Birmingham remarks were intended as an invitation for a German alliance. As for Salisbury: "The latter may differ in points of detail or prefer a slower tempo, but on the major issue he is certainly in agreement with Chamberlain."[67]

Shortly thereafter, at a dinner given by the Kaiser, Sir Frank Lascelles, the British Ambassador to Germany, was seated next to his host. Lascelles reported to Salisbury that William carried on a virtually nonstop conversation "with his usual vivacity and amiability." He was cool to an Anglo-German alliance, questioning, somewhat tongue-in-cheek, "whether it was judicious to proclaim so openly the necessity of an alliance for England, as it might make the Power with which she might seek an alliance demand heavy terms." The Kaiser emphasized that "Germany did not intend to go to war with Russia for the purpose of driving her out of China." In short, while he "would view with pleasure a thoroughly good understanding with England," that was as far as he would go.[68]

The Kaiser's private views were somewhat different. As expressed in a memorandum that William wrote in late May:

"At the beginning of the next century we should have a battle fleet which, in alliance with others which will also have grown, could represent a real danger to England's....Hence the intention either to force an alliance or to destroy us before we have become strong, like Holland in times past."[69]

When Holstein read the memorandum, he asked Hatzfeldt to do his best to remove this suspicion from the Kaiser's mind. He prophetically recognized that a failure to do so could raise serious problems in the years ahead.[70]

Meanwhile, the Kaiser was using Chamberlain's alliance offer as the basis for trying to blackmail Russia. In a letter dated May 30 written in English to "Nicky,"..."my old and trusted friend," "Willy" told the Tsar that a request for an Anglo-German alliance by "a Celebrated Politician"

"...has been renewed for the third time in such an unmistakable manner, putting a certain short time to my definite answer and accompanied by such enormous offers showing a wide and future opening for my country that I think it is my duty to Germany to reflect before I answer.

"..I am informed that the Alliance is to be with the Triple Alliance and with the addition of Japan and America, with whom pourparlers have already been opened!

"Now...I beg you to tell me what you can offer me and do if I refuse...May God help you to find the right solution and decision! It is for the next generation! But time is passing, so please answer soon..."[71]

Although the German Foreign Office recognized that the Russians were likely to communicate to the British the contents of the Kaiser's amazing letter and thus further worsen relations between the two countries, Holstein's reaction was surprisingly restrained. He wrote Hatzfeldt: "Our Kaiser, who is a talented and impulsive man, has already accustomed his relatives to surprises and unexpected conclusions." Holstein probably was amused by the Tsar's June 3 response to the Kaiser's letter, which was a masterful turning of the tables on his "esteemed friend and cousin." Russia also had received "tempting proposals" from England, but

"(W)ithout thinking twice over it, their proposals were refused...It is very difficult for me, if not impossible, to answer your question whether it is useful or not for Germany to accept these often repeated English proposals, as I have not got the slightest knowledge of their value.

You must, or course decide what is best and most necessary for your country...—Believe me ever, your loving cousin and trusting friend.

Nicky"[72]

The Tsar's report of British overtures was greatly exaggerated. Whether or not intentionally, however, it served to reinforce German suspicion of

Chamberlain's alliance proposals. Thus, several days after Wilhelm received Nicholas's letter, Bülow wrote Hatzfeldt:

"Here we have the proof of His Imperial and Royal Majesty's oft-repeated opinion that England, if she had been able, would long ago have reached an agreement with Russia at the expense of the interests of third parties. The Kaiser was therefore absolutely correct in wanting to wait calmly until Britain made positive proposals through responsible official authorities."[73]

While Salisbury and Chamberlain were considering the possibility of an Anglo-German alliance, other observers were concerned that the growing German naval strength would make more likely a German alliance with some other power against England. Writing in the June 17 *Fortnightly*, in an article titled "Our Navy Against a Coalition," a commentator raised the possibility of a German alliance with France. In that event, "(t)he neutrality of Holland and Belgium would not stand for a week", and "(t)he Scheldt and the Texel might then, as in the days of the great Napoleon, harbour a flotilla, destined for the transport of an army of invasion." An even greater concern, the author suggested, was that Germany might ally itself with Russia as well as France. In that event, Britain would have to be sure "that in battleships we are equal to the three powers," i.e., the "two power" rule would no longer suffice.[74] The recently planted seeds of naval rivalry between England and Germany were thus already germinating into a primary cause of the conflict that would become war sixteen years later.

By 1898 England's long-standing ally Portugal was on the verge of bankruptcy, with the French government a major creditor. The Salisbury Government was concerned that the Portuguese monarchy might fall and be replaced by a republic. In the process Portugal might be willing to sell its South African possessions, Angola to the west and Delagoa Bay, at Mozambique's southern end directly east of the Transvaal. Should the Transvaal's Boer population revolt, it was essential that an unfriendly power not possess the Bay and use it as a base to supply the rebels.[75]

In 1897 the British had proposed to lend Portugal the money to pay off its existing debt, with certain customs duties and African railroad receipts serving as collateral security. An integral part of the proposal was that

Britain would assume practical control of Delagoa. As the Portuguese disliked this loss of sovereignty, the Lisbon government initially demurred.[76]

Matters remained at an impasse until mid-1898. At this point, Germany, with its increasing colonial appetite, determined that Britain should not be permitted to acquire any more African territory unless the Reich did so as well. Thus, on July 9, Hatzfeldt proposed to Salisbury that the two governments should make a joint loan to Portugal, with the collateral being the customs duties of the territories that each power would possess in the event of a default. For this purpose Germany wanted all of Angola. Salisbury disagreed: "the preemptive claim would have to be divided."[77]

On July 13 and 18 Hatzfeldt had indicated to Salisbury that as the price for German acquiescence in a British-Portuguese loan, Germany might be interested in acquiring the portion of Mozambique north of the Zambesi River. Germany would also obtain a part of the British territory of Nyasaland which thrust south into Mozambique and the Cape Colony's enclave of Walfish (now Walvis) Bay on the coast of German Southwest Africa. In return, the Germans would give Britain a free hand in dealing with the Transvaal.[78]

The two countries were negotiating at cross purposes. The Germans believed that they had a legitimate interest in looking out for the future of the Boers in the Transvaal, and that they should receive a quid pro quo for surrendering it. The British, on the other hand, admitted nothing of the sort. Thus, on July 20, Salisbury told Hatzfeldt that the Cabinet had concluded that only the cession of Togoland would be adequate recompense for what the British were being asked to give up.[79]

According to Salisbury, Hatzfeldt expressed a fear that this decision might bring the negotiations to an end. The German ambassador even resorted to a threat: "In the position occupied by Germany she could not stand alone; if she could find no recourse in the friendship of Great Britain she must turn to Russia."[80] The Kaiser for his part treated Salisbury's position as an insult:

"Lord Salisbury's conduct is quite Jesuitical, monstrous and insolent! ...One can see again how the noble Lord plays with us and shifts around, merely because he does not fear us since we have no fleet—which that fool Reichstag has continually refused me in ten years of government."

Instead of making further concessions, it was "better to resign ourselves to the unavoidable and to use it for the fleet."[81]

Meanwhile, the possibility of some kind of alliance continued to intrigue both governments. In a conversation in early June between Lascelles and Bülow, Bülow asked the Ambassador whether Chamberlain's proposal would include an English guarantee to support Germany if the latter were attacked by both Russia and France. Shortly thereafter Lascelles was in London on leave, and Chamberlain invited him and several other Conservative leaders to lunch on June 18 at the Colonial Secretary's home. Neither Salisbury nor Balfour was present. Although it is almost certain that Lascelles relayed Bülow's question to the group, there is no contemporaneous record of what transpired.[82]

As a result of the June 18 meeting, Lascelles had concluded that a Anglo-German alliance was still possible. The Kaiser's mother, Empress Victoria, helped him arrange a meeting on August 21 with her son at her castle of Friedrichshof at which he could discuss this and other matters.[83] At the outset, William complained that no progress was being made regarding the Portuguese colonies. Lascelles replied that Balfour was now in charge of the British side of the negotiations, and that he was likely to adopt a more conciliatory posture than Salisbury. Then, as reported by the Kaiser and generally confirmed by Lascelles four months later, the British Ambassador said that England understood that Germany would not want to endanger its relations with Russia by siding with England if she and Russia went to war over China. There was, however, another kind of alliance that Chamberlain and several other ministers had approved at a meeting held following Lascelles' lunch with them on June 18. It would be implemented only if either England and Germany were attacked at the same time by two other powers. As the Kaiser described Lascelles' explanation:

"one of us is strong enough to fight any other Power, who should attack him, but in case of two Powers attacking, the issue is at least very doubtful; therefore, should Germany be assaulted by any two Powers at once England is ready to assist with every armament in her power to knock down one of her antagonists, while Germany is fighting the other one; the same England would wish Germany to do should the case be the reverse."[84]

The Kaiser noted to Lascelles that this was a new idea, and one that he would carefully consider. His initial reaction was favorable, and Bülow was not at all pleased when he received the Kaiser's description of the conversation.[85] The German Foreign Minister continued to oppose any form of Anglo-German alliance. Knowing how William liked to be flattered, on August 24 he immediately wrote him, congratulating him for so clearly describing German foreign policy to Lascelles, but then reiterating his own position that Germany should never side with England against Russia. Indeed, any alliance should be confined to matters relating to the Portuguese colonies. The Kaiser was irritated with this response, and marginally scribbled on Bülow's memorandum: "We are free to make as many agreements as we like with anybody, and we don't have to answer to the Russians." William, however, did not pursue the matter further, and Chamberlain and Lascelles received no reply to their proposal.[86]

Meanwhile, the Germans were trying every possible means of involving themselves in a Portuguese loan. The Kaiser even induced his mother, with whom he was not overly friendly, to write her mother, Queen Victoria, stressing the German desire for an agreement and intimating that Salisbury was the major obstacle. This effort almost backfired when Victoria told Salisbury about the letters and he became annoyed at the Germans for going around him to the Queen. He was especially irritated that the German Queen Mother had suggested that "Mr. Chamberlain is anxious to meet the wishes of Germany, while Lord Salisbury is opposing them." On August 19 Salisbury wrote Victoria that "this view...is not correct; it is the very opposite of the truth."[87]

When ill health forced Salisbury to leave London for the south of France in early August, Balfour took over responsibility for the negotiations. By the time Salisbury departed, he had convinced Hatzfeldt and, through him, the German Foreign Ministry, that they would have to scale down their demands if there was to be any chance of an agreement. When the Germans advised the British that they would no longer ask for Walfish Bay, and that security for the Portuguese loan would be arranged so that Britain's interest would include Delagoa Bay and the railroad to the Transvaal, Balfour decided to support a joint loan. Salisbury was not happy, writing Balfour on August 19 that "Germany is trying to induce us to join in putting the knife into Portugal." Balfour, however, was in charge of the negotiations, and by now was convinced that they would succeed.[88]

On August 30 Balfour and Hatzfeldt signed a "Convention" in which England and Germany agreed on the conditions on which they would make a loan to Portugal. Among other things, it set forth the basis on which Angola and Mozambique would be divided as security for Portugal's obligations. The German security would also include the East

Indian island of Timor. This document was accompanied by two secret agreements which made it clear that the security interests the two countries would obtain were really spheres of influence.[89]

For Britain, these agreements assured its control of Delagoa Bay and the Transvaal railroad. Chamberlain for one, regarded these as important enough to justify the agreements' concessions to Germany, which he referred to as blackmail.[90] Others in Britain believed that concerns that Germany might support the Boers against England were unjustified and that Balfour had conceded too much. This was Salisbury's opinion, which may have been why Balfour had the agreements rushed for signature just before the Prime Minister's return to London.[91]

The Anglo-German loan was never made. Portugal obtained the necessary funds from French sources with the security of only domestic revenues. The Germans suspected Balfour and his colleagues of helping implement that result. Thus, although the agreements brought a temporary improvement in relations between the two countries, in the long run they left sour tastes in the mouths of both.[92]

During the evening of July 30, Otto von Bismarck, age eighty-three, died at his country home outside Hamburg. During his last months, his breathing had grown increasingly difficult, and he rarely left his wheelchair.[93]

Although he had been out of power for more than eight years, in Europe his death was viewed as marking the end of an era. The next morning's London *Times* editorialized:

"Since Napoleon passed away in his island prison, death had claimed no greater figure in the higher fields of politics than the statesman who died on Saturday night."

His "life-work," wrote the *Times*, was "the unity of the German people, under the aegis of the German Empire."[94]

Bismarck had become successful by building up the power of the emperor and the army, while at the same time using his personal ability and will power to control them. His successors were already proving themselves unable to do so. The eventual consequence would be the destruction in less than fifty years of the superstate that Bismarck had created.[95]

TEN

Preparing For Battle

Now that it had declared war on Spain, the United States was considering the best way to fight it. On April 18 the President met with the Secretaries of War and the Navy, and the senior officers of the two services. The navy, due to the efforts of Roosevelt and others, was ready for hostilities. The army, however, was not. A successful invasion of Cuba would require the addition of volunteers to the regular forces in order to provide an army large enough to defeat the estimated 80,000 Spanish troops on the island. It would take time to train them. General Miles told the group that he would need two months. That meant that the invasion would commence at the end of June when the rainy season, with the risk of yellow fever, would be about to start. Miles therefore urged that the invasion be postponed until fall. McKinley and his advisors tentatively agreed.[1]

At 6:30 A.M. on April 22, Rear Admiral William T. Sampson's North Atlantic Squadron formed outside Key West and set off for Havana, which it reached at 3:30 P.M. the same day. The fleet consisted of two battle-ships, one armored cruiser, three monitors, five gunboats, three cruisers, and seven torpedo boats. The blockade of Cuba that it now commenced was the first act of the war.[2]

The preceding day, thirty-five days after leaving San Francisco, the *Oregon* steamed out of the Straits of Magellan into the South Atlantic.[3] It could not have been lost on any perceptive observer that had there been a canal across either Nicaragua or Panama, she already would have joined the blockading fleet. As it was, she arrived in Florida in time to support the invasion of Cuba.

Pursuant to an authorization voted by Congress, on April 23 McKinley issued a call for 125,000 volunteers. A million men showed up at informal recruiting stations that blossomed in post offices, vacant stores, and even

156

at desks and tables on sidewalks. The Army thus was able to reject more than seventy-five percent of the potential enlistees. Only ten percent of the men seeking officers' commissions were accepted.[4]

The President's call for volunteers included a provision for three regiments "to be composed exclusively of frontiersmen possessing special qualifications as horsemen and marksmen." Secretary of War Alger offered Roosevelt command of the first regiment. Surprisingly, Roosevelt turned down the offer on the basis that he had no experience in military organization or leadership. He suggested that he instead serve as lieutenant colonel under his friend Leonard Wood.[5] Wood, a doctor by profession but a soldier by choice, had won military fame as victor over the Apache chief Geronimo. The Secretary agreed to Roosevelt's proposal.[6]

Roosevelt's decision to leave the Navy Department and go to war was widely criticized. Some of his friends doubted his sanity and one suggested, "... of course this ends his political career." Nearly every major newspaper urged him not to leave at a time when his services would be increasingly valuable to the country.[7] The Assistant Secretary, however, was adamant. He wrote New York *Sun* editor Paul Dana, in response to an editorial praising "the instinctive glowing chivalry of his nature," but contending that the country needed him to remain at his desk:[8]

"... I have been able to accomplish a great deal in getting the Navy ready. It is not of course in exactly the shape I should like to see it, but still it is in very good shape indeed, and will respond nobly to any demand made upon it."

Roosevelt continued:

"I want to go because I wouldn't feel that I had been entirely true to my beliefs and convictions, and to the ideal I had set for myself if I didn't go. .. For two years I have consistently preached the doctrine of a resolute foreign policy, and of readiness to accept the arbitrament of the sword if necessary; and I have always intended to act up to my preaching if the occasion arose. Now, the occasion has arisen, and I ought to meet it."[9]

In the course of this long letter, Roosevelt wrote with apparent sincerity that he was "entirely certain that I don't expect any military glory out of this Cuban war, more than what is implied in the honorable performance of duty."[10] The events of the coming months would demonstrate the inaccuracy of this observation.

On April 23 McKinley reluctantly asked Secretary of State Sherman for his resignation. Assistant Secretary Day would succeed him.[11] As Ambassador Hay wrote Henry Adams from London shortly after, "... the crisis was precipitated by a lapse of memory in a conversation with the Austrian Minister of so serious a nature that the President had to put in Day without an instant's delay—I need not tell you how much to my relief."[12]

Three days earlier Hay had given the major speech at the London Lord Mayor's banquet. After referring to the growing friendship between Britain and the United States, he said:

"The good understanding between us is based on something deeper than mere expediency. All who think cannot but see there is a sanction like that of religion which binds us in partnership in the serious work of the world ... We are joint ministers in the same sacred mission of freedom and progress, charged with duties we cannot evade by the imposition of irresistible bonds."[13]

Hay's speech was widely reported in the British press and was greatly appreciated by the British public. The McKinley Administration was doing its utmost to encourage British popular and press support for the United States in the war with Spain. On April 21 the London *Times* had written:

"Whether the struggle be brief or protracted, there can be as little doubt of the result as there is of the direction in which lie the sympathy and hope of the English people."

McKinley promptly responded in a letter that the *Times* printed on the twenty-third: "You can say that the whole of the United States responds to the expression of British friendship."[14]

On the twenty-ninth the *Times* noted American concessions on matters relating to North Atlantic fisheries, the Canadian boundary commission, and the Bering Sea as proof of a desire "to consider English interests wherever possible." Its comment concluded:

"Finally the President is not only willing that his good will toward Great Britain should be made known, but he desires that there may be some way provided by means of which cooperation on a large scale may be carried on between the United States and Great Britain."[15]

Queen Victoria, however, had a different view of the United States. She wrote in her diary:

"21st April—War seems hopeless declared, and the respective Spanish and United States Ministers have left their posts! It is monstrous of America."[16]

The war with Spain was bringing together the North and South to an extent not seen since the Civil War. McKinley saw a way to help the process along by appointing former Confederate generals to high military positions.

Fitzhugh Lee's selection as a major general of volunteers was predictable, not only because of his background as a cavalry general under his uncle Robert E. Lee, but also because of his recent Cuban experience during his two-year Havana consulship.[17] More surprising, and seemingly of purely political motivation, was the invitation to Congressman Joseph Wheeler of Alabama to see McKinley at the White House at 8:30 on the evening of the twenty-sixth. Wheeler, a West Point graduate, had been a renowned Confederate cavalry general, but more recently had been primarily concerned with revenue matters as a member and former chairman of the House Ways and Means Committee. At their meeting, McKinley asked him to don a U.S. Army uniform for the first time in thirty-eight years. Since Wheeler, with his slight build and snowy white hair and beard looked even older than his sixty-one years, the President qualified his request by adding, "and if you feel able to go." Wheeler immediately replied that he was both happy and able to once again see military service under the United States flag.[18]

Although Leonard Wood was its commanding officer, it was Roosevelt's role that excited the country over the formation of the proposed regiment of cowboys and frontiersmen. What *The New York Times* described as "Roosevelt's dashing band of Western cowboys" was "to be picked from the best fighting and riding herders and ranchers of the West." The press was already suggesting names for the regiment, referring to "Teddy's Terrors" and "Teddy's Cowboy Contingent," finally settling on "Roosevelt's Rough Riders." Fortunately, Colonel Wood seemingly did not object to the fact that his subordinate was getting all the publicity, so long as Roosevelt obeyed orders. Meanwhile, applications for the regiment were pouring in from all part of the United States, eventually numbering twenty-three thousand, from which Wood and Roosevelt could have formed a complete division.[19]

This response was indicative of the war fever that was sweeping the country. The patriotic surge was heightened by a sense of moral righteousness that the nation had gone to war to free Cuba from a tyrannical oppressor. It extended to all classes, with wealthy citizens like the Astors offering to outfit entire regiments at their own expense. The patriotic fires were constantly being stoked by the newspapers and their growing phalanxes of war correspondents, whose efforts were leading to record press runs such as the 1,300,000 copies that Joseph Pulitzer's New York *World* sold on April 26.[20]

A few thoughtful Americans were saddened by what was occurring, although for the most part they expressed their opinions only privately. Typical was former President Cleveland, who wrote his Secretary of State Richard Olney of "a feeling of shame and humiliation" and of foreboding over

"...a depreciation of national standing before the world abroad, and, at home, demoralization of our people's character, much demagogy and humbug, great additions to our public burden and the exposure of scandalous operations."[21]

A major United States concern was that Admiral Cervera's fleet would attack any American invading force on its voyage between the United States and Cuba.[22] At the war's outbreak, the Spanish force, on paper strong in number but actually in poor condition for battle, was riding at anchor at St. Vincent in the Portuguese-owned Cape Verde Islands, approximately 3,500 miles due east of Cuba. Minister Bermejo had ordered it to sail west and defend Puerto Rico from attack, but the Admiral and his officers feared the loss of the fleet in the West Indies, and that its departure for the Caribbean would leave the Spanish coast undefended. They therefore asked Bermejo to change his orders and send the fleet back to the Canaries, several hundred miles to the northeast.[23]

Bermejo failed to respond to the Admiral's appeal. On April 29, the local Portuguese officials, realizing that their country had declared neutrality in the war, ordered the Spaniards to leave St. Vincent. Cervera's prearranged coded cable to Madrid read "Am going North," but meant he was following orders and steaming west toward Puerto Rico. The code was unnecessary. A correspondent of the *New York Herald* who had been sent to the island to monitor the Spanish fleet chartered a small steamer and followed Cervera until nightfall. He then returned and cabled his paper that the fleet, consisting of four armored cruisers and six torpedo boat destroyers, was steaming west. He estimated that it would arrive off Puerto Rico in between twelve and fourteen days.[24]

With Cervera's fleet at large somewhere in the Atlantic, rumors spread that his destination might not be Cuba or Puerto Rico, but the East Coast of the United States. The result was widespread panic. As Roosevelt later recalled:

"The governor of one State actually announced that he would not permit the National Guard of that State to leave its borders, the idea being to retain it against a possible Spanish invasion. So many of the business men of the city of Boston took their securities inland to Worcester that the safe deposit companies of Worcester proved unable to take care of them. In my own neighborhood on Long Island clauses were put into leases to the effect that if the property were destroyed by the Spaniards the lease should lapse."

Roosevelt also described one congressman who wanted a navy ship stationed off Jekyll Island "because it contained the winter homes of certain millionaires" and an "influential" woman who made a similar request "because she had a house in the neighborhood" of "a huge seaside hotel."[25]

On May 6 Roosevelt wrote Secretary Long, enclosing a letter of resignation to be delivered to the President. Overlooking the differences that had marred their relationship from time to time, the outgoing Assistant Secretary could not have been more positive:

"I don't suppose I shall ever again have a chief under whom I shall enjoy serving as I have enjoyed serving under you, nor one toward whom I shall feel the same affectionate regard."[26]

Earlier, like any well turned out New York patrician, he had ordered from Brooks Brothers an "ordinary cavalry lieutenant colonel's uniform in blue Cravenette."[27]

The euphoria caused by Dewey's painless victory led to pressure to move at once against the Spanish forces in Cuba. Taking the lead was Secretary Long, who seemed to believe that since the Navy had already vanquished one Spanish force, the Army should not delay in defeating another. He wrote Army Secretary Alger to that effect, and, perhaps to needle Alger, presented the letter to him at a May 6 Cabinet meeting. Alger was clearly annoyed, but the prodding may have been effective. Two days later, on May 8, General Miles was ordered to assemble an invasion army of up to 70,000 men and proceed, with the help of the Navy, to attack Havana.[28]

Miles, who opposed an immediate Cuban invasion, was incensed at this preemptory treatment, and immediately went to the White House. Among other things, he told McKinley that there was not enough ammunition in the country to support an invasion, and that the necessary supply could not be manufactured for several weeks. Miles was partly successful, for the attack on Havana was suspended. There would be no change, however, in the decision to invade Cuba before the onset of the rainy season. To that end, a large force with the necessary supplies was to be assembled as soon as possible at Tampa, Florida.[29]

General William R. Shafter was to lead the invasion army. Shafter was a sixty-three-year-old Civil War winner of the Congressional Medal of Honor. Unfortunately, whatever military skill he possessed was largely offset by the fact that he by now weighed 300 pounds. On May 10, he was directed to move a large part of his forces to Key West, which would be the jumping-off point for a landing at Mariel, a port on Cuba's north shore, twenty-six miles west of Havana. On the eleventh however, a telegram from Tampa informed Shafter's superiors in Washington that there was no water for the assembling army in Key West. For the time being, the invading forces would continue to be organized at Tampa.[30]

May 11 also brought the first American fatalities of the war. An American torpedo boat ventured too close to Spanish batteries at Cardenas, on Cuba's north coast. They riddled the American vessel, killing one officer and wounding several seamen. The same day, two gunboats cutting cables off Cienfuegos on the south shore suffered seven casualties, two fatal. The cable cutting mission was only partly successful.[31]

Concern over the whereabouts and destination of Cervera's ships led the Americans to divide their Atlantic naval forces. The larger North Atlantic Squadron, under the command of Rear Admiral Sampson, was stationed off the north coast of Cuba, blockading Havana and other ports. A smaller Flying Squadron, commanded by Commodore Winfield

Scott Schley, was sent to Hampton Roads, Virginia, where it could move either north or south if necessary to protect America's eastern coast from Cervera, should his squadron suddenly appear there.[32]

Sampson and Schley were officers of widely different personality. The fifty-eight-year-old Sampson was a cool, somewhat frail intellectual type whose modesty had not prevented Secretary Long from recognizing his merit and naming him to replace Rear Admiral Sicard as squadron commander when the latter had to retire because of ill health earlier in the year.[33] Schley, a year older than Sampson, was described by a mid-twentieth century historian as "a hearty old sea dog,"[34] with a strong ego and an aptitude for self-promotion. He had achieved the status of a popular hero in defending a group of American seamen from a Chilean mob seven years earlier and did all he could to keep himself in the public eye.[35] Future conflict between these two officers seemed almost inevitable.

In early May Sampson's squadron was ordered to steam eastward to Puerto Rico, where he could intercept Cervera, who was expected to make a coaling stop there before proceeding west to Cuba. It was not until the early morning of May 12 that he arrived outside San Juan harbor, taking almost four days longer than expected due to the antiquated equipment and poor repair of some of his vessels. Unfortunately, Cervera was not there. Not wanting to leave without showing some positive result, the Americans conducted a two-and-a-half-hour generally ineffective cannonade of the port's batteries.[36] Then, concerned that Cervera had eluded him and would be able to attack the small flotilla that he had left behind to blockade Havana, Sampson immediately reversed his course and proceeded west as rapidly as possible.[37]

Sampson need not have worried. The day before, Cervera had appeared off the French island of Martinique, several hundred miles southeast of San Juan. The Spanish Admiral sent one of his ships to the port of Fort de France for any information that could be obtained regarding the military situation in the Caribbean. It returned with news of the Manila disaster, as well as reports of American blockades of Havana and San Juan. On the morning of the twelfth, without entering the port, Cervera continued his voyage to the west, in the direction of Curaçao.[38] Before he departed, however, his ships were spotted by an officer from an American ship that had arrived at another port on the island, who wired word of what he had seen to the Navy Department in Washington. It was received on the evening of the twelfth and was reported in the next morning's American newspapers.[39]

The next sighting of Cervera's fleet was by the American consul on the

Dutch island of Curaçao, off the Venezuelan coast. He reported its arrival on the fourteenth and its departure on the fifteenth but no one knew where it had gone. American scouting ships were stationed off the east and west coasts of Haiti and others were sent to Venezuelan waters. Meanwhile, Schley's Flying Squadron had arrived at Key West from Hampton Roads early on May 18, and Sampson reached there several hours later in the cruiser *New York,* which had pushed on ahead of the rest of his squadron. On the assumption that Cervera was bringing supplies for Havana and was unlikely to try to run the American blockade of that port, the Navy Department's best guess was that he would be moving north from Curaçao to Cienfuegos, on Cuba's south-central coast. Accordingly, at a meeting between the two commanders, the Admiral ordered Schley to leave for Cienfuegos the next morning with his strength to be augmented by Sampson's best ship, the battleship *Iowa.* Sampson would return to his previous assignment of blockading Havana and the north-west Cuban coast.[40]

While the American commanders were deliberating and trying to ascertain his whereabouts, Cervera was off the east coast of Jamaica, steaming north from Curaçao. His destination was Santiago de Cuba, on Cuba's south coast, but well to the east of Cienfuegos.[41] His ships had gone to Curacao in the hope that they could obtain substantial amounts of coal to replenish their rapidly depleting supply. On their arrival, however, the local authorities advised them that conditions of neutrality permitted only two ships to enter the port and remain for no longer than forty-eight hours. Even worse, only 400 tons of coal were available, far from enough to permit the fleet to continue on an extended voyage. Cervera's only course was to find the nearest Spanish port at which he could confidently resupply. He knew that Havana was blockaded by the Americans, and feared that San Juan and Cienfuegos were as well. According to his chief of staff:

"There remained as the only solution, going to Santiago de Cuba, the second capital of the island, which we had to suppose, and did suppose, well supplied with provisions and artillery, in view of the favorable condition of the harbor entrance."[42]

Steaming north slowly so as to conserve fuel, Cervera was off Santiago the morning of the nineteenth. The trip was uneventful, with no American ships in sight.[43]

Unbeknown to all but a few Government officials, the United States had access to all important messages transmitted and received by the

Admiral Pascual Cervera y Topete

Havana telegraph office. Martin Luther Hellings, the manager of Western Union's Key West office, had arranged with Domingo Villaverde, a Cuban patriot who was one of the Havana telegraphers, to send him copies of such messages over the Havana-Key West Cable, which had been kept open by mutual agreement with Spain. Thus, when Cevera telegraphed the authorities in Havana on May 19 that he had arrived in Santiago, Villaverde immediately sent the news to Hellings, who passed it on by early afternoon to the command center at the White House.[44]

If the report was accurate, it offered the Americans a golden opportunity to bottle up Cervera's squadron and help bring a quick end to the war. It was difficult, however, for McKinley and his advisers to believe that Cervera would have ended his trans-Atlantic voyage at a port several hundred miles from Havana and San Juan, to which he was supposedly carrying supplies. Moreover, the auxiliary cruiser *St. Louis* had been off Santiago at the time that Cervera reportedly had arrived, and her crew had seen no Spanish ships. At last, at about midnight, Secretary Long telegraphed Sampson in Key West that since the report that Cervera was at Santiago "might very well be correct, the department strongly advises that you send word immediately by the *Iowa* to Schley to proceed at once off Santiago de Cuba with his whole command."[45]

Despite Long's "strong advice," Sampson decided not to order Schley to Santiago. Instead, on May 20 he sent Schley a copy of Long's telegram, but instructed him to remain at Cienfuegos for the present:

"If the Spanish ships have put into Santiago, they must come either to Havana or Cienfuegos to deliver the munitions of war which they are said to bring for use in Cuba. I am therefore of the opinion that our best chances of success in capturing these ships will be to hold to two points—Cienfuegos and Havana—with all of the forces we can muster. If, later, it should develop that these vessels are at Santiago, we can then assemble off that port the ships best suited for that purpose, and completely blockade it."[46]

Later in the day, Sampson received more definite word that Cervera was at Santiago. Accordingly, around midnight he wrote Schley that Cervera was

"probably at Santiago de Cuba ... If you are satisfied that they are not at Cienfuegos proceed with all dispatch, but cautiously, to Santiago de Cuba, and if the enemy is there, blockade him in port."[47]

Unfortunately for the Americans, the first radio messages had been sent by Marconi only three years earlier, and communication between naval forces at sea was still only by ship. Since Cienfuegos was more than 500 miles from Key West, Sampson's instructions to Schley to proceed to Santiago were not delivered to the Commodore until 7:30 A.M. on May 23.[48] Schley, who was unaware of the source of Sampson's information that Cervera was at Santiago, responded that he was remaining off Cienfuegos for the time being. Reports that he had received, as well as his instinct, made him almost certain that Cervera had left Santiago and was likely at Cienfuegos.[49] The next day, however, Schley received a further report that convinced him that Cervera was not at Cienfuegos. That evening, the Flying Squadron started east for Santiago, but, following Sampson's admonition to proceed "cautiously," only at hourly speeds ranging from 7 to 9 knots.[50] Later, because the bow compartment of the converted yacht *Eagle* was filling with water and had to be bailed out with buckets, Schley's for the moment misnamed "Flying Squadron" slowed to an average speed of less than 6.6 knots per hour.[51]

Schley was lucky, for his delay was not proving costly. Cervera's ships had been at sea for nearly two months. Their boilers needed cleaning and their engines overhauling. Even worse, they were in acute need of coal. Like most other necessaries, including food, it was in short supply in Santiago. Three thousand tons of good Welsh coal were on the way to Santiago aboard an English ship, but it would be several days before it could arrive.[52] Cervera called a council of war to decide whether his ships should leave for San Juan, probably the only harbor that remained open to them. As he reported to Madrid:

"In view maximum speed this squadron reduced to 14 knots, account of Vizcaya bottom fouled, lack of coal, location of hostile fleets, and condition of harbor, certain danger of sortie greater than advantages gained by reaching San Juan..."[53]

Perhaps because they were aware of the likely significance of this decision to remain at Santiago, Cervera and his officers wrote and signed detailed minutes of their council. As recorded, they had agreed to

"...remain at Santiago, refit as far as possible from the stores to be had here, and take advantage of the first good opportunity for leaving the harbor, at present blockaded by superior forces."[54]

Far to the West, the Rough Riders were receiving their initial training at the Texas state fair grounds, two miles out of San Antonio. Roosevelt arrived there by train on the morning of April 15. The group of recruits that greeted him was a strange mixture of hard bitten Westerners and Eastern aristocrats. Although the former predominated, Roosevelt believed that the publicity value to the regiment would be heightened by adding a small contingent of college athletes and patricians. Since he had lived on equal terms with Westerners such as these, there was no reason why other bluebloods could not do the same. Thus, the recruits included his Harvard classmate and yachtsman Woodbury Kane, the world's leading polo player and the United States tennis champion. There were football players from Harvard and Princeton, high-jumpers from Yale, a Wadsworth, a Tiffany, and Hamilton Fish, the ex-captain of the Columbia crew, whose forebears had been prominent in New York politics and society since the Revolutionary War and included a United States Secretary of State. These men were accorded no special favors, and were expected to cook and wash dishes on an equal basis with their cowboy comrades.[55]

After Roosevelt had been with the Rough Riders for only ten days, already, as he wrote McKinley, "we are in fine shape." From morning roll call at 6:00 until 8:30 at night, the thousand-man regiment was kept busy with riding, skirmish practice, caring for horses and night school for the officers.[56] The new lieutenant colonel was having the time of his life. He was proud of his men, and delighted at his nascent skill as a commanding officer. As he wrote Henry Cabot Lodge:

"I have been both astonished and pleased at my own ability in the line of tactics. I thoroughly enjoy handling these men, and I get them on the jump so that they execute their movements at a gallop."[57]

Although Colonel Leonard Wood was the regiment's commanding officer, the men as well as the country at large regarded Roosevelt as its de facto leader. This impression was created not only by Roosevelt's obvious energy and drive, but also by his enthusiastic supervision of the hour and a half daily mounted drill, while Wood stayed in his tent working on administrative matters. But the colonel was capable of holding his second-in-command in check, as when he made clear his disapproval when Roosevelt treated one of the regiment's squads to unlimited beer.[58]

Due largely to Roosevelt's influence, the Rough Riders were well organized and equipped. The Army in general was less fortunate. In a month, it was expected to expand from 25,000 men to 250,000, who were to be provided with qualified officers, clothing, guns, and ammunition. The difficulties of accomplishing this were exacerbated by the politicians, who regularly intervened regarding officer commissions and the posting of their home state regiments. Although Roosevelt complained of the "stupidity" of the Ordinance Department and that the War Department had "no head, no management whatever," it is hard to see how either could have done much better.[59]

Notwithstanding these difficulties, an army of more than 20,000 men was assembling outside of Tampa, which was to be the jumping off point for an attack on Cuba. There were only two single-track railroad lines into Tampa. Port Tampa, where the troops were to be loaded onto the ships that were to take them to Cuba, was nine miles away and connected to Tampa by only a single railroad track. Unlike today's metropolis, the Tampa of 1898 was a small town of nondescript wood buildings surrounded by uninhabited sand and swamp.[60]

The single exception to this dreary location was the elegant, five-hundred-room Moorish-style Tampa Bay Hotel, built by railroad, hotel, and shipping magnate Henry B. Plant as a mecca for the west coast of Florida in its earliest days of tourism. In addition to housing Army officers and the press, it served as office space for General Shafter and his staff. Correspondent Richard Harding Davis dubbed it "a real oasis in the real desert." As they waited for the troops to arrive and be trained, and for Cervera's fleet to be contained so that it could not attack the invasion armada, the Army's commanders whiled away their leisure hours in elegant rockers on the hotel's broad veranda. Davis described this time as "the rocking-chair period of the war."[61]

McKinley was taking seriously his responsibilities as commander-in-chief. He had installed a "war room" next to his White House office, where maps covered the walls and pins marked the positions of the opposing forces, and participated in all meetings at which strategic decisions were reached.[62]

At a three-hour-long conference on May 26, the President and his advisers discussed what use should be made of the large force that was assembling in Florida. Commanding General Miles was in favor of first capturing Puerto Rico. This would be followed by an invasion of Cuba's eastern end by cavalry and light artillery, who with guerilla support would push westward toward Havana during the rainy season. When the dry weather arrived, this force and a now-well-trained volunteer army from the mainland would assault the capital.[63]

McKinley's other advisors viewed this proposal with trepidation, in part because the war was being fought over Cuba and the country would likely regard a Puerto Rican expedition as a sideshow. Miles then amended his proposal. Since Santiago was on the way to Puerto Rico and as Cervera was apparently in that port and likely to be confined there, why not stop the army that was en route to Puerto Rico at Santiago, help the Navy take that port, and either capture Cervera or drive him out into the gunfire of the blockading American fleet. This satisfied everyone's desire for prompt military action in Cuba. Secretary of War Alger was thus instructed that as soon as Cervera's presence there was confirmed absolutely, "the movement to Santiago should be made without a moment's delay, day or night."[64]

⟞⟩◦⟨⟝

At 5:25 P.M. on May 26, Schley's squadron stopped twenty-six to thirty miles south of Santiago, where it was joined by three American vessels that had already been in the area. The day before, just outside Santiago harbor, one of them, the *St. Paul*, commanded by Captain Sigsbee, formerly of the *Maine*, had stopped the British steamer *Restormel* which was carrying coal to Cervera. This should have indicated to Sigsbee that the Spanish ships were in the port but, according to Schley, Sigsbee reported that there was no evidence to that effect. Because Schley was running short of coal, he decided to return to Key West and in the early evening turned west.[65]

At the same time that Schley was deliberating whether to remain outside Santiago, Cervera and his captains once more debated whether to try to leave for San Juan. Initially, they decided to sail at 5:30 P.M., but at 2:30, the three American scout ships that were about to leave to rendezvous with Schley were spotted offshore. When a pilot sent by the Admiral reported a swell that might cause one of the Spanish ships to strike a large rock just outside the harbor, the council, with two captains dissenting, decided to delay their departure. The decision turned out to be fatal.[66]

By the next morning, Schley was troubled. By leaving Santiago, he could be viewed as disobeying orders, including a message that had been delivered to him on the twenty-sixth. The deciding factor may have been a report from a press boat from Key West that he overhauled at 1:15 P.M. on the twenty-seventh that Sampson "had sailed," presumably for Santiago. In any event, Schley changed his mind and at 7:10 P.M. ordered his ships to stop and fill up with all available coal. Early the next afternoon, May 28, the squadron turned east toward Santiago, stopping ten miles outside the harbor at 8:00 P.M.[67]

On the same afternoon, Schley's message that he was returning to Key West was telegraphed to Washington from Kingston, Jamaica, where one of the Commodore's ships had delivered it. McKinley and his advisers had believed Schley had by now bottled up Cervera. The report was therefore met with consternation. As Secretary Long later recalled:

"It was the most anxious day in the naval history of the war and was the only instance in which the Department had to whistle to keep its courage up ... The feeling that the Spanish fleet might leave the harbor off Santiago ... its movements might be lost track of, and that it might appear at any time on the coast of the United States, was depressing beyond measure."[68]

Immediate action was called for. At midnight a telegram was sent to Sampson in Key West, asking if he could leave for Santiago, seize Guantanamo Bay, about forty miles to the east, and use it as a coaling station.[69] Sampson wasted no time in responding three hours later with affirmative answers. He estimated that it would take him two days to reach Santiago, and proposed that he leave immediately on the *New York*. Having received no response by noon, he sent the Navy Department a follow-up telegram, stating that Schley's failure to blockade Santiago "must be remedied at once if possible." Two hours later he received the cheering news from Schley via telegram from Jamaica that the latter had reversed course. Nevertheless, in passing this information on to Washington, he renewed his recommendation that he go to Santiago. Later in the afternoon he received an affirmative reply, and at 11.00 P.M. left on the *New York* to meet the squadron off Havana, and then proceed to Santiago.[70]

Schley's conduct left a sour taste in everyone's mouth. Because he had at last obeyed orders and since Cervera had not taken advantage of his dereliction to escape, there was no effort to pursue the otherwise likely court-martial. Sampson, however, disbelieved Schley's report of a coal shortage, which the Admiral did not bother to investigate. He regarded Schley as incompetent, and treated him accordingly. Schley, for his part, conveyed the impression that the Flying Squadron was his own independent command, over which Sampson had no authority.[71] Meanwhile, excited by the news that Cervera had been bottled up, the public praised Schley as an authentic naval hero. The Navy Department, unwilling to admit to the near failures of the past few weeks, maintained a discreet silence.[72]

⸻◉⸻

Now that it was clear that Schley at last had blockaded Santiago, orders went to General Shafter to commence immediately loading his men on the ships that would take them to Cuba for a joint military and naval attack on Santiago. General Miles, wanting to be in the middle of whatever action took place, left Washington by special train for Tampa, accompanied by an entourage that included his wife, son, and daughter. As a historian later wrote, "it was a civilized war."[73]

The Rough Riders would be part of that war. After spending most of the previous day trying to get twelve hundred stubborn horses and mules aboard the seven trains that were to take the regiment to Tampa, they left San Antonio at 6:00 A.M. on May 30. Thus commenced a sweltering four-day cross-country journey, interspersed with stops at stations where "girls in straw hats and freshly starched dresses of many colors" passed watermelons and jugs of iced beer through the car windows to the suffering troops. As the trains passed groups of what appeared to be former Confederate veterans waving American flags, Roosevelt reflected on how this war with a foreign country was bringing together the North and South. At each stop, everyone wanted to see "Teddy."[74]

There was no cheering or flag waving in Florida. The War Department could command Shafter to load his troops on the ships that would take them to Cuba, but it would take more than its orders to accomplish that task. At Tampa and on other Florida railroad sidings, freight cars were sitting full of supplies that had not yet been inventoried.[75] Thus, as Miles discovered when he arrived in Tampa on June 1,

"... officers are obliged to break open seals and hunt from car to car to ascertain whether they contain clothing, grain, balloon material, horse equipment, ammunition, siege guns, commissary stores, etc. To illustrate the embarrassment caused by present conditions, 15 cars loaded with uniforms were side-tracked 25 miles away from Tampa and remained there for weeks while the troops were suffering for clothing. 5,000 rifles which were discovered yesterday were needed by several regiments."[76]

It would take several days to bring even partial order out of this chaos.

ELEVEN

"Don't Cheer Boys! Those Poor Devils Are Dying."

A t 6:30 A.M. on June 1, Admiral Sampson in the *New York* joined Schley's Flying Squadron as it steamed back and forth on an east-west course outside Santiago. The Admiral immediately assumed command of the blockading forces.[1]

Before the *New York* left Key West, Sampson asked Richmond P. Hobson, a twenty-seven-year-old officer whose specialty was naval architecture, to develop a plan to sink a collier in the channel into Santiago harbor, making it impossible for Cervera to escape. If successful, this would allow Schley's Flying Squadron to turn from the blockade to other duties.[2]

Hobson immediately turned his full attention to the problem. Before the *New York* joined Schley off Santiago, he returned to Sampson with a detailed proposal. He agreed with the Admiral that the channel was narrow enough to block successfully, and picked the collier *Merrimac* from the Flying Squadron as the vessel to be sunk. It had a length of 333 feet, and Sampson's charts showed that the channel at its narrowest point ranged from 352 to 450 feet. Thus, if the *Merrimac* with its explosives attached were anchored athwart the channel before the charges were fired, it would effectively forestall any escape attempt by Cervera.[3]

As soon as Sampson arrived off Santiago, he decided to carry out the mission shortly after 3:00 A.M. on the third, during the hour and a quarter of darkness between the setting of the moon, which then was full, and daybreak. The *Merrimac* would be manned by a crew of volunteers, of whom there was no shortage. After the ship was sunk, they were either to row out to sea or swim to shore. Although the *Merrimac's* commander, James Miller, asked to lead the expedition, Sampson picked Hobson, because, as Sampson explained in a letter to Miller intended to assuage the latter's feelings, "Hobson has done the work."[4]

At 3:00 A.M. as planned, with the *Merrimac* about 2,000 yards from the harbor entrance, Hobson called for full speed ahead. With its crew of six enlisted men and a stowaway, the collier charged forward at nine knots into an artillery barrage that strengthened as she steamed into the channel.[5]

When the *Merrimac* reached the point at which she was expected to turn hard to port and straddle the harbor entrance, Hobson found her steering gear had been shot away. As she drifted into the harbor, he unsuccessfully tried to detonate the mines that would sink her and partially block the channel. Under a hail of fire, she moved with the tide further into the harbor until torpedoes from two Spanish ships finished her off, too far from the channel to impede an escape attempt by Cervera's squadron.[6]

Hobson and all of his crew escaped from the sinking ship and swam to the floating debris, onto which they held until daybreak. Since there was no chance of escape, they decided to surrender. Identifying themselves to a passing launch, they were permitted to climb on board. Hobson, who was in the lead, was helped up by an elegant middle-aged officer, who turned out to be Admiral Cervera. When the Admiral learned the identity of his captive, he looked at Hobson in amazement and then, a gentleman even to the enemy, looked straight at him and with admiration exclaimed "Valiant."[7]*

In Washington, fueled by rivalry between the two services, official impatience over the delay in launching the Cuban expeditionary force was increasing. The Navy Department took every opportunity to point out that its ships were waiting for the Army to board: where were the troops? A clearly annoyed Secretary of War Alger wired Shafter on June 6:

"Twenty thousand men ought to unload any number of cars and assort contents. Better to leave a fast ship to bring balance material needed than delay longer."

Lieutenant Colonel Roosevelt, perhaps biased because of his recent Navy Department affiliation, was just as upset. On June 5 he wrote in his diary:

"No word can paint the confusion. No head; a breakdown of both the railroad and military system of the country."[8]

---

* The next month, after being afforded every courtesy by their captors, Hobson and his crew were exchanged for double the number of Spanish prisoners.

During the morning of June 7, the Navy Department received a dispatch from Sampson that the previous day his forces had conducted a two-and-a-half hour bombardment of Santiago. It stated:

"If 10,000 men were here, city and fleet would be ours within forty-eight hours. Every consideration demands immediate army movement. If delayed, city will be defended more strongly by guns taken from the fleet."[9]

This was too much for official Washington. After the War Department sent telegrams almost hourly to Shafter urging immediate action, but with no apparent result, at 8:50 P.M. McKinley's name was invoked:

"Since telegraphing you an hour since the President directs you to sail at once with what force you have ready."[10]

Shafter had no alternative but to obey. He immediately issued orders that the ships would sail the next day with such troops as had managed to board them. The rest of his army would follow later.[11]

Shafter's order had an immediate effect. On June 8, although the night was already well advanced, each of his regiments rushed to seize any available means of transport to take it to the steamers at Port Tampa, some nine miles away. It was "first come, first serve," and every regiment for itself. As one example, an advance contingent of the 71st New York volunteers "captured" an arriving train intended for the 13th Infantry, and held it at bayonet point until the balance of the regiment arrived and the train was fully loaded with supplies.[12]

Not surprisingly, the Rough Riders and their second-in-command demonstrated special talents in this free-for-all. Unable to find a train to commandeer, just after dawn they took over a group of approaching coal cars, and persuaded the engineer to steam to the port in reverse gear. When, covered with soot, they reached the harbor, Colonel Wood grabbed a passing launch and, steaming to mid-harbor, boarded the transport *Yucatan* which was coming in to carry two other regiments to Cuba. When Roosevelt heard the *Yucatan* had not been assigned to the Rough Riders,

"...I ran at full speed to our train, and leaving a strong guard with the baggage, I double-quicked the rest of the regiment up to the boat, just in time to board her as she came into the quay, and then to hold her against the Second Regulars and the Seventy-first, who had arrived a little late, being a shade less ready than we were in the matter of individual initiative.[13]

Rear Admiral William T. Sampson on the *New York*

Roosevelt listened to the outraged protests of the displaced troops, to which he gave the unanswerable response: "Well, we seem to have it."[14]

By 2:00 P.M. most of the transports were loaded and were steaming down the bay so as to be ready to enter the Gulf of Mexico early the next morning. On the headquarters ship, an exhausted Shafter had just commenced a well-earned nap, when his adjutant awakened him with an urgent telegram from Secretary of War Alger: "Wait until you get further orders before you sail."[15]

Only later did Shafter learn the reason for this abrupt command. The previous evening, the converted yacht *Eagle*, patrolling the St. Nicholas Channel off Cuba's north shore, thought she espied a Spanish armored cruiser and torpedo-boat destroyer. The channel is only a little more than one hundred miles from Key West, and lay on the intended route of the American expeditionary force.[16] Since the Americans were not yet sure that all of Cervera's ships were bottled up in Santiago harbor, both Sampson and the authorities in Washington were concerned that at least two of them were still at large and free to attack the transports carrying Shafter's army to Cuba. Some of the warships that were to protect the expeditionary force were sent immediately to the St. Nicholas Channel to investigate the *Eagle's* report, and Sampson was ordered to find out whether the entire Spanish fleet was at Santiago. Until the concern raised by the *Eagle's* report could be dispelled, Shafter's departure was indefinitely postponed.[17]

By June 8 Sampson was becoming increasingly concerned that Cervera would try to escape from Santiago under cover of darkness. For the past few days the full moon had precluded a surprise departure, but it was now on the wane.[18] The Americans imaginatively devised a system of searchlights that would brighten the harbor's entrance and thus permit them to foil an attempted escape. Each two hours from dusk to dawn, the *Iowa*, *Oregon*, and *Massachusetts* would take turns beaming a single light on the harbor, occasionally also sweeping the horizon. The lights of other ships patrolling the shore made the initial effort less than completely successful, but the next night this was remedied.[19]

If Sampson had been able to listen in on Cervera's councils, he would have been pleased at the deterrent effect of his action. On June 8, the Spanish Admiral met with his captains to consider whether to attempt a sortie, but opinions were divided and no decision was reached. As it turned out, this was the Spaniards' last chance to escape undetected. As Cervera wrote the Spanish Army commander at Santiago, General Arsenio Linares on June 11, as a result of Sampson's searchlights, "...it will be absolutely impossible for the squadron under my command to go out without being seen."[20]

———※◎※———

During June 10, while the Navy was trying to assure itself that Cervera's entire force was at Santiago, Shafter's expeditionary force remained crammed aboard their transports, and suffered all the discomforts of a hot late Florida spring. Roosevelt described their agonies to Lodge:

"We are in a sewer; a canal which is festering as if it were Havana harbor. The steamer on which we are contains nearly one thousand men, there being room for about five hundred comfortably. We have given up the entire deck to the men, so that the officers have to sit in the cabin, and even so several companies are down in the lower hold, which is unpleasantly suggestive of the Black Hole of Calcutta."[21]

There was little that Shafter could do to remedy the situation. To disembark and wait for an "all clear" before reembarking would entail further delay, and the orders from Washington were to leave as soon as possible.

It therefore was the Marines and not the Army that made the first landing in Cuba. Although Guantanamo Bay, forty-five miles east, was too far from Santiago to guard it if a storm led Sampson's fleet to take refuge there, it was a large landlocked harbor that in future years would be a perfect naval base. When a contingent of Marines arrived from Key West on the morning of June 10, they were immediately sent to Guantanamo and landed without opposition at the east end of the bay.[22]

———※◎※———

On June 10, in response to a Liberal attack in the House of Commons on Chamberlain's May 13 Birmingham speech, the Colonial Secretary responded in what Balfour described to Queen Victoria as "a speech of characteristic vigor." After replying to "the suggestions of differences in the Cabinet with sarcastic allusions to the notorious differences which existed in the Cabinet which preceded it,"[23] he stated that the objective of the speech "was to state the facts:"

"...as long as you are isolated, can you say that it is ...not probable, that some time or another you may have a combination of at least three Powers against you? It seems to me that you have to look forward to the possibilities of the next ten or twenty years, and now is the time to decide how you will meet the contingencies which are evidently ahead.

"... I ...most earnestly desire, a close, a cordial and intimate connection with the United States of America...Well, nothing in the nature of a cut-and-dried alliance is at this moment proposed. The Americans...do not ask for our assistance, and we do not want theirs.

"But will anyone say that the occasion may not arise, foreseen as it has been by some American statesmen, who have said that there is a possibility in the future that Anglo-Saxon liberty and Anglo-Saxon interests may hereafter be menaced by a great combination of other Powers? Yes, Sir, I think that such a thing is possible, and, in that case, whether it be America or whether it be England that is menaced, I hope that blood will be found to be thicker than water."[24]

On June 12 Shafter's forces were still waiting aboard their transports for the order that would send them off to Cuba. Roosevelt spent some of the time writing Lodge a long letter in which he set forth the many faults he had found with the operation and its leadership and asked him if possible "to tell the Administration, that is, the President, and if necessary the Secretary of War, just what is going on here and the damage that is being done." If this were not enough, Roosevelt then urged his old friend:

"You must get Manila and Hawaii; you must prevent any talk of peace until we get Puerto Rico and the Philippines as well as secure the independence of Cuba."[25]

At the same time that a frustrated Roosevelt was pouring out his thoughts to Lodge, Navy Lieutenant Victor Blue was climbing with a Cuban revolutionary officer up a jungle covered hill northwest off Santiago Bay. Blue had been sent by Sampson to ascertain whether Cervera's entire force was anchored in the harbor. At an opening in the undergrowth, he looked down on the bay and counted the ships that were lying there, comparing their size and strength with the details he had been given of the Spanish fleet. All were present and accounted for. Earlier, it had been determined that the suspicious ships that the *Eagle* had seen were American vessels. Shafter's forces could safely leave for Cuba.[26]

Although Shafter had received word the next day that he could sail for Santiago, the transports' water supplies had been seriously depleted by the several days' delay, and had to be replaced. Thus, it was not until 9:00 A.M. on June 14 that the entire armada left port and steamed to the entrance of Tampa Bay. There, the forty-eight transports formed in three columns and, escorted by ships of the North Atlantic Squadron, moved south over a calm sea.[27]

Shafter's force was impressive—more than 16,000 enlisted men commanded by more than 800 officers. It consisted of two divisions of infantry and one of cavalry, but the latter, including the Rough Riders, were largely dismounted due to inadequate transport for the horses. Even so, in this last American war without motor transport, there were some 2,300 animals to serve as beasts of burden and to pull the artillery, wagons, and ambulances.[28]

On the morning of June 19, after five days at sea, the flotilla entered the Windward Passage between Cuba and Haiti and turned south on the last leg of its trip to Santiago.[29] Shafter's voyage had been blessed by fair weather and a glassy sea. Its pace was slow, between four and seven knots, encumbered as it was by two landing-scows and a huge tanker filled with drinking water. The speed of the ships varied considerably, resulting in a column that at times was more than twenty-five miles long. From time to time Shafter would have to order the ships in the van to stop until the rear of the column could catch up.[30]

For Roosevelt and his fellow officers the voyage was pleasant, especially the tropical evenings under star-filled skies, with regimental bands playing ragtime music. For the men below, it was a different story—hard bunks and air that was not only warm and close, but also increasingly bore the smell of horses and mules, as well as their manure. Yet to the large majority of both officers and men the expedition was the beginning of a great adventure in an exotic foreign land.[31]

After sailing through the Windward Passage, Shafter's armada turned west, and by the morning of June 20 anchored several miles south off Santiago. Shortly before noon, one of Sampson's ships came by and escorted the troopships north among the blockading force, with the seamen lining the rails of the naval vessels and cheering the troops as the transports steamed up.[32] Sampson immediately came aboard Shafter's ship and advised him that the Cuban rebel leader Calisto Garcia was camped near the coast about twenty miles west of Santiago. It would be well to meet with him without delay so as to plan a joint strategy of attack. Uppermost in everyone's minds was that the rainy season, with its threat of disease, was fast approaching. If Santiago was to be taken, it must be done in the next few weeks.[33]

The meeting with Garcia took place at his camp a mile up a steep jungle trail from the beach. The 300-pound Shafter was by now suffering seriously from the sweltering heat, but this did not lessen his determination to take Santiago, and on his own terms. Thus, when Sampson suggested that the attack should be on Morro Point, at the entrance to the harbor, with the Navy then steaming in to attack Cervera's ships, Shafter demurred. He did not have the high-powered artillery that was needed to batter down the Morro's fortifications, and his men would be easy targets as they tried to climb the steep 230-foot bluff atop which sat the Spanish fort. The Army would suffer the losses and, even if the assault was successful, the Navy would get the glory of defeating Cervera and taking the city, either by shellfire or intimidation.[34]

Shafter therefore urged that Santiago itself, five miles northeast of the entrance to the bay, should be his target. This required a landing somewhere east of the city. Guantanamo Bay would provide a perfect site, but the forty-five miles of difficult and largely roadless terrain between it and Santiago quickly removed it from consideration. However, at two villages, Daiquiri, eighteen miles east of Santiago and Siboney, ten miles east of the provincial capital, there were beaches which appeared suitable for landing. A coastal road ran between the two hamlets, and from Siboney turned inland west northwest to Santiago. Garcia reported that although there were as many as 1,600 Spanish troops at Siboney, there were only 300 at Daiquiri. On his recommendation, the American leaders decided to land at Daiquiri the next morning.[35]

The morning of June 21 opened with wind, rain, and heavy seas, too rough to allow the scheduled landing to take place that day. In the afternoon, however, the weather cleared, and at 6:00 A.M. on the twenty-second, the first wave of Shafter's invasion force began to be loaded into the landing craft that would be towed by Navy cutters close to the shore. In part due to a still-choppy sea, the landing process was lengthy. It was not until 9:40 A.M. that the Navy was ordered to begin its bombardment while the landing ships readied themselves for their mile or so trip.[36]

Although the land beyond Daiquiri was fairly level and thus offered a good spot to group the landing parties for a move inland, it was otherwise not an ideal place for an amphibious invasion. It was commanded by a high hill, atop which sat a Spanish blockhouse. Further, a wooden pier and a small shingly beach offered the only realistic landing spots. Thus, while the naval bombardment of the village would soften up any defending forces, it would only partially weaken them. Moreover, although the Navy was carrying out further shelling down the coast at Siboney in order to confuse the Spaniards, any observer of the lengthy landing preparations at Daiquiri would not have been fooled.[37] The Spaniards therefore had a golden opportunity to inflict at least significant casualties on Shafter's forces as they came ashore. This would probably not have altered the ultimate outcome of the conflict, but might have lessened the political popularity of what John Hay was later able to refer to as "a splendid little war." For some inexplicable reason, however, there were no Spanish forces at Daiquiri and not a shot was fired on the Americans.[38]

By evening, approximately 6,000 men and their supplies were on shore. The only casualties were a few horses that, when tossed into the ocean from the transports, headed out to sea instead of in to land. Needless to say, the troops on shore included the Rough Riders. Although not slated to disembark until after most of the regulars, their lieutenant colonel spotted a former Navy Department aide steaming by on a converted yacht and persuaded him to tow the *Yucatan* to within a few hundred yards of shore. Unfortunately, after the Rough Riders had landed, the *Yucatan* steamed off with most of the regiment's supplies. However, the near-sighted Roosevelt carried with him his most important possession—several extra pairs of spectacles sewn into the lining of his hat.[39]

The first troops to land were from the division of infantry commanded by General Henry W. Lawton. General Joseph Wheeler, however, displaying the agility that had won him Civil War fame, managed to follow soon thereafter. It was "Fighting Joe" instead of Lawton who sent a few Rough Riders to plant their flag above the Spanish blockhouse that commanded Daiquiri. The combined American forces, including those on the naval vessels and transports, cheered lustily as they participated in what late-twentieth-century America would have regarded as a unique "photo opportunity."[40]

Lawton's advance guard was halfway to Siboney by the evening of the twenty-second, and the next morning reached the village. Apart from a single volley from the departing Spanish rear guard, its advance was unopposed.[41] Shafter, who was still aboard ship, at once directed that the chief operation should be transferred from Daiquiri to Siboney and that Lawton should hold the gap in the hills on the inland road to Santiago until the full invasion force was assembled. However, the commanding general had not reckoned with Wheeler, whose Civil War reputation was "never staying still in one place long enough for the Almighty to put a finger on him," and who probably relished any opportunity to upstage

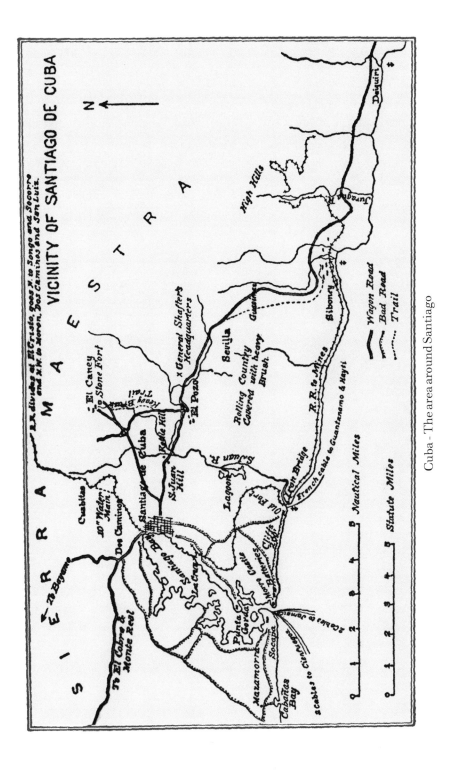

Cuba - The area around Santiago

Lawton, a Union Medal of Honor winner. During the afternoon of the twenty-third, Wheeler pushed some of his dismounted cavalry, including the Rough Riders, to Siboney. He then conceived the idea of out-flanking his superior officer and putting some of his troops further than Lawton's men up the road to Santiago, so that he instead of Lawton would lead the first land fight of the war. Under cover of darkness and before Lawton knew what was happening, he was able to place the Rough Riders and two dismounted cavalry squadrons, nearly 1,000 men in all, ahead of Lawton.[42]

Three miles up the Santiago road from Siboney was a mountain pass called Las Guasimas, after the guacima, or hog nut trees, that grew there. Spanish General Antero Rubin, commanding about 1,500 men, had placed an advance guard at Las Guasimas, while his main body was at the village of Sevilla, another half mile up the road.[43] Wheeler planned to attack this force on the morning of the twenty-fourth. He split his command in two, with the Rough Riders advancing up a trail that paralleled the road on the west and the remaining troops under his direct command proceeding up the main road. They set off at 5:40 A.M. Both bodies ran into the Spaniards at almost the same time about two hours later. The Spanish fire, usually in volleys, was heavy, and it was hard for the Americans to spot the defenders, hidden as they were in the jungle. Both wings of the attacking force were suffering casualties, with the first to be killed being the New York patrician and ex-Columbia University crew captain Sergeant Hamilton Fish.[44]

At about 8:30, one of Wheeler's aides suggested that it might be advisable to ask Lawton for help. Reluctantly, Fighting Joe agreed, and a courier was sent to Lawton, who had already heard the sounds of the conflict and then saw wounded men stumbling down the hill to Siboney. Meanwhile, the Rough Riders' fire seemed to be having effect, and forced the Spanish advance guard facing them back to Sevilla. Just as the Rough Riders joined up with Wheeler's force and the head of Lawton's supporting column came into sight, the Spaniards retreated from their position, prompting Wheeler to cry, "We've got the damn Yankees on the run!" Thus, at the cost of sixteen men killed and fifty-two wounded, the Americans had eliminated any possible interference with their landing efforts and had secured the initial approaches to Santiago.[45]

For Roosevelt, the victory was especially satisfying. Three days later, he wrote Lodge:

"Well, whatever comes I shall feel contented with having left the Navy

Department to go into the army for the war; for our regiment has been in the first fight on land, and has done well."[46]

Meanwhile, Richard Harding Davis, whom Roosevelt cited for bravery in his official report, gave the impression in the New York *Herald* that "Roosevelt's Rough Riders" had won the battle almost single-handed. In New York there was immediate talk of nominating this new hero to run for Governor in the fall.[47]

Following their victory at Las Guasimas, the Americans had advanced their lines to within five miles of Santiago. Their major problem was a shortage of supplies. There was plenty of salt pork, hard bread, coffee, and sugar, but more popular items like onions, potatoes, and tobacco were largely unavailable. The tobacco shortage was especially hard to take, since most of the insurgents with whom the Americans came into contact were smoking their own cheroots.[48] Roosevelt acted to remedy the situation. When he heard a rumor that beans could be found at the beach, eight miles from his camp, he led a squad down the hills to investigate. Advised that the beans were available only to officers, he briefly considered the issue and then demanded 1,100 pounds "for the officers mess." When the commissar protested that this was too much for any group of regimental officers to eat, Roosevelt replied: "You don't know what appetites my officers have." Told that such a requisition would have to go to Washington and that, if denied, it would be taken out of his salary, he replied, "That will be all right, only give me the beans." The commissar did so and the entire regiment of Rough Riders enjoyed the feast.[49]

Roosevelt was in his element. Like a small boy temporarily freed of parental discipline, on June 15, he wrote his sister Corinne:

"I am personally in excellent health, in spite of having been obliged for the week since I landed, to violate all the rules of health which I was told I must observe. I've had to sleep steadily on the ground, for four days I never took off my clothes, which were always drenched with rain, dew or perspiration, and we had no chance to boil the water we drank."[50]

Meanwhile Cervera and his squadron had become pawns in a dispute between Captain General Blanco in Havana and General Linares in Santiago. The Captain General argued that the Spanish fleet should be able to escape without serious damage, while Linares contended that he could not spare Cervera's men and guns, at least until a relief expedition from the north, still several days away, could provide assistance. On June 28 the hapless Admiral agreed to help Linares in the defense of Santiago, but on the understanding that if matters looked hopeless, his seamen who had been aiding in the land fighting would rejoin their ships before they sought to break Sampson's blockade.[51]

Shafter would have liked to follow up the victory at Las Guasimas with an immediate attack on Santiago's outlying defenses. His troops could not advance without munitions and other supplies, however, and these had to be moved to the front by pack train and wagon up a narrow mountain road. To make things worse, in the hurry to establish a beachhead and drive inland, there was no time to get many of the necessary supplies off the transports. Thus, many medical officers had left their chests and supplies behind, and these had to be located, collected, and brought ashore before further military action could commence.[52]

Shafter initially had planned to continue his advance on June 28. On June 26, however, he received word that 4,000 more troops were about to arrive, and decided to wait for them. Thus, his attack on the Spanish lines outside Santiago was rescheduled for July 1.[53]

On the morning of the thirtieth, Shafter managed to get his vast bulk up a hill named El Pozo, east of the Spanish lines, where he surveyed the scene. A mile and a half in front of him across to the west was a series of hills called the San Juan Heights, the most dominant of which was San Juan Hill. The main road to Santiago, the Camino Real, crossed the heights to the north of the hill. About two miles beyond them was Santiago itself. Four miles to the north was a small fortified hill named El Caney.[54] Linares's defending forces totalled some 6,600 men with another 3,800 within twenty miles of Santiago. Unfortunately for the Spaniards, instead of concentrating his troops on what seemed to be the obvious points of attack, their commander had spread them at various places around the city. The result was that he would have only slightly more than 1,000 men on El Caney and San Juan Heights to meet the concentrated power of the attacking army.[55]

Shafter planned to deploy his 15,000-man army in a two-pronged attack. Lawton's division would turn north and attack El Caney. At the same time, after an artillery bombardment, the other American infantry division, under Brigadier General Jacob Kent, together with Wheeler's dismounted cavalry would attack the San Juan Heights. This coordinated effort would prevent the Spaniards on and around the Heights from reinforcing El Caney. After Lawton had taken the latter position, his troops would turn southwest and assist Kent and Wheeler.[56]

In mid-afternoon, the Americans started their move to be in position for the morrow's attack. Lawton marched up the road to El Caney, while the rest of the troops were advanced up behind El Pozo. Wheeler had been felled by fever, as had Leonard Wood's superior, Brigadier General S.B.M. Young. As a result, the command of Wheeler's division shifted to Brigadier General Samuel Sumner and that of Young's brigade upon Wood. Thus, Theodore Roosevelt would command the Rough Riders.[57]

July 1, 1898, which Roosevelt always thereafter referred to as "the great day of my life," dawned cloudless and clear. The American troops were up well before dawn, and many were on the move. To the north, one of Lawton's brigades had advanced to within a mile of El Caney. To the south, an artillery battery was struggling up El Pozo in order to support the troops that were massing behind the hill to be ready for the attack on the San Juan Heights. Among them was the Tenth Cavalry, a regiment of black troops led by Lieutenant John J. Pershing, who was to command the American Expeditionary Force in France twenty years later.[58]*

At 6:30 A.M Lawton's guns began their bombardment of El Caney. Their fire was generally ineffective; the guns were too far away. Shortly thereafter the infantry began its advance. It soon became apparent that El Caney's capture would be much more difficult than anticipated. The only protection for the Americans was the brush through which they were advancing. The Spanish defenders, on the other hand, occupied a fort, a church and well prepared trenches. The fort, named El Viso, stood atop a 100-foot-high steep, conical hill.[59]

By 1:00 P.M. Lawton's troops were still unable to advance in the face of the heavy Spanish gunfire. An hour later Lawton received a dispatch from Shafter suggesting that he disengage and move his forces to the right of the attack that was then to be made on the San Juan Heights. This was easier said than done, however, and Lawton decided it was preferable to try to finish the battle at El Caney. By 3:00 P.M. his artillery managed to get close enough to batter the walls of El Viso. The charge and hand-to-hand fighting that followed gave the Americans possession of the Spanish lines between 4:00 and 5:00 P.M., more than six hours after they had expected to complete an easy victory. The main American force would have to advance directly on Santiago without their support.[60]

---

* Pershing's evident admiration for his men led his fellow officers to nickname him "Black Jack," which remained with him the rest of his life.

Colonel Theodore Roosevelt

At 8:00 A.M., Captain Charles Grimes' four gun battery on El Pozo had opened that attack. After a short while, the Spanish artillery on the San Juan Heights returned their fire and its heavier guns got the better of the duel, which eventually stopped. During the remainder of the morning, the 8,000 men who were to attack the Heights were slowly making their way up the steep jungle trail and deploying in the woods to the east. As this force grew, it came under an increasingly destructive Spanish fire, which the Americans were in no position to return.[61]

Morning passed and turned into early afternoon, but Kent's infantry and Wheeler's dismounted cavalry remained in this exposed position, with no orders of any kind. In the Rough Riders, "man after man...fell dead or wounded," and other regiments were also suffering heavily. Shafter, at his headquarters a mile-and-a-half to the rear, may have been waiting for word that Lawton would be free to join in the attack on the Heights. Perhaps he assumed that the division commanders could commence the assault on their own. It finally became obvious to Lieutenant John D. Miley, who was Shafter's representative at the front, that neither the commanding officers there nor Shafter at the rear were willing to take the initiative to extricate the army from its pinned down position. To remain or retreat would be a disaster; the only course was to advance. Shortly after 1.00 P.M. he ordered the attack to begin.[62]

Kent's troops had already reached this conclusion on their own. Thus, when a battery of Gatling guns providentially appeared and opened fire on the Spaniards' trenches and many of their occupants were seen running, the Americans spontaneously charged over the open ground. They paused at the foot of the Heights until their artillery ceased firing at the heights above, and then resumed the attack. When they reached the crest they found its defenders in flight.[63] Describing their charge, correspondent Richard Harding Davis wrote:

"They had no glittering bayonets, they were not massed in regular array. There were a few men in advance, bunched together, and creeping up a steep, sunny hill, the tops of which roared and flashed with flame. The men held their guns pressed across their breasts and stepped heavily as they climbed. Behind these first few, spreading out like a fan, were single lines of men, slipping and scrambling in the smooth grass, moving forward with difficulty, as though they were walking waist high through water, moving slowly, carefully, and with strenuous effort."[64]

To the right, Sumner's dismounted cavalry was also attacking, in its case up an elevation to the east of the northern end of the Heights called Kettle Hill. The Rough Riders were on the right of this charge. They quickly reached the top, where they came under fire from the Spaniards on the Heights to the southwest. They also saw Kent's troops moving up to attack that position. "Obviously," wrote Roosevelt later, "the proper thing to do was help them." For ten minutes he directed a rifle fire on the Spanish position and then decided to add his force to Kent's attack.[65]

No sooner was Roosevelt's decision made than he started to run down Kettle Hill. In his excitement he forgot to issue an order. When he noticed that he had only five followers, two of whom were quickly felled by bullets, he turned and roared to his regiment, "What, are you cowards?" The response was immediate: "We didn't hear you. We didn't see you, colonel." Roosevelt immediately ordered the charge, and the Rough Riders and other dismounted cavalry followed him in a mad rush down Kettle Hill and up the grassy slope beyond. By the time they neared the top of San Juan Heights, they saw the defenders fleeing west toward Santiago. Together with Kent's troops to their left, they had won the day.[66]

Especially considering the alternative of defeat, it was a major triumph. Sadly, it was expensive, with 420 Americans killed and 1,180 wounded—one tenth of Shafter's army. The Spanish defenders suffered fewer casualties—215 killed but only 376 wounded. But Shafter's forces had accomplished their immediate objective, and Roosevelt for one was "reveling in victory and gore."[67]

Next day, however, Shafter's force was anything but elated. Exhausted from their efforts of the previous day, his troops remained all day in the trenches they had dug on the San Juan Heights and other spots to the east of Santiago. Meanwhile, Wheeler, who could never be accused of congenital pessimism, studied the city's defenses and concluded that a successful attack might cost the Americans up to 3,000 casualties.[68] As losses of this size would be unacceptable, Shafter wrote Sampson asking him to force the entrance to the harbor on the basis that the Navy "could now operate with less loss of life than I can." Sampson immediately replied that he was more concerned as to a possible loss of ships than of men. He added:

"If it is your earnest desire that we should force the entrance, I will at once prepare to undertake it. I think, however, that our position and yours would be made more difficult if, as is possible, we fail in our attempt."[69]

Even Roosevelt shared the general concern. On July 3 he wrote Lodge:

"Tell the President for Heaven's sake to send us every regiment and above all every battery possible. We have won so far at a heavy cost, but the Spaniards fight very hard and charging these entrenchments against modern rifles is terrible. We are within measurable distance of a terrible military disaster; we must have help....men, batteries, food, and ammunition."[70]

That evening, Shafter called a council of war to decide on his army's future course of action. Prostrated by the heat, he had to be carried to the meeting on a detached door borne by six men. With discouraging prospects of attacking Santiago from both land and sea, and with a relief column of 3,000 men approaching the city from the north, he was giving serious though to ordering a retreat. His fellow officers disagreed, with only Kent supporting withdrawal. For twenty-four hours, the Americans would retain their present positions. After that, the council would reconvene.[71]

The word of potential reinforcements that concerned the Americans had given the Spanish forces in Santiago a lift in their otherwise downcast spirits. Nonetheless, their position was not good, with shortages of ammunition and of food, and a recognition that the anticipated arrival of more troops would likely exacerbate the latter.[72]

For more than a week, Cervera had been under constant pressure from his superiors in Havana and Madrid not to let his fleet be captured by the Americans. On June 28 he was ordered to take any opportunity to try to leave, and do so in any event if the city was in danger of falling. The night of the Spanish defeat at El Caney and the San Juan Heights, Cervera called a council of war, at which his captains unanimously agreed that the time had come to try to force an escape. The next day the Spanish seamen were withdrawn from the defensive lines where they had been "loaned" to the army, and returned to their ships. The fleet was ready to leave by late afternoon, but Cervera decided that the escape channel was too narrow to risk a night departure. The attempt would be made in the morning.[73]

On July 3, while Shafter was sending a letter to the Spanish commander threatening to shell the city the next day unless it surrendered, the blockading force was enjoying a sunny, warm Sunday morning. The fleet extended in an eight-mile semicircle, with each ship maintaining a position about three miles from the harbor entrance. The crews, in their dress whites, were about to attend church services. Sampson had gone ashore to confer with Shafter regarding the possibility of a naval attack on the city, leaving Schley in temporary command.[74]

Early in the morning, Captain Concas of Cervera's flagship *Maria Teresa* had paid a visit to the harbor's mouth several miles from Santiago.

He observed that Schley's flagship *Brooklyn*, stationed at the western end of the blockading arc, seemed farther out to sea than usual. When he reported his finding to the Admiral and their fellow officers, they agreed that after leaving the bay, the fleet would swung sharply to the west and try to elude the Americans by fleeing along the coast toward Cienfuegos. They recognized that the lead vessel would bear the initial brunt of the American fire. Cervera, both courageous and in his mind a captive of fate, volunteered the *Maria Teresa* for the assignment.[75]

Shortly after 9:00 A.M., the Sunday calm on the American ships was broken by a shot from a signal gun on the battleship *Iowa*, the second blockading ship east of the *Brooklyn*. The Spanish fleet was attempting to escape! As Captain Robley "Fighting Bob" Evans and his crew watched, there first appeared the *Maria Teresa* bright in the sunlight with its fresh paint and large blood and gold battle flags at its mastheads. There followed in a single line the armored cruisers *Vizcaya*, *Cristobel Colon*, and *Almirante Oquendo*. The torpedo-boat destroyers *Furor* and *Pluton* brought up the rear. In a short while, Cervera's entire fleet was out of the harbor.[76]

Even before it cleared the headland at the western end of the bay, the *Maria Teresa* had opened fire with its long-range guns. The Americans were quick to respond. At the same time, Commodore Schley on the *Brooklyn* began to revel in his good luck. With Sampson several miles to the east in the *New York*, having first flown the signal "Disregard movements of the flagship," the Commodore and not the Admiral was the senior officer in charge of a battle that would be moving ever further to the west, away from Sampson.[77]

Schley had little time to congratulate himself on his good fortune. The *Maria Teresa* was rapidly approaching, and apparently seeking to ram the *Brooklyn*. To avoid her, the *Brooklyn* swung sharply to the east. As the *Brooklyn* did so, the *Texas*, which was next in the line of pursuers, slowed to avoid her. Thus, the two American ships that should have been leading the pursuit were now behind the *Iowa*, with the powerful *Oregon* closing fast on their heels.[78]

The American confusion provided Cervera's ships an unexpected opportunity. Further, the American gunfire was causing no structural damage. The shells were causing fires to erupt, however, and the combination of the wind caused by their speed and their wooden decks was the Spaniards' undoing. The *Maria Teresa* was the first to suffer as projectiles from the *Iowa* burst a steam pipe and one of her fire-protecting water mains. As a result, her crew was unable to fight the spreading flames.

Cervera, who had assumed command of the flagship when Captain Concas was wounded, swung her toward shore so that as many of her crew as possible could escape.[79]

The next Spanish ship to be disabled was the *Oquendo*. Again it was the *Iowa*, hit in two places by the *Colon*, but still functional, that inflicted most of the damage. The *Brooklyn* and other ships came up to add their guns. As Evans later recalled, "She rolled and staggered like a drunken thing." The *Oquendo's* interior was soon burning like a furnace, and most of her gun crews were either dead or wounded. Eventually, her crew was able to get her to shore, where she lay burning near the *Maria Teresa*.[80]

Next to go were the two Spanish destroyers, which received the full fire of the American ships as they steamed by to reach Cervera's cruisers. The *Pluton* was run on the rocks and blew up. After going out of control and steaming in circles, the *Furor* blew up at sea.[81]

The *Vizcaya* and *Colon* remained afloat. Schley's *Brooklyn*, seeking to make amends for her earlier failure to attack the *Maria Teresa*, quickly closed on the *Vizcaya*. The American ship's punishing fire caused an armed torpedo to explode, blowing out a large section of the *Vizcaya's* bow. As an observer described the scene:

"We could see men's bodies hurled into the air, and see others dropping over the sides. One end of her bridge tumbled down as though her underpinning was driven out, and then at 11:06 o'clock she turned and ran for shore, hauling down her flag, her deck one mass of flames, and the ammunition, which had been brought up to supply her deck guns, exploding in every direction."[82]

As the *Texas* came up, with her men cheering at the sight of the *Vizcaya* in flames, her Captain J.W. Philip, horrified at the suffering of the brave Spanish seamen, called out, "Don't cheer, boys! Those poor devils are dying!"[83]

Meanwhile the *Colon*, steaming inshore and shrouded by the battle's smoke, had escaped in good shape. Perhaps the swiftest Spanish ship, she was six miles ahead of the *Brooklyn*, her nearest pursuer, and apparently gaining. But the *Colon* was not to be spared. She had used up her good coal, and was forced to turn to her poorer supply. This reduced her speed, and at about 11:30 she spied the *Oregon* slowly closing in on her from the east. Unlike the other American ships, that powerful battleship had kept her boilers lit and hence was able to make better time than the other pursuers.[84] At 12:20, the *Oregon* opened fire with her long-range guns.

Her shots fell short, but to the *Colon's* Captain Paredes it was only a matter of time before they would begin to hit his ship. Her heavy guns, ordered before the war from an Italian manufacturer, had not arrived when she had hastily left Cadiz and no substitutes had been found. Paredes concluded that it would be futile to either try to escape or fight. At 1:15, fifty miles west of Santiago, he headed for shore. The *Oregon* held her fire as he beached his ship.[85]

The Spanish fleet had been completely destroyed at the cost of one American ensign killed and no one wounded. The brave but outclassed Spaniards suffered 323 lives lost and 151 wounded. The Americans did their best to show their admiration and sympathy for their courageous opponents. As Admiral Cervera was brought on board the *Iowa*, he was accorded full honors. Captain Evans wrote:

"As the brave old admiral came over the side...without shirt or hat, yet an admiral every inch of him, the officers saluted and the marines presented arms, and the buglers sounded the salute for an officer of his rank. As he bowed and extended his hand to me, my men burst into cheers."[86]

Definitive news of the American naval victory did not reach Washington until 1:00 A.M. on July 4. Thus, when the American public opened its morning papers, it realized that this Fourth of July would warrant a celebration more heartfelt than any since 1863, when news of the twin victories of Gettysburg and Vicksburg arrived on this national holiday.[87]

Only six hours before, the mood in the capital had been gloomy. At seven o'clock on the evening of the third, McKinley and his advisers had received a preliminary account of the naval battle from Shafter which indicated that Cervera had escaped. Earlier the same day, the General had shocked his civilian superiors by advising that he was "seriously considering withdrawing about five miles and taking up a new position..." Against the background of these depressing reports, the news of the naval triumph was all the more welcome. It looked as if the war might be almost over.[88]

TWELVE

Moving Toward Peace

Cervera's defeat initially seemed to make a new man of Shafter. On July 3, even before learning of the results of the sea battle, at the suggestion of one of his officers he had demanded the surrender of Santiago. Shortly thereafter, however, he became concerned over the casualties that an attack on the city would inflict on both his men and the civilian population. At the request of the local foreign consular officials, he agreed to postpone it until July 5. He then provided Spanish commanding General Jose Toral, who had succeeded the wounded General Linares, a further extension of time to respond to the American surrender proposal. By now, a truce had taken effect.[1]

On July 9 Toral wrote Shafter that he would surrender Santiago if he and his men were allowed to depart to a town about seventy-five miles northwest of the port. Shafter suggested to Washington that he should approve the proposal, since it would free the Americans for action elsewhere. It also would permit the return to the city of the civilian population, which the Americans had been feeding since it fled the port several days earlier out of fear of a bombardment. Shafter also worried over the risk of a yellow fever epidemic. Cases of the disease were increasing daily now that the summer rains had commenced.[2] Shafter wanted to pull out most of his troops before conditions worsened.

The War Department was shocked at Shafter's apparent timidity. Secretary Alger at once responded that Shafter "should accept nothing but an unconditional surrender." Even McKinley weighed in with his concern that if Shafter allowed Toral's army to evacuate, "you must meet it somewhere else."[3]

On July 13, the President called an emergency Cabinet session to consider a recommendation from General Miles regarding the Spanish force in Santiago. Like Shafter, the Commanding General, who had just arrived in Cuba, was concerned over the increasing rate of sickness, primarily malaria, in the American camps. A promptly arranged surrender "with honor" would allow the American troops to leave the Santiago area before an epidemic developed. Notwithstanding this risk, the President and his advisers agreed that an easy "out" for the Spaniards would look like an American defeat and was out of the question. Miles was advised that the choices were to obtain a prompt surrender or take the city by storm.[4]

On July 13, at the same time that the Cabinet was meeting, the American and Spanish commanding officers had resumed their negotiations. When Toral pleaded that the time required to communicate with Madrid made it impossible to respond to the American surrender proposal, Shafter answered that he could delay no longer. If there was not a positive response by 5:00 A.M. the next day, the Americans would open fire on the city. After an appeal by Toral to their "soldierly feelings," Miles and Shafter agreed to extend the truce to noon. Meanwhile the seriously wounded General Linares was urging his superiors in Madrid to recognize that "there is a limit to the honor of arms." He himself would give up the city if Toral or other officers believed that their reputations would suffer if they were to do so.[5]

After what seemed to be interminable negotiations, the Spanish army at Santiago surrendered on July 17. Shafter managed to heave his 300-pound bulk onto a horse, which he rode, with Wheeler alongside and the other officers behind him, to an open plain between the lines. As a correspondent described it, what followed was as amicable an event as could be imagined:

"General Toral rode forward and smilingly saluted General Shafter, who stretched forth his hand and heartily shook that of the Spanish general. He congratulated General Toral upon the bravery of his men and of their gallant defense of Santiago, and both expressed satisfaction that the campaign had closed.[6]

The Spaniards had been better negotiators than fighters. They persuaded the Americans that the written agreement should refer to "capitulation" rather than the more humiliating "surrender." More important, to the displeasure of Shafter's superiors in Washington, Toral obtained a promise that the troops' arms would be sent back to Spain with the prisoners. There were mutterings in Washington of having to fight these soldiers again on some other field, but eventually it was conceded that this would never happen. For these men, the war was over.[7]

Meanwhile, yellow fever was beginning to spread among Shafter's army. On July 19 Roosevelt wrote Lodge that he had "over one hundred men down with fever in my own camp." There was not enough nourishing food, "nothing...but hardtack, bacon, and generally coffee without sugar." The cause, he complained, was the lack of transportation "including lack of means to land from the ships." Thus, despite their military victory, "our condition is horrible in every respect."[8]

At 3:00 P.M. on July 21, Miles and an army of 3,314 men left Guantanamo Bay for Puerto Rico. This had been Miles's goal from the outset of the war. It now had the added advantage that the rainy season, and thus the yellow fever season, did not begin in Puerto Rico until mid-August.[9] Miles was taking no chances in this respect. His force was made up entirely of volunteers, who had not been permitted to land in Cuba for fear of contracting the disease. His fear of yellow fever was so great that later, when two paymasters for his command were sent to Puerto Rico by way of Santiago and fell ill aboard ship, he had the money they were carrying impounded and a fresh supply of presumably uninfected currency sent from the mainland.[10]

There was another reason besides the upcoming rainy season for a quick conquest of Puerto Rico. Washington expected that peace negotiations would shortly commence. The United States should possess as much of the island as possible before they began. As a potential naval base and coaling station, it would be important to any United States adversary in a future war. American occupation would prevent this.[11]

Although there reportedly were 8,000 Spanish regulars and as many more ill-trained militia on the island, Miles was hopeful of a successful operation. He was taking no chances, however. He augmented his small army by a powerful naval flotilla, even obtaining approval to suspend an expedition to the Philippines that was forming up at Guantanamo so that some of those ships could be added to his force. His ostensible goal was Cape Fajardo, on the northeast tip of Puerto Rico, forty miles from San Juan.[12]

Cape Fajardo, however, was not Miles's real destination. Instead, on July 25 once the expedition had left Guantanamo, he announced that the landing would be made at Guanica, a port near Puerto Rico's second largest city, Ponce, on the island's southern coast. It is unclear whether he had decided on this course before he left Cuba, and thus intentionally deceived Secretary of War Alger and others in Washington, or whether he changed his mind while the expedition was at sea.[13] Miles apparently changed course in order to fool the Spaniards. He believed, probably correctly, that reports that he would land at Fajardo had already leaked out, thus, a landing there could be met with stout opposition. Whether or not he was right, the landing at Guanica encountered only a token defense. The town's inhabitants fled in terror when the attack commenced. They soon returned and welcomed the Americans with seeming enthusiasm.[14]

On July 13 an Anglo-American League had been formed in London. Its goal was to exert "every effort...in the interests of civilization and of peace to secure the most cordial and constant cooperation on the part of the two nations." Its General Committee was headed by James Bryce, and other eminent Englishmen served as its officers.[15]

In response, an Anglo-American Committee was formed on July 27 in New York. Publisher Whitelaw Reid was its chairman. Its members included former presidential cabinet members of both parties and the chief Roman Catholic and Episcopalian dignitaries of New York. It applauded

"...the recent demonstrations of sympathy and fellowship with this country on the part of citizens of the various countries comprised in the British Empire."

The Committee's statement concluded:

"We earnestly reciprocate these sentiments, recognizing as we do that the same language and the same principles of ordered liberty shall form the basis of an intimate and enduring friendship between these two kindred peoples—a friendship destined to hasten the day of peace and good-will among all the nations of the earth."[16]

The address was sent to about fifteen hundred prominent Americans. Reportedly, very few refused to sign.[17]

Even before the formation of the Committee, the improved relations between the two countries were receiving journalistic praise. Typical was an editorial in the July edition of the *Century* magazine. Referring to the Fourth of July celebrations that year, it read:

"The day will be distinguished by the omission of the occasional tirades against England. There is no progress in the world that is not marked by somebody's change of mind, and in the last three months even the most violent prejudices among our people against our English kinsmen have disappeared in the face of unmistakable evidence of her sympathy with America in the irrepressible conflict between the ideas of the sixteenth century and those of the nineteenth...the two great divisions of the Anglo-Saxon race are in greater sympathy than ever before."[18]

=—◉)(◉—=

On July 27, from London Ambassador Hay summed up to Roosevelt his impression of the events of the past few weeks:

"It has been a splendid little war; begun with the highest motives; carried on with magnificent intelligence and spirit, favored by that fortune that loves the brave. It is now to be concluded, I hope, with that fine good nature which is, after all, the distinguishing trait of our American character."[19]

=—◉)(◉—=

On July 28 Ponce fell to the Americans without opposition. A naval contingent secured its surrender early in the morning. By the time Army units arrived later in the day, the Stars and Stripes were flying from the city hall, raised there by temporary midshipman George Cabot Lodge, whose father had been doing so much to insure American annexation of the island. The local population gave Miles's forces a wildly enthusiastic welcome. The same day the General issued a proclamation to the residents of the island which made it clear that they were to become subjects of the United States government, and that political independence was not an option. No Aguinaldos would be allowed to surface in Puerto Rico.[20]

American occupation of the entire island was about to become a *fait accompli*. By August 5, the invading army assembled on the island's southern coast numbered almost 15,000. Miles shortly commenced a four-pronged advance on San Juan, with the main body moving without major opposition northeast on the paved main road that linked Ponce and the capital.[21]

Shafter was not as fortunate. Yellow fever was spreading among his troops. He cabled the War Department on August 2 that "at any time a yellow fever epidemic is likely to occur" and urged that his troops be moved as soon as possible. He hoped to send the major part of his army back to the United States.[22] Washington's response was anything but positive. Based on confusing earlier reports, Secretary Alger and his colleagues had believed that, instead of increasing, the number of cases was declining. Because they were unaware of the cause of yellow fever, they also were afraid that bringing the sick troops home would introduce the disease onto the American mainland. Thus, Alger's response was to suggest that Shafter move his troops by train to the hills above Santiago and keep them there until the sickness had run its course.[23]

Alger's recommendation was unrealistic. The railroad that was supposed to transport the sick soldiers to the higher elevations had not operated since it was damaged in the recent fighting. To make things worse, the supposedly dry area where the troops were to go was even rainier than the army's present location. Roosevelt later described it as "a perfect hotbed of malaria." Shafter's response to the War Department was therefore both prompt and alarming: if his army were not promptly shipped back to the United States, "I believe the death rate will be appalling."[24]

Shafter was far from confidant that his superiors would follow his recommendation. Then, after writing Alger, he called a meeting of his top officers, and included Roosevelt. They decided to take their case to the American public. In part because Roosevelt, as a volunteer, would not be subject to the same insubordination risks that they would face, Shafter asked him to prepare a letter describing the medical situation and give it to the press. Roosevelt's superior officer, Leonard Wood, looking out for his friend's future interests, suggested that he merely draft a letter which would be signed by Shafter and all his leading officers.[25] The result was an August 3 "round-robin" letter that expressed the army's plight in the strongest possible language:

"We...are of the unanimous opinion...that the army is disabled by malarial fever to the extent that its efficiency is destroyed, and that it is in a condition to be practically entirely destroyed by an epidemic of yellow fever, which is sure to come in the near future...

"The army must move at once, or perish. As the army can be safely moved now, the persons responsible for preventing such a move will be responsible for the unnecessary loss of many thousands of lives."[26]

Roosevelt wrote Shafter a separate letter expressing similar opinions. Both letters were handed to an Associated Press reporter. Thus, when McKinley, Alger, and the American public opened their newspapers the next morning, they were shocked by reports of an incipient disaster.[27]

It was all unnecessary. Shafter's letter of earlier in the day had had its desired effect. By the close of the day he had been ordered to move to the mainland all troops not required in Cuba. This was followed by instructions to "begin the movement at once, using the ships you have to their limit."[28]

On the morning of August 7 the first transports carrying Shafter's army to the United States left Santiago. The departing troops included the Rough Riders. Their destination was Camp Wikoff, which was being hastily thrown up at the end of the Long Island Railroad on the sandy soil of Montauk Point on Long Island's eastern tip. Its first occupants were more than 4,000 men from Florida, some ill with typhoid and malaria. They arrived to find an encampment in the frantic throes of early construction, with tents yet to be pitched, inadequate water supplies, and freight cars backed up as far as Amagansett, fifteen miles to the west.[29]

At approximately noon on August 15, the troops from Cuba began to arrive at Montauk. A large crowd was there to greet them. When Fighting Joe Wheeler led the soldiers off the ship, there was loud cheering, but it was dwarfed by the shouting that erupted when Roosevelt stepped ashore. Always the publicist, he immediately made his way over to a group of reporters and started to discuss the campaign and his exploits in it. The question the newsmen wanted answered was whether he would run for Governor of New York in the fall, but Roosevelt would have none of that. All he wanted to talk about was his regiment.[30]

The forest of tents and other structures that had been rapidly put up at Camp Wikoff would probably have met the needs of a healthy, well-supplied army. However, the sick and emaciated men who arrived almost simultaneously at Montauk needed much more than shelter. Inadequate transport forced many of the troops to walk the several miles from the landing areas to the camp. Some fell by the wayside, thus delaying disembarkation. Hospital facilities and medical supplies were insufficient, and even the distribution of food was held up by bureaucratic red tape.[31]

Needless to say, the press raised a loud hue and cry. Hearst's *Journal* announced "Starving Men at Montauk Point," and other newspapers sounded similar alarms. The public response was instantaneous, with ladies' aid societies and Red Cross groups hurrying to the rescue. William K. Vanderbilt and other wealthy New Yorkers sent their cooks to Montauk, together with such delicacies as pheasant and champagne, which had only been dreamed of by most of the troops but hardly provided the nourishment they needed.[32]

Fighting Joe Wheeler was put in charge of the camp, and did his best to break the logjams. By August 24, when Alger responded to the criticism by visiting Camp Wikoff, conditions had substantially improved. Alger tried to put the best light possible on the situation, asserting that only 126 men dying out of 22,000 was not a bad record. The public disagreed, and the ensuing reaction against the military would not be helpful in furthering the Administration's expansionist policy.

The Queen Regent and many in the Spanish government were angry with England because she had refused to take sides with Spain against the United States. Nevertheless, Sir Henry Drummond Wolff, the British Ambassador in Madrid, was asked if Britain could take the initiative to end the war on terms reasonably favorable to Spain. On July 16 Salisbury advised Wolff that only one of the warring sides could initiate a successful peace negotiation. "It is obvious," he added, "that the other Powers will not take an active part in a quarrel in which they are not concerned."[33]

Less than a week later the Spanish Government was ready to begin peace discussions. In a letter to McKinley of July 22, sent on behalf of the Queen Regent, the Duc d'Almodovar del Rio suggested that the two countries "might mutually endeavor to find upon which conditions the present struggle could be terminated otherwise than by force of arms." The letter concluded:

"And so do we wish to learn from the President of the United States upon which basis might be established a political status in Cuba, and might be terminated a strife which would continue without reason should both Governments not agree upon the means of pacifying the island."[34]

The letter did not refer to the Philippines or any other Spanish possessions. It was sent to French Ambassador Jules Cambon in Washington for him to deliver to the President. Unfortunately, it arrived in cipher so that the French Embassy had to send it to the nearest Spanish consul, in Montreal, for translation.[35] Finally, on the afternoon of July 26, Cambon brought the translated proposal to McKinley at the White House. When the Ambassador suggested that if the issue of Cuba was resolved there would be no further excuse for hostilities, Secretary Day made it clear that the American reply would not be limited to the future of that island.[36]

The next four days were filled with intense discussions among the President and his advisers. It had long been understood that Cuba would be given its independence. There was also general agreement within the Administration that Spain must cede Puerto Rico and the Ladrone (Mariana) Islands. The only question before the group was the future of the Philippines. The issue was whether to claim possession of the entire group of islands or only the port area of Manila. Three Cabinet members, led by Attorney General John W. Griggs, favored the first course, whereas three others, including Day and Long, advocated the more limited approach. Day's initial draft of the American reply took this position.[37]

McKinley's role was to preside and encourage a full exchange of views as impartially as possible. Yet, as the debate continued, Secretary Day began to sense which way the wind was blowing. After one of the meetings, he noted to the President, "...you didn't put my motion for a naval base." "No, Judge," McKinley answered, with a twinkle in his eye, "I was afraid it would be carried." The President had not yet made up his mind, and was unwilling to abandon the ability to decide later to annex the entire archipelago.[38]

Thus, the note that was delivered to Cambon on the afternoon of the thirtieth required that Spain consent to American occupation of "the city, bay and harbor of Manila pending the conclusion of a treaty of peace which shall determine the control, possession and government of the Philippines." The Ambassador was disturbed by the scope of the American demands, but McKinley and Day were not moved by his strongly expressed objections. Their only concession was to change the reference to "possession" of the Philippines to their "disposition," which Cambon believed would be less threatening. They also agreed to declare an armistice as soon as the Spaniards had agreed to the American terms.[39]

The issue of the Philippines was uppermost in McKinley's mind. His secretary, George Cortelyou, had given him an article in an English journal by John Foreman, a long-term resident of the Islands who was reported to be particularly knowledgeable on conditions there. Foreman had concluded that the Philippine people were incapable of self-government, and that the insurgents were not representative of the population. If Spain were not to retain the Islands, the alternative was either the United States or a European power. England had strongly expressed the view that the Philippines should come under American control, and the ambitious Germans would not challenge the two English-speaking powers.[40]

On the morning of August 3, Cambon saw the President to protest what he considered to be overly harsh American peace terms. He especially questioned the United States's insistence on keeping Puerto Rico. According to his summary of the conversation, he argued that that island "had not for a moment been an element of conflict between Spain and the United States; its inhabitants have remained loyal to the crown..." McKinley, however, "showed himself inflexible, and reiterated that the question of the Philippines was the only one which was not definitely resolved in his mind." This was to be left to the negotiators.[41] McKinley's only concession, made in a reply delivered to Cambon that evening, was that the peace negotiations could take place on neutral ground in Paris instead of Washington, as the Americans preferred. Otherwise, McKinley and his advisers remained firm in their position. Cambon advised the Spanish government to accept the American terms: "I cannot but persist in the idea that all vacillation will further aggravate the severity of the conditions."[42]

Spain, however, was not yet prepared to follow Cambon's advice. On August 9 the French Ambassador delivered to McKinley a letter addressed to the Secretary of State in which the Spaniards complained that the American demand for Puerto Rico "strips us of the very last memory of a glorious past." The communication also noted with displeasure the "indefinite" terms proposed regarding the Philippines. It argued that "the Spanish standard still waves" over Manila and that "the whole archipelago of the Philippines is in the power and under the sovereignty of Spain."[43] McKinley and Secretary of State Day were "visibly annoyed" by the Spanish response. They were especially disturbed by the letter's statement that any agreement to cease hostilities would require the approval of the Spanish Cortes. McKinley refused to "lend myself to entering into these considerations of domestic government." Cambon later reported that his attempts to smooth matters over were proving fruitless and that McKinley "was on the point of terminating the conversation."[44]

At this point Cambon asked "what pledges of sincerity Spain could give." The President's prompt response was that the Americans would draft "a protocol which will set forth the conditions proposed to Spain on the same terms in which I have already formulated them" and calling for the appointment of peace treaty negotiators. Cambon would send the protocol to Madrid for signature by the Spanish Government. McKinley concluded, "Then, but only then, will hostilities be suspended."[45]

The next day, Secretary Day delivered the draft protocol to Cambon, who sent it to Madrid. As expected, it embodied the precise terms of the previously presented American proposal. In his report of the prior day's meeting, Cambon had told the Spanish Government to expect no change in the American position. He added:

"...if it were proper for me to express myself here, however much it may cost me, I would express my conviction that if the Madrid cabinet does not think it possible to accept this document Spain will have nothing more to expect from a conqueror resolved to procure all the profit possible from the advantages it has obtained.[46]

The Spanish Government finally decided to follow Cambon's advice and accept McKinley's proposals. Thus, at 4:23 P.M. on Friday, August 12, with a storm raging outside, Day and Cambon signed four copies of the proto-col, two in English and two in French. The White House ceremony was a private one, witnessed only by McKinley, seven White House and State Department officials and the First Secretary of the French Embassy. After the signing, the President warmly thanked Cambon and France for their efforts in ending the hostilities. He then signed a proclamation ordering an end to the fighting. Word was immediately sent to all American military and naval forces that the war was over.[47]

That the protocol was not signed in public did not detract from the event's importance. As a McKinley biographer wrote after the passage of more than sixty years, it marked

"...the entrance of the United States on the stage of the world. The great challenge of that event was guessed by few then living, and would be resisted by millions in generations yet to come...The passionate young dream of untrammeled independence was not ended, but the period of American isolation had quietly drawn to a close in a shabby room on a rainswept August afternoon of 1898.[48]

Day had not been happy as Secretary of State. He looked forward to returning to the judiciary, where he eventually became a Supreme Court justice. He was therefore pleased when McKinley decided to name him to head the American Peace Commission, with a judgeship to follow. To replace him the President wanted a man with diplomatic experience to face the difficult international issues that loomed on the horizon. On August 13 he picked Ambassador John Hay.[49]

The anglophile Hay had been very happy in England. According to his close friend Henry Adams,

"...he would gladly have found a valid excuse for refusing...His only ambi-tion was to escape annoyance, and no one knew better than he that, at six-ty years of age, sensitive to strain, and even more sensitive to brutality, vindictiveness or betrayal, he took office at cost of life."[51]

Nonetheless, on August 13 Hay cabled McKinley his acceptance of the post because, as Adams observed,

"...old habits of the Civil War left their mark of military drill on every one who lived through it. He shouldered his pack and started for home."[52]

Hay's appointment as Secretary of State was widely viewed as a further potential enhancement of Anglo-American relations. From Washington, on August 16, German Ambassador Holleben wrote to his superiors in Berlin, "Day's leaving the Department means a great loss to us, all the more so because his...successor, Col. John Hay, wholly belongs to the British direction."[52] Hay was sorry to leave England, later writing his wife, "All the fun of my life ended on the platform at Euston." But he realized his liking of England could go only so far. As he wrote his former subordinate, Henry White, a year after assuming his new duties:

"As long as I stay here, no action shall be taken contrary to my conviction that the one indispensable feature of our foreign policy should be a friendly understanding with England. But an alliance must remain, in the present state of things, an unattainable dream."[53]

Looking back on Hay's accomplishments in England against the background of his own family history of two Presidents and an Ambassador to England, each of whom had tried to encourage better relations between the two countries, Adams later wrote ecstatically in his autobiography:

"After two hundred years of stupid and greedy blundering,...the people of England learned their lesson just at the moment when Hay would otherwise have faced a flood of the old anxieties. Hay himself scarcely knew how grateful he should be... He saw only the necessary stages that had led to it, and to him they seemed natural; but to Adams...the sudden appearance of Germany as the grizzly terror which in twenty years effected what Adams had tried for two hundred in vain—frightened England into America's arms,—seemed as melodramatic as any plot of Napoleon the Great. He could only feel the sense of satisfaction at seeing the diplomatic triumph of all his family, since the breed existed, at last realized under his own eyes for the advantage of his oldest and closest ally."[54]

On August 26 McKinley announced the names of the five members of the commission that was to go to Paris to negotiate the peace treaty with Spain. As already announced, Day was to be its chairman. Three of the remaining four members were Republicans—Senators Cushman Davis and William Frye, and New York *Tribune* publisher Whitelaw Reid. Reid, a former American minister to France, was an ardent imperialist. Davis, the chairman of the Foreign Relations Committee, also had expansionist leanings, and Frye, the next ranking Republican member, could be expected to follow suit.[55]

The President wanted the fifth member of the commission to be a well-respected Democrat, and first turned, respectively, to Supreme Court Chief Justice Melville Fuller and Justice (and later Chief Justice) Edward D. White. When both turned McKinley down on the basis that the assignment would be inconsistent with their judicial duties, he turned to Senator George Gray, a conservative Democrat and a minority member of the Foreign Relations Committee. Since Gray had opposed the annexation of Hawaii, he could be expected to take a similar position on the Philippines.[56]

McKinley was criticized for appointing three senators to the commission since their independence would be compromised when they later voted on the treaty they had just negotiated. More important to the President was the other side of this coin—he wanted the treaty ratified and its negotiators would prove persuasive advocates on its behalf.[*] Although the President had announced that he was leaving the question of Philippine annexation to the treaty negotiations, the composition of the American team was a clear indication of the way he was leaning.[57]

In mid-September, the five commissioners were in Washington, meeting with the Cabinet and the President. On September 15 he tendered them a departure dinner at the White House.[58] The lengthy instructions that Mckinley gave them opened with the high-minded platitude that the United States "should be as scrupulous and magnanimous in the concluding settlement as it was just and humane in its original action." They then generally repeated the terms contained in the protocol that ended the fighting. In the case of the Philippines, the instructions stressed "the duties and responsibilities" that the war had brought the United States as well as "the commercial opportunity to which American statesmanship cannot be indifferent." At a minimum, "the United States cannot accept less than the cession in full right and sovereignty of the Island of Luzon." How much more would be required would depend on future events.[59]

---

[*] Woodrow Wilson's failure, twenty years later, to include any senators in the American delegation that negotiated the World War I peace treaty has been viewed as one reason it was not ratified by the Senate.

THIRTEEN

A Pacific Empire For America

O n May 22 Major General Wesley Merritt had left Washington for San Francisco, where he would take command of a force of 10,000 regulars and militia that was gathering in San Francisco for departure to the Philippines. Merritt was a sixty-two-year-old Civil War veteran, who, among other duties, had been superintendent of West Point from 1882 to 1887. He had a reputation for decisiveness and had won McKinley's respect.[1]

Insofar as Merritt's orders involved dealing with the Spanish military forces in the Philippines, they could be reasonably straightforward. There was no American precedent, however, for what was to be done with the Islands after the Spanish had been defeated. The United States had never occupied a territory that it did not intend to become a state at some point in the future.[2]

Drafted with the assistance of the thirty-eight-year-old First Assistant Secretary of State John Bassett Moore, who had already become recognized as a leading authority on international law, the President's instructions to Merritt did not directly confront this question. In addition to defeating the Spanish forces, he was to give "order and security to the islands while in the possession of the United States." How long the occupation would last and for what purpose were not discussed. As for Aguinaldo and his insurgents, although Merritt's role was to include "the establishment of a new political power," there was no suggestion of what it was to be. His only instructions were to make clear to the native population that the American occupation was not intended "to make war upon the people of the Philippines nor upon any party or faction among them."[3]

At this stage of the war, McKinley's interest in acquiring the Philippines was limited. Ambassador Hay had received unofficial feelers for an armistice, and asked Secretary of State Day what was American policy regarding Spain's overseas territories. On June 3, Day replied that "at the present juncture" although the United States should claim Puerto Rico and Spain should surrender Cuba, the Philippines were "to be allowed to remain with Spain except a port and necessary appurtenances, to be selected by the United States." Significantly, he added, "Prolongation of the war may change this materially."[4] Thus, on June 14 he cabled Hay in London that his earlier suggestion to that effect "will probably have to be modified." He added, "it is most difficult without further knowledge to determine as to disposition of Philippine Islands."[5]

The President's perplexity reflected the uncertainty on the subject in the country at large, even among imperialists. In an article in the June issue of the influential *North American Review*, Alabama Senator John T. Morgan referred to the Islands' future as the "question of greatest difficulty." He conceded that "under the laws of nations...we may lawfully govern the Philippines, or any part of them..., if we find it necessary for the welfare of those people, or our own, so to govern them." On the other hand, were the natives not of an inferior race and would not American occupation lead to possible conflict with other countries? Further, "(a) policy of colonization by conquest, or coercion, is repugnant to our national creed."[6] In the same issue, however, American diplomat Truxton Beale argued forcefully for annexation, stressing the Islands' strategic importance:

"Their position controls the channel of the China Sea—the road to Europe. They would flank the communications between any European power and her colonies on the China coast with whom we were at war. Our cruisers, with them as a coaling station, could always infest the narrower passages of the Malay Archipelago...They have, besides, for us one accidental advantage, almost equidistant as they are from both Singapore and Hong Kong, which would always enable us to cooperate with England, our natural ally, to defend the trade that Anglo-Saxon enterprise has won. Their importance cannot be overemphasized."[7]

At a June 14 meeting at Faneuil Hall called by two distinguished Bostonians, Moorfield Story and Gamaliel Bradford, an Anti-Imperialist League was founded. Its president was eighty-year-old George Boutwell, a former Massachusetts senator and Secretary of the Treasury in the Grant Administration. Boutwell's major concern was that American expansion in the Pacific would lead to war with Japan or, more likely, Russia. Others feared that the acquisition of overseas possessions would distract the public from facing political and social needs at home, and might increase the power of the central government at the expense of states rights and personal liberties.[8]

Many prominent persons either joined or supported the goals of the league. They included Presidents Eliot of Harvard, Angell of Michigan, and Jordan of Stanford, Mark Twain, and novelist William Dean Howells.[9] In a Founders' Day address at Lawrenceville School a few days later, former President Cleveland, consistent with his position when he was in the White House, condemned "temptations so dangerous as those which now whisper in our ears alluring words of conquest and expansion and point out to us fields bright with the glory of war."[10]

Influential though these voices of caution were, they would be waging an uphill fight against the popular enthusiasm for an expanding American role in the world that was whetted by the patriotic fever brought on by a victorious war against an allegedly despotic foreign power. These same emotions made annexation of Hawaii inevitable. Speaker Reed had done his best to hold up consideration of the proposal by the House, but by early June the pressures of the majority had become too great. His position was not helped by the fact that most of them were coming from members of his own Republican Party, including the Republican President.[11]

Reed agreed that debate on the annexation resolution would commence on June 10, with the vote to take place on June 15. Knowing that principled argument at this point was futile, Missouri's Democratic Congressman Champ Clark, a future House Speaker, attempted ridicule, drawing the picture of a future "Chinese Senator from Hawaii, with his pigtail hanging down his back" who shall rise from his curule chair and in pigeon English proceed to chop logic with ... Henry Cabot Lodge." It was to no avail, for on the fifteenth the resolution passed by a mostly party line vote of 209 to 91. It was too much for Speaker Reed, who absented himself "on account of illness," at the same time making clear that if he had been present his vote would have been "No."[12]

Although the Spanish forces in the Philippines had proved ineffective thus far, the native population might be another matter. Admiral Dewey, waiting for Merritt's forces to arrive from San Francisco, viewed with evident approval insurgent leader Aguinaldo's success in clearing the Spaniards from Cavite Province and even his formation of a civil government. Former United States Consul Williams was not so easily deluded. Believing that the Philippines should become part of the United States, he saw Aguinaldo as a kind of Trojan horse that the Americans had gullibly brought into the Islands. He was therefore pleased when Secretary Day wrote him on June 16:

"This Government has known the Philippine insurgents only as discontented and rebellious subjects of Spain and is not acquainted with their purposes...The United States is entering upon the occupation of the islands as a result of its military conquest,...and will expect from the inhabitants...that obedience which will be lawfully due from them." [13]

Two days later, at Cavite, Aguinaldo issued a declaration of independence and made clear his desire that the Islands and its people should be free from foreign powers. With Merritt and his army of occupation about to arrive in Manila Bay, a confrontation appeared likely. [14]

The Spanish Government was not yet ready to give up possession of the Philippines. On June 16 a task force under Admiral Manuel de la Camara left Cadiz for the Islands, steaming east through the Mediterranean to the Suez Canal. It consisted of one large battleship, three cruisers, three destroyers, and four colliers, together with two transports carrying 4,000 troops. [15]

When he learned of Camara's departure, William Randolph Hearst decided to take this aspect of the war into his own hands. He cabled a European representative of the *Journal* to

"...make preparations so that...we can buy some big English steamer at the eastern end of the Mediterranean and take her to some part of the Suez Canal where we can then sink her and obstruct the passage of the Spanish warships." [16]

Fortunately, nothing came of the suggestion.

On June 25 Camara's squadron arrived at Port Said and requested coal for its long voyage down the Red Sea and across the Indian Ocean. It was refused, on the basis that a neutral power could provide only enough fuel to permit belligerent ships to reach a home port. Meanwhile the deputy American Consul-General in Cairo, apprised of Camara's imminent arrival, had placed a lien on the coal supply. [17]

On June 29 Camara was told he must leave Port Said. The balance of his story is quickly told. His coaling efforts in the Eastern Mediterranean were beset by rough seas, and were largely unsuccessful. By July 5 he concluded that his three destroyers could not make the trip east, and sent them back to Spain. On July 8, after proceeding through the Suez Canal into the Red Sea, but with the Philippines still 6,300 miles away, he received orders to return to Spain. As an American historian wrote:

"The one wise order given was to direct his return home. Spain got off cheaply with the expenditure of the coal used and of the $264,000 which she paid for the useless promenade to and from through the Suez Canal."[18]

<hr />

The German Government would have been happy if Spain had remained in the Philippines. She was a weak power and no threat to Germany. Given the American victory at Manila Bay, however, this did not seem to be a likely alternative. The United States might be acceptable, but her history argued against a permanent American occupation of the islands. This left a major European power as the only long-term possibility, and in that event Germany should play a role at least as great as England.[19]

The arrival of the *Kaiser* late on June 18 meant that there were five German naval vessels in Manila Bay—four warships and one relief transport. Their commander, Vice-Admiral Otto von Diedrichs, had entered the bay six days earlier on his flagship, the *Kaiserin Augusta*. In a courtesy call on Diedrichs, Dewey commented that the size of the German fleet seemed excessive in light of the limited German commercial interests in the Philippines. The German officer snapped his heels together in true Prussian style and curtly replied, "I am here by order of the Kaiser, sir!"[20]

Diedrichs and his officers made no secret of their sympathy with the Spaniards, visiting and fraternizing with the Spanish troops. The German commander and the Spanish Captain General exchanged visits, and the Germans often acted as if they, rather than the Americans, controlled the Bay. The general view in Manila, no doubt in part the product of wishful thinking, was that Germany would help Spain retain at least part of the Islands.[21] At the same time, elements of the German press were advancing the idea that Germany was in the Philippines to stay, with the *Berlin Marine Politische Correspondenz* contending on June 17:

"For the same reasons which justified us in demanding the cession of a harbor from China, we must claim one from the 'Republic of the Philippines' which to all appearances will be the issue of the present affairs."[22]

On June 4 the first contingent of Merritt's forces, approximately 2,500 men and officers under Brigadier General Thomas Anderson, left Honolulu accompanied by a strong naval escort. At dawn on June 20, the expedition anchored off Agana, the capital of Guam, 3,337 miles west of Oahu. The protected cruiser *Charleston*, under Captain Henry Glass, entered the harbor unopposed. It shelled the shore fortifications, but there was no return fire. The small group of Spaniards that put out from shore in a small boat told the Americans that no ships had arrived from the outer world since April 14. The Spaniards were thus unaware that the United States and Spain were at war. Taking the garrison aboard as prisoners, the Americans continued on their westward course, leaving the Stars and Stripes flying over the island.[23] It was the United States's first Pacific possession and, except for a brief occupation by the Japanese after Pearl Harbor, one that she would keep throughout the upcoming century.

On June 30, Merritt joined Dewey. As soon as his full complement arrived, the Americans would be able to attack Manila and take over the surrounding territory. They would have to reckon with Aguinaldo and his insurgents, however.[24]

As the summer progressed, the debate over United States policy toward the Spanish colonies was intensifying. On August 26, in a speech delivered at Saratoga, American Federation of Labor President Samuel Gompers argued that annexation of the Philippines would likely result in cheap oriental labor flooding the United States and competing with domestic workers, a danger that would also be created by the annexation of Hawaii. Gompers also feared that the occupation of overseas territories might lead to the creation of a large standing army, which the government could use for strike breaking, such as had occurred with the Pullman strike of 1894.[25]

From the other end of the economic spectrum, Andrew Carnegie was providing strong financial aid and vocal support to the anti-imperialist movement. He argued that American occupation of the Philippines would likely lead to war against the native population. Thus, a war fought to free the people of one island would lead to the oppression of people on another island. Carnegie also contended that imperialism would divert American energy from industrial development at home and would make it more difficult for the United States to gain respect in the world on the basis that it was different from the other major powers.[26]

These and other like-minded persons were unlikely to carry the day. Perhaps because of imperialism's patriotic trappings, a large number of union members did not agree with Gompers on the issue. Likewise, much of the business community hoped that annexation of the Philippines would provide a potential market for American goods and a stepping stone to customers on the Asian mainland. This pressure was not only coming from interests on the West Coast, where the potential commercial benefit was obvious. Southern business men, for example, saw occupation of the Islands as a boon to expanded sales of American cotton goods in China.[27]

Indeed, in an alliance of mutual convenience between God and Mammon, religious groups also favored American expansion. Protestant leaders in particular saw the conquest of Spain's overseas possessions as an excellent opportunity for missionary activities in lands from which they had largely been barred under Spanish rule. The Philippines also could be a gateway to China, which, according to the Presbyterian journal *Interior* of June 30, "as everyone perceives, is on the eve of the most fateful crisis." A week earlier, *Interior* articulated another widely held reason why the United States should not give up the conquered territories:

"The work of emancipation has providentially been thrust upon us. The question is, shall we back out of, and back down from, our responsibility and duty, and selfishly abandon peoples who are holding up their manacled hands to us and praying us not to desert them?"[28]

On July 6, the Senate debate on the Hawaii annexation resolution, which had commenced on June 20, finally came to an end. The senators wanted to vote and adjourn to escape the heat of a pre-air-conditioning Washington summer.[29]

Opposition came primarily from Democrats and Populists who feared that annexation of Hawaii would be a first move toward worldwide expansion. Thus, Louisiana Senator Caffery asked:

"Is not this but the opening of a grand avenue of conquest and of power? The Philippines next. Part of Asia next. What will be the limits? The Hawaiian scheme is but the entering wedge that cleaves a way open for empire."[30]

Despite attempts from Senators such as George F. Hoar of Massachusetts

to show that Hawaii could be viewed differently from the Spanish possessions, Caffery was right. The expansionist fever was too powerful. It had
infected even Senator Teller, whose amendment had promised independence for Cuba. That Colorado senator was now announcing that wherever the Stars and Stripes flew "by right of conquest or by the consent of
the people," it should remain;

"...and the party or the men who propose to take it down will reckon with
the great body of the American people, who believe that it is the best flag
and the best Government, better calculated to bring peace and prosperity
to men than any other flag and Government under the sky."[31]

It was no surprise that the annexation resolution passed by the strong
majority of 42 to 21. McKinley signed it on July 17 and the Navy Department ordered the cruiser *Philadelphia* to take possession of the islands.
The United States had acquired its first overseas territory.[32]

After approving Hawaiian annexation, Congress adjourned. It would
not return until after the fall elections. Although the Democratic members had fully supported every measure for prosecuting the war, the
McKinley Administration was receiving most of the credit for the American victories. Those triumphs also were helping promote support for
overseas expansion which, at least in the case of Hawaii, many Democrats opposed. All this could only help the Republicans.

On June 21 Foreign Minister Bülow sent word to the Kaiser that the
Spanish Government had proposed to him that Manila should be turned
over to the commanders of the neutral forces then in Manila Bay. Similar approaches reportedly had also been made to France and Russia,
where they were coolly received. The proposal apparently went no
further.[33] However, on July 4, the London *Times* Berlin correspondent
reported "on the best authority" that Germany, France, and Russia had
agreed that when the war was over "the whole Philippine question will
be submitted to an international congress."[34]

Meanwhile Holstein's fertile brain was calculating whether the
United States could be drawn away from England and toward Germany.
His goal was to convince the Americans they had more to gain from an
alliance with Germany than with the British even though at the same
time, the Kaiser and his ministers continued their strong interest in an
increasing German role in the Far East, including the Philippines.[35]

On July 1 Holstein had asked Ambassador Holleben in Washington to ascertain the strength of support in the United States for Philippine annexation, together with anything he could learn as to what the McKinley Administration expected England would demand for its support in the matter. On July 4, Holleben responded that he could offer no help, since the Americans had not yet decided what they wanted to do with Spain's Pacific colonies. He added that anti-German feeling in the United States was so strong that neither the Administration nor the congressional leadership would be likely to take any kind of public stand that supported Germany.[36]

From London, Ambassador Hatzfeldt had suggested that American Ambassador to Germany Andrew White might be able to shed light on future United States policy in the Far East. White was an outspoken proponent of closer American-German relations. In a speech in Leipzig on July 4, he had predicted that the apparent hostility between the two countries was only temporary. Accordingly, on July 6, Foreign Under Secretary Baron Oswald von Richtofen had a lengthy discussion with White, during which the Ambassador expressed his personal opposition to Philippine annexation. Richtofen left the meeting with the impression that this view might eventually prevail in Washington.[37]

Meanwhile, the Americans were becoming increasingly irritated by the large German naval force in Manila Bay. Thus, later in the week, the London *Times* reported from Hong Kong, "The Germans are fraternizing with the Spaniards, and German officers are often seen in the Spanish trenches."[38]

Some days earlier, British Captain Chichester had supported the American position that any neutral naval vessel entering the harbor should first report to Dewey and satisfy him as to its intentions. On July 9, when the German cruiser *Cormoran* failed to do so, Dewey sent the *McCulloch* to board the German ship. When the *Cormoran* apparently paid no attention to the *McCulloch*'s signal, the *McCulloch* fired a shot across the *Cormoran*'s bow. At this point the Germans complied with the American order.[39]

The next day, Diedrichs sent an officer to Dewey to complain about the *McCulloch*'s actions as well as other irritants. After listening to the German officer for a while, the naturally hot-tempered Dewey, in a voice of increasing pitch and intensity that could be heard in the officers' quarters below, exclaimed, according to the official German report:

"Why, I shall stop each vessel whatever may be her colors! And if she does not stop I shall fire at her! And that means war, do you know, Sir? And I tell you if Germany wants war, all right, we are ready. With the English I have not the slightest difficulty, they always communicate with me..."[40]

According to an American officer who overheard the conversation. Dewey concluded the interview by shouting:

"If the German Government has decided to make war on the United States, or has any intention of making war, and has so informed your Admiral, it is his duty to let me know."

Dewey then reportedly added:

"But whether he intends to fight or not, I am ready."[41]

By the next day Dewey had cooled off. The German failure to follow the rules of naval blockade was generally viewed as the result of inexperience rather than enmity toward the United States. In any event, Dewey reported no further interference.[42]

From London, Ambassador Hay continued to warn Washington of German aspirations in the Pacific. In mid-July Hatzfeldt had suggested to Hay that the United States should be willing to cede to Germany "a few coaling stations" and recognition of her claim to the Caroline Islands in return for German acceptance of American annexation of Hawaii. As Hay reported the conversation to a journalist, the German Ambassador had contemptuously requested the American: "You had so many islands; why could you not give us one." Hay's emphatic response was: "Not an island—not one!"[43]

Hay's attitude towards Germany was undoubtedly colored by additional reports he was receiving from Spring-Rice in Berlin. Shortly after the Hatzfeldt interview, Hay received a letter from Spring-Rice and passed on its substance, with evident approval, to Lodge:

"The jealousy and animosity felt towards us in Germany is something which can hardly be exaggerated... They hate us in France, but French hate is a straw fire compared to German. And France had nothing to fear from us while the Vaterland is all on fire with greed, and terror of us. They want the Philippines, the Carolines, and Samoa—they want to get into our markets and keep us out of theirs.

"There is in the German mind, something monstrous in the thought that war should take place anywhere and they not profit by it."[44]

Not surprisingly, the view of the matter from the German capital was somewhat different. Although the Government would have liked to occupy some part of the Philippines, it was not prepared to fight if the United States strongly asserted its right of annexation by conquest. On the other hand, if the McKinley Administration decided to occupy only part of the archipelago, Germany wanted to share the rest of the spoils.[45]

That possibility was appearing less and less likely as July drew to a close. Nevertheless, perhaps unwittingly, Ambassador White continued to encourage this line of thinking. To that end, in a personal capacity, on July 30 he suggested to Under Secretary Richtofen that the impression of Germany in the United States would be greatly improved if the German squadron in Manila Bay could be moved about from time to time, presumably by sailing occasionally to non-Philippine locations. When Richtofen reported his conversation to Bülow, the Foreign Minister, always the sycophant when the Kaiser was concerned, instructed his assistant to tell White that his proposal should not be made formally, since it would touch William on a "tender spot." When Richtofen did so, the American Ambassador at once backed off and told the German diplomat to ignore his earlier suggestion. Thus, Diedrichs was permitted to remain in a position which gave the American public the impression that his purpose was to thwart Dewey and Merritt, whereas the German Government in fact was losing hope that it could make major inroads in the Philippines.[46] Meanwhile McKinley's views on the future of the Spanish colonies were hardening. On July 13 he reportedly said to the publisher of the New York *Sun*:

"We will first take the Philippines, the Ladrones, the Carolines and Puerto Rico. Then when we have possession undisputed, we will look them all over at our leisure and do what seems wisest. Personally, I am in favor of keeping Luzon and fortifying Manila...I think the United States possessed of all Spain's colonies would do well to act with great magnanimity and show European governments the lofty spirit that guides us. Apart from that idea I favor the general principle of holding on to what we got."[47]

On July 17 a second body of United States troops, 3,500 strong, arrived in Manila Bay. The Americans were now in a position to attack Manila itself if its defenders were unwilling to surrender. The major problem was that Aguinaldo's insurgents were stationed between the Americans and the city. They were showing no signs of moving, or otherwise cooperating with the invaders. On July 22 the increasingly frustrated American commander, General Anderson, wrote Aguinaldo that "your fine intellect must perceive... that I cannot recognize your civil authority."[48]

Auginaldo's response to Anderson's appeal was to protest against the Americans' landing, without written notice to his "Government," in places already occupied by the insurgents. Dewey, who had brought Aguinaldo to the Philippines and initially had encouraged him, cabled Washington on July 26 that the rebel leader "has become aggressive and even threatening towards our Army." Fortunately for the Americans, Merritt had arrived the day before with the third army contingent, swelling the ranks of the attacking force to nearly 11,000 men. Merritt decided that he needed no rebel assistance in taking Manila, and put a temporary end to all correspondence with Aguinaldo.[49]

In the days that followed, relations between Aguinaldo and the American forces became increasingly strained. On August 1 the Filipino leader and his officers had signed a declaration of independence of the "Philippine Republic." He wrote former American Consul Williams, whom he regarded as his friend, that he recognized that annexation by the United States might bring benefits to his fellow islanders, but asking, "Will my people believe it?" He asked Williams "to entreat the Government at Washington to recognize the revolutionary government of the Filipinos." Not having received a favorable answer, on August 6 he published the independence declaration as well as an appeal to other countries to recognize his "government."[50]

Meanwhile, informal negotiations between Dewey and the Spanish commander General Firmin Jaudenes for the surrender of Manila had been taking place through the Belgian Consul Edouard André. A major difficulty was how to effect a peaceful capitulation of the city without an attack by Aguinaldo's Filipinos. The arrival on July 31 of 4,400 additional troops under General Arthur MacArthur[*] and their deployment on shore gave the Americans added assurance that they could take Manila and at the same time keep Aguinaldo at bay.[51]

A certain amount of stage management was required to fool the

---

[*] The father of World War II Philippine defender and liberator Douglas MacArthur.

insurgents and also to satisfy Spanish honor. The first step was the delivery on August 7 of a letter to Jaudenes from Merritt and Dewey stating that "operations of the land and naval forces of the United States against the defenses of Manila may begin at any time after the expiration of forty-eight hours...or sooner if made necessary by an attack on your part." The letter was sent to afford the Spaniards "an opportunity to remove all non-combatants from the city." In a reply delivered the same day and closing, "Very respectfully, and kissing the hands of your excellencies," Jaudenes wrote "that finding myself surrounded by insurrectionary forces, I am without place of refuge for the increased number of wounded, sick, women, and children who are now lodged within the walls."[52]

The American attack on Manila initially had been scheduled for August 10, but since Merritt's troops were not yet ready, it was deferred until the thirteenth. Although the peace protocol had just been signed in Washington, because the telegraph wires were still cut, it would be three days before Dewey and Merritt would receive word of the truce by steamer from Hong Kong.[53]

The attack was to be preceded by a naval shelling of the flank of the Spanish lines that was closest to the bay.[54] At 8:45 A.M Dewey's ships began to steam to their stations. At about the same time, the two English warships under Captain Chichester moved to a position between Dewey and the German squadron, which had failed to honor Dewey's suggestion of four days earlier that all foreign vessels should move out of range of the forthcoming attack. Chichester also ordered the *Immortalite*'s guard paraded as Dewey's ships passed by and its band to play his favorite march, "Under the Double Eagle." These German and British actions led to the surmise that Diedrichs was putting his ships in a position to interfere with Dewey's bombardment and that the British were signaling that any attack on the Americans would also involve Chichester's ships. Although it is likely that Diedrichs did not intend to cause trouble, the belief that he did, based on Dewey's report of the day's activities, did nothing to further amicable United States-German relations. At the same time, Chichester's actions led the Americans to believe that the English would support them in case of trouble.[55]

At 9:35, Dewey's ships commenced firing. As expected, the Spanish guns remained silent. An hour later, the bombardment stopped and the land forces commenced their advance. Although there was not supposed to be any fighting, not all the American soldiers were aware of this understanding between the United States and Spanish commanders. Neither were Aguinaldo's insurgents, who tried to participate in the attack. Thus, particularly on the right of the advance, there was shooting by both attackers and defenders. After a little more than an hour, however, white flags were raised and the firing gradually ceased. Sadly, what was supposed to be a bloodless attack had resulted in six American dead and forty-three wounded.[56]

Another casualty was American relations with the insurgents. Neither the Americans nor the Spanish wanted them in Manila. However, it took a determined effort by Merritt's forces to secure that result, including the planting of artillery to command Aguinaldo's positions. The insurgent commander strongly protested, but soon recognized that the Americans had the upper hand and did not challenge Merritt's forces. The rebuff rankled, however, and the rebel leader was prepared to fight the Americans when the odds were more favorable.[57]

Before the day was over, Diedrichs took another step that would irritate the Americans. Spanish General Augustín had been removed as Governor General of the Philippines a few days earlier. He had escaped from Manila and boarded the German cruiser *Kaiserin Augusta*. As soon as the city had surrendered, the ship left for Hong Kong, without Dewey's approval and apparently to convey word of the battle before Dewey could do so. When the cruiser reached Hong Kong, its officers exacerbated the situation even further by trying to keep the American victory secret from the British. The American and British press took umbrage, and the German newspapers, already openly hostile to the United States, responded in kind. This was especially unfortunate, since by now the Kaiser and his ministers had generally conceded the inevitability of American annexation of the Philippines.[58]

On August 15 Diedrichs received orders, apparently issued at his suggestion, to leave the Philippines for Java, where he would take part in the coronation ceremonies honoring the new Dutch Queen Wilhelmina. On his departure, the Kaiser congratulated him on the manner in which he represented German interests in the islands. In this instance, a historian may legitimately excuse the Emperor on the basis that he was half the globe away. In fact, giving Diedrich's actions their most favorable interpretation, he clearly did German-American relations no good. The contrast with the friendly attitude manifested by Chichester and his fellow officers and men made the German gaffes appear even more serious.[59]

———⚫———

Just as Germany was despairing of obtaining any Spanish possession, an opportunity presented itself. The United States decided that with the exception of Guam, it had no interest in acquiring any of the Ladrones (now the Marianas) and the Carolines. Secretary of State Hay advised a surprised Ambassador Holleben that if Germany wanted to acquire these islands from Spain, there would be no American objection. Although Germany would obtain little economic or strategic value from their ownership, it would prevent the Kaiser and his government from losing face. Accordingly, on September 10, the Germans agreed to buy the islands from Spain.[60]

The United States would later rue the day it had made this concession. After World War I, Japan acquired the islands as a protectorate, and used them as naval bases against the United States after Pearl Harbor.

=—◦)◦(◦—=

Although Japan's official position was friendly, American annexation of the Philippines and Hawaii had placed the two countries on a potentially explosive collision course. Only forty years after United States Commodore Matthew Perry had opened Japanese ports to Western trade, her victory in the 1894-1895 Sino-Japanese War initiated her efforts to become a major power on the Asian mainland and the Western Pacific. United States acquisition of the Philippines, however, would block Japanese expansion south from Taiwan, one of the spoils of the victory over China.[61]

In the mid-1890s, some Japanese had hoped for eventual acquisition of Hawaii, where the 20,000 Japanese inhabitants easily outnumbered the white residents. Prior to the American occupation of the islands, the Japanese cruiser *Naniwa* had occasionally visited Honolulu to indicate a concern for them. United States's awareness of Japan's interest was an important reason for the McKinley Administration's push for annexation. Although the Japanese Government viewed the American acquisition with deep concern, it decided that a protest would be ineffective and that Japanese interests in Hawaii were not worth war.[62]

These apparent frustrations of future Japanese expansion were not the only seeds of the confrontation that would eventually lead to war. Profound cultural and racial difference were also involved. Further, although most Americans were impressed by Japan's rapid emergence as a major industrial and military power, the white supremacy ethos that permeated Western culture at the time relegated even the Japanese to "lesser breed" status. The American failure to grant Japanese residents equal status with the white population of both island territories would anger Japan in the coming decades.

On September 15 a Philippine congress convened in the market town of Malalos, about thirty miles north of Manila. Its ninety-five members included leading Filipino intellectuals and businessmen. Dressed in a swallowtail coat, Aguinaldo opened the first session with a short statement that proclaimed that the islands belonged to the Filipinos and no one else. The next day, the congress formally ratified his declaration of independence.[63]

By now Aguinaldo's forces controlled all of Luzon outside of Manila and Cavite. On September 12, a *New York Times* correspondent reported from Manila that they "have recently captured several thousand rifles, some cannon, a large quantity of ammunition, and several small armed steamers." He added that they had "annihilated their every claim to be considered in any respect as the allies of the Americans."[64]

Until December, matters remained relatively calm. At that point, the news that the United States would acquire the Philippines from Spain was greeted with open hostility by Aguinaldo and his allies. One of their newspapers, the *Independencia*, announced that the Filipinos would "decline to permit their homes to be bought and sold like merchandise." Spain could not cede the archipelago "because it was never hers."[65]

The threat of war between the insurgents and General Elwell Otis's American army rapidly increased. Conservative Filipinos who had joined with the insurgents against Spain but were willing to accept American rule could no longer influence Aguinaldo and his advisors.[66] Indeed, Aguinaldo himself was losing control to the military and radical elements who favored war even if it would lead to certain defeat.[67]

As of mid-December, Iloilo, the chief port and capital of the important southern island of Panay, was still occupied by a Spanish contingent. It was hard pressed by the insurgents, however. Otis and Dewey recommended prompt intervention before the Spaniards abandoned the city. Accordingly, on December 21, McKinley ordered Otis "to send necessary troops to Iloilo to preserve the peace and protect life and property." Then, recognizing the tightrope on which the Americans were walking, the President added:

"It is most important that there should be no conflict with the insurgents. Be conciliatory but firm."[68]

But the United States could no longer delay its decision on what to do with the insurgents. On December 26, before American troops had reached Iloilo, the Spanish garrison had evacuated the city and Aguinaldo's forces took over.[69] Otis's problem was not confined to Iloilo. On December 26 he was instructed, now that the peace treaty had been signed, to extend his military government "with all possible dispatch to the whole of the ceded territory." He was "to announce and proclaim in the most public manner that we come, not as invaders or conquerors, but as friends."[70]

On December 28 Otis received more specific instructions—"to occupy all strategic points in the islands before the insurgents get possession of them." It was too late. On December 30 he reluctantly replied:

"All military stations, outside Luzon, with exception Zamboanga, turned over by Spaniards to inhabitants, who may be denominated insurgents, with more or less hostility to the United States."

Indeed, several thousand of Aguinaldo's forces remained outside Manila. In the city itself there were "large numbers of sympathizers who have threatened uprising."[71] It was therefore not surprising that Under Secretary of State Alvey Adee wrote on December 30:

"Since the treaty of peace was signed, Aguinaldo is virtually at war with the United States...I strongly favor immediate coercive action against Aguinaldo as a disturber of *our* peace."[72]

FOURTEEN

"I Did What I Did For The Good Of The Country"

The French Army wasted no time in following up on the Zola decision. For his role in reopening the Dreyfus case and testifying for Zola, Colonel Picquart was promptly discharged because of "grave misdeeds while in service" and was denied his pension.[1] On March 5 he engaged Major Henry in a duel apparently resulting from the Zola trial. It was fought with swords at the Riding School of the Military Academy. Henry was slightly wounded in the wrist and arm, while Picquart apparently was untouched.[2]

The duel was a relatively insignificant manifestation of the deep divisions in French life created by l'Affaire. The issue had become much broader than Dreyfus's personal fate. To a large and diverse body of liberal intellectuals, Zola's involvement and the cover up they believed had occurred provided a basis for an attack on the established order. They included well-recognized figures like Claude Monet and the writer Anatole France, who had always worshiped the Army but now sensed that a conspiracy against truth was at work there. Mostly, however, the group consisted of younger men like Marcel Proust, as well as social activists and others with concerns for individual rights.[3] Not all intellectuals were pro-Dreyfus, however, and in what one writer has described as "a kind of class struggle," many writers supported the Army.[4]

By spring there was gloom in the Dreyfus camp. There had been no legislative initiative for a reopening of the case. Although one might have expected politicians of the left to use the case as a basis to attack the establishment, Jean Jaurés was the only Socialist deputy to fight for revision. The primary reason for this silence apparently was the anti-Semitism which had infected the working classes as widely as the aristocracy. It had been three years since Dreyfus had arrived on Devil's Island, and the end was nowhere in sight.[5]

On April 2 an appeals court quashed Zola's February conviction on technical grounds after the eighty-year-old public prosecutor had virtually conceded his case when he denounced anti-Semitism and asserted the revisionists were "the honor of the country." The Army, however, would not be put down so easily. Zola was immediately sued for slander over his statement in *J'Accuse* that Esterhazy's court-martial acquittal was "a supreme offense to all truth and justice..." The Government brought the suit in a court that would sit at Versailles, where the large military garrison stationed there could be expected to intimidate the judge and terrorize Zola.[6]

The hearing on May 23 did not proceed as planned. Zola avoided the mob that had gathered at the Versailles train station to hurl insults at him by driving by automobile from the suburb of Saint-Cloud, where he had spent the prior night at a friend's house. Then, as soon as the case was called, Zola's lawyer, Fernand Labori, questioned the court's competence to hear a case involving a misdemeanor that took place outside its jurisdiction. When the judge, who showed open bias against the defendant, denied Labori's motion, the lawyer immediately filed an appeal. This stayed the proceeding. Thus, after only an hour and a quarter, Zola and his coterie emerged from the court into a waiting automobile. It cut through a mob that pelted it with stones and drove back to Paris.[7]

The May elections to the Chamber of Deputies had apparently resulted in little change in the makeup of that body. The number of Centrists was the same at 270, and the Méline government remained in power. There was increasing concern, however, among many Centrists over what seemed to be increasing efforts from the right, especially the military and the Church, which could pose a threat to the future of the Republic. Thus, when Henri Brisson, a distinguished anticlerical republican deputy, prompted two Radical members to move that in the future the Chamber would approve "solely policies based on a strictly Republican majority," the motion was passed over Méline's strong opposition by a 295 to 246 vote. The Center, which was Méline's power base, had split, and on June 14 he was forced to resign. President Faure had the thankless task of trying to form a new Government.[8]

On June 27 Brisson was named to head the new Government. Although the Dreyfus camp had hoped that this would lead to a reopening of the case, their hopes were cruelly dashed when he appointed, as the new Minister of War, Godefroy Cavaignac. As strong a nationalist as he was a republican, Cavaignac was convinced of Dreyfus's guilt, and had made himself a leader of the anti-revision forces. His reputation as a man of honor who was scrupulously fair gave his words particular weight. He was also self-confident and ambitious, with the presidency of France his long term goal.[9]

On June 28 Cavaignac announced that he wanted to bring an end to the Dreyfus controversy. He immediately asked for the "secret file" so that it could be examined by two army officers in whom he had complete trust. He hoped that their thorough review would uncover material that would establish Dreyfus's guilt so conclusively as to silence even the captain's most vociferous supporters.[10]

Those who knew of the forgeries that the file contained were deeply disturbed. They feared that Cavaignac's investigators would stumble upon the truth and, with the rectitude that was his trademark, he would feel himself obligated to expose the forgers and their accomplices. Army Chief of Staff de Boisdeffre and his deputy, General Gonse, did their best first to discourage Cavaignac from reviewing such a large file. Failing that, they tried to steer his investigation into less dangerous channels. It was to no avail; Cavaignac would do things his own way. Esterhazy, in particular, started to panic, and feeling that if necessary he would be made a sacrificial scapegoat, threatened to commit suicide and thus expose his supposed friends.[11]

In pursuit of his efforts to establish Dreyfus's guilt once and for all, Cavaignac planned to make a "major address" in the Chamber of Deputies on July 7. In preparation, he reviewed a report of an alleged confession by Dreyfus that had been included in the dossier that had been prepared to prove his guilt. After spreading out the "secret file" and explaining it with an officer's assistance to Prime Minister Brisson and several other ministers, he was authorized to go ahead with his address.[12]

At the outset of Cavaignac's speech he created a sensation by contending that Esterhazy had collaborated with Dreyfus and would be "stricken tomorrow with the punishment he deserves." This did not exonerate Dreyfus, however, whose guilt he would now prove.[13] To that end, Cavaignac brought out three letters from the "secret file," including one of Henry's forgeries, and the statement of Dreyfus's alleged confession. He announced with all the fervor he could summon: "I have assessed the material authenticity and the moral authenticity" of the documents and then summarized the papers as he understood them. He closed by urging all Frenchmen "to come together tomorrow to proclaim that the Army which is their pride and their hope is not only mighty with its own strength...is not only strong with the nation's trust, but strong as well in the justice of the acts that it has accomplished." Cavaignac left the rostrum to a standing ovation. With only a few abstentions, the Chamber voted unanimously to post the text of his speech outside every town hall in France.[14]

To most of the Dreyfusards, Cavaignac's speech seemed the final blow. Here was a man, who, whatever were his faults, was universally conceded to be fair and honest. If he would not see the truth, who would? Léon Blum had been sitting with Dreyfus's brother Mathieu and another Dreyfus supporter when they heard the news of the speech. Blum later described their feelings:

"We were silent, immobile. Were we crying? Did the oppression constrain our tears? I search in vain for words to convey that burden of despondency, consternation, and mourning."[15]

At this point Jean Jaurès joined the group. An already famous thirty-nine-year-old Socialist member of the Chamber from the south of France, Jaurès was intelligent, energetic, and famed for his eloquence. Even his political opponents would flock to hear him speak. A guest at a dinner party where he was holding forth on a scientific subject reported: "The women forgot to re-powder their faces, the men to smoke, the servants to go in search of their own supper."[16]

Jaurès loved a good fight, and today he was even more excited than usual. His friends should not be discouraged for

"...now, now for the first time we are certain of victory! Méline was invulnerable because he said nothing. Cavaignac talks, so he will be beaten...Now Cavaignac has named the documents and I, yes I, tell you they are false...They are forgeries...I am certain of it and will prove it. The forgers have come out of their holes; we'll have them by the throat."[17]

Jaurès was as good as his word. The next day, July 8, *La Petite République* published an open letter from him to Cavaignac, which, together with later letters on this subject, were titled "*Les Preuses (The Proofs)*." It opened:

"Yesterday in the Chamber you performed both a useful labor and a criminal labor. You performed a useful labor in presenting to the country a part of the dossier."

The letter continued with a detailed analysis of the supposed proof of Dreyfus's guilt and the War Minister's failure to examine all the evidence. Thus,

"The 1896 document contains the crudest errors. The forger wanted to imitate a foreigner's style, took delight in fabricating the most pitiful French."

Jaurès closed:

"Have you ever thought about these things? Have you taken the time to study and compare. No, for what you needed was an immediate success, a success on the tribune and with public opinion... Be careful, though: law, justice, and truth cannot always be violated with impunity. The acclamations will pass; the truth will remain."[18]

Cavaignac's speech had other repercussions. On July 9 Picquart wrote Prime Minister Brisson that until then he had not felt free to comment "...on the subject of the secret documents on which it has been claimed to base Dreyfus's guilt." He then stated:

"Since the minister of war has quoted from the tribune of the Chamber of Deputies three of those documents, I consider it a duty to inform you that I am in a position to establish before any competent jurisdiction that the two documents dated 1894 cannot be applied to Dreyfus and that the one dated 1896 has every appearance of being a forgery. It will then appear that the good faith of the minister of war has been caught unawares."[19]

As Picquart anticipated, Cavaignac was furious. On July 12 he sought the colonel's arrest on the charge of divulging secret materials. The next day Picquart was incarcerated in the La Santé Prison.[20]

Esterhazy already occupied a cell in the same building. His nephew, Christian, had previously given him money to be invested, supposedly with the Rothschilds. When Esterhazy never returned the money and Christian discovered that his uncle had duped him, he decided to expose him. To the Dreyfusard lawyer Fernand Labori he admitted his role the previous fall as a go-between between his uncle and du Paty de Clam. He provided Labori with all available information and incriminating documents. Then, based on his recollection that one of the telegrams that had sent Picquart to Tunisia had been written by Esterhazy's current mistress Mlle. Marguerite Pays, Labori sent her flowers from an alleged admirer. The handwriting on her note of profuse thanks and on the telegraph form was the same.[21]

Examining Magistrate Paul Bertulus was already investigating Picquart's charges that the Tunisian telegrams were forgeries. When Labori contrived to have Esterhazy's testimony and documents brought before the judge, Bertulus immediately advised the public prosecutor that he would have both Esterhazy and his mistress arrested for swindling and forgery. He did so on the evening of July 12. The military establishment was stunned. Boisdeffre suddenly became ill and went on leave. Gonse followed suit several days later.[22]

At this point, Cavaignac decided that someone from the War Office should examine Esterhazy's papers. Before going on leave, Gonse suggested Henry, and the War Minister, having no inkling of the major's involvement in the coverup, readily agreed.[23] On July 18 Henry met with Judge Bertulus, who already knew him, and fully described the situation to him, including the charges that likely would be pressed against Esterhazy and du Paty de Clam. During their conversation, Henry gave an indication of personal fear that at once led the Judge to suspect that he also might be part of the conspiracy against Dreyfus. As Bertulus spoke of forged telegrams as well as indications in the papers that the major was one of Esterhazy's accomplices, Henry lost control of himself. According to Bertulus's later description, he started to cry, and, throwing his arms around the startled Judge, sobbed, "Save us! save us!" When the magistrate asked whether Esterhazy was the author of the *bordereau*, Henry replied: "Don't ask any more. Before all, the honor of the Army." Although Henry's behavior was becoming more and more suspicious, Bertulus did not pursue the matter further.[24]

As expected, Zola's jurisdictional appeal was rejected. On July 18 he again appeared before the Court of Assizes at Versailles. This time, when Labori asked for an appeal, it was summarily denied. The trial would commence the next day.[25]

On their way home, Labori urged Zola to flee France. Otherwise he was sure to be convicted and sent to prison, where his voice would be stilled. At the home of his publisher, Georges Charpentier, they were joined by Clemenceau. All agreed that Zola should leave for England that evening; if he were convicted at tomorrow's trial, escape would be impossible. When Zola reluctantly agreed they summoned his wife, who arrived at the Charpentiers with only a nightshirt folded in a newspaper; a valise would likely have caused the police, who were watching Zola's home, to become suspicious. As Zola wrote in his diary:

"This was the sum total of luggage that we took, she and I, in a hackney cab, to the Gare du Nord. The suddenness of the event bowled us over. I had grasped her hand, my heart went out to her, we exchanged only a few choked words. Charpentier, who was following us in another carriage, bought my ticket. Both accompanied me to the train and stayed a quarter hour, disguising the interior of the compartment until departure time. What an abrupt separation. My dear wife, her eyes clouded, her trembling hands joined, watched me leave."[26]

The train headed north as evening turned into night. It finally arrived at Calais, where Zola boarded the Channel steamer for Dover. He spent much of the cloudy night on deck, later writing that he "had never yet experienced such distress," yet was sure that "I would return in several months..." His abrupt departure shocked many of his friends: yet even they sensed that the tide would somehow turn in their favor.[27]

Zola's friends were concerned that, despite an English solicitor's opinion to the contrary, he might be served with notice of a judgment by a French court and that a British court would order his return to France. Zola thus went into hiding using the name M. Pascal, which after a week he changed to Jacques Beauchamp. Even under an alias, however, he did not stay in London, where he might be recognized. His English publisher found him a secluded villa south of the capital in Surrey, to which he moved in early August.[28] As soon as he had settled into his new home, Zola commenced work on a new novel. It had been eight months since he had completed his last book. Although he did not in the least regret his recent struggles "on behalf of truth and justice," he was happy to resume his old routine. His life was further brightened on August 11, when his mistress Jeanne Rozerot arrived from Paris with their two children.[29]

On August 12 the grand jury investigating the forgery charges against

Esterhazy and his mistress found for the accused. Undoubtedly influenced by pressures from the public prosecutor and others, it refused to accept the evidence regarding Mlle. Pays's handwriting, and found Christian Esterhazy's testimony too contradictory to be believed. Once more the anti-Dreyfusards had triumphed. A discouraged Zola wrote from London: "My only hopes are now with the unknown, the unexpected. We need a lightning bolt falling from the sky."[30]

⸺⬥⸺

By early August, Cavaignac's frustration over the Dreyfus Affair was increasing daily. Instead of resolving the matter, he had stirred up a hornets nest. At a dinner given on August 11 by Premier Brisson for the Cabinet, he announced his intent to take all the leading Dreyfusards to court on charges of attempts against the national security. When someone suggested that he should also include their lawyers, he answered, "Of course." Brisson and his other guests were shocked. The Premier's immediate response was, "It's mad, preposterous." Even if such a proposal were to be made to him officially, he would not consider it.[31]

On August 14, Cavaignac was given the shock of his life. He received an urgent visit from General Guadérique Roget, the head of his cabinet, and Captain Louis Cuignet, who on the War Minister's instructions had been going through the secret file.[32] At about ten o'clock the previous evening, the diligent Cuignet had been examining by lamplight the letter to von Schwarzkoppen that referred specifically to Dreyfus, and that Cavaignac had read with such telling effect in his July 7 speech to the Chamber of Deputies. He suddenly realized that although the document was entirely on ruled paper, the lines on the portions containing the heading and signature were of a different color than those on the letter's body. It dawned on him that the sheet of paper was made up of parts of two letters joined together. On what apparently was its first close inspection by anyone, this document, which Henry claimed had been discovered in von Schwarzkoppen's trash, was an obvious forgery.[33]

Although Cuignet was a friend of Henry, his duty as a soldier seemed clear. The next morning, he promptly reported his discovery to Roget. When the two men first examined the document in daylight, the color difference was much less obvious. However, once the blinds were drawn and they studied it by lamplight, Roget agreed that it was not authentic. They immediately met with Cavaignac, who also was convinced.[34]

Although the discovery significantly undermined the case he thought he had built against Dreyfus, Cavaignac decided that he must take some action. He would bide his time, however. Henry was about to go on leave, and Cavaignac would await his return and deal with him personally. Meanwhile, he would continue his public attacks on the Dreyfus forces. Indeed, since the forged document was dated more than a year after Dreyfus's trial, the forgery did not prove him innocent.[35]

Meanwhile, the War Minister decided the time had come to "execute" Esterhazy. He was brought before a military court on August 24 and charged with habitual private misconduct and a failure of military honor and discipline.[36] In his defense, Esterhazy admitted that his private life had been far from blameless. His alleged misdeeds as an officer, however, were not his fault; he had acted under the orders of the Cabinet and the General Staff. Among others, he named Generals Boisdeffre and Gonse, and Major Henry. Esterhazy also alleged that Jewish elements had offered him 600,000 francs to betray his military superiors, but that he had refused to do so. In the face of this barrage, a few days later the court found that Esterhazy should be dismissed from the Army, but only for personal misconduct. Cavaignac immediately carried out the order.[37]

By late August Cavaignac had again reviewed the forged letters and continued to believe that they were not authentic. When he learned that Henry would pass through Paris on August 30, he ordered the Lieutenant Colonel to report to him at the War Office. He also asked Boisdeffre and Gonse to be present at the interrogation, which Roget recorded.

At the outset, the War Minister toyed with Henry, who admitted that he had ungummed and put together pieces of the same letters, but that he had never taken pieces of one letter and put them together with pieces of another. Finally, after continuing to deny that he had "forged" the 1896 letter, Henry admitted that he "added to the 1896 piece words which were in the other," and that he "got out of the 1894 piece some words which completed the sense" of the 1896 letter. Acting "in the interest of my country," he had "added the end to make it more cogent."[38]

After Henry continued to assert that he had added "only the phrase at the end", Cavaignac asked him to leave the room for a moment. On his return, the questioning resumed:

Cavaignac: Let us see. One of the pieces has crosslines of pale violet, the other of bluish grey, which shows that portions of it were regummed. But your explanation is impossible. The intercalations do not answer to what you say.

Henry: What portions do you say were intercalated?

Cavaignac: I do not wish you to ask me questions, but to answer mine. You forged the whole letter?

Henry: I swear I did not. I must have had the names which are in that of 1896 to do so. Why should I have taken a fragment of the 1894 piece to insert it in the other?

Cavaignac: You will not tell the truth?

Henry: I can tell you nothing else. I cannot say that I wrote the whole of it. As to the first letter, I found it; the second I intercalated, and only added the end.

Cavaignac: All you could have received was the heading and the signature.

Henry: I received the first part.

Cavaignac: You received nothing at all.

Henry: I had the first part, the heading and the signature.

Cavaignac: Impossible! You aggravate your situation by these concealments.

Henry: I did what I did for the good of the country.

Cavaignac: That is not what I asked. What you did was based on the documents themselves. Tell everything.

Henry: I cannot say I did what I did not. When I got the first part....

Cavaignac: Impossible! I tell you it is written on the piece. You had better tell all.

Henry: Then you are convinced it is I.

Cavaignac: Say what is the case.... So then, this is what happened: You received in 1896 an envelope with a letter inside it, a letter of no importance. You suppressed the letter and forged another instead of it.

Henry: Yes."[39]

Henry had admitted the forgery. As soon as Roget led him out of the room, Boisdeffre went to a nearby desk and wrote out a letter of resignation as Chief of Staff. When Cavaignac, unaware of the General's role in the affair, tried to dissuade him, Boisdeffre replied that although anyone "can be led into error,...not everyone has had the misfortune of affirming before a jury that a document was authentic when it was not..."[40]

For the moment, instead of charging Henry with forgery, Cavaignac merely ordered that he be put under "fortress arrest" and sent to a cell at Mont-Valerien prison. In the carriage on the way to Mont-Valerien Henry broke down, crying: "What I did I am ready to do again...It was for the good of the country and of the Army. I have always done my duty...In all my life I never met with such a pack of wretches...They are to blame for my misfortune..."[41]

Later in the day, Cavaignac issued a brief communiqué:

"Today in the office of the minister of war, Lieutenant Colonel Henry was acknowledged and acknowledged himself to be the author of the letter dated October 1896 in which Dreyfus is named. The minister of war immediately ordered the arrest of Lieutenant Colonel Henry who has been taken to the Fortress of Mont-Valerien."[42]

The War Minister immediately told Prime Minister Brisson and the Cabinet what had transpired. When one of them exclaimed that "this means revision," the War Minister shot back, "Less than ever." Without a further investigation, perhaps including further questioning of Henry, he was not ready to admit his error.[43]

The next day, August 31, Henry had spent a troubled morning in his cell. After eating a light lunch, he wrote a short note asking General Gonse to see him and a letter to his wife in which he asserted his innocence. By now Henry's sunlit room was sweltering and he had been drinking heavily. He started a second letter to his wife: "I am like a madman; a frightening pain is gripping my brain. I am going to take a swim in the Seine..." There the letter ended. Henry took off his clothes and at about three o'clock, spread out on the bed, he slit his throat twice with a razor. In fifteen minutes he had bled to death.[44]

Henry's suicide was discovered three hours later by an orderly who was bringing his supper. By the time the news reached Cavaignac that evening, the Cabinet had met four times to discuss the Government's reaction to Henry's forgery admission. The major topic was whether to accept Boisdeffre's resignation and, if so, the form it should take. Tempers were high. Brisson demanded a major reorganization at the War Office, which Cavaignac rejected. The ministers' concern over the forgery was so great that the news of Henry's death seemed to make only a slight impression.[45]

Shortly thereafter, however, the Cabinet and most of France recognized its significance. In the aftershock of Henry's death, even the French right wing press conceded that a new trial for Dreyfus was almost a foregone conclusion. L'Echo de Paris expressed the general sentiment when it stated, "All is changed; the revision is a necessity. It is desired by a large number of officers." The Dreyfusards were ecstatic. Léon Blum recalled that when he heard the news, "I don't think that ever in my whole life I felt an equal excitement...The truth had actually won."[46]

But had it? Premier Brisson apparently did not feel politically strong enough to call on his own for a revision commission. On September 3, he instead asked Lucie Dreyfus's friends to prepare a written request for her to sign. The same day, when Brisson told Cavaignac that the Government could not avoid commencing a revision procedure, the War Minister resigned, announcing, "I remain convinced of Dreyfus' guilt."[47]

To Esterhazy it would make no difference whether or not there was revision. As soon as he learned of Henry's suicide, he took a train to the Belgian border, which he crossed on foot after shaving off his large mustache. After a short stop in Brussels, he crossed the Channel, and settled in London under an assumed name.[48]

After a few days, the anti-Dreyfusards recovered from their initial shock over Henry's suicide. Their leading spokesman was a writer named Charles Maurras. On September 5 and 6 in a royalist newspaper he claimed that Henry's only offense was "patriotic forgery." He had acted "for the public good, confiding his deed to no one, not even to the leaders whom he loved, consenting to run the risk entirely on his own." The real crime was that France did not

"...give you the great funeral that your martyrdom deserved. We should have waved your bloody tunic and the sullied blades down the boulevards; marched the coffin, hoisted the mortuary banner like a black flag."[49]

To this praise of Henry, others added threats. *La Libre Parole* intoned:

"Revision means war. For this war we are not prepared. Yes, it will be war and a debacle. And that is precisely the plan and the hopes of the Jews."[50]

Meanwhile Premier Brisson was searching for a successor to Cavaignac as Minister of War. On President Faure's recommendation, he named General Emile Zurlinden, an Alsatian who was serving as Military Governor of Paris. Zurlinden was reputed to be sympathetic to the Dreyfusard cause. One of his first acts was to ask the Minister of the Navy to prepare orders that would transport Dreyfus back to France for another hearing. Before taking any action, however, he announced that he would personally study the case to assure himself as to where the truth lay.[51] After what must have been only a cursory review, he recognized that there had been at least one forgery, but was convinced by the officers who showed it to him that Henry was not the guilty party. Instead, he concluded that it had been Picquart, who had altered the papers in an attempt to implicate Esterhazy.[52]

Zurlinden reported his conclusion at a Cabinet meeting on September 17. Brisson and a majority of the ministers disagreed, and decided to initiate revision of the Dreyfus case. Accordingly Zurlinden resigned, explaining as he left the meeting:

"An exhaustive study of the papers in the Dreyfus case had convinced me too fully of his guilt for me to accept, as the head of the army, any other solution than that of the maintenance of the judgment in its entirety."[53]

Later the same day Brisson named as Zurlinden's successor General Charles Chanoine, who also was thought to be a revisionist and agreed to support the Cabinet's revision decision.[54] No sooner had Chanoine moved into his new office, however, than, on September 20, he signed the order prepared by Zurlinden just before he resigned that commenced legal proceedings against Picquart for alleged forgery. Zurlinden, who conveniently had resumed his post as Military Governor of Paris, swiftly acted to implement the order.[55]

Picquart was already required to appear on September 21 before a Court of Summary Jurisdiction to face a charge of divulging documents. The prosecutor asked for a postponement on the basis that the Colonel had just been accused of forgery. Before this motion to adjourn was granted, Picquart asked to address the court. Looking directly at Gonse and Pellieux, who had been called as witnesses, he said:

"It is probable that this is the last time, before being accused in secret, that I shall be able to speak in public. I wish it to be known that should there be found in my cell...Henry's razor, it will be murder; for a man such as I am could never for one instant think of suicide.[56]

Picquart was returned to the Santé Prison, where he spent his seventy-second night. On September 22, pursuant to Zurlinden's order, he was sent to the Cherche-Midi Prison, to be held in isolation. Brisson may have been Prime Minister, but he had not established control over his Government.[57]

On September 24 the commission that Brisson had appointed the preceding week divided evenly as to whether to accept Lucie Dreyfus's request and thus was unable to make any recommendation. At this point,

Brisson at last intervened. He argued that, for the good of the country, the recent developments made it essential to redetermine Dreyfus' guilt or innocence. On September 26, after a four-hour debate, the Council of Ministers voted six to four to transmit the revision request to the High Court of Appeal. The Minister of Justice did so immediately. The same day, Lucie Dreyfus joyfully wrote her husband, on Devils Island:

"And so we have arrived at the last stage of our journey, at the final crisis, which should restore to us what we have unjustifiably been deprived of— our honor.

"I hope with all my heart that this is the last letter that I will send to you in that wretched place."[58]

By now, France seemed on the verge of civil strife. On October 2 the Paris police broke up a revisionist demonstration, with many persons injured. As *The New York Times* Paris correspondent reported, the demonstrations "have created intense alarm among the foreigners at the hotels, and it is possible that an exodus will occur, the guests fearing grave developments."[59]

Two weeks later the French capital was agog with rumors that a military coup against the government was scheduled for October 16. The unconfirmed reports included an alleged meeting of generals in Versailles, and an invitation to Prince Victor Bonaparte, who until recently had led the Imperialist Party, to be the titular head of the revolt.[60] The construction and railway workers were on strike, and the Army was occupying the railroad stations. The leading revisionists were alarmed, and several of them cautiously moved to new addresses until the crisis had blown over.[61] Although the anti-revisionist forces strongly denied the rumors, the Brisson Government took such measures as it deemed necessary to protect the Republic. For whatever reason, October 16 passed without incident.[62]

In another week, on October 25, the Chamber of Deputies was scheduled to reconvene. Moderate deputies were becoming concerned over the Government's increasingly radical complexion. Meanwhile, the anti-Dreyfusards and the Socialists were organizing counter-demonstrations. In light of the Brisson Government's vacillation on most issues, these reports led to predictions that it would not last beyond the opening of parliament.[63]

When the Chamber convened, its building was protected by troops and police against a noisy mob of anti-Dreyfusards. Proceedings had barely commenced when the anti-Dreyfusard leader, Paul Déroulède, called for the Government, specifically including Minister of War Chanoine, to resign. As if on cue, Chanoine rose to protest that his views on the Dreyfus case were the same as those of his predecessors. He closed by announcing his immediate resignation as Minister of War.[64] This abrupt action threw the Chamber into confusion. For a short time it appeared that anger at Chanoine's action and support for the Republic might permit the Government to survive. By the time that the session ended, however, a confidence vote had been defeated and the Brisson government was forced to resign.[65]

On October 27, the Court of Appeals began its consideration of Lucie Dreyfus's request to have her husband's conviction reopened. The proceeding took place under the gilded ceiling of a chamber in the Palais de Justice on the Ile de la Cité and was purely legal in nature. The police prevented the entry of the anti-Dreyfusard demonstrators who wanted to attend the hearing. In this atmosphere, the emotions were on the side of the accused. The elderly Public Prosecutor's address set the tone:

"O! Sacred laws for the protection of the accused, and even of the convicted, what have they done to you...let the Republic's justice then proceed; let it cross the seas!"

Lucie Dreyfus's lawyer, Henri Mornard, very different from the emotional Labori, was especially effective as he calmly and precisely argued the case for revision.[66]

On October 29, by a ten-to-four vote the Court ruled that Madame Dreyfus's request was "admissible in its present form" and that the matter "will proceed to a supplementary judicial investigation." Although the Court had refused to suspend Dreyfus's sentence, the revisionists had scored a major triumph. From London, still in exile, Zola wrote: "For me this supplementary inquest means the certain acquittal of an innocent man."[67]

In forming a new Government, President Faure's task was a difficult one. The new Premier must not be viewed by the Army as its enemy, yet he should be at least willing to let the revision process continue. On October

31 Faure named Charles Dupuy, a manipulating but otherwise mediocre politician, who had been Premier at the time of the Dreyfus trial but was not an idealogue. The important post of War Minister went to Charles de Freycinet, who had held the same post prior to the Panama scandal. A Protestant who was acceptable to the Catholics, he had shown Dreyfusard sympathies.[68]

Up to now all correspondence to and from Dreyfus had been heavily censored. News of family affairs and other noncontroversial matters was allowed to filter through, but nothing of the efforts of his wife and others to secure a new trial. It was not until early November that the prisoner received the September 26 letter from his wife that the Council of Ministers had sent his case to the High Court of Appeal.[69] The Colonial Office reportedly was still rejecting her request to send her husband warm clothing for his anticipated return home for a new trial. Its excuse was that the Government would do whatever was necessary.[70]

On November 10, Lucie Dreyfus received a letter from her husband indicating that he had not been informed of the October 29 Court decision to proceed with its investigation of his case. She protested to the Minister of Justice, and the Dreyfusard press raised a hue and a cry. When the Court learned that the Dupuy Government was denying Dreyfus this important information, it ordered that he be promptly informed. Thus, on November 16, the prisoner on Devil's Island was handed a telegram which read:

"To inform you that the Criminal Chamber of the High Court of Appeal has declared admissible in present form request for revision of your verdict and decided that you would be informed of this decision and invited to produce your means of defense."[71]

Commencing November 8, the Criminal Chamber of the High Court of Appeal conducted the initial phase of its investigation by hearing each of the five Ministers of War who had been in office since Dreyfus's arrest. They all asserted his guilt, and Mercier and Cavaignac tried to prove it on November 17. Cavaignac argued that Esterhazy was Dreyfus' accomplice in copying the *bordereau*. Mercier's testimony was especially aggressive. When asked why he had not prepared a report explaining his acceptance of secondhand testimony regarding Dreyfus' "confession," he responded: "It was a closed case. It could not be foreseen that a whole race would later line up behind Dreyfus."[72]

The anti-Dreyfusards believed that the Court's invitation to Dreyfus to prepare his defense was a sign of how it would decide the case. They were furious. An article in *Le Gaulois* by an anti-Semitic Jewish columnist charged that "the judges of the Court of Appeal have undertaken...to cast aspersions on the Army out of hatred for the sabre." This comment was mild compared to the suggestion in another paper that the judges' eyes should be gouged out and that they then should be sent off to be pilloried with a sign on their chests reading: "This is how France punishes traitors who try to sell her to the enemy."[73]

Across the English Channel, after Jeanne Rozerot had returned to France in mid-October, Zola decided that he would fare better in an urban environment. With the aid of friends, he took rooms at the residential Queen's Hotel in Upper Norwood, near Dulwich, a southern London suburb, registering as "M. Richard." He continued his routine of writing in the morning, and walked around the town after lunch.

The arrival of Zola's wife, Alexandrine, in late October only partly dispelled the author's increasing gloom. The fall weather was unpleasant, with fog, rain, or both on most days. Equally depressing was the English food. Alexandrine complained that "boiled potatoes are the only thing they do well," and that on Sundays, when the kitchen staff sought "to avoid work," the bill of fare consisted largely of "stale bread."[74]

Meanwhile the military proceeding against Picquart was being conducted before a Captain Tavernier, who was predisposed to find the accused guilty of forgery. Picquart was confronted with no witnesses, and was not permitted to consult Labori, who was acting as his lawyer. When Labori objected, Minister of War Freycinet upheld Tavernier on the basis that the law that provided prisoners a right to counsel did not apply to military proceedings. Finally, on November 13, after Picquart had spent 122 days in prison, 49 of them in solitary confinement, the Minister of Justice allowed Labori to see his client. It was too late. On November 16, apparently ignoring Henry's admission of forgery, Tavernier followed the line of his superiors and recommended a court-martial.[75] On November 24 Military Governor Zurlinden approved Tavernier's recommendation and set the formal court-martial for December 12. Picquart would be charged with forgery and the communication of secret documents to an unauthorized person.[76]

The Picquart court-martial raised the issues initially presented by the Affair to a different level. No longer was the question one of an individual miscarriage of justice. Instead, as exemplified by the crude effort to destroy Picquart, it was the role of the Army in the affairs of the Republic. Thus, the November 26 London *Times* referred to the "premeditated, intentional conflict between the military oligarchy and the civil democracy."[77]

The outrage against the Army's treatment of Picquart was so strong that Dupuy ordered a discussion of the matter in the Chamber of Deputies. The Dreyfusards and their allies opened the November 28 debate by arguing that the Government had the power to halt the court martial while Lucie Dreyfus' appeal was still pending, and that it should do so.[78] In the midst of this discussion, Raymond Poincaré, who had been Minister of Finance in the Dupuy Government at the time of the Dreyfus court martial, exclaimed, "Really, enough of this!" and rose to speak. Poincaré was a thirty-eight-year-old Republican deputy whose future career included the French presidency during World War I. Completely honest and impartial, his indignation at what was occurring caused him to unburden himself of any part he had played in Dreyfus' conviction:

"At the present moment, silence on the part of some of us would be undisguised cowardice. If it were true that a judicial error had been committed, those of us who were in charge in 1894 would have the imperious obligation not to do anything or let anything be done that might impede its discovery."[79]

Poincaré continued by claiming that the *bordereau* was the only evidence he and his 1894 Cabinet colleagues had ever heard of against Dreyfus at the time of the captain's conviction. There had been no references to a "secret file" or a "confession." Poincaré's clear implication was that these had been developed later to justify the Army's position. He concluded:

"I am well aware that today, in breaking this silence which weighed on me, I am exposing myself to attacks, insults and slanders. That does not concern me. I am happy to have taken from this tribune the all too long awaited opportunity of freeing my conscience.[80]

Poincaré's outburst did not sway the Government. Dupuy conceded that it had the right to postpone Picquart's court-martial, but that even if the

Chamber ordered him to do so, he would not obey. Given this position as well as the anti-Dreyfusard sentiment of many of the deputies, a Socialist motion requesting the Minister of War to order a postponement was defeated by the lopsided vote of 338 to 83.[81]

The apparent inability of France to see justice done was not lost on the outside world. In England, concern was mixed with a sense of moral superiority. Thus the November 28 London *Times* intoned:

"The United Kingdom, like all civilized communities, is deeply interested, on moral as well as material grounds, in seeing France rescued from disastrous courses that can only lead to revolution and anarchy. It is with a kindly and honest concern for the interests of the French themselves that we look with pain and alarm on the prospects of new scandals casting discredit on the securities for liberty and fair-dealing in France, even more flagrant than those which have theretofore disfigured the squalid history of the Dreyfus case."[82]

By now, December 12, the date of the Picquart court-martial was fast approaching. On December 1 the Senate, by a tie vote, failed to approve a resolution that would have authorized the Court of Appeal to suspend other legal proceedings on matters that were already within its purview. Legislative relief denied, resort to the courts seemed the only alternative.[83]

The proponent of the defeated Senate resolution, René Waldeck-Rousseau, was perhaps the greatest French civil lawyer of his day. Together with Poincaré, he consulted with several other leading French lawyers who had realized that something must be done to prevent a clear miscarriage of justice. They noted that Picquart was to be court-martialed for espionage as well as forgery, and that the Court of Summary Jurisdiction was also to try him for communicating the secret Esterhazy file. Here was an overlap between the two proceedings. Picquart's lawyers at once asked the High Court of Appeal to defer the court-martial until the Court of Summary Jurisdiction had acted.[84] On December 8 a judge of the Criminal Chamber of the High Court of Appeal held a hearing on their petition. He postponed action until he could review the court-martial dossier on the matter. When the public prosecutor agreed, the High Court of Appeal ordered the transmission of the military file to the Criminal Chamber, thus effectively staying the court-martial indefinitely. Picquart remained in prison, but at least he was now assured of an impartial trial.[85]

On December 12 a crowd of anti-Dreyfusards headed by two members of the Chamber of Deputies marched to the Cherche-Midi Prison, where Picquart was incarcerated, and then to the Hotel des Invalides, General Zurlinden's official residence. Throughout, they shouted monotonously, "Spit upon Picquart." The demonstrators eventually disbanded, but the French capital's military garrison remained under arms.[86] Meanwhile, the support for Picquart and the outrage that the Army was trying to ruin him was growing daily. Although there was sympathy for Dreyfus and his role as a kind of scapegoat, there had been little enthusiasm for him as a person. Picquart, however, was widely viewed as a hero for risking the prospects of a brilliant career in order to prevent a miscarriage of justice.[87]

⚜

On December 19 the Chamber of Deputies debated whether the secret Dreyfus dossier could be transmitted to the Court of Appeal. Minister of War Freycinet asserted that some of the documents in the secret file related to national security matters, and that if forced to turn them over to the Court, he would resign. Premier Dupuy then announced that the Government would not allow the file to be shown to either the Court or Dreyfus's lawyers unless there were assurances of absolute secrecy. Former Premier Brisson disagreed:

"There is no document in the Dreyfus dossier that could affect the security of the State. I examined the entire dossier after the discovery of the Henry forgery and considered them all suspicious."

Former Minister of War Cavaignac then added more fuel to the fire by contending that Brisson had not seen all the relevant documents which had been offered to him but which he had "thought it useless to examine." After further heated debate, the Government's position was approved by a 370 to 80 vote.[88]

This inability of the French Government to allow a full review of the Dreyfus case continued to outrage foreign observers. Commenting on the previous day's debate, the London *Times* said:

"There was reason to hope of late that the investigation to be conducted by the Court of Cassation would go to the very bottom of the business. The debate yesterday in the Chamber of Deputies does not, we are afraid, make it certain that proceedings will follow this rational and prudent course. The Premier and Minister of War appear to have been impressed with the difficulty—perhaps the danger—of insisting on a full disclosure of the facts."[89]

Emile Zola was suffering the discomforts of the early English winter. His wife, Alexandrine, who had gone back to France for three weeks, returned on December 23 and four days later became seriously ill with bronchitis. The author, already frustrated over the slow pace of the Court of Appeal's review, had the new worry of nursing his wife until, after a fortnight, her health began to improve.[90] Although it was generally known that Zola was somewhere in England, his exact whereabouts had remained a well-guarded secret. A London correspondent of *The New York Times* reported that he was "recently stopping at the Grosvenor Hotel," which the author had left for the London suburbs five months earlier.[91]

Although a London *Times* correspondent had recently reported from Paris that "owing to the state in which matters now stand, no one dreams any longer of disturbing his sojourn abroad," affairs in France were sufficiently volatile that Zola probably was wise to keep his location unknown. It was not until December 30 that the Court of Appeal was given access to the "secret file." Even this would not be a full-scale review that the judges could make as they saw fit. Instead, each morning Captain Cuignet would bring in the nearly-400-document file, show and explain a portion to the judges, and take it back at the end of the day. The Court could not publish any of the documents in the file without the Minister of War's consent.[92]

The anti-Dreyfusard press was full of charges that at least some of the judges were showing partiality towards the Dreyfus camp. The accusations came from none other than the presiding judge of the Civil Chamber of the High Court of Appeal Jules Quesnay de Beaurepaire. After making several comments to the press, on December 28 he wrote the presiding judge of the Criminal Chamber enumerating seven acts which demonstrated the "favoritism" of two of the judges. They included such trivia as offering Picquart a beverage and asking the court clerk to apologize for keeping him waiting.[93]

At year end, with professed concern but probably secret enjoyment, the Kaiser was observing the troubles of his country's major rival. On December 29 he wrote to Queen Victoria, his "Most Beloved Grandmama":

"France is in a terrible plight, and the fight about Dreyfus, etc, has disclosed a fearful amount of corruption and injustice in the Government and Army circles. The longing for scandal, the perpetual, startling "disclosures" have created a most deplorable state of excitement, which may one day ease itself in some sort of explosion towards inside or outside! Voltaire saw his countrymen were "half apes and half tigers." It seems to me as if they were in the act of changing from the first to the latter."[94]

FIFTEEN

"This Affair May Set France And England At War"

As the spring dragged on, Marchand's force was still waiting at Fort Desaix for the rains to come and raise the water level of the streams and rivers that would take it to Fashoda. Tired of the long delay, the commander had made a 400-mile exploratory expedition to the south. He returned to Fort Desaix in early May to find the water level unchanged. Exhausted and depressed, Marchand came down with a serious case of malaria, occasionally becoming delirious. When he began gradually to recover, he decided to send Lieutenant Charles Emmanuel-Marie Mangin, who was the most difficult of his officers to control, on an expedition to confirm that when the waters finally rose, the channels to the Nile would be clear. On May 17 Mangin and fifty men left on an overland march to the northeast.[1]

Although the last half of May brought steady and heavy rain, the Sué barely rose. Finally, on June 4 at 10:00 A.M., Marchand, with four officers and about seventy soldiers and boatmen in a number of small boats, set out down the Sué on the first lap of their final push to Fashoda. He had wanted to leave with his entire force, including the well armored *Faidherbe*. It was becoming increasingly clear, however, that the ship's draught would not permit it to move down the Sué until the river had risen substantially, probably not for many days. Any further delay would further weaken the already depleted morale of both Marchand and his men. The captain also was concerned over Kitchener's movement up the Nile. It was essential that the French should reach Fashoda before the Sirdar.[2]

Seeing no other alternative, Marchand decided to divide his force. He would lead an advance guard in small boats and try to reach Fashoda as rapidly as possible. His remaining troops would follow in the

243

Faidherbe and the remaining boats as soon as the Sué had risen to an acceptable level.[3]

For Marchand, pale, haggard, and frustrated almost to the point of collapse, the prospect of immediate movement acted as a tonic. He viewed his expedition as akin to a noble quest. As he wrote a friend just before he set out on June 4:

"At least don't go and think I believe I am carrying the world on my shoulders and that I'm exaggerating the role that we're playing here....It is always respectable when it has for a motive the task of reminding the country of its true greatness, of its mission in the world, begun nearly 20 centuries ago, the mission which we all have the unavoidable obligation of continuing on pain of being guilty of national cowardice."[4]

Thus, as Baratier described their departure: "Vive la France! Le grand voyage est commence."[5]

By June 11 Marchand and his party reached the edge of the great swamp that separated them from the Nile. Their journey until now had been relatively easy, as they sailed or paddled down the Sué at an average rate of forty kilometers a day. True Frenchmen, they broke their journey every day for a two-hour midday meal, which, with a good cook and game, wild duck, and crocodiles to eat, was a pleasant repast. The only mishap occurred when Marchand's dugout was smashed to pieces by a hippopotamus. There were no signs of human life except for occasional white-painted naked Dinkas standing on the shore saluting them with the open palms of their right hands. At the edge of the swamp, a group of Dinka men indicated that the French should go no further, but while they patiently waited under a shady tree the Dinka women persuaded their men to let the party continue.[6]

The Ethiopian force that had left Gore in full panoply on March 10 was only a shadow of its former self when it finally reached the White Nile on June 22. After proceeding part way, its commander had decided that only 800 men would accompany Faivre and Potter on their expedition to join Marchand, whom they expected to find already established on the Nile. Like Bonchamps the previous year, this force struggled through deserted villages, high grass, mud, and swamp. The heat was too much for many Ethiopians. The stragglers were the prey of the ever-lurking crocodiles.[7]

When the decimated force reached the Nile about sixty miles south of Fashoda, Faivre and Potter were bitterly disappointed to find no sign of Marchand and his men. They proposed that the expedition retain its position until scouts could be sent to Fashoda to find out whether Marchand was there. The Ethiopian commander emphatically refused, stating:

"We have not enough food. My men are sick. The river is rising. We will die in the swamps. Let us go."[8]

Faivre and Potter could not prevail on the Ethiopians. On June 25, before they departed, the two Frenchmen decided to plant the tricolor on the far bank, 150 yards away, thus identifying it as French soil. Potter was so ill, however, that he could hardly stand, and Faivre was unable to swim. They persuaded one of the native soldiers to swim the flag across the Nile, for a suitable reward. He was about to do so with the tricolor attached to a floating crate that he would push in front of him, when a Russian adventurer, Colonel Artamanov, who was accompanying the expedition, intervened. With the prejudice that was so typical of the times, and shouting, "Now it shall not be said that only a nigger dared plant the French flag!," he jumped into the Nile and with the Yambo native put up the flag and returned to the east bank.[9] The expedition then returned to Ethiopia.

On the same June 25, Marchand and his men finally emerged from the high grass and swamps through which they had been laboriously making their way for the past twelve days, averaging only two daily miles. It had been a terrible ordeal. For almost one entire day they had lost the water channel in the high grass. On the nineteenth, first blocked by hippopotami, and then, in torrential rain, finding the channel apparently ending before a wall of reeds, they progressed only ninety yards. The only living land creatures were rats, snakes, millipedes, and ants. At night they were attacked by clouds of mosquitoes, with no dry land on which to pitch tents and spread protective netting. But at last they were through, and the worst of their many trials seemed to be over.[10]

For several days, the main body of Marchand's forces camped on an island in the Bahr al-Ghazal while their commander and Baratier went south to Meshra'er Req to bring back Mangin and his men. On July 2 they returned, and the French force was united for the final push to

Fashoda. At seven o'clock the next morning they set out. Marchand was becoming increasingly concerned that the dervishes would oppose their arrival, in contrast to his earlier hope that the French would be seen by the Khalifa as allies against the hated British. Thus, their boats proceeded in military formation, with orders never to be more than 200 meters apart.[11]

At five o'clock in the afternoon of July 12, under a pale blue sky, Marchand's lead boat rounded a bend in the Nile and saw Fashoda. It was an almost completely ruined fort sitting in an island of maize fields in the midst of a large marsh. It was an inauspicious spot, but to Marchand and his men it was the Holy Grail. Their arduous journey of almost two years had ended in triumph. They had won the race to Fashoda![12]

From the Shilluk, a large tribe inhabiting the Nile Valley near Fashoda, the French had learned that Kitchener was north of Khartoum, and that the Mahdist army still stood between him and the Sudanese capital. Sadly, however, there was no sign or news of Bonchamps's force of French and Ethiopians that they hoped would greet them.[13]

Since the seasonal rise in the Nile would not occur until mid-August, Kitchener would not attack Khartoum until then. Thorough as always, he took the opportunity to send for an additional British infantry brigade, as well as a cavalry regiment and a field artillery brigade. He then left in early June for a month's leave in Cairo. His request for more troops may have been a case of overkill, for he told Lord Cromer that he was "inclined to think that his force is inconveniently large" and that "the real dervish opposition is quite broken."[14]

Although Kitchener's concern was the defeat of the dervishes, Cromer's thoughts were turning to issues relating to the Sudan after the British-Egyptian force had won their anticipated victory. Cromer believed in a post-war Anglo-Egyptian role in the southern Sudan. Perhaps because of his background as a member of the Baring family of bankers, he was concerned that a long-term occupation might adversely affect the Egyptian financial stability that he was working to establish and maintain. On June 15 he therefore proposed in a memorandum to the Government in London that after Khartoum's capture only two gunboat flotillas should complete the conquest of the Sudan, one going up the Blue Nile and the other, under Kitchener, up the While Nile to Fashoda. Interestingly, Cromer thought it was more likely that Kitchener would find Ethiopians at Fashoda than French. In either case, the

Sirdar should claim the entire White Nile valley, but he would need instructions whether in the name of Britain, of Egypt, or of both countries combined.[15]

On July 2 Kitchener returned to the front after his leave in Cairo. The War Office in London had complied with all his requests for reinforcements, and these were now arriving. In preparation for his final assault, he was concentrating his army at Wad Hamed, only sixty miles north of Omdurman.[16]

The Khalifa was making no attempt to disrupt Kitchener's preparations. Instead, the Dervish leader had decided to make his final stand at Omdurman, just north of Khartoum. By early July his force consisted of 20,000 men, including 4,000 horsemen. By the time that the British were ready to attack, he could summon nearly twice as many more. Kitchener's army at full strength would number 8,200 British and 17,600 Egyptians and Sudanese regulars. All of them would be much better armed than their opponents, however.[17]

By late spring, Winston Churchill had determined to see action in Egypt without regard to the consequences. On May 22, still in India, he wrote his mother:

"...Egypt. Please redouble your efforts in that direction...I am determined to go to Egypt and if I cannot get employment or at least sufficient leave, I will not remain in the army. There are other and better things ahead. But the additional campaign will be valuable as an educational experience—agreeable from the point of view of an adventure—and profitable as far as finance goes as I shall write a book about it—easily and without the blunders which disfigure my first attempt."[18]

When Churchill started his three-months leave on June 18, however, and departed from Bombay for London, his Egyptian prospects looked bleak. Despite all her efforts, Lady Randolph apparently had accomplished nothing. She and her good friend Mary, Lady Jeune, a leading London hostess, had made some headway in the War Office, but Kitchener was impervious to feminine charms. Moreover, he had no use for Churchill, whom he believed was behaving in unmilitary fashion in criticizing his superior officers in *The Malakand Field Force*. Thus, the most that Lady Randolph's Egyptian visit elicited from the Sirdar was a reply to one of her many letters: "I have noted your son's name and I hope I may be able to employ him later in the Sudan." If this was not frustrating enough, on returning unexpectedly one day to her Cairo hotel room, she discovered the major who was her current lover in her bed with the wife of another army officer.[19]

Just as Churchill's prospects were looking hopeless, Lord Salisbury invited him to see him on July 12 at his spacious office overlooking the Horseguards Parade. The Prime Minister had read and been impressed by *The Malakand Field Force*. He told Churchill:

"I myself have been able to form a truer picture of the kind of fighting that has been going on in those frontier valleys from your writings than from any other documents which it has been my duty to read."[20]

Churchill's account continued:

"I thought twenty minutes would be about the limit of my favour, which I had by no means the intention to outrun, and I accordingly made as if to depart after that period had expired. But he kept me for over half an hour, and when he finally conducted me again across the wide expanse of carpet to the door, he dismissed me in the following terms, 'I hope you will allow me to say how much you remind me of your father, with whom such important days of my political life were lived. If there is anything at any time which would be of assistance to you, pray do not fail to let me know.'"[21]

Salisbury's offer seemed to provide Churchill a last chance to get to Egypt, and he accepted it. He wrote the Prime Minister on July 18 that he wanted to go to Khartoum, first, because its recapture "will be a historical event: second, because I can, I anticipate, write a book about it which from a monetary, as well as from other points of view, will be useful to me." Churchill asked Salisbury to write Cromer "and say that on personal grounds you wish me to go."[22]

While he was pondering the next move in his private Egyptian campaign, Churchill was also testing the political waters. On July 14 at Bradford, he delivered a speech of an hour's length which, as he wrote his mother the next day, "was listened to with the greatest attention..." The experience excited and pleased him:

"The keenness of the audience stirred my blood—and altho I stuck to my notes rigidly I certainly succeeded in rousing and amusing them.

Lieutenant Winston Churchill

The conclusions I form are these—With practice I shall obtain great power on a public platform. My voice sufficiently powerful, and—this is vital—my ideas & modes of thought are pleasing to men."[23]

Only twenty-three, Churchill, according to his biographer son, already

"had become an object of conversation and controversy. It was facile to say that he was trading on his father's reputation, that he pulled all the strings he could and made use of all the influence he had inherited. But none could gainsay his courage or the ardor of his ambition. All this, however, did not make him very popular...

"He recognized all this, but with his eyes open decided to run the risks. After all, he had nothing to lose. He was penniless, indeed in debt. He was a soldier of fortune. He had to make his way, he had to make his name. Many people, ... who had important transactions with Lord Randolph, were prepared to help him. But their help would have been of no avail without his own primordial thrust."[24]

Shortly thereafter Churchill learned that he could go to the Sudan. Salisbury had asked Cromer to write Kitchener on his behalf, but it is unclear whether Cromer did so. It is likely that the immediate cause of Churchill's good luck was a conversation between Lady Jeune and her friend Adjutant General Sir Evelyn Wood. At the same time that Lady Jeune told Sir Evelyn that Salisbury had telegraphed Cromer and asked him to follow up on the matter, word arrived at the War Office that a young officer of the Twenty-first Lancers had died in Cairo and had to be replaced. Wood and Cromer chose Churchill, and Kitchener said nothing.[25]

Churchill did not wait for official permission from his regiment in India to transfer to the Sudan. Taking no chances that the answer might be negative, he simply vanished, leaving on the 26th by train for Marseilles, and from there by tramp steamer to Egypt. Once he had arrived in the Sudan, it would be almost impossible to recall him.[26]

On July 25 the British Cabinet met to decide the course that Kitchener should follow after he had taken Khartoum. Cromer was present by invitation. The instructions for Kitchener, which Cromer drafted after the meeting as a memorandum to himself from Salisbury, directed the Sirdar personally to lead a flotilla up the White Nile. If he met either

French or Ethiopian forces, he was to do nothing that might be viewed as recognizing their claim to any part of the Nile Valley. At this point the instructions differed. Kitchener should avoid "by all possible means, any collision with the forces of the Emperor Menelik." On the other hand, if the forces he met were French, "he should endeavor to convince" them that their presence "in the Nile valley is an infringement of the rights both of Great Britain and of the Khedive." Thereafter,

"the course of action to be pursued must depend so much on local circumstances that it is neither necessary or desirable to furnish Sir Herbert Kitchener with detailed instructions."

Salisbury apparently was unwilling to risk a war with Ethiopia over the Upper Nile, perhaps because of the difficulty of maintaining a long-term presence there in the face of opposition from a neighboring power that only two years earlier had soundly defeated a supposedly invincible Italian invading army. He was more confident as to England's ability to win a conflict with France, either on the Nile or worldwide. As later events would prove, Salisbury was willing to fight France for the Nile.[27]

On July 12 in the presence of the Reth, or king of the Shilluk, and his council, Marchand officially took possession of Fashoda: "Au nom de la France." As the French tricolor was going up the makeshift flagstaff, the halyard broke and the flag dropped to the ground. In jest, an officer commented that in the face of such an omen, "If we were Romans we would give up and go home." As it was, the rope was replaced, and the ceremony went forward without further incident.[28]

The French may have become more superstitious when that same day, the Reth described how, three weeks earlier, he had received the news that the Ethiopians and their European fellow travelers had reached the Nile at its junction with the Sobat. He had sent messengers to meet them and invite them to visit him at Fashoda. However, his men could find no one – only two flags, one on the right bank and the other on the island in the Nile where Potter and Faivre had managed to have it planted it with such effort. There seemed little hope for support from that quarter.[29]

Their initial euphoria now gone, Marchand and his men soon realized that they were in a precarious position. With one-third of their force away on the *Faidherbe* in the Bahr al-Ghazal, they could muster only six French officers, two NCOs, ninety-eight Senegalese armed with light rifles, and ten native boatmen with old-fashioned muskets which frequently failed to fire. They faced not only an eventual attack by Kitchener's advancing army, but, of more immediate concern, a possible encounter with the dervishes to the north.[30]

Another problem was Fashoda itself. The fort that twenty to thirty years earlier had been garrisoned by 800 English and Egyptians was in ruins. Apart from a few palm trees, the island it occupied was bare, brutally hot, and mosquito ridden. Apart from its location on the Nile, it had nothing to recommend it as a defensible position.[31]

Initially, reports from the local population had provided hope that there were forces, including Europeans, not far distant in the Valley of the Sobat. Using couriers provided by the Reth, Marchand sent them a request for help. He also put his entire force to work constructing a brick and masonry fort that would accommodate his expedition. The French planted vegetables and fruit trees in the rich Nile soil, and set up a market to which the natives could bring produce.[32]

On August 1 the couriers returned with bad news. They had found no indication that there were any Europeans in the Sobat Valley. All that the French could do was hope that the *Faidherbe* and its supporting force would arrive before too many days had passed, and that in the meantime they could withstand any attack by the Khalifa, who was likely to regard them as invaders of his lands.[33]

By August 5 Churchill had reached Luxor, some 300 miles up the Nile from Cairo. He finally felt safe from a recall to his regiment in India. He wrote his mother: "As there has been no canceling order and a fortnight has already passed, I think I may now conclude with certainty that 'silence has given consent.'"[34]

The Twenty-First Lancers, which Churchill had just joined, was the newest cavalry regiment in the British Army. In its forty-year life, it had never been in battle. For that reason, other regiments had suggested that its motto should be "Thou shalt not kill." This, of course, did not sit at all well with the regiment's officers and men. They hoped to earn a different reputation in the Sudan.[35]

By mid-August the Twenty-First Lancers had left their river steamer and were proceeding by land to join Kitchener. When the troops began the morning's march on August 16, Churchill was left behind to hand over surplus stores. He was to catch up with the regiment at its next camp, about fifteen miles away.[36] His work took Churchill longer than expected, and it was dusk before he was able to start out. He was told he would have no trouble finding the camp; he should "just go due south until you see the campfires and turn towards the river." For a time, all went well, but then "the sky began to cloud over and the pointers of the Great Bear faded and became invisible." It soon became clear to Churchill that he was lost in the desert.[37]

The only thing to do was wait until the clouds broke or dawn arrived. With his senses sharpened by his plight, he soon obtained a vivid sense of his surroundings:

"The resolution of its utter waste and desolation grew. A hot, restless, weary wind blew continuously with a mournful sound over the miles and miles of sand and rock, as if conscious of its own uselessness: a rainless wind over a sterile soil. In the distance there was a noise like the rattle of a train. It was more wind blowing over more desert."[38]

Fortunately, at about 3:30 A.M. the clouds broke and with the aid of Orion, and then the lightening eastern sky, Churchill made his way to the Nile, only to find the camp site deserted. At a nearby village, with the aid of sign language and the outline of a lancer he drew with his sword point in the sand, he learned that his regiment had moved south. Fortified by dates and fresh and sweet, but dirty milk, he spent the seventeenth riding through the riparian bush along the Nile. Joining the Lancers in the evening, he "washed away the taste and recollection of native life with one of the most popular drinks of the western world."[39]*

On August 24, about two o'clock on a very hot afternoon, the Twenty-First Lancers "emerged from the scrub, trotted across the open space which had all around the zeriba been cleared of bushes, and entered the camp at Wad Hamed."[40] After they had settled in, Churchill found time to write his mother:

"...Within the next few days there will be a general action—perhaps a very severe one. I may be killed. I do not think so. But if I am you must avail yourself of the consolation of philosophy and reflect on the utter insignificance of all human beings. I want to come back and shall hope all will be well. But I can assure you I do not flinch—though I do not accept the Christian or any other form of religious belief...

---

* Churchill did not identify the drink.

"But I shall come back afterwards the wiser and stronger for my gamble. And then we will think of other and wider spheres of action."[41]

Although he had given every outward indication that he was friendly to the French, the Reth of the Shilluk had become concerned as to their strength relative to that of the dervishes. Marchand had received no reinforcements from either the east or the west, and there was no assurance that any would arrive in the near future. The Reth therefore sent details of Marchand's strength to the Khalifa, correctly assuming that the dervishes would take his hint and attack the French.[42]

On the morning of August 25 a Shilluk rival of the Reth brought word to the French that a Mahdist flotilla carrying a large body of troops was steaming towards Fashoda, and was only an hour away. This gave Marchand time to prepare for the forthcoming attack. At 6:00 A.M. the gunboats appeared, followed by seven lighters carrying about 1,000 men.[43]

At Fashoda the Nile was divided by islands of reeds into two channels. The dervishes slowly steamed up the farther, eastern channel, so that their long-range cannon could hit the fort without being harmed by the shorter-range French guns. Their aim was so bad and their shells were of such poor quality, however, that they inflicted little damage.[44] Once the dervishes had steamed out of range to the south, Marchand seized the initiative, taking thirty-six men through the millet fields to a position where from good cover they could effectively attack the gunboats. At close range they were able to pierce the steamers' armor and also inflict heavy casualties on the Mahdist soldiers on the lighters. After two hours, with their boilers badly damaged, the gunboats retreated downstream with the lighters in tow, passing through a destructive fire as they passed the French fortifications.[45]

The French were ecstatic over their victory over a force more than ten times their size. When someone recalled that August 25 was the special day of Saint Louis, they renamed Fashoda, Fort Saint Louis. They were realistic enough, however, to recognize that the dervishes were likely to return, and that they had used up nearly a third of their ammunition in repelling this initial attack.[46]

The dervishes did so on August 29. This time, with their boats disabled, they came on foot from the north. However, just as they were about to attack, the *Faidherbe* arrived, after a grueling twenty-four day journey from Fort Desaix. The attackers quickly withdrew.[47]

To Marchand and his men, the *Faidherbe's* arrival was an act of salvation. Most of the French were in tears as the boat steamed by the fort, with its sirens and horns at full blast. In addition to its reinforcements of officers and men, the *Faidherbe* brought badly need ammunition and other supplies. The entire expedition was united for the first time since it had left France two years earlier.[48]

⸻⬦⸻

On August 25 and 26, Kitchener's army moved almost halfway from Wad Hamed to Omdurman, and camped at Royan on the west bank of the Nile at the head of the Sixth Cataract. The army's total strength was 8,200 British and 17,000 Egyptian soldiers. Their firepower was augmented by the guns of the Nile steamers and gunboats and by a small force of Arab irregulars, who would advance up the east bank of the Nile and clear away any dervishes who happened to be there. The troops would carry with them two days of supplies, with another nineteen days of provisions on the river barges and transports. The cavalry, which had remained at Wad Hamed to rest the horses, had now arrived. The army was fully concentrated and would begin its final advance on the morrow.[49]

The dervish army, some 50,000 strong, was waiting for them outside Omdurman. The Shabluka Heights, which commanded the Sixth Cataract and around which the army had to march, would have been a strong defensive position for the Khalifa's troops. However, the dervish leader announced that the Mahdi had told him in a dream that the infidel army would be totally destroyed on the Kerreri Plains in front of the Mahdi's Omdurman tomb. The final battle would be fought there and nowhere else.[50]

At four o'clock the afternoon of August 28, Kitchener's army left Royan and commenced its final advance on Omdurman. The British marched along the Nile in a large square. The Egyptian infantry was in the desert to the west, and the Egyptian camel corps covered the army's right flank. The cavalry was in the lead, searching out any possible ambush. The advance was unopposed. At night the army camped at Wady el Abid, on the Nile six miles south of Royan.[51]

After resting on the twenty-ninth at Wady el Abid, Kitchener's army resumed its advance the next day. On the evening of the thirty-first it camped just north of a slight elevation called the Kerreri Hills, the last natural defense line before Omdurman, less than ten miles away.[52] Except for a few patrols, there had been no sign of the Mahdist forces. On August 30 Kitchener had sent the Khalifa a note, stating his intent to

bombard Omdurman and suggesting the removal of all women and children from the city. He received no reply.[53] The lack of any contact with
the dervishes led some of the British to suspect that they would abandon
Omdurman without a fight. In any event, as Churchill later wrote:

"Everyone that night lay down to sleep with a feeling of keen expect-
ancy. One way or the other all doubts would be settled the next day. The
cavalry would ride over the Kerreri Hills if they were not occupied by
the enemy, and right up to the walls of Omdurman. If the Dervishes
had any army—if there was to be any battle—we should know within
a few hours."[54]

At dawn on September 1, Kitchener's army began its advance
through the Kerreri Hills. Later in the morning the British gunboats
steamed up the Nile, and around eleven o'clock began a heavy bombardment of Omdurman's river forts. These were soon rendered ineffective,
and the dervish gunners fled to the city streets. The English then turned
their attention to the gleaming ninety-one-foot-high dome of the Mahdi's tomb, and quickly tore great holes in what had been Omdurman's
leading architectural landmark.[55]

Meanwhile the Anglo-Egyptian army had passed through the Kerreri Hills. On the plain to the south it formed in a crescent with the Nile
at its back. There it awaited the attack that likely would be coming.
Earlier that morning, the British and Egyptian cavalry, patrolling the
Kerreri Plain, suddenly discovered, as described by Churchill, that what
seemed to be

"...a high dense zeriba of thorn-bushes...was made of men, not of bushes. Behind it other immense masses and lines of men appeared over the
crest; and while we watched, amazed by the wonder of the sight, the
whole face of the slope became black with swarming savages. Four
miles from end to end and, as it seemed, in five great divisions, this
mighty army advanced—swiftly. The whole side of the hill seemed to
move. Between the masses horsemen galloped continually; before them
many patrols dotted the plain; above them waved hundreds of banners,
and the sun, glinting on many thousand hostile spear-points, spread a
sparkling cloud."[56]

As the dervishes came closer, Churchill's commanding officer, Colonel Rowland Martin, ordered him to ride post haste back to Kitchener

and warn him that his army would soon be attacked. Churchill did so, identifying himself only as an officer of the 21st Lancers. Without indicating whether he recognized the young officer who had created such a stir to join his army, the Sirdar asked Churchill how long he had to prepare the army for battle. On hearing "at least an hour," Kitchener seemed satisfied, and rode to a nearby hill to take a look for himself. He ordered his troops to prepare for an attack early that afternoon.[57]

The expected assault never came. At about 1:45 P.M., the dervish hordes halted, the front line discharged its rifles into the air, and then the entire force lay down on the plain. There they remained until dark. Fearing a night attack, the British sent spies posing as deserters into the Khalifa's camps to spread word that it would be Kitchener who would take advantage of the darkness to steal upon the dervishes. As a further precaution, searchlights from the boats on the Nile continuously swept the area in front of the Anglo-Egyptian lines, searching for any sign of activity. There was none. Less than four miles apart, the two armies took what rest they could prior to the conclusive battle that was almost sure to be fought the next day.[58]

The Khalifa had divided his large army into three parts. The first, the 14,000-man Army of the White Flag, would advance from Omdurman on the south and attack Kitchener's left flank. The Army of the Green Flag, 20,000 strong, had slipped away and was waiting behind the Kerreri Hills, two miles to the northwest of Kitchener's crescent shaped line. The 17,000-man Army of the Black Flag, to which the Khalifa had attached himself, was stationed behind the black hill to the southwest, named Jebel Surgam. If the charge of the White Flags was successful, these two forces would move in to complete the victory. If it was repelled, their actions would depend on Kitchener's exploitation of his triumph.[59]

Kitchener expected that the dervishes were most likely to attack his left flank, since it was closest to Omdurman. He accordingly stationed his British regiments there, with the Egyptians on the right. At about ten to six in the morning of September 2, Churchill and other British scouts saw the enemy masses advancing. In another hour, Kitchener's artillery opened fire. As the Khalifa's troops drew closer, the infantry joined in, firing shoulder to shoulder, with the front rank kneeling and the second rank standing. It was the same defense that Wellington had employed against the French at Waterloo, eighty-three years before.[60] Against the dervishes it was devastating. As Churchill described the awful scene:

General Herbert Kitchener

"...bullets were shearing through flesh, smashing and splintering bone; blood spouted from terrible wounds; valiant men were struggling on through a hell of whistling metal, exploding shells, and spurting dust—suffering, despairing, dying. Such was the first phase of the battle of Omdurman."[61]

It was a self-inflicted massacre. By 8:30 P.M., when the dervishes broke off the engagement, some 2,000 of their men lay dead or dying on the plain in front of the British lines. Many more wounded managed to follow their retreating comrades back to their camps.[62]

At this point Kitchener made what could have been a disastrous strategic error. He decided to take advantage of his repulse of the dervish attack and take Omdurman before his foe could regroup and organize the town's defense. He was apparently unaware of the size of the enemy force north of the Kerreri Hills and behind Jebel Surgam. He left his rear protected only by a single Egyptian brigade commanded by Brigadier General Hector MacDonald.[63]

At the first step in the grand advance, Kitchener ordered the 21st Landers to reconnoiter the ground to his front and "use every effort to prevent the enemy entering Omdurman." To its commander, Colonel Martin, this was a golden opportunity for his command to make a name for itself. Thus, when the 400-man regiment spotted a force of dervishes ahead on their right, instead of sideswiping them, the Lancers, including Lieutenant Churchill, made a right turn and charged. As Churchill described what followed:

"The collision was prodigious. Nearly thirty Lancers, men and horses, and at least two hundred Arabs were overthrown. The shock was stunning to both sides, and for perhaps ten wonderful seconds no man heeded his enemy. Terrified horses wedged in the crowd, bruised and shaken men, sprawling in heaps, struggled, dazed and stupid, to their feet, panted and looked about them...Meanwhile the impetus of the calvary carried them on...They shattered the Dervish army and, their pace reduced to a walk, scrambled out of the Khor on the further side, leaving a score of troopers behind them."[64]

After taking five minutes to regroup, the regiment was about to mount a second attack and "cut their way back through their enemies." But then

"...some realization of the cost of our wild ride began to come to those who were responsible. Riderless horses galloped across the plain. Men, clinging to their saddles, lurched helplessly about, covered with blood from perhaps a dozen wounds. Horses, streaming from tremendous gashes, limped and staggered with their riders. In 120 seconds, 5 officers, 65 men, and 119 horses out of 400 had been killed or wounded."[65]

Shocked at what had transpired, Martin and his fellow officers decided against a further charge. Instead, they sent the Lancers around the enemy flank. After a period of rifle fire, the dervishes withdrew, and the regiment remained in possession of the battlefield. It had won three Victoria Crosses and earned a reputation for courage. In retrospect, however, the charge was unnecessary, and so decimated the regiment that Kitchener would be unable to use it to pursue the dervishes after the eventual British victory.[66]

Like Theodore Roosevelt on the San Juan Heights, Winston Churchill had felt the thrill of the wild surge of battle. In a letter written two weeks later to his friend Ian Hamilton, he described it as likely to have been "the most dangerous two minutes I shall live to see." As a pre-World War I Englishman, he "was very anxious for the regiment to charge back...pour la gloire."[67] It would take the slaughter of the Somme eighteen years later to change that attitude.

While the 21st Landers were licking their wounds and Kitchener's main body was nearing Omdurman, MacDonald's Egyptian-Sudanese brigade was about to be attacked by the Khalifa's remaining forces, numbering more than 30,000 men. Fortunately, MacDonald was a hard-fighting Scot who had risen from the ranks and had drilled his men into a well disciplined force. When his excited troops started shooting at random at the first dervish onslaught, he stopped them until they could fire effectively and in unison. Their volleys decimated the Khalifa's troops.[68]

Fortunately for MacDonald's men, the dervish attacks were not well coordinated. Thus, they were first able to repulse the assault from the west by the masses under black banners, and then wheel about to meet the howling hordes coming from the north under green flags. After initial skepticism on hearing that MacDonald was in trouble, Kitchener changed his mind and sent reinforcements, which arrived just as it looked as if the dervishes might overwhelm the beleaguered Egyptians and Sudanese. The Khalifa's men fell in droves under their withering fire, and the rest of his forces fled the scene.[69]

The battle over, Kitchener resumed his advance to Khartoum. He entered the city in mid-afternoon. The only resistance was from wounded dervishes. Kitchener's order to kill several hundred of them to prevent further attacks on his men was strongly criticized in some quarters, but the Sirdar believed that it was necessary.[70]

Kitchener was lucky. His decision to advance his main army to Omdurman without ascertaining the whereabouts and size of the Khalifa's remaining forces could have cost him the battle. Instead, he had won a decisive victory. The dervishes' futile attacks had left more than 11,000 corpses on the battlefield. The British counted another 16,000 wounded and prisoners. By contrast, Kitchener's losses were 48 killed and 434 wounded. More than half of the dead were from the 21st Lancers.[71]

The Khalifa had escaped. After trying in vain to organize resistance in the city and praying to Allah under the shattered dome of the mahdi's tomb, he left by camel. He made his way to El Obeid, 150 miles to the southwest. Efforts at pursuit proved futile, but they were unnecessary. He would cause the Anglo-Egyptians no further trouble.[72] Kitchener was taking no chances, however. The Mahdi's tomb, which had developed into a kind of shrine, had already been seriously damaged by British gunfire. The Sirdar now ordered it destroyed, and the Mahdi's body, except for the skull, thrown into the Nile. Certain segments of the British public, as well as Queen Victoria, complained, especially when Kitchener proposed that the Mahdi's skull should be sent to the museum of the College of Surgeons in London for display beside the guts of Napoleon. Kitchener responded to the criticism by secretly burying the skull in a Moslem cemetery.[73]

A much happier event was the memorial service that Kitchener organized on September 4 outside the palace in Khartoum where Gordon had been killed thirteen years before. Five hundred British, Egyptians, and Sudanese selected from the army's different regiments stood hushed through a ceremony conducted by the army's Anglican, Presbyterian, and Catholic chaplains, which closed as a Sudanese band played Gordon's favorite hymn, "Abide with Me." Even the consistently stone-faced Kitchener was moved to tears.[74]

The foreign diplomatic contingent in Paris had been abuzz with speculation over the effects on French foreign policy of the governmental shakeup in late June, and especially the views of the new Foreign Minister, Theophile Delcassé. Originally a journalist, Delcassé was first elected a deputy in 1889. He at once became a strong supporter of colonial expansion, including the Marchand expedition. Count Munster, the German Ambassador to France, viewed him unfavorably as "a keen supporter of the Russian alliance," who would prove to be no friend of Germany. Delcassé's seven years as Foreign Minister were to confirm the accuracy of this prediction.[75]

On July 1, British Ambassador Sir Edmund Monson wrote Salisbury regarding Delcassé that

"...I cannot say that his antecedents at the Ministry of the Colonies inspire me with any other expectation than that Her Majesty's Government will find him a very combative minister."

Monson added that an

"...Anglophobe writer in the 'Figaro' welcomes this morning his advent at the Quai d'Orsay in the confident hope that he will signalize it by vigour in dealing with the Egyptian question."[76]

On September 7 Monson met with Delcassé. The French Foreign Minister noted that if Kitchener were to continue up the Nile, as seemed probable, he likely "would fall in before long with Captain Marchand." The latter had been told to consider himself "an emissary of civilization," with no power "to decide questions of right." Delcassé hoped that Kitchener also "might be instructed to take no steps which might lead to a local conflict with regard to such questions ...." In reply, Monson asked whether the French had had any news from Marchand himself or where his expedition was. Delcassé's somewhat evasive response was that within the past forty-eight hours he had received news "of" Marchand, but that it was not recent.[77]

Delcassé's position on the Sudan was changing. Several years earlier, he had been willing to risk confrontation with England on the issue. Now, as he wrote his colleagues on September 7, the situation was different:

"On the one hand the capture of Khartoum and, on the other, Germany's rapprochement as much with Turkey as with England, have profoundly modified the situation which existed at the moment of the Marchand expedition's departure."[78]

The Foreign Minister was especially concerned over the possible implications of the recent Anglo-German agreement regarding the Portuguese colonies. The same day, he wrote to his wife:

"In exchange for the concessions which she has made, has England received from Germany carte blanche in Egypt? Ought one to conclude that she is going to take advantage of the capture of Khartoum by proclaiming her protectorate over the valley of the Nile? I can well see that this spectacular declaration would delight English chauvinists and perhaps consolidate Salisbury's government... The powers of the Triple Alliance might remain silent and thus in effect give their tacit approval— but this would not alter the fact that the British occupation would continue to be in defiance of international law. That, however, is a question with which I have been unceasingly concerned since I became foreign minister. It is not easy to restore a situation defined for sixteen years and which daily becomes more remote."[79]

Salisbury was on holiday at a German spa, but on September 9, he immediately responded to Monson regarding Delcassé's comments on a possible British-French confrontation in the Sudan:

"If M. Delcassé should revert to this subject, I request you to point out to him that, by the military events of last week, all the territories which were subject to the Khalifa passed to the British and Egyptian Governments by right of conquest. Her Majesty's Government do not consider that this right is open to discussion..."[80]

Shortly after his victory at Omdurman, Kitchener opened the sealed orders instructing him to proceed up the White Nile to Fashoda and beyond. On September 10, he started out with a company of Cameron Highlanders, two battalions of Sudanese infantry, a battery of artillery and four machine guns. The river transports that would carry the expedition up the Nile were accompanied by five gunboats. Kitchener anticipated that this small army should be able to defeat any opposing French force it might meet, should it choose to give battle.[81]

Reports that the French had established themselves on the Upper Nile were widely circulating in the British press, and were generally believed to be true. The Liberal papers were taking a "wait and see" attitude, but the Conservative press had no doubts regarding what British policy should be. As the September 13 *Evening News* explained:

"If a householder finds a man in his back garden, he does not go to arbitration about the matter or enter into elaborate arguments to show that he, the householder, is the owner of the garden. He simply orders the trespasser out, and if he will not go of his own accord, he has to go in another fashion."[82]

If anyone had been gardening on the Upper Nile, it was the French. Immediately on their arrival at Fashoda, they had planted not only flowers, but also peas, cabbages, and haricots verts. They had apparently settled in for a long stay.[83] Marchand's two victories over the dervishes had convinced the Reth that the French were at Fashoda to stay and were worth having as allies. Although he was aware of the strong British force advancing on Omdurman, Marchand apparently had convinced him that the French and English were friends, and that his real need was the protection from other tribes that the French could provide. On September 3 he signed a treaty, written by one of Marchand's officers in French and Arabic, putting the Shilluk nation under French protection.[84]

On September 7 Marchand signed a second treaty of protection and friendship with the chiefs of the nearby Dinkas. On the fifteenth, he issued an Order of the Day declaring that the French had accomplished their goals of "occupying the Bahr al-Ghazal and establishing French domination at Fashoda." The next day the *Faidherbe* left for Meshra, where word could be sent to the French in Ubangi for more men and military armaments and supplies. If Marchand's force could only hold out until these had arrived and there was time to train their new native allies, they might be a match for either the Mahdists, should they return, or the British.[85]

Marchand's wish would not be granted. On September 18 Kitchener's flotilla reached Babiu, a small village only a few miles north of Fashoda. The trip from Khartoum had generally been peaceful and uneventful. The sole encounter had been with a Mahdist gunboat, which had not yet received word of the Khalifa's defeat. It was quickly subdued, and its captain was taken on board to help the British navigate the occasionally treacherous channels of the Upper Nile.[86]

Since the Mahdist boat had been engaged in the earlier dervish battle with the French, Kitchener now knew that a force of Europeans was at Fashoda. However, the Mahdists could not tell whether they were French or nationals of some other country. So as to reduce the risk of an accidental battle and also to let the force at Fashoda know of his victory over the dervishes, Kitchener's chief of intelligence, Colonel Francis Wingate, prepared a letter of explanation, written in French, but addressed to the "Chief of the European expedition at Fashoda." It was sent by runner late in the day, in time to arrive at Fashoda early the next morning. Otherwise, September 18 was spent in anxious waiting and negotiating with the Shilluks who, seeing the size and power of the Anglo-Egyptian force, tried to explain their alliance with the French on the basis that they mistakenly believed that those Europeans were English.[87]

═══◯▶◀◯═══

The same day, in a meeting "conducted on both sides with perfect calmness," Delcassé and Monson made clear each other's position regarding Fashoda and the Sudan. The French Foreign Minister was the more conciliatory of the two, opening the discussion by suggesting that if the feeling on the matter was the same in London as in Paris, "there can be no real danger of a conflict between the two powers, even upon so delicate a question as that which seems to be imminent on the Upper Nile." Monson replied that although England wished to "live in perfect amity" with France, Delcassé "was as well aware as I that Her Majesty's Government had very openly let France understand that any incursion of them into the Upper Nile would be considered by us as an unfriendly act."[88]

As the conversation continued, Delcassé reiterated that France had never recognized the British claim, but again stressed "that if Her Majesty's government would meet that of France in a friendly spirit, there could be no reason why a satisfactory arrangement should not be swiftly arrived at." To this, the Ambassador replied "that the situation on the Upper Nile is a very dangerous one," adding "categorically" that the British "would not consent to a compromise on this point." He then concluded:

"For the rest we had no wish to pick a quarrel; but having long ago given a warning, I could not see how we could now cause surprise if we resent a step which we had cautioned France not to take."[89]

═══◯▶◀◯═══

Marchand received Kitchener's letter shortly after dawn on September 19. In an hour, he composed and sent off his reply in a whale boat displaying what one of the British officers described as "an immense French flag." After congratulating Kitchener on his victory over the dervishes, the letter outlined the exploits of the French expedition and the treaty with the Shilluk that placed Fashoda and its surrounding area under French protection. It then welcomed Kitchener to the Upper Nile "au nom de la France."[90]

Upon receipt of the letter, and now assured that the occupants of Fashoda were French, the British proceeded up the Nile. When they reached Fashoda, Kitchener invited Marchand aboard his steamer. After repeating the mutual congratulations already expressed in their exchange of letters, they got down to business. According to Marchand's later description:

"'I have come to resume possession of the Khedive's dominions,' Kitchener began.

"Mon General, I, Marchand, am here by order of the French Government. I thank you for your offer of conveyance to Europe, but I must wait here for instructions.'

"Major, I will place my boats at your disposal to return to Europe by the Nile.'

"Mon General, I thank you, but I am waiting for orders from my Government.'

"I must hoist the Egyptian flag here,' Kitchener next said.

"Why, I myself will help you to hoist it—over the village.'

"Over your fort.'

"No, that I shall resist.'

"Do you know, Major, that this affair may set France and England at war?'

I bowed, without replying."[91]

At this point, Kitchener scanned the horizon, comparing his force of 2,000 men and several gunboats with the French contingent of slightly more than 100 and their fort, which one of his officers later described as "a puny little thing." He then observed "We are the stronger," and announced his intention to hoist the Egyptian flag over an outlying part of the fort. Perhaps because it was not the Union Jack that would be raised, and since Kitchener did not insist on the French flag being lowered, Marchand did not object. The two soldiers tacitly agreed that the dispute between their countries was not for them to resolve. That could be left to the diplomats in London and Paris.[92]

Watching from a nearby gunboat, British Major (later General) Smith-Dorrien vividly remembered the proceedings twenty-four years later:

"After much bowing and scraping and saluting, what I supposed to be a map was spread on the table, and there followed much gesticulation and apparently angry conversation. Distinct signs of hostility on both sides. I was beginning to think there could be only one ending to such forcible discussions, and that I should see negotiations broken off, when up the ladder moved a native servant bearing a tray of bottles and glasses, and these, full of golden liquid, were soon being clinked together by the two central figures, who until that moment, I had believed to be engaged in a deadly dispute."[93]*

At three in the afternoon, Kitchener and his staff returned Marchand's visit. This time, the toasts were drunk in sweet champagne and, as the conviviality increased, became more frequent. Several French officers admitted their relief when they learned that their "attackers" were the British and not the Mahdists. Perhaps to undermine the French morale, Kitchener had obtained from Cairo copies of the most recent Paris newspapers. According to Marchand, after they had read the news of the Dreyfus case and the continuing French government crisis, "the French officers were trembling and weeping...and for thirty-six hours none of us were able to say anything to the others."[94]

The friendly atmosphere and mutual admiration reached its peak as the gathering ended and the French presented the departing British with a basketful of vegetables they had grown since their arrival in Fashoda two months earlier. Realism returned, however, when Kitchener asked Wingate to hand Marchand a sealed envelope and told the French commander that it contained a formal protest of the French presence in British and Egyptian territory. Without waiting for a reply, the Sirdar informed Marchand that he would be leaving immediately to plant his flag upstream where the Sobat joins the Nile. He left behind a well-armed battalion of 400 Sudanese under Major H.W. Jackson and a gunboat.[95]

The same day, after resting for the night twenty miles south of Fashoda, Kitchener's force reached the mouth of the Sobat, forty-two miles further upstream. There, it ceremoniously hoisted flags of occupation. Leaving behind half of a Sudanese battalion as a garrison, the armada immediately reversed course, and headed for Omdurman, steaming by Fashoda without stopping.[96]

On September 21, Jackson delivered a second "protest" to Marchand.

---

* Marchand later commented that having to drink toasts in lukewarm whisky and soda— "cet affreux alcool enfumé"—was one of the greatest sacrifices he ever made for France.

It referred to an alleged oral statement by Kitchener to the French commander that since the Anglo-Egyptians had placed Fashoda and the surrounding area under martial law, any movement of "munitions of war" was forbidden. Marchand replied that he could recall no such discussion and pointed out that the *Faidherbe* would be returning from Meshra'er Req without any knowledge of Kitchener's order. He warned that Kitchener would be responsible for any attack on the steamer.[97]

The first of Churchill's reports from the Sudan was published in the August 31 *Morning Post*. Because Lady Jeune had written Kitchener that if Churchill joined his army: "Guarantee he won't write" a subterfuge seemed necessary. The dispatches were written as letters from a soldier to a friend or relative, who was so impressed that he turned them over to the newspaper. Thus the first letter, dated August 8, commenced: "You would rightly call me faithless, my dear..., if I were to make no effort to carry out my promise to give you some account of the features and the fortunes of the war on the Nile."

In fact, Churchill mailed the dispatches directly to Oliver Borthwick, the *Morning Post's* proprietor. When printed, they were preceded by an explanation of their supposed origin. In all there were fifteen letters, which were printed between August 31 and October 13. By October, the author's identity was generally known.[98] But by then it made no difference as the fighting was over.

The 21st Lancers did not accompany Kitchener to Fashoda. Instead, three days after its charge at Omdurman, the regiment left for England, going to Cairo first by boat and then by rail.[99] Waiting in Cairo for transport to England, Lieutenant Churchill visited a fellow officer whose arm had been seriously wounded by a sword cut during the charge at Omdurman. While they were talking, the officer's doctor came in to dress his wound and decided that it should be skinned over. He suggested to Churchill that to this limited extent he should volunteer to be "flayed alive." Churchill agreed, and gamely managed to hold out as "a beautiful piece of skin with a thin layer of flesh attached to it" was cut from the inside of his forearm and "grafted on to my friend's wound." To the end of his life, Churchill proudly wore his scar as a memento of the campaign.[100]

SIXTEEN

Building France
A 'Golden Bridge'

O n September 25 the British Government received two dispatches from Kitchener, wired from Omdurman via Cairo. After describing his discussions with Marchand, Kitchener wrote:

"The position in which Captain Marchand finds himself at Fashoda is as impossible as it is absurd. He is cut off from the interior, and his water transport is quite inadequate; he is, moreover, short of ammunition and supplies, which must take months to reach him; he has no following in the country, and nothing could have saved him and his expedition from being annihilated by the Dervishes had we been a fortnight later in crushing the Khalifa."

"The futility of all their efforts is fully realized by Captain Marchand himself, and he seems quite as anxious to return as we are to facilitate his departure." [1]

Kitchener's second message confirmed that if the French

"...will at once give telegraphic instructions for the explorer M. Marchand and his expedition to leave Fashoda and come down Nile, I can now send special steamer with such orders to fetch them." [2]

In several respects, Kitchener's report was misleading. The arrival of the *Faidherbe* in August had provided the French with plenty of ammunition, and on its return from Meshra they would have ample water mobility. Especially with their vegetable gardens, they had adequate and nourishing food. In that respect they were better off than the garrison that Kitchener left behind. As its commander, Major Jackson later wrote "...it must be admitted that, while the French were admirably equipped for service in a tropical climate, the Anglo-Egyptian force was

267

lacking in practically everything which might ameliorate the conditions of service in such a country..."[3]

—◦※◦—

Pursuant to Salisbury's instructions, on September 26 Monson met with Delcassé and watched as he twice read over "carefully" a French translation of Kitchener's two telegrams. The Foreign Minister asked the Ambassador to furnish him with a "French paraphrase," which he would read and discuss at a Cabinet meeting which was already scheduled for the next day. All that he could do at this point was to speak of "his gratification that the meeting between the Sirdar and M. Marchand has passed off in a manner creditable to the chivalrous sentiments of the Representatives of the two Nations."[4]

After the September 27 French Cabinet meeting, Delcassé sent for Monson. Initially, he asked the British to forward to Marchand a French request for an official report, and to facilitate the report's transmission to the French Government. After both diplomats restated their countries' positions, Delcassé said that all he wanted at this time was "some clear and explicit definition of what Her Majesty's Government consider to be the territories to which, on the part of Egypt, they lay claim for her." He urged Monson not to "drive him into a corner" by refusing to entertain this request. Monson reported that "his Excellency showed me some of the papers in which he is held up to execration as the 'author of national disgrace.'"[5]* Monson advised Salisbury that "I yielded only to his pressing appeal not to drive him to extremities."[6]

On September 28 Salisbury instructed Monson to tell Delcassé that the British would transmit any message that the French Government wished to send to Marchand. He added that Monson should warn his fellow ministers that "if the present situation is prolonged, great uneasiness will be caused here..."[7]

The same day Delcassé "initiated" a further discussion with Monson on Fashoda, advising him that the French Minister in London had been instructed to discuss the crisis directly with Salisbury. According to Monson, Delcassé then

"...reiterated that it is the desire of the present French Government to make a friend of England, adding that between ourselves he would much

---

* The morning's headlines included: "Marchand Cannot Be Disavowed or Recalled!" and "The Honour of the Flag Is at Stake!"

prefer an Anglo-French to a French-Russian alliance. He again entreat-ed me to take account of existing excitement in France, which is becom-ing dangerous and might in an instant break out into overt acts ..He admitted that he knew feeling in England is strong, but he argued that Englishmen are not so excitable as the French, and felt sentimental con-siderations less deeply. I replied that he could not exaggerate strength of feeling in England on this subject, both on the part of Government and the public, and the knowledge of this caused me great apprehension. He said: 'You surely would not break with us over Fashoda?' To which I answered that it was exactly that which I feared..."[8]

Delcassé was in a very difficult position. A group of approximately 100 deputies was becoming increasingly vocal in support of Marchand's position. On the other hand, the Foreign Minister recognized that Eng-land held the stronger hand for, as he wrote his wife on September 28 "All we have is arguments, and they have soldiers on the spot."[9]

Observers outside England and France were beginning to take note of the impending crisis. The September 28 London *Times* quoted a Cologne newspaper as predicting that the relative negotiating positions of the two countries would be influenced by the fact that "England has her hands free while the energies of France are paralyzed by the Dreyfus case."[10]

When Monson called at the Foreign Ministry on the Quai d'Orsay in September 30, Delcassé took a firm stand. The Ambassador reported to Salisbury that the Foreign Minister "wishes me to let you know unoffi-cially that it is impossible for the French government to give up Fasho-da..." It would be "an insult to the national honour" and "France would, how-ever unwillingly, accept war rather then submit."

Before the meeting, Delcassé had received a deciphered copy of a telegram from the Italian Ambassador to his Government stating that Monson had been instructed to deliver an ultimatum at their next meet-ing. Delcassé mistakenly believed that the report was accurate, and was elated when Monson failed to present the nonexistent demand in re-sponse to the firm stand that Delcassé took in their conversation. This belief that he had scored a diplomatic triumph would affect French policy in the days ahead.[12]

Reports from other sources seemed to confirm Delcassé's optimism.

September 30's London *Times* carried a report from Vienna that "all expect England for the sake of peace to sacrifice interests which no Continental Power would think of surrendering." The *Times*'s correspondent added that "there is a general conviction that the British Government is committed to a policy of peace at any price."[13]

Queen Victoria was taking an active interest in the Fashoda controversy. On October 2 she telegraphed Lord Salisbury that the reports from Ambassador Monson "are most unsatisfactory." She suggested that England "delay" until the French Government received Marchand's report, "which can, I believe, come only through us."

On October 3, the Prime Minister sent the Queen a sympathetic reply that he and his ministers

"...are doing nothing, but only waiting, and we cannot do anything else. No offer of territorial concession on our part would be endorsed by public opinion here."

Victoria quickly answered:

"...Quite agree. We cannot give way. If we wait, I think the force of circumstances will bring the French to their senses."[15]

French Ambassador Courcel had been in France on leave pending his upcoming retirement. Delcassé sent him back to London to negotiate personally with Salisbury. Their first meeting, on October 5, lasted two hours, and was devoted to statements of position. Courcel argued that the British and Egyptians had abandoned any rights they may have had to the Southern Sudan, and that France's position at Fashoda was as much hers by right of conquest as that of the Anglo-Egyptians at Omdurman. The Prime Minister responded that England's cession of the Sudan had been involuntary. Now that Kitchener had defeated the Mahdists and retaken the territory's capital city, the Anglo-Egyptian position was the same as though they had continuously occupied it. Indeed, Britain had regularly made clear that she had not abandoned the Sudan.[15]

Of more importance than these legalistic justifications was Salisbury's reference to the relative weakness of Marchand's position:

Queen Victoria

"I pointed out to him that such an occupation as that of M. Marchand, with an escort of 100 troops, could give no title to the occupying force, and that, in point of fact, but for the arrival of the British flotilla, M. Marchand's escort would have been destroyed by the Dervishes."

After both men noted the "strength of feeling" that existed on the subject in their respective countries, they parted. Clearly, the last words had not been spoken.[16]

The real French position would be less inflexible than Courcel had indicated. Delcassé had concluded that Fashoda was not worth a war with England. What he wanted was a British concession of a French right to some part of the Bahr al-Ghazal, which the French government could use as a sop to public opinion. However, it would have been premature for Courcel to suggest this in his first meeting with Salisbury. The fact that the British Prime Minister was amenable to continuing discussion made Delcassé cautiously optimistic that France would not be forced into a complete surrender of its position in the Sudan.[17]

In public, the French Government was taking a strong stand. Thus, *Le Matin*, which was generally regarded as its "mouthpiece," proclaimed on October 7:

"The Government...will not retreat before menaces from the press or any other menaces...If the Foreign Office were to adopt and make its own the theories of the London press, and meet the offer of imminent negotiations by the previous question of the recall of M. Marchand, we are in a position to affirm that the reply of our Government would be the only one worthy of France—No..."[18]

A nervous Ambassador Monson described these and other French newspaper comments in an October 7 note to Salisbury. After assuring the Prime Minister that he had no doubt "of the policy which the safeguarding of British and Egyptian rights imposes upon us," he cautioned:

"I shall not be surprised, should the present situation continue, to see that at least one Great Power...assumes the right to submit to Europe that...this grave controversy should be made the subject of deliberation by other Powers besides the two most immediately concerned."[19]

Salisbury also was trying to put nondiplomatic pressure on France to abandon Fashoda. In an October 7, telegram to Cromer in Cairo, after noting that Kitchener had imposed martial law and prohibited the transport of war material on the Nile, he emphasized that the Sirdar "has of course authority to take whatever measures he thinks necessary to enforce this decision." He added that the French "have been informed of the Sirdar's action and will understand what it implies."[20]

On October 9 the Foreign Office issued a "Blue Book" on the Fashoda crisis. It contained copies of official documents and correspondence commencing in December 1897 and running to the publication date. The papers apparently had been released so that the British public would be aware of the issues involved, and the strong stand that their Government was taking.[21]

By the next day, if the expressions of the editors of *Le Matin* were any guide, the French Government appeared to be reversing course on Fashoda. Monson sent Salisbury a "leading article" in the October 10 issue which "in view of the tone previously adopted by that organ with regard to the question, almost verges on the ludicrous, so sudden and complete is the change of front taken up." The article's "pith," according to the Ambassador, was: "The abandonment of Fashoda is perfectly compatible with the preservation of the national honour." Among other things, the editors referred to "useless and extravagant territories, practically inaccessible from the French possessions on the Atlantic coast...which might, for all the good they do to us, as well be in the moon itself." Monson's dispatch concluded:

"If a hint from the Government has inspired this article, the writer has carried out his instructions with a vengeance, and it will be interesting to observe whether this is but a solitary note, or whether the cry will be taken up by the whole pack."[22]

On October 9 the British gunboat *Kaiber* arrived at Fashoda. Its captain promptly gave to Marchand Delcassé's dispatch asking the French commander to send Paris as promptly as possible a report describing his condition and recommendations. The next day the *Kaiber* turned back downstream, with Lieutenant Baratier aboard, carrying with him not only Marchand's report but also personal letters sent home by other expedition members.[23]

On October 11, Monson met again with Delcassé, who, "for the first time, became excited in our conversation." He was annoyed at the jingoist response in much of the British press to the publication of the diplomatic papers on the Upper Nile, contrasting it with what he described as the more moderate tone of the French newspapers. Monson wrote Salisbury that

"...I am inclined to believe that there must have been some unpleasant things said to him to-day at the Cabinet Council in regard to his having allowed such a clear intimation to be given to him about the impossibility of the retention of Fashoda by France, for he talked of the possibility of retiring, and said that another Minister would not be so accommodating."

Having thus cleared the air, the French Foreign Minister stated, as a "private and unofficial" matter, that "if we would make things easy for him in form he would be conciliatory in substance." Specifically,

"...he was quite willing to discuss the evacuation of Fashoda in connection with the delimitation of the Franco-Egyptian frontier, and he seems to me to be resigned to the inevitable, but not immediate, retreat of Marchand's expedition if unaccompanied by any incident which might be considered humiliating to France..."

Delcassé added "that the greater part of the Bahr al-Ghazal is effectively occupied" by France. Monson concluded optimistically that Delcassé "is prepared to retreat eventually, and after negotiation,...if we can build him a golden bridge for that retrograde movement."[24]

The October 9 "Blue Book" may have had a greater effect than Salisbury would have wished. By solidifying popular support for the Government's policy, its publication may have made it harder for the British to provide the French a sop that would permit them to make a graceful retreat. Thus, the October 11 London *Times* reported that the "reception by the country of the Fashoda papers has been all that the Government could desire..." Its own leading article, or editorial, on the matter affirmed that the Government's policy "is the only course a British Government could have taken." Elsewhere, the paper carried a report from its Paris correspondent that the Paris Municipal Council had proposed to rename a street "Fashoda." The reporter commented:

"This is the entry of the mob into international questions. The object of the proposal is evident. It is impossible for a Government to evacuate a place after which, as a sign of conquest, a street has been named."[25]*

Three days later, the October 14 *Times* asserted that Marchand had committed "an Unfriendly Act against England." Its Paris correspondent quoted a conversation between a Frenchman and an Englishman:

"The Frenchman: 'Sir Edward Grey's warning was like a notice board posted on the boundary of an estate, but England was not the proprietor when she set up that board.'
The Englishman: 'That may be, but when the board was put up poachers alone cross the boundary, whereas sportsmen in broad daylight begin by arguing the right and do not cross till afterwards.'"[26]

Following up the previous day's conversation between Delcassé and Monson, on October 12 Courcel met again with Salisbury. After what were becoming obligatory restatements of position, the Prime Minister suggested that if Marchand would withdraw from the Nile, the British would not object if the French at the same time were to assert that they were not abandoning any rights they had in that area. Courcel countered by proposing that if Marchand left Fashoda, the British would concede the right of France to some part of the Bahr al-Ghazal that would provide it with navigational access to the Upper Nile. After responding that he and his colleagues would consider this proposal, Salisbury suggested that Courcel state it precisely in writing.[27]

This development looked promising. However, in the short letter that Courcel wrote and delivered later in the day, he told Salisbury that the French claim included the entire region between the Bahr al-Ghazal on the south and the Bahr al-Arab to the north. This was more than Salisbury had anticipated. The next day he quickly responded that without Courcel's clarifying letter "I think I should have misunderstood the effect of the observations which you made during our conversation yes-

---

* On a recent perusal of a Paris street directory, the author found no reference to a "Rue Fashoda."

terday." He added that Courcel's territorial claim "is quite new to me, and, as far as I know, has never been officially made on behalf of the French Government."[28]

Archibald Philip, Fifth Earl of Rosebery, had served as the leader of the Liberal Party and Prime Minister from 1894 to 1895. Unlike many of his fellow party members, he was an ardent imperialist. Wealthy by birth, he also had inherited the property of his deceased wife, the only daughter of Austrian Baron Meyer Amschel de Rothschild.

As the owner of a large estate at the Durdans, near Epsom, south of London, Rosebery was president of the Surrey Agricultural Association. As reported by the London *Times*, on October 13 he "strolled across the fields from the Durdans, and after examining the plough horses and witnessing a portion of the competition for straw binding, presented the prizes to the successful competitors." That evening, at a dinner at the Epsom Town Hall marking the sixty-ninth anniversary of the Association, he spoke in support of the Government's policy regarding "the very critical condition of affairs which exists in a remote district of Central Africa.":

"Behind the policy of the British Government in the matter there is the entire and united strength of the nation. It is the policy of the last Government deliberately adopted and sustained by the present Government. That is only a matter of form, but this is the policy of the nation itself."[29]

Some Government officials were taking on even more strident public stances. Sir Michael Hicks-Beach, as Chancellor of the Exchequer, was one of the most important of Salisbury's ministers. On October 19, in a speech before the Conservative Association in the northern English town of North Shields, his main topic was the Fashoda crisis. He began by stating that although he believed that "the question is capable of a friendly and an amicable solution, ...this country must put its foot down." He then asserted, "to loud cheering."

"It would be a great calamity, I do not understate it, that, after a peace of more than eighty years, during which I had hoped that unfriendly feeling had practically disappeared between two neighboring nations, those friendly relations would be disturbed and we should be launched into a great war. But there are greater evils than war. We have to do our duty."[30]

The opinion in Great Britain was nearly unanimous: the French must abandon Fashoda. The feeling cut across all classes. Although some Liberals held out, that party's rank and file, no less than aristocrats like Lord Rosebery, backed the Government. Typical was the October 20 resolution of the Yeovil Working Men's Liberal Association that praised the Government for its stand.[31] As Churchill wrote two months later, if the French did not depart, "we were all agreed...all the might, majesty, dominion and power of everything that could by any stretch of the imagination be called 'British' should be employed to make them go."[32]

Hicks-Beach's talk of war led to concern that emotions might be getting out of hand. For example, the October 21 London *Times* warned:

"The time has come when it is absolutely necessary to dispel French dreams on this subject, unless very dangerous consequences are to result; but the Chancellor of the Exchequer might have performed the operation more dexterously.[55]

The same issue of the *Times* that contained the text of Hicks-Beach's speech quoted a Paris newspaper as announcing that, "if Great Britain threatens us with an ultimatum...France from that moment is ready to make every sacrifice rather than suffer such humiliation." The same day, *The New York Times* contained reports of the movement of troops from Paris to French coastal ports and of "the embarkation of war materials and supplies" at the French Mediterranean port of Toulon.[34]

During the morning of October 21, Delcassé met with Monson and complained that Hicks-Beach's speech had caused "the greatest irritation" to "men representing almost every shade of opinion" in the Senate and the Chamber of Deputies. Delcassé was convinced "that war between England and France over such a question as Fashoda would be an unparalleled calamity" and "he had all along been ready to discuss M. Marchand's recall, provided that it was not forced upon him as an ultimatum." Monson concluded that the French "will be unable to maintain their contention as regards M. Marchand, but that until they can announce that negotiations have begun on their claims to the west of the Nile, they will decline to withdraw him."[35]

Monson had an additional concern. Russian Foreign Minister Count

Muraviëv had just left Paris, which he had visited for the apparent purpose of assuaging French concerns over Tsar Nicholas II's proposal for a worldwide disarmament conference.[*] The British Ambassador had heard from his fellow diplomats that, to placate France, the Russian Foreign Minister had announced that Russia would support her on the Fashoda issue.[36] Like many rumors, this one had no substance. Russia, short of funds, with an army which was undergoing reorganization, had no interest in fighting England. If Muraviëv had given any advice to Delcassé, it was to reach a settlement.[37]

On October 21 Baratier arrived in Cairo and promptly telegraphed Marchand's report to Delcassé. The Foreign Minister, however, was not satisfied to base his Fashoda decision only on written evidence. Thus, when Baratier reached Cairo, he was handed an order to proceed to Paris immediately. He started out the next morning.[38]

Delcassé was wise in not expecting too much from Marchand's report. It made clear that the French had sufficient ammunition and supplies, but expressed concern as to the long-range health of the officers and men. Of greater importance, Marchand was finding it "impossible to put up any longer with the conditions of isolation and imprisonment which the English have imposed on us here..." Thus, if he received no orders in the next twelve days, Marchand would try to get to Khartoum "to demand communication with Paris. I think I would be of more use to you in Paris."[39]

By now, the crisis seemed to be escalating to a dangerous degree. On Saturday, October 22, the British Government announced that the Cabinet would hold a special meeting as early the next week as the ministers could return from their early fall holiday. Under the headline "BRITISH NAVY IS READY TO STRIKE" in the next day's *New York Times* its London correspondent reported: "Never since the two countries began to dispute over Egypt...has the situation looked so ominous as today." French military and naval authorities reportedly were "making feverish preparations for war." Further,

"...though calm reigns at the British dockyards...it is only the calm of

---

[*] *See* Chapter Seventeen.

preparedness, and significant orders have been arriving there from the Admiralty, indicating the belief that Great Britain and France are on the brink of war."[40]

In response to the British "Blue Book" of papers on the Fashoda controversy, the French Government on October 21 published a "Yellow Book," containing its own documents on the subject. What the next day's London *Times* described as the Yellow Book's "most striking passage" was the statement in Ambassador Courcel's report to Delcassé that in their October 12 conversation Salisbury "pressed me, with insistence, to make proposals to him, if my instructions permitted it." This looked as if, despite its denials, the British Government was "negotiating" with France.[41]

Matters were rapidly moving to a head. During a generally quiet Sunday, October 23, Delcassé wrote his wife:

"This week will very likely bring the denouement of the Anglo-French crisis. My course of action is decided and I have let it be known: "Recognize an outlet for us on the Nile and I shall withdraw Marchand."[42]

Privately, Delcassé had reluctantly concluded that Marchand must withdraw even if England refused to concede France a Nile outlet. The next day, he wrote his wife: "If England does not accept my proposition, I shall publish Marchand's journal and recall the heroic little band."[43]

On October 24 the Salisbury Government reacted quickly to the French Yellow Book by publishing a further set of papers regarding the Sudan. Among them was Salisbury's October 12 report to Monson of that afternoon's conversation with Courcel. As an article in the October 25 London *Times* noted, it contained no indication that the Prime Minister had suggested he would welcome a French proposal on Fashoda.[44]

All this diplomatic activity was taking place against continuing military buildups by both sides. *The New York Times* carried a report from London that British dockyards had been ordered to prepare six torpedo boat destroyers for immediate sea duty, and that overtime had been ordered to put two first-class cruisers in shape for action. The English North

Atlantic Squadron received orders to mobilize at Halifax, Nova Scotia. Several battalions of French troops were gathering at Toulon, where the schools had been closed to house them.[45]

Notwithstanding these alarming reports, there appeared to be a growing belief in both London and Paris that war would be averted. Perhaps, both countries were following the maxim, one must "arm to parley."[46]

Monson was closely observing the newest French Government crisis resulting from the Dreyfus case and considering its possible effect on the Fashoda crisis. He unexpectedly received from an "entirely trustworthy" source a copy of the advice which the recently departed Russian Foreign Minister had given Delcassé. According to Monson's October 25 report to Salisbury, it "was almost textually as follows":

'Do not give England any pretext for attacking you at present. At a later date an opportunity will be found by Russia for reopening the whole question of Egypt.'

Monson added his "own opinion" that the Russian minister "neither categorically refused, nor contingently promised, the support of Russia in the present controversy."[47] He continued to worry that Russia might provide France with more than moral support. On October 27 he telegraphed Salisbury that he could "now state with positive assurance" that this would be the case.

The feeling in London was to the contrary: Russia was unlikely to intervene. However, the British Mediterranean Fleet had been alerted to be prepared for action if a Russian fleet were to steam through the Dardanelles into the Eastern Mediterranean.[48] From October twenty-sixth through the twenty-ninth the Admiralty prepared and delivered detailed orders under which the Mediterranean Fleet would concentrate at Malta and the Channel Fleet at Gibraltar. In this way, the French fleet, which was in port at Toulon, would be boxed in whether it chose to go either east or west. Meanwhile, the British Home Fleet's cruisers and destroyers would protect English Channel shipping and ports from the French torpedo boats that seemed to present the greatest danger to them.[49]

⚜

In the evening of October 26, Lieutenant Baratier arrived by train at the Gare de Lyon. He was enthusiastically greeted by a large crowd. His initial joy that his reception indicated widespread popular support for

Marchand's position on the Nile soon disappeared when he realized that the demonstration had been arranged by private citizens representing a leading colonialist group and that no leading Government members had been at the station to welcome him.[50]

Baratier immediately underwent two days of debriefing by Delcassé. Not long after the first day's session had gotten under way, he became suspicious that notwithstanding the Foreign Minister's praise for the expedition's accomplishments, his purpose was to find excuses for ordering Marchand to withdraw. As Delcassé continued to press him as to the real state of the troops' health and supplies, Baratier vigorously replied that, notwithstanding intimations to the contrary in Marchand's written report, the French were in good shape on all counts. He finally broke off the interview, and later in the day reported his frustration to a group of colonialist deputies.[51]

On October 27 the British Cabinet met on Fashoda. There apparently was no serious thought of compromise. Instead, the general feeling was that at some point there would have to be a serious colonial confrontation with France and that it might just as well be over Fashoda, where Britain had the stronger position. Chamberlain, for one, was apparently in favor of war. Salisbury, however, still thought that a peaceful solution was possible, and he had the Queen behind him. Probably at his suggestion, the Cabinet decided to tell the French that although Marchand must withdraw immediately without any British concessions to possible French access to the Nile, it would be possible later on to consider whether the French claims were worth discussing. If Marchand did not depart, he would not be attacked, but no reinforcements would be permitted to reach him. At that point, France rather than England would be the country that would "adopt any active measures that would precipitate a conflict."[52]

Shortly after the conclusion of the October 27 Cabinet meeting, Salisbury reported its conclusions to Courcel. At the Ambassador's request, the next day the Prime Minister provided him with an "unofficial aide-memoire" confirming that "whatever was at present abnormal in the diplomatic relations between the two countries would cease" as soon as the French ordered Marchand's withdrawal. At that point, the French claims could be considered "without prejudice," but without any commitment as to the outcome of that discussion. The Ambassador also received from Sir Thomas Sanderson of the Foreign Office a written statement that England "had never made any official request for the removal of M. Marchand and his party from Fashoda." With these assurances, on October 29 Courcel recommended to Delcassé that the French should now agree to leave Fashoda, and that they could do so "avec honneur et la tête haute."[53]

Marchand was no longer at Fashoda. As he had warned, having received no instructions from home, on October 24 he secured passage aboard a boat steaming north and was now on his way down the Nile to Cairo.[54] On October 28 he arrived at Khartoum.[55]

On October 29, Monson had dropped in on Delcassé, whom he found "a little irate at the 'escapade' of M. Marchand" in leaving his post without permission. Very confidentially, he told Monson that he was immediately sending Baratier back to Cairo with orders for Marchand to return to Fashoda.[56] Delcassé then reiterated that his continuation in office in the new government that was being formed depended on a favorable British response to the French request that "their order to M. Marchand to evacuate Fashoda would be followed by an understanding that England will negotiate on the principle of the grant to France of an outlet for her commerce to the Nile." If this proposal were rejected, a war with England, "which is the only alternative," would be "so repulsive to his principles" that he could no longer continue as Foreign Minister. Monson found it "quite impossible to shake these obstinate views" and left "disappointed at being able to make no impression upon him."[57]

Marchand's trip to Cairo was viewed in London as "a rift in the clouds overhanging Anglo-French relations." On October 29 the Associated Press reported from London that whether or not Marchand had been officially recalled,

"...M. Delcassé and the Government of France have got over a great difficulty from a diplomatic *amour propre* point of view. M. Delcassé has declared that the French Government could not do the impossible, that is to say, recall Major Marchand. Therefore, the latter's return has enabled the French Government to 'save its face,' as the saying goes."[58]

Salisbury apparently shared this opinion, and determined to keep Marchand away from Fashoda for as long as possible. During the afternoon of October 30, he telegraphed Cromer in Cairo that he concurred with Kitchener as to

"...the inexpediency of letting either Marchand or Baratier go back to Fashoda. I concur with him in urging that the gunboat now at Khartoum should start at once without delay, so that if you are asked to send these two officers back you may reply with truth that there is not likely to be any gunboat starting south from Khartoum for some time." [59]

On October 30, Queen Victoria telegraphed Salisbury of her continuing concern over a possible war with France:

"I feel very anxious about the state of affairs, and think a war for so miserable and small an object is what I could hardly bring myself to consent to..."

"We must try and save France from humiliation. Would it be safe to promise commercial access to the Nile and delimitation of that position suggested in Sirdar's letter of 8th October to Lord Cromer on condition of French withdrawal from Fashoda?" [60]

Throughout the world, British war preparations continued. Among the proposals being considered was the suggestion of Sir John Fisher, Commander-in-Chief of the North American sector and a future First Lord of the Admiralty, that a British force should attack Devil's Island and kidnap Dreyfus. The Captain would then be sent by a fast ship to France, where he would be landed to sow dissension. On October 30, a news report from Victoria, British Columbia, stated that ships were being ordered from that port to Tahiti and from Halifax, Nova Scotia to the West Indies "to show the French how utterly her colonies would be at the mercy of the British should she make any warlike movements." [61]

Here was the reality of the matter. With the French fleet at Toulon bottled by the British Mediterranean and Channel Fleets and the British Home Fleet lying off Brest to attack the French squadron there should it emerge, other British naval forces would be able with impunity to attack the French colonies, including those in West Africa, which were on the top of the British list. [62] As Mahan had predicted, sea power was in the ascendancy. The stunning United States naval victories in the just concluded Spanish-American War, which were fresh in everyone's minds, seemed irrefutable confirmation of that conclusion. Thus, if the French colonialists had their way and France went to war over Fashoda, the ironic result was likely to be that France, like Spain, would lose her overseas possessions.

═══◦✕◦═══

The political instability created by the Dreyfus case was hobbling the French. For nearly a week, when decisions that would lead to peace or war had to be made, France had been without a functioning Government. President Faure had no constitutional power to act and it was unclear whether Delcassé would continue to serve in the new Government that was yet to be formed.

Finally, when the Dupuy Cabinet was announced on October 31, Delcassé retained his post as Foreign Minister. Faure had convinced him that at such a time of crisis, his scruples over surrendering Fashoda without any recompense should be subordinated to the national interest. As Faure later wrote:

"...I had to tell him that I would accept full personal responsibility and that as soon as the new cabinet was formed I would absolve him from responsibility for this action." [63]

The President was also prepared to convince others in the new Government and in the Chamber of Deputies that the evacuation of Fashoda was the only realistic course to take. [64]

With the Dupuy Government now formed and in a position to act, a decision to leave Fashoda seemed almost inevitable. The November 2 London *Times* contained a report from its Paris correspondent that "the new government recognizes, as the French public at large recognizes, that the French interests at Fashoda are not worth a conflict with Great Britain." [65] This same day Delcassé advised Courcel of his "disposition" to send Marchand back to lead his force from Fashoda "sur un autre point." [66] On November 3, under pressure from Faure, the new Cabinet agreed to evacuate Fashoda without further delay. Monson telegraphed the news to Salisbury, and told him to expect official word from Courcel. [67] The British were taking no chances, however, and pending official word of the French decision, war preparations continued at a feverish pace. Thus, First Lord of the Admiralty George Goschen abruptly canceled his appearance as the "principal guest" at November 3's Cutlers' Feast in Sheffield, because his "continuous presence at the Admiralty was required." [68]

Courcel had already called on Lord Salisbury to announce the French decision. He suggested, as a kind of sop, that the announcement could be made as a joint communique that hinted at further discussion of the future of the Upper Nile. Salisbury refused, on the basis that at the moment public opinion was too wrought up; further negotiations should be deferred to a calmer day.[69]

For some time the Prime Minister had been scheduled to be the principal speaker at a November 4 banquet at the Mansion House, honoring Lord Kitchener. It was widely anticipated that he would have something important to say regarding Fashoda. No doubt savoring his triumph, Salisbury chose to sandwich the news of the French capitulation into the middle of a long chronological report of recent events:

"I received from the French Ambassador this afternoon the information that the French Government has come to the conclusion that the occupation of Fashoda was of no sort of value to the French Republic, and they thought that, in the circumstances, to persist in an occupation that only cost them money and did them harm, merely because some bad advisors thought it might be disagreeable to an unwelcome neighbor, would not show the wisdom by which I think the French Republic has been uniformly guided, and they have done what I believe the Government of any other country would have done in the same position - they have resolved that that occupation must cease... I do not wish to be misunderstood as saying that all causes of controversy are resolved by this... It is probably not so; ...but a cause of controversy of a somewhat acute and dangerous character has been removed, and we cannot but congratulate ourselves on that."[70]

The same day the French Government's Fashoda decision was published as an official announcement in the Paris newspapers. It had been taken only "après un examen approfondi de la question."[71]

Notwithstanding the French announcement that Marchand would evacuate Fashoda, the British were taking no chances. A London dispatch to the November 7 *New York Times* reported that naval preparations were continuing unabated, and that the War Office had ordered immediate mobilization of all troops in the Western District of England.[72] The same day the London *Times* reported from Paris that most of the French papers were responding to the Fashoda settlement with "less irritation than the first impulse might have dictated." Similarly, expected challenges in the Chamber of Deputies to the Government's decision were withdrawn to "unanimous" applause.[73]

After several days the French reaction was less positive. Monson wrote Salisbury on November 11 that "although the immediate effect of your Lordship's speech at the Lord Mayor's Banquet was a decided relief to pressing anxiety here, the views which you expressed as to the possibility of complications in a not very distant future have not generally lightened the gloom which generally oppresses France at this moment." Thus, although there was no evidence that the French Government was thinking of changing its decision to evacuate Fashoda, Monson reported that

"France appears to me to be staggered; and in consequence calls herself humiliated. I should like to think that the feeling of resentment is transitory; but the contrary is, I fear, the more likely. What she would probably like would be to utilize the next two or three years' respite with which the obligations imposed by the preparations for, and the carrying out of, the coming International Exposition may offer her, for the purpose of increasing her naval strength."[74]

In a second memorandum to Salisbury written the same day, primarily regarding an issue relating to Crete involving England, Russia, and Italy. Monson stated that the "gist" of what Delcassé told him

"was that, in order to maintain the accord among the four Powers, France would agree to anything to which the other three assented.

"In fact, his tone seemed to be pitched in the 'humiliation' key, and his meaning to be—'What is the use of France having an opinion on her own about anything now-a-days.'"[75]

On November 13 Marchand and Baratier left Cairo for Khartoum and then to Fashoda to supervise the evacuation. Initially, the French Government had agreed to the British suggestion that the expedition should take the most expeditious course of leaving, i.e., by way of the Nile. Marchand had violently objected. To leave Fashoda voluntarily was bad enough, but even more humiliating would be to do so in full view of the British and Egyptians on the lower Nile and the European community in Cairo. He insisted that the expedition should depart without outside assistance by continuing east on the *Faidherbe* up the Sobat and then on through Ethiopia to Jibuti at the head of the Gulf of Aden. The French Government let Marchand have his way, and the English also assented, subject to working out the details.[76]

The Fashoda crisis had been defused, but that would not lead to immediate Anglo-French amity. In a November 15 speech at Manchester's Free Trade Hall, Chamberlain attacked the policy of "pin-pricks" which the French allegedly had been pursuing wherever they came into contact with Britain. As for the Sudan: "Fashoda is only a symbol: the great issue is the control of the whole valley of the Nile."[77] Salisbury also was not allowing the apparent resolution of the Fashoda crisis to relax British pressure on France. He wrote Queen Victoria on November 17 that if the Kaiser were to indicate that he would like to visit his grandmother, "it certainly would do good" to invite him. Not only had the German Emperor "shown himself disposed to be friendly to this country," but "the attitude of France makes it desirable that the world should believe in an understanding between Germany and England.[78]

Feelings on the other side of the Channel also continued to be sensitive. When a French official suggested that French-speaking schools should be established at Khartoum and Fashoda, the usually calm and correct Ambassador Monson exploded. At a December 6 dinner of the British Chamber of Commerce in Paris, he called on France to abstain from its "policy of pin-pricks," and threatened that England might have to abandon its policy of "forbearance" unless the French became willing to "profit from the lesson of Fashoda [and] to appreciate the friendly consideration with which they had been treated." Moreover, the British naval buildup had not been halted. Thus, it was little wonder that three days later Delcassé expressed to Monson his concern that England would soon present France with a series of unacceptable demands, and go to war when the French rejected them.[79]

The Salisbury Government saw things differently. Chancellor of the Exchequer Hicks-Beach, probably the most bellicose member of Salisbury's Cabinet prior to the French decision to evacuate Fashoda, was reported as stating on November 23 that "what had occurred with regard to Fashoda had materially cleared the air." Speaking in Edinburgh, "he looked upon the prospects of any serious difficulty with France as much further removed at the present moment than they had been for some years past."[80] One likely reason for this conciliatory expression was a quiet confidence that France had accepted the fact that

England was almost sure to prevail in any colonial conflict between the two countries. As the London *Times* editorialized on November 22:

"In 1878 we sang, vaingloriously enough, 'We've got the ships, we've got the men.' In 1885 we found we had neither in sufficiency. Now that we have both we sing no songs, but we indulge in no scares. In quietness and in confidence...we have awaited the issue trusting in our right, but also in our power, to vindicate it."[81]*

⸺◉⟊◉⸺

At year end, after a short stay in England, Winston Churchill was back in India for a final series of polo matches before he returned home and his future career as author and politician. When he was not practicing for the games, he was devoting all his time to his book on the Nile campaign. On December 21, he wrote his mother:

"I work all day & every day at the book and have done about a third. You must forgive my short letter on that account. Time is so precious and there is so much to do...My hand gets so cramped! I am writing every word twice & some parts three times. It ought to be good since it is the best I can do..."[82]

During his English stopover Churchill had received friendly advice from the Prince of Wales, who was among those who had learned the identity of the author of the letters in the *Morning Post*. On October 6, he wrote Churchill:

"...I fear in matters of discipline in the Army I may be considered old fashioned—& I must say that I think that an officer serving in a campaign should not write letters for the newspapers or express strong opinions of how the operations were carried out...

"Your writing a book with an account of the campaign is quite another matter...I cannot help feeling that Parliament & literary life is what would suit you best as the monotony of military life in an Indian station can have no attraction for you..."[83]

While waiting to return to India, Churchill made three political

---

* The 1878 reference presumably was to the Balkan crisis that led to the Congress of Berlin, and the citation of 1885 was likely to Gordon's defeat and death at Khartoum.

speeches. The *Morning Post* reports of his experience in the Sudan had given him public recognition, and the Conservative Party at once moved to use him to its advantage. The ambitious Churchill was only too happy to oblige. After the second speech, at Dover, he wrote his mother on October 27 that the press had reported it as "successful." He added:

"I had one moment when I lost my train of thought—but I remained silent until I found it again—and I don't think it matters."[84]

The twenty-three-year-old Churchill also was trying to restore himself in the good graces of a young lady with whom he professed to be in love. The woman in question was Pamela Plowden, the well-born granddaughter of a British general, whom Churchill had met in India two years before. Pamela had written him with several complaints, including the most important one of all—that he really did not love her. On November 28, he responded:

"...I will admit that you are quite right and that I make unnecessary enemies. The question is—Is it worth it? I confess I think so in many cases.
    One thing I take exception to in your letter. Why do you say I am incapable of affection? Perish the thought. I love one above all others. And I shall be constant. I am no fickle gallant capriciously following the fancy of the hour. My love is deep and strong. Nothing will ever change it."[85]

Churchill was wrong. His love at that moment was not for Pamela Plowden or any other woman. For him, the all consuming goal was to make a name for himself as a public figure. Until then, romantic love and marriage would have to wait. When they did come ten years later it would be to another woman, Clementine Hozier, and he would be constant.

Marchand and Baratier returned to Fashoda on December 4, and sadly commenced preparations for their departure. By now, the necessary approvals for their passage through Ethiopia had been obtained, although it had been suggested that they should leave their "heavy baggage" behind. If anyone in Jackson's Anglo-Egyptian force had thought that the French were about to run short of supplies, they were surprised when Marchand handed over twenty tons of perishable goods as well as a number of cases of champagne and wine.[86]
    During the two-and-a-half months the French and Anglo-Egyptians

had co-existed side-by-side, relations between them had been polite and on occasion friendly. From time to time the French sent vegetables and game to Jackson's troops, while the British and Egyptians provided the French with newspapers, books, and help in sending private letters back to France. Over frequent drinks of wine and brandy, the two doctors attached to the opposing forces discussed in great detail the treatment of diseases such as beri-beri and hookworm and the treatment of the serious bites of Nile crocodiles.[87]

December 13 was the date set for Marchand's departure. Two days earlier, the French tendered the British a farewell dinner, which was reciprocated by a festive luncheon on December 12. At the latter, the French accepted with great emotion Jackson's gift of the flag of the Mahdist gunboat that they had repulsed in August. As Marchand took the flag, Jackson's band played the Marseillaise.[88]

The next morning, the French left Fashoda. There was a slight delay when Marchand asked Jackson to postpone replacing the Tricolor with the Union Jack until the French were out of sight. The British commander, who had developed a great admiration for Marchand and his men, was happy to oblige. Then, as the French convoy of the *Faidherbe* and five small boats moved into the river, they passed an Anglo-Egyptian honor guard, which presented arms as the British band once more played the Marseillaise.[89]

Jackson's courtesy and respect could not erase the sadness and sense of betrayal felt by Marchand and his men. After all they had accomplished, it was humiliating for their undefeated force to abandon Fashoda without a fight, on orders from Paris politicians. Thus, when one of their Senegalese soldiers asked French doctor Jules Emily why Marchand's force was leaving, his only reply was, "The white man doesn't know."[90]

SEVENTEEN

"I See Nothing But A Terrible Heritage Of Revolutionary Anarchy"

In early March, in the Russian city of Minsk, the first Congress of the Russian Social-Democratic Workers Party (the future Communist Party) had just ended after a meeting of nearly two weeks. There were nine delegates, each representing a local organization, e.g. Moscow and St. Petersburg. Although they appointed a central committee and agreed to start a party journal, their plans came to naught, largely because each of the delegates was arrested as he left for home at the Congress's close.[1]

The Congress presented no program for action. What remained other than the party's name was a manifesto which provided an important ideological underpinning for future revolutionary activities. It noted the need for the Russian working class to possess in the struggle for "a share of what the bourgeoisie in the West had already won in the administration of the state"—"freedom of the speaker and written word" and "freedom of organization and assembly."[2] Then came the following paragraph:

"The farther east one goes in Europe, the weaker, meaner and more cowardly in the political sense becomes the bourgeoisie, and the greater the cultural and political tasks which fall to the lot of the proletariat. On its strong shoulders the Russian working class must carry the work of conquering political liberty. This is an essential step to the realization of the great historical mission of the proletariat, to the foundation of a social order in which there will be no place for the exploitation of man by man. The Russian proletariat will cast off from itself the yoke of the autocracy in order with all the greater energy to continue the struggle with capitalism and with the bourgeoisie until the final victory of socialism."[3]

In 1848 Karl Marx had set forth the concept of the two-step revolution, the first coming from the middle class or bourgeoisie, and the second, building on the first, that of the working classes. Thus, at the very time that Marx and Engels were writing *The Communist Manifesto,* middle-class revolutions were in progress in France and in what later became Germany. In their opinion, the fact that these largely aborted did not invalidate Marx's theory. In Russia, however, the middle class seemed incapable of a similar exertion. If revolution was to come in Russia, the proletariat would have to create it on its own.[4]

The Congress was also important because it marked the first attempt to create a Russian Marxist party in Russia. Until the mid-1890s, the major revolutionary force had been the narodniks, a series of groups that believed in peasant revolts and terrorism against members of the aristocracy. In the 1880s, a revolutionary named Georgi Plekhanov had broken with the narodniks on the terrorism issue and fled to Switzerland, where he became a convert to Marxism. There he formed a Marxist group made up of other Russian exiles. This led to the founding in Russia of similar groups, who organized the Minsk Congress.[5]

One of Plekhanov's most enthusiastic followers during the late 1890s was Vladimir Ilyich Lenin. Since the twenty-eight-year-old Lenin had been exiled to Siberia for revolutionary activities, he could not attend the Congress. In the early years of the coming century, however, he was to embrace the dogmas agreed on at Minsk and use them to great advantage.[6]

In 1898 the smell of anarchism was in the air and was not confined to Russia. For a number of years, there had been a growing belief that something must be done to right the disparity of living conditions between the rich in their palaces and mansions, and the poor who were not sharing in the abundance of wealth from the Industrial Revolution that others were amassing. The resulting anger manifested itself in labor unrest, which could lead to violence, as in the 1892 steel workers' strike at Homestead, Pennsylvania. In a more extreme form, it was directed personally against the heads of government, both monarchical and elected. Thus, in 1881, an anarchist's bomb killed the current Tsar's grandfather, Alexander II. This was followed by the assassinations of President Carnot of France in 1894 and Premier Canovas of Spain in 1897. In late August 1898 a would-be assassin's bullet had narrowly missed Holland's young Queen Wilhelmina.[7]

Empress Elizabeth of Austria-Hungary, a deeply troubled woman, was preoccupied with thoughts of death. Not only was she still mourning the suicide of her son Rudolf at Mayerling almost ten years before, but she had more recently lost two sisters, one of whom had been burned to death in a fire at a charity bazaar the previous year. Some years before, her brother-in-law Maximilian had been killed by a Mexican firing squad. Elizabeth tried to escape from her morbid thoughts by incessant travel, returning occasionally to Vienna to visit her husband. Emperor Franz Joseph did not join his wife on her journeys, but remained in his capital, busy with affairs of state and enjoying the company of his long-time mistress, Katherina Schratt.[8]

During 1898 Elizabeth had not been well, and moved from spa to spa and cure to cure. In late summer she was staying at a villa at Caux, near Montreaux at the east end of Lake Geneva. There, the unusually fine weather revived both her health and spirits. She reportedly was considering a trip to Sicily, but was dissuaded when she read a book describing Sicilian vendettas and related killings that had been given her by nervous members of her entourage.[9]

On September 9, another beautiful day, the Empress left Caux by lake steamer for Geneva and then on to the nearby estate of her sister's very good friend, Baroness Julie de Rothschild. She refused the use of the Rothschild yacht, saying it would be too much trouble. She and her companion, Countess Sztáray, enjoyed a pleasant lunch with the Baroness, and then visited the estate's aviaries, aquarium, and greenhouses, where she was especially impressed with the orchids. Since it was too late to return by steamer to Caux, she and the Countess had reserved rooms at the Hotel Beau-Rivage in Geneva, where they spent the night following an uneventful stroll through the city.[10]

Elizabeth's chamberlain had learned that Geneva was a favorite base for terrorists and urged her not to spend the night there. The Empress not only refused, but also rejected special police protection, scoffing, "Who would want to harm an old woman like me?" She was enjoying her outing, and spent a pleasant morning with the Countess visiting a nearby shop where she bought a music-box-like contraption called an "Orchestration." When it was time to return to Caux, Elizabeth lingered for so long at her hotel room window gazing at an especially clear Mont Blanc that the Countess feared they would miss their steamer.[11]

At 1:35 P.M., as the two women were walking to the dock, a man darted across the street and, appearing to stumble against the Empress, plunged a stiletto-like knife into her chest. At first, neither Elizabeth nor the Countess seemed to realize that anything serious had happened, and the Empress boarded the ship unaided. Once she had done so, however, she collapsed and lost consciousness. Only at this point did the Countess notice the bloody spot on her chest where the assassin's blade had been plunged. The steamer had already left land, but quickly returned to shore, and Elizabeth was carried back to her room at the hotel. Doctors were promptly summoned, but to no avail. The Empress died at 2:40 P.M.[12]

The assassin was quickly apprehended. He was Luigi Lucheni, a twenty-five-year-old Italian day laborer who lived in Lausanne. He had come to Geneva to kill the Prince of Orleans, the pretender to the French throne. When he learned on arrival that the Prince had left town, Lucheni decided "to kill some high-placed person or another, prince, king, or president of a republic—it's all the same." He read in the Geneva newspapers that Elizabeth was staying in the city, and took her as his victim. When he was told that she had died he exclaimed, "All hail to anarchism!"[13]

In Vienna, Franz Joseph was shattered by the news. He reportedly shuddered, sank into a chair and cried, "I see I am not to be spared any misfortune in this world!"[14] He could not foresee that one final misfortune was yet to fall on him—sixteen years later at Sarajevo.

For the past few years there had been increasing concern over the spread of armaments and their increasingly destructive power. The firepower of infantry had increased more than five times since Waterloo, and smokeless powder, invented by Alfred Nobel, had increased the accuracy of artillery and its range from 1,000 to 6,000 yards.[15] The naval expansion that Tirpitz had pushed through the Reichstag earlier in the year was but one manifestation of the arms race that was developing among the major powers. In a speech the previous November, Lord Salisbury, not an alarmist, voiced the fear that it would end in a "terrible effort of mutual destruction which will be fatal for Christian civilization." His only answer was some form of agreement among the great powers which at a future date could "be welded in some international constitution."[16]

In St. Petersburg, the concerns of Tsar Nicholas II's ministers were much more immediate. Already engaged in a major upgrading of the firepower of its infantry, Russia suddenly was faced with reports that its major rival, Austria, was planning to introduce field guns with six times the firing speed of Russia's artillery. At the same time, Finance Minister Witte was valiantly attempting to turn Russia into a modern industrial nation. In that effort, each ruble spent for arms would be wasted. However, a bilateral arms reduction agreement with Austria, even if honored, would betray the relative weakness of those powers to the rest of the world and would do nothing for Russia against England or Germany. Witte therefore suggested, first to Foreign Minister Muraviëv, and then to their fellow ministers, that Russia propose an international moratorium on new weapons. They agreed and the thirty-year-old Tsar accepted their recommendation.[17]

Thus it was that on August 28 Muraviëv, in the Tsar's name, called for an international conference to consider the limitation of armaments. His statement observed that despite the seemingly almost universal desire for peace, "the intellectual and physical strength of nations, labour and capital alike, have been unproductively consumed in building terrible engines of destruction." Echoing Salisbury's fears of the previous year, the Tsar warned that this

"...is transforming the armed peace into a crushing burden that weighs on all nations and if prolonged will lead inevitably to the very cataclysm which it is desired to avert."

The conference, on the other hand

"...should be, by the help of God, a happy passage for the century which is about to open. It would converge in one powerful focus the efforts of all States which are sincerely seeking to make the great idea of universal peace triumph over elements of trouble and discord."[18]

Reaction to the Tsar's disarmament proposal varied, unsurprisingly, on its potential effect on the country involved. In England, already the world's foremost naval power, comment was generally favorable. As an example, on August 29, the London *Times* editorialized that the proposal showed "a spirit of generous, perhaps, indeed, of almost quixotic, humanity." It continued:

"Never perhaps in modern history have the aspirations which good men of all ages have regarded as at once ideal and unattainable found so responsive an echo in the councils of one of the greatest and most powerful of the world's rulers...For this country...they point to an object which, if

Tsar Nicholas II

it could be attained, would promote the greatest of our national interests and satisfy the most abiding of our national aspirations."[19]

The French reaction to the Tsar's proposal was very different from that in England. However strong may have been the French desire for peace, the country's leading long-range priority was the reconquest of Alsace-Lorraine. Only a victorious war in which France would have an ally such as Russia was likely to accomplish that goal. On August 30 the Paris correspondent of the London *Times* reported that the Tsar's message

"...has surprised public opinion in France like an unexpected peal of thunder, and this constitutes the real gravity of the event. Either France has not been consulted—and people ask themselves bitterly what is the nature of this singular alliance in which it is possible for one of the allies to spring upon the world such a surprise without consulting the partner to the alliance—or France has been consulted, and the world as a whole will ask itself what is and what must be the primary condition which would induce France to adhere to a proposal of this sort."[20]

That condition of course would be Germany's cession of Alsace-Lorraine. And France had not been consulted.[21]

The initial German press comment was that "the proposal of the Tsar is one of the greatest events of recent times."[22] This euphoria soon was replaced by the recognition that, as the Kaiser stated a few days later, "Our future lies upon the ocean."[23] Germany would not abandon its recently adopted program of naval expansion unless England substantially reduced the size of her fleet. Since the two-for-one doctrine was a cardinal tenet of British national policy, there seemed little chance that, in this area at least, the Tsar's proposal would make any difference.

Proponents of the conference also had to confront a post-Darwinian view of war as not only an inevitable event in which the "fittest" survived, but one that ennobled its participants. This attitude was manifested not only in Roosevelt's 1897 Newport Naval War College speech, but also in an 1895 address, 'The Soldier's Faith," which Massachusetts Supreme Judicial Court Justice Oliver Wendell Holmes gave to the Harvard graduating class, in which he praised

"the faith...which leads a soldier to throw away his life in obedience to a blindly accepted duty, in a cause which he little understands, in a plan of campaign of which he has no notion, under tactics of which he does not see the use."[24]

Nevertheless, the broad popular appeal for the Tsar's disarmament proposal could not be ignored. During 1898, the British Foreign Office received more than 750 resolutions from public groups urging, in the words of one of them, that the Government do its utmost to assure "that something practical may result" from the conference.[25] Popular support in England culminated in a large meeting on December 18 at London's St. James Hall, where English peace advocate William T. Stead reported on his recent meeting with Nicholas II, at which the Tsar had expressed his worry over "the heaping up of fleets and armies in order to take part in a scramble with the world." The Russian ruler then reportedly made this prophetic remark:

"What with disconnection caused by mobilizing, what with empty exchequers, what with the decimated ranks of leading and governing men, I see nothing before any nation but a terrible heritage of revolutionary anarchy."

Although the meeting appears to have been organized under the auspices of religious groups, it was supported by leaders of both political parties, including Rosebery and Balfour. Balfour wrote Stead that if the peace proposal's "effects for mankind are even a fraction of what you hope, it is surely worthy of international sympathy."[26]

It was easy for Balfour and his colleagues to support the Tsar's proposal because it was unlikely to hurt the English. Their navy already controlled the seas. A restriction on new armaments would prevent other countries such as Germany from trying to match it. The French and Germans privately had no desire to limit their military development, but neither country wished to antagonize the Russians, and thus were willing to give lip service to the Tsar's proposal. The conference would therefore take place, but prospects for its success were not bright.

EIGHTEEN

Playing It In "Bull Luck"

B y August the New York State political pot was busily boiling. Republican Governor Frank S. Black was up for reelection, but was unpopular with good government forces for allegedly weakening the civil service. On August 4 his already poor prospects were dealt a major blow when a special investigating committee reported an "improper expenditure" of at least a million dollars on a project to improve the Erie Canal that was dear to upstate voters.[1]

New York Republican Senator Thomas Collier Platt sensed that Black would not do as a candidate. On August 14, the "easy boss" was visited at his seaside vacation hotel by Republican State Committee Chairman Benjamin B. Odell and New York City Committee Chairman Lemuel Ely Quigg. They argued that dropping Black would be viewed as an admission of corruption, and that the only way to avoid an electoral defeat was to replace him with Roosevelt as the party nominee. The advice did not please Platt, who feared that Roosevelt would use the Governorship as a stepping stone to the Presidency. He nevertheless agreed that Quigg could speak with Roosevelt about a possible candidacy.[2]

On August 19, the day before Roosevelt took a short leave at his Oyster Bay home at Sagamore Hill, Quigg visited him at Camp Wikoff. He told the Colonel, as Roosevelt would be known for the rest of his life, that he and Odell were trying to convince Platt that Roosevelt should be the party's nominee. Was he interested? Roosevelt responded affirmatively, and added that although if elected he would act "as my own judgment and conscience dictated," he would consult with the organization and did not envision that he would "make war on Mr. Platt."[3]

The previous day Roosevelt had had another political visitor. He was John Jay Chapman, an incorruptible but impractical good government advocate and leader of New York's small Independent party. Chapman urged Roosevelt to agree to be that party's gubernatorial nominee. He reasoned that in that event, to keep the good government vote, the Republicans also would be forced to nominate the Colonel. Roosevelt would be elected with a large Independent Party vote, and its leaders could legitimately claim a major role in his administration. Roosevelt accepted Chapman's suggestion that he take time to think the offer over.[4]

On September 4 McKinley visited Camp Wikoff, which by now was operating in reasonably good order. Roosevelt managed to head the cavalry escort that would accompany him from the railroad station to the camp. As soon as the President saw the hero of San Juan Hill, he left his carriage and walked over to greet Roosevelt, cordially shaking hands and with a broad smile on his face and exclaiming. "Colonel Roosevelt, I'm glad to see you looking so well."[5] Once more, the potential Republican nominee for Governor, who already was being mentioned as a 1904 Presidential candidate, had garnered free publicity for himself. In a letter to his good friend Henry Cabot Lodge, however, he was realistic regarding his political future:

"If I am nominated, well and good; I shall try to be elected, and if elected I shall try to rise to the extremely difficult position in which I shall find myself. If I am not nominated, I shall take the result with extreme philosophy and with a certain sense of relief, and shall turn my attention to the literary work which is awaiting me."[6]

Shortly after 1:30 P.M. on September 13, Roosevelt was quietly working in his tent when an honor guard summoned him to come outside where the entire regiment of Rough Riders was assembled in a hollow square. In an emotional ceremony, his men presented him with a bronze replica of Frederic Remington's sculpture "The Bronco Buster," the cost of which had been borne equally by every man in the regiment. On their behalf, one of the troopers presented it as a "very slight token of admiration, love and esteem" to a leader whose acts "have always been of the kindest." For once, Roosevelt was temporarily speechless. After he had collected himself, he said to his comrades:

"Nothing could have possibly happened to touch and please me as this does... I have never tried to coddle you, and I have never hesitated to call upon you to shed your blood like water. This is something I shall hand down to my children, and I shall value it more than the weapons I carried through the campaign."[7]

Following the ceremony, the Rough Riders, including their Colonel, were mustered out of the Army.

Under the heading "ROOSEVELT PAST A DOUBT," the September 17 *New York Times* reported that the Rough Rider's nomination was a sure thing, and that Superintendent of Insurance and Black ally Louis F. Payn "returned to Albany yesterday afternoon discouraged and despondent, to tell the governor that the task is hopeless."[8]

The same day, now almost assured of the Republican gubernatorial nomination, Roosevelt paid a visit to Platt at the latter's headquarters at the Fifth Avenue Hotel on lower Fifth Avenue. The meeting had been announced in advance, so that a large crowd, including representatives of the press, was waiting for Roosevelt, who arrived in civilian clothing but with a hat "of the army type which gave him a semi-military air."[9] After a two-hour meeting, Roosevelt emerged to announce, as expected, that he would accept the Republican nomination.[10]

Many reformers were worried that Roosevelt had joined company with Platt and his machine. The Reverend Charles H. Parkhurst of the Madison Square Church, a leader of New York City's good government forces, expressed disbelief when he returned from Europe a week later:

"I do not believe that Teddy Roosevelt...has so far humbled himself as to go to Mr. Platt. Mr. Platt must have gone to him."[11]

Parkhurst was mistaken. When it counted, Roosevelt was always a party man. Otherwise he would have had no chance of the nomination. Thus, pursuant to his understanding with Platt, he wrote John Jay Chapman that "I do not see how I can accept the Independent nomination and keep good faith with the other men on the ticket."[12]

Black was not ready to concede to Boss Platt and his candidate. On September 11, two weeks before the Saratoga convention would convene,

his supporters claimed 426 of the 971 delegates. The Platt camp scof-
fed at these numbers, and announced that Roosevelt was assured of the
support of at least 650 delegates "beyond the shadow of a doubt."[13]

On September 24, the Black forces dropped a bombshell that threatened to derail the Roosevelt candidacy.As reported in all the major
newspapers, earlier in the year the prospective nominee had signed
and filed an affidavit affirming that he was a resident of the District of
Columbia and thus was not liable for New York City personal property
taxes. Prepared by Roosevelt's New York lawyer and dated March 21,
1898, the affidavit stated that since October, 1897, "I have not had any
domicile or residence in New York City ... and since then I have been
and now am a resident of Washington."[*] However—New York's Constitution specifically provided that no one could serve as Governor unless that person "shall have been five years next preceding his election
a resident of this state."[14] The affidavit had been discovered by Payn
and other allies of Governor Black, probably with the assistance of
Tammany Hall opponents of Roosevelt. They had delayed its disclosure until the eve of the Republican convention, which was to open
only three days later on September 27.[15]

Although Roosevelt immediately affirmed his New York residence,
he was deeply worried. Platt, however, was convinced that the nomination should go forward. Thus, when Roosevelt suggested at a hastily
called meeting he should withdraw from the race, as Platt later wrote:

"In order to emphasize my determination and to restore his courage, I
said with brutal frankness: 'Is the hero of San Juan a coward?'

"He replied with his customary vehemence: 'No, I am not a coward.'"[16]

At this point Platt turned to two of New York's most distinguished
lawyers. The sixty-six year old Joseph Choate, perhaps believing Roosevelt was truly ineligible, turned Platt down. Elihu Root, however,
thirteen years younger and more ambitious than Choate, agreed to
help. As he later recalled:

"Roosevelt was a youngster. He didn't know much about business or
business affairs. He got caught in a little inconsistency of an affidavit

---

* Fortunately for Roosevelt, the Black forces did not uncover an earlier affidavit, filed
with the Oyster Bay town clerk on August 24, 1897, in which he affirmed his residence in
New York City to avoid the higher Oyster Bay taxes.

about his tax... It was a question of using the word "residence" in one of several senses."[17]*

Fortunately, Root located a helpful letter that Roosevelt had sent his lawyer a few days before he signed the affidavit, in which he had written,

"I don't want to lose my vote this fall and therefore I will just pay the penalty and pay those taxes in New York—if it is not practicable to alter matters so as to have me taxed in Oyster Bay—Would this be practicable or not? If not, then I will pay in New York anyway. I don't want to sneak out of anything nor do I wish to lose my vote at Oyster Bay two years in succession."[18]

Although the Republican State Convention did not open until September 27, many delegates had arrived at least two days earlier. By 12:25 P.M., when the convention was called to order, the Platt organization had done its work, and Roosevelt was the assured nominee. Governor Black would not concede, however, and his was the first name placed in nomination. *The New York Times* reported that one of his seconders drew unintended "paroxysms of laughter" when he pleaded: "Let us say to Governor Black, 'well done, good and faithful servant,' not 'good and faithful servant, we will see that you are well done.'"[19]

Roosevelt was placed in nomination by the leading Republican orator and after-dinner speaker, Chauncey M. Depew, who raised cheers with his description of the exploits of the Rough Riders. Depew's reference to the problem of his candidate's residence was humorous, drawing "uproarious laughter...when he said that on the day San Juan Hill was taken Roosevelt was 'an influential citizen of Santiago de Cuba.'"[20]

It was the speech by Elihu Root, however, which followed Depew that effectively disposed of that troublesome issue. In a lengthy argument which he later admitted included "a lot of ballyhoo," Root explained the difference between physical residence and "domicile or legal residence," which Roosevelt had never surrendered. At one point,

---

* Root subsequently became Secretary of War under McKinley and Roosevelt, and Secretary of State under Roosevelt. He received the 1912 Nobel Peace Prize for his work on behalf of the peaceful settlement of international disputes.

Root read from a letter in which Roosevelt had written that he would like to reduce his taxes because his capital had become seriously impaired. "Yes," said Root to loud cheers, "impaired raising a regiment of rough riders to defend his country." The speech was so effective that Edward Lauterbach, a Black ally who had been involved in circulating the nonresidency affidavit, confessed, "I have been a bad boy and I want to be forgiven."[21]

Roosevelt was nominated on the first ballot by a margin of nearly three to one. On October 3 he paid New York City taxes of $995.28 by personal check.[22]

≡⊚≡

Roosevelt's opponent was Augustus Van Wyck of Brooklyn. Van Wyck was a judge on the New York Supreme Court (the state's principal trial court), and the brother of New York City's mayor. Although he had been put forward by Tammany Hall boss Richard Croker, he had a reputation for honesty as well as competence. His chief drawback seemed to be that he was an uninspiring stump speaker.[23]

≡⊚≡

On October 5, as large an audience as ever filled Carnegie Hall heard Roosevelt deliver his first campaign speech. *The New York Times* reported that, as several thousand more people waited outside, inside the auditorium, "Men and women stood in the aisles, leaned over the platform edges, and pressed against the walls." The *Times* described the meeting as "a brilliant scene, formed by thousands of faces, framed in the profuse drapery of flags." However, for a political rally

"...it was too fashionable. Magnificently dressed women occupied the boxes in the galleries and men in evening dress sat or stood beside them. It looked like a grand opera night..."[24]

As he spoke of "the fact that we occupy a new place among the people of the earth" and "the guns of our warships in the tropic seas of the West..." the candidate sounded as if he were running for national rather than state office.[25]

≡⊚≡

By October 9 the Roosevelt campaign was not going well. Upstate, which the Republicans must carry by a heavy majority, the voters seemed apathetic. Roosevelt's case was not helped by the alleged scandals relating to canal improvements, which had been given credence by the Republican failure to renominate Governor Black.[26]

Until now, Platt and Republican State Committee Chairman Odell had been opposed to capitalizing on Roosevelt's war record, and had been keeping the "hero of San Juan Hill" under wraps. Something had to be done however, and only the candidate himself could do it. Thus, on Monday, October 10, the Colonel announced that beginning the next week he would make a campaign tour of the state:

"I don't know how often I shall speak, but probably almost every day. It is not going to be a hurrah campaign from the rear platform of a train, however." [27]

Under the headline "TROY SNUBS ROOSEVELT," *The New York Times*'s lead story on October 15 described what was undoubtedly the low point of the Roosevelt gubernatorial campaign.[28] Roosevelt had not planned to start his upstate swing until the following week. A few days earlier, however, Governor Black had suggested that the Colonel address the Rensselaer County fair, to take place at Troy. Since Troy was the Governor's home, Roosevelt decided it would be politic to accept the invitation. Rising at dawn on October 14, he went by train from Oyster Bay to New York and by another train to Albany, where Governor Black seemed surprised to see him and regretted that a prior engagement would make it impossible to accompany the candidate to Troy.[29]

This did not stop Roosevelt, who went by trolley to Troy, and, with a hastily assembled welcoming committee, to the fair grounds. *The Times* described what ensued:

"When the grounds were reached, at 1:15, a band preceded the party in carriages and a parade was made about the track. There were less than 500 persons present, and scarcely one-third of them appeared to be aware of the personality of the visitor. A few men raised a cheer, and then Col. Roosevelt, pulling out his watch, said: 'I will not speak. It is late, and I must catch the 3:10 train from Albany.'

"Mr. Knickerbocker of the local committee asked him to say a few words from the carriage, but he declined with some asperity."

It was difficult to know who was more indignant—Roosevelt or the

Troy Republicans who had failed to attract a crowd to an event of which they had been unaware. The Black forces tried to put the blame on State Chairman Odell. Whoever was at fault, from this point the candidate would take an active role in running his campaign.[30]

New York Supreme Court Justice Joseph F. Daly had been on the bench for twenty-eight years. He had won a reputation for competence and honesty. However, he had incurred the displeasure of Tammany Hall's Croker when he refused to appoint a clearly unqualified politician as court clerk. On October 16, Croker retaliated by announcing that the Democrats would not nominate Daly for reelection, even though he had already been endorsed by the Republicans in what had been expected to be an uncontested election. Roosevelt could not have wished for a better piece of luck. Based on personal experience, he knew of the importance that New Yorkers of both parties placed on an impartial, incorruptible judiciary. When coupled with an attack on Tammany Hall, the issue could be especially effective with upstate voters.[31]

The Republican candidate returned to New York late on October 19 from his first upstate tour and made four speeches in Brooklyn. The highlight was a rally at the Academy of Music, where *The New York Times* reported that "a crowd of several thousand persons stood up and waved their hats and handkerchiefs at him and cheered and shouted campaign cries for more than ten minutes at a time."[32] The Colonel's reception upstate had been equally enthusiastic. By the time he closed his first day's efforts north of Albany at Glens Falls, crowds estimated at more than 25,000 had either heard or seen him. The next day his train took him through the Adirondacks to Ogdensburg on the St. Lawrence, where the 2,000-seat auditorium was filled to capacity and hundreds had to settle for a glimpse of the candidate as he entered and left the hall.[33]

At the seventeen stops on his upstate swing, Roosevelt discussed state issues, but drew the greatest applause when he described the exploits of the Rough Riders and the importance of retaining the territories America had taken from Spain. This aspect of his campaign was highlighted by the inclusion in his entourage of six Rough Riders in full uniform, one of whom frequently blew a trumpet to announce the candidate's appearance.[34] An admiring political ally described the stop at a small town just west of the Adirondacks:

"At Carthage, in Jeff. County, there were three thousand people standing in the mud and rain. He spoke about ten minutes—the speech was nothing, but the man's presence was everything. It was electrical, magnetic. I looked in the faces of hundreds and saw only pleasure and satisfaction. When the train moved away, scores of men and women ran after the train, waving hats and handkerchiefs and cheering, trying to keep him in sight as long as possible."[35]

Roosevelt's skills involved more than personal magnetism. He also had become a sophisticated political organizer. Just before his upstate campaign, he suggested to New York County Committee Chairman Quigg that "there should be an immediate effort" to arrange meetings "in the German, Jewish, and Scandinavian communities" in which non-organization men would participate. He also asked Quigg to see to it that at his Brooklyn speeches "we could have one or two men who are not identified with the organization."[36]

Meanwhile, Croker had clearly developed a bad case of "foot in mouth disease." Not content to try to let the storm over Justice Daly blow over, the Tammany boss sought to justify the judge's rejection on the basis that he had "a right to expect proper consideration" from anyone he helped put on the bench.[37] On October 22, speaking in the Mohawk Valley town of Little Falls, Roosevelt took advantage of the opening as he pressed the issue of judicial independence for all that it was worth. He pointed out that "my party...possessed the wisdom this year to renominate Judge Daly for the bench." He then scornfully turned on Croker and the Democrats:

"But his own party—and when I speak of the Democratic Party in the State of New York, I never know whether to speak of 'him' or 'it'—but his own party, speaking on this occasion in the singular, failed to nominate him, as Mr. Croker said that Judge Daly could not be renominated because while on the bench he had failed to show a proper sense of his obligations to Tammany Hall."

Roosevelt then brought the issue home to his audience of upstate voters:

"Remember that Mr. Croker's Governor could send Mr. Croker's Judge to sit in judgment anywhere from Buffalo up to Plattsburg and down to New York."[40]

Only by electing Roosevelt could the voters avoid such a dire result.

In some quarters, including the New York National Guard, there were adverse reactions to Roosevelt's constant emphasis on his war record. Indeed, a rumor was circulating that he had not actually stormed San Juan Hill.[39]

Shortly after that historic event, Roosevelt developed the idea that he should be awarded the Medal of Honor. As it became clear that the gubernatorial vote would be close, he believed that an award of the medal prior to the election might swing some votes to him. To that end, from his Massachusetts seaside home on October 25 Lodge wrote McKinley

"...in regard to giving Colonel Roosevelt this time the medal for distinguished gallantry for which he was recommended by General Wheeler. I assume that there is no doubt that that medal will be conferred upon him sooner or later. Just now it would have a very important meaning and value and would put at rest many stories which are being circulated by the Democrats. In view of the immense importance of the New York election, I feel justified bringing this matter to your attention and desire to express my most earnest hope that this medal may be awarded to Colonel Roosevelt in the course of the next few days."[40]

There is no record of any reply. Roosevelt was never awarded the medal. Later, in his *Autobiography*, he agreed that the authorities had taken "exactly the right position."[41]

On October 29 Roosevelt concluded a six-day campaign trip through central and western New York. His stamina was amazing. By the time he returned to New York City, he had made a total of 102 speeches, all but twelve of them formal. He clearly was enjoying himself, and the crowds responded in kind.[42]

Although Roosevelt continued to stress national as well as state issues, he had reduced the size of his entourage of Rough Riders from six to two, and these were dressed in mufti. They would frequently come on the platform to warm up the audience with a few words. They were loudly applauded and cheered, even when their use of the language was not what it might have been, as in the case of Sergeant Buck Taylor's endorsement at Port Jervis:

"I want to talk to you about mah Colonel. He kept ev'y promise he made to us and he will to you... He told us we might meet wounds and death and we done it, but he was there in the midst of us, and when it came to the great day he led us up San Juan Hill like sheep to the slaughter and so he will you."[43]

By November 2, with the gubernatorial election less than a week away, both sides were swinging their hardest punches. Stung by Roosevelt's attacks, Croker charged that when Roosevelt was police commissioner, while the police were

"...hunting women...in hired dress suits, when children of tender age were being used to induce saloonkeepers to violate the law by selling cases of beer, murder after murder was being committed, and in the hurly-burly of Roosevelt's fanatical policy nearly every murderer escaped."

Under Roosevelt, the Tammany boss asserted, the police were "making a splendid record in the capture of men who sold soda water on Sunday."[44]

If Croker had confined his attacks to Roosevelt personally, he might not have gotten himself further into trouble. Once he started, however, he could not stop, striking out at anyone he thought was in his way. He thus offended independent-minded voters who otherwise might have voted for Van Wyck. *The Nation*, for example, described his allegations as

"...the talk of a blackmailing criminal. He threatens most prominent opponents with exposure of various sorts, just like the strolling extortioners who so often make erring citizens pay smartly lest their sins find them out. Most of his stories are either evident exaggerations, or silly trivialities, or plain lies."

Roosevelt seized this opportunity to isolate Van Wyck, and, in his own words, "to fix the contest in the public mind as one between Croker and myself..." As a New York historian wrote twenty-five years later:

"The Colonel was in his element, and for the first time, perhaps, came into full consciousness of his peculiar power. Speaking straight to the people, often with the downward stroke of a clenched fist, with teeth disclosed, and squinting eyes that seemed to vision the cloud of a great misfortune hanging over the State, he told them things already familiar, but in words and tones that vibrated in the very centre of their being." [45]

As the November 8 election approached, each of the New York gubernatorial candidates extended his campaign into what was purportedly the other's territory. Stressing the alleged "scheme to defraud the State for the benefit of favored contractors" reported by the canal investigation commission, on November 5 Justice Van Wyck drew an enthusiastic crowd that was reportedly one of the largest that had ever attended a political meeting in Troy. [46]

Roosevelt's experience the same day on New York City's Lower East Side was very different. Although warned in advance that he would face a hostile mob, he took his campaign to the Bowery, where he underwent what *The New York Times* described as "an experience that was second only to his famous ascent of San Juan Hill." After his party was pelted with bricks and stones, "in Mott Street came the volley of feline remains. It was not dangerous, but it did not have the odors of Araby." Before any real damage was done, the police arrived, and the candidate left for the more hospitable surroundings of Stuyvesant Square. [47]

By November 7 there was a growing belief that, although the margin would be narrow, Roosevelt would be New York's next Governor. As the day progressed, odds in his favor of between ten to six and ten to nine were being quoted. [48]

The Republican candidate closed his campaign at 10:30 P.M. at Dunkirk, in the western part of the state. His train then took him overnight to New York City, from where he would go to vote in Oyster Bay. Roosevelt was hoarse, but satisfied that he had done all he could. In a thirteen-day effort unmatched by any prior candidate, he had spoken 127 times from the rear of his railroad car, as well as on numerous other occasions from platforms in cities and towns across the state. [49]

The bookmakers had guessed right. On a generally pleasant November 8, New York's voters turned out in large numbers to elect Roosevelt by a margin of 17,794 votes. Van Wyck's New York City plurality of more than 80,000 was outmatched by Roosevelt majorities elsewhere.[50]

Roosevelt carried with him the entire Republican ticket, as well as a GOP majority in both houses of the legislature. His victory was a personal triumph in an uphill fight. Although an editorial in the next morning's Democratic leaning *New York Times* blamed Croker and "his brutal and selfish will on the judiciary nominations" for the outcome, it took the vigorous and imaginative Roosevelt to seize the opportunity that Croker provided.[51] Boss Platt later conceded that "no man besides Roosevelt could have accomplished that feat in 1898."[52]

Following the election, the Governor-elect took time to reflect on his victory. On November 11, in a response to a congratulatory cable from his good friend Cecil Spring-Rice, he spoke of his good fortune:

"I have played it in bull luck this summer. First, to get into the war; then to get out of it; then to get elected. I have worked hard all my life, and have never been particularly lucky, but this summer I *was* lucky, and I am enjoying it to the full. I know perfectly well that this luck will not continue, and it is not necessary that it should. I am more than contented to be Governor of New York, and shall not care if I never hold another office..."[53]

In a letter to British historian and diplomat James Bryce, Roosevelt was more specific. The Republican machine, he said

"...would not have nominated me if I had not been a straight Republican, one who while always acting ultimately on his own best judgment, was yet anxious always to consult with the party leaders. In other words I had what the Mugwump conspicuously lacks, and what the Frenchman, and in fact all people who are unfitted for self-government, likewise lack, mainly the power of coming to a consensus with my fellows. But, of course, the Machine never dreamt of asking a promise of me of any kind or sort. I had a big burden of scandals, both of the National and State administration, to carry; and I was opposed by the professional Independents, like Carl Schurz, Godkin, Parkhurst, and the idiot variety of 'Goo-Goos', partly because they objected to my being for the war with Spain, and partly because they feared lest somebody they did not like might vote for me. However, we took the aggressive, and got a great many not only of the Independents proper but of the Independent Democrats away from them, and, after a very close, uphill fight, we won."[54]

The seven and a half weeks following Roosevelt's election were busy ones. In addition to starting to organize his new administration, he made significant progress in the dictation of his war memoirs, "The Rough Riders," and delivered eight Lowell Lectures at Harvard.[55]

Under New York law, a new Governor takes office on New Year's Day. January 1, 1899 fell on Sunday. In observance of the then current practice that no important work should be done on the Sabbath, Roosevelt was sworn in as Governor of New York at noon on Saturday, December 31, in the Albany office of the Secretary of State.[56] He had embarked on a new great adventure.

NINETEEN

"A Peace Treaty Can Contain Anything Which The Victors Put Into It"

A s the American peace commissioners sailed for France on September 17, it was becoming increasingly likely that the United States would insist on annexation of all the Philippines. The influential new Secretary of State John Hay had come to that opinion.[1] He and others of the McKinley Administration were becoming concerned that even if Germany decided not to acquire any territory that the United States did not want, Japan might try to do so. Given Japan's geographical proximity to the Philippines, this might be a greater threat to American interests in the Pacific and the Orient than would a German presence in the area.[2]

Early off-year elections in the rock-ribbed Republican states of Maine and Vermont had given the GOP reduced majorities. The primary reason was public blame on the War Department for the intolerable conditions at Camp Wikoff and other military establishments, after reports of mismanagement. The Administration feared that if this trend continued, the Democrats might capture the House or the Senate in November. The loss of either would likely put a stop to McKinley's expansionist policy.[3]

Imperialism might be the issue that would turn the tide, especially if it could be dressed in patriotic garb. Fortunately for the Republicans, that case had just been forcefully made. Albert J. Beveridge, whose April 27 speech in Boston had won him a national reputation, was planning to run for an Indiana Senate seat. On September 16, in a speech before a large and enthusiastic Indianapolis audience, he argued that the doctrine that a people should not be ruled without their consent did not apply to a territory like the Philippines which was not capable of self- government, and where the alternative to American government would be "the savage bloody rule of pillage and extortion from which we have rescued them."[4]

Beveridge then turned to the theme that gave his oration its name and made it famous: "The March of the Flag." During the past hundred years, the American flag had advanced from the Atlantic seaboard across the continent to the Pacific so that "from ocean to ocean the folds of glory blazed." And now,

"...William McKinley plants the flag over all the islands of the seas, outposts of commerce, citadels of national security, and the march of the flag goes on...And the question you will answer at the polls is whether you are marching onward with the flag."[5]

It is difficult today to appreciate the impact that these sentiments had at the time. Philippine annexation had found its spokesman, and the Republican National Committee distributed 300,000 copies of Beveridge's speech around the country.[6]

General Francis V. Greene was a New York militia officer who had commanded the second installment of Merritt's military expedition to the Philippines. He had been sent back to Washington to present his and Dewey's views on future United States policy toward the islands.[7]

Although Greene had spent only six weeks in the Philippines, his background in business and engineering and his acute powers of observation made him an excellent choice to provide McKinley with first-hand information. His lengthy report with appendices and exhibits was delivered to McKinley on September 30. It concluded that returning the Islands to Spanish rule would lead to civil war and likely foreign intervention. On the other hand, a government headed by Aguinaldo would almost certainly be a South American type dictatorship which would not command the support of most educated and propertied Filipinos. Further, the Philippines had natural resources which could be "exploited with American energy." For these reasons, he recommended United States annexation.[8]

Greene's report was the first reasoned analysis of the issue that

McKinley had seen. He read it carefully, and discussed it several times with Greene. It would be an important factor in his ultimate decision.[9]

The peace conference between the United States and Spain opened at 2:00 P.M. on October 1. The hospitable French had provided the conferees with a suite of three magnificent rooms at the Foreign Ministry. On the north side, overlooking the Seine, were five large windows draped with silk and priceless lace curtains. The other walls were covered with Gobelin tapestries.[10] Foreign Minister Delcassé took time off from the Fashoda crisis to formally welcome the delegates. The first session adjourned for a reception at which the hosts provided Spanish songs and dances.[11]

The only sour note of the opening day was the demand of the Spanish conferees that the United States forces in the Philippines should retreat to the positions that they held when the peace protocol was initialed a month and a half earlier. The American delegates rejected this proposal when the conferees next met on October 3.[12] If the Spanish intelligence operations were at all perceptive, this would have been no surprise. For example, the October 2 *New York Times* quoted McKinley's close friend and advisor Senator Mark Hanna as predicting that the peace conference would have "no other result than that Spain will have to relinquish her sovereignty over not only Luzon Island, but the entire Philippine Archipelago." The real issue "relates to the form of government which we will give the islands."[13]

During the next week, at their Paris headquarters at the Continental Hotel, the American peace conferees were briefed by Merritt, who had been summoned to provide his and Dewey's views on the Philippines. Merritt was a disappointment. He had had no direct conversation with the Admiral on the subject. As for himself, the conclusion that the United States should annex the entire archipelago probably was largely "sentimental."[14]

The fate of the Philippines was not the first major issue confronted by the American and Spanish conferees, however. It instead involved the more than $4 million of Spanish debt relating to Cuba. On October 12 the Spaniards proposed that, as part of Spain's surrender of Cuban sovereignty, the United States should assume this liability. The American delegates promptly rejected the suggestion, particularly since much of the debt had been incurred in trying to put down the insurrection activity on the island. The discussion reportedly was "very animated."[15]

On October 12 McKinley was in Omaha, Nebraska to speak at the city's Trans-Mississippi Exposition. At brief stops in Iowa, the President had drawn large and enthusiastic crowds as he expressed high-minded sounding platitudes such as "the courage of destiny." He never failed to refer to the recent American military and naval victories and the country's responsibilities to the native populations of the lands that the United States had conquered. Thus, in Omaha, McKinley asked rhetorically, "Shall we deny ourselves what the rest of the world so freely and so justly accords to us?"[16]

The President's trip was as political as it was ceremonial. The patriotic fervor that had drawn the country into war still lingered west of Chicago. McKinley was trying to turn it into Republican votes in next month's election. His choice of Omaha to deliver a major address also was probably no accident. McKinley's 1896 opponent, William Jennings Bryan, was a Nebraskan. Bryan was now in Florida serving as a volunteer Army colonel. The President undoubtedly enjoyed making a strong and unchallenged policy statement on his rival's home ground.[17]

By the close of an inconclusive meeting with the Spaniards on October 14, the peace conference was at an impasse over the Cuban debt. The United States delegates were beginning to conclude that their opponents were working for a total negotiating breakdown, in the hope that all issues could be turned over to European arbitrators presumably sympathetic to Spain. However, they were adamant on the issue. They shared Whitelaw Reid's view, as expressed by his biographer:

"The question of the Cuban debt was a thing which he couldn't consent to arbitrate under any circumstances, any more than he could consent to arbitrate a question whether we should or should not obey the moral law."[18]

Morality aside, the Americans knew that they held all the bargaining chips. They had already won the war. As the victors, they were entitled to the spoils.

The American conferees were not permitting the Cuban debt issue to postpone their continuing consideration of future United States policy towards the Philippines. The major issue was still whether the United States should annex all the islands, or only a few, including Luzon. By

October 15 the need for a prompt decision was highlighted by a report from Dewey that "general anarchy prevails" throughout Luzon except for Manila and its environs. He urged that "the disposition of the Philippine Islands should be decided as soon as possible and a strong government established." His reference to a "strong government" clearly was to the United States. Since only a few months earlier Dewey had contended that the Filipinos were more capable of self-government than the Cubans, his negative assessment was especially significant.[19]

On October 15 the testimony of Commander R.B. Bradford buttressed the case for annexation of all the islands. Chief of the Bureau of Naval Equipment, Bradford was also a naval strategist who had made three visits to the Philippines. He argued that it would be a mistake to acquire only Luzon, since it could be easily attacked from the neighboring islands. If Spain were allowed to retain any portion of the Philippines, it would likely sell those islands to Germany. Bradford agreed when Commissioner Frye observed that Germany was "about as troublesome a neighbor as we could get."[20]

Bradford's testimony clearly impressed Day, who previously had taken no position regarding the Philippines. His thinking was also influenced by the comments of John Foreman, whose article on the Philippines had previously interested McKinley. When Day asked Foreman: "Would it not be as well to take the entire property and be done with it?" the Englishman made the surprising, but not unreasonable response: "By taking the whole of the islands, it would be a favor to Europe by setting aside all chances of rivalry."[21]

By October 17 discussions at the Peace Conference were growing acrimonious. A London news agency reported that Commissioner Day told the Spanish delegates that the United States would no longer "tolerate" their attempts to have the United States assume the Cuban debt. When one of the Spaniards responded that his country would rather give up the Philippines than pay the debt (or more likely repudiate all or part of it), Day rejoined that the United States probably would want the Philippines regardless of the debt issue.[22] However, in their October 26 meeting with the American peace negotiators at the Foreign Ministry, the Spanish delegates at last agreed to discuss the future of the Philippines without a prior agreement on the Cuban debt question. This meant that they were giving up on that issue.

Their concession followed a last ditch effort the prior evening. The

Spanish Ambassador to France, not an official delegate but an old personal friend of Whitelaw Reid, met him at his hotel to plead the Spanish case one more time, but in vain. By the time the Ambassador left, Reid later described him as

"...obviously greatly depressed. He said in saying good-bye: 'My dear friend, it is cruel, most cruel; pray God that you may never be likewise vanquished.' Shaking hands again at the door, for perhaps a second or third time, I closed with the words 'Do not break off,' and with every expression of cordiality but obviously with great sadness the Ambassador disappeared in the corridors of the hotel."[23]

Spain was accepting the inevitable. The United States had the upper hand and would have its way. The once mighty Spanish empire was disappearing into history.

This left the Philippines, and American policy on that issue was finally about to be resolved. On October 25 the five commissioners telegraphed their separate recommendations to Washington. As expected, Reid's opinion, in which Senators Davis and Frye joined, favored annexing the entire archipelago. Day agreed, but only to the extent of Luzon and certain neighboring islands, "thus controlling the entrance to the China Sea with additional harbors and ports of call."[24]

Senator Gray dissented in a cogently reasoned statement. The acquisition of Puerto Rico and, despite the Teller Amendment, of Cuba, could be justified by their "propinquity" to the continental United States. On the other hand, to annex the Philippines "would be to reverse accepted continental policy of country declared and acted upon throughout our history and introduces us into European politics and...entangling alliances." Further:

"It will make necessary a navy equal to largest of powers, a greatly increased military establishment, immense sums for fortifications and harbors, multiply occasions for dangerous complications with foreign nations, and increase burdens of taxation.

"But even conceding all benefits claimed for annexation, we exchange the moral grandeur and strength to be gained by keeping our word to the nations of the world and by exhibiting a magnanimity and moderation in hour of victory that becomes the advanced civilization we claim, for doubtful material advantages and shameful stepping down from high moral position boastfully assumed."[25]

These persuasive arguments apparently fell on deaf ears. The next day, October 26, Hay telegraphed the delegates:

"The cession must be of the whole archipelago or none. The latter is wholly inadmissable, and the former must therefore be required. The president reaches this conclusion after most thorough consideration of the whole subject, and is deeply sensible of the grave responsibilities it will impose, believing that this course will entail less trouble than any other, and besides will best subserve the interests of the people involved, for whose welfare we cannot escape responsibility."[26]

For more than a month, McKinley had been leaning towards acquisition of the entire archipelago. Even before his Western trip, he had been subjected to a continuous barrage of annexation demands from business and religious leaders. Strategic and foreign policy considerations pointed in the same direction. Finally, the enthusiastic response of his Western audiences to his references to "duty" and "destiny" convinced him that, at least in that part of the country, annexation would find broad popular support.[27]

A year later the President explained what he believed was the primary reason for his decision. As a visiting delegation from the General Missionary Committee of the Methodist Episcopal Church was starting to depart from a White House visit, he stopped them:

"...Before you go, I would like to say just a word about the Philippine business...The truth is I didn't want the Philippines, and when they came to us as a gift from the gods, I did not know what to do with them...I sought counsel from all sides—Democrats as well as Republicans—but got little help. I thought first we would take only Manila; then Luzon; then other islands, perhaps, also. I walked the floor of the White House night after night until midnight: and I am not ashamed to tell you, gentlemen, that I went down on my knees and prayed Almighty God for light and guidance more than one night.

"And one night late it came to me this way—I don't know how it was, but it came: (1) That we could not give them back to Spain—that would be cowardly and dishonorable; (2) that we could not turn them over to France or Germany—our commercial rivals in the Orient—that would be bad business and discreditable: (3) that we could not leave them to themselves—they were unfit for self-government—that they would soon have anarchy and misrule over them worse than Spain's was; and (4) that there was nothing left for us to do but to take them all, and educate the Filipinos, and uplift and civilize and Christianize them, and by God's grace do the very best we could do by them, as our fellow men for whom Christ also died. And then I went to bed and went to sleep and slept soundly."[28]

On October 28 Hay telegraphed more complete instructions to the peace delegation in Paris. While emphasizing that under no circumstances could the Philippines be returned to Spain, the Secretary of State left to the commissioners "how these instructions should be carried out and whether to be presented as a peremptory command." Hay reported that the President "is not unmindful of the distressed financial condition of Spain, and whatever consideration the United States may show must come from its sense of generosity and benevolence, rather than from any real or technical obligation."[29]

Pursuant to these instructions, on October 31 the conferees formally presented to their Spanish opposites the American demand for the entire Philippine archipelago. The initial response was negative, but an official reply would come later after the Spanish delegates had conferred with the government in Madrid.[30]

To say that the Spanish commissioners were displeased with the American proposal on the Philippines would have understated the case. On November 1 Don Eugenio Montero Rios, who headed the Spanish delegation, telegraphed Madrid that

"...the said proposition which is wholly outside the protocol of Washington and in contradiction to its provisions causes amazement because, as it is drawn, it is equivalent to proposing to Spain that she present to the United States the Philippine archipelago, doubtless as a demonstration of our gratitude for its course in the Cuban question."[31]

On November 4 the American and Spanish conferees met for two hours to hear and discuss the Spanish response. As expected, the Spaniards asserted that it went beyond the protocol that had terminated hostilities. Indeed, since the Americans had not taken Manila until after the protocol had been initialed, the United States had no right even to the

John Hay

Philippine capital. Despite the impasse, the negotiations were not broken off, as the Americans had earlier feared.[32]

Despite their initial concern, the Republicans were satisfied with the November 8 national election results. They significantly increased their Senate majority, and retained control of the House, although by a slimmer margin.[33] Unlike today, when a new Congress commences in January, the 56th Congress would not convene for several months. Thus, the existing Congress would consider and presumably act on the peace treaty when it returned in December for a short session ending in early March. Nevertheless, the impressive support for McKinley's policies demonstrated by the election results would undoubtedly affect the Senators in their treaty vote.

Amid the continuing praise for his success on the Fashoda question, Salisbury delivered another Guildhall speech, this time on November 9 at the annual Lord Mayor's Banquet. In a review of the foreign scene and "the dangers that surround us," the Prime Minister rejected "for the present" the declaration of a British protectorate for Egypt and welcomed the Tsar's disarmament conference proposal. The portion of his address that drew that most comment related to the United States in this

"...first year in which the mighty force of the American Republic has been introduced among the nations whose dominion is spent, and whose instruments, to a certain extent, are weakened. I am not implying the slightest blame—far from it—I am not refusing sympathy to the American republic in the difficulties through which they have passed, but no one can deny that their appearance among the factors at all events of Asiatic and possibly of European diplomacy is not a grave and serious event, which may not conduce to the interests of peace, though I think in any event they are likely to conduce to the interests of Great Britain."[34]

Salisbury's speech provoked widespread comment. The London press viewed it as an invitation for closer Anglo-American relations. The *Times* commented that the Prime Minister's remarks on the new United States role in world affairs "obviously meant that America and England would stand together in a friendship based upon community of aims, sentiments and interests."[35] Not surprisingly, observers on the European continent were concerned that any British-American entente would be directed against one or more of the other great powers. Thus, one Paris journal called Salisbury's speech "an invitation to America to make an alliance against Europe." Another suggested that any agreement by the two countries would be directed against Germany regarding the Philippines.[36]

═══◦)◦(◦═══

The impasse over the Philippines and the resulting possibility that there might be no peace treaty led the American commissioners to ask for further instructions. Among their individual views was the suggestion of Senator Frye that the United States might agree to pay Spain for the entire archipelago. In his November 13 reply Hay accepted this suggestion:

"Willing or not, we have the responsibility of duty which we cannot escape. You are therefore instructed to insist upon the cession of the whole of the Philippines, and, if necessary, pay to Spain $10,000,000 to $20,000,000."[37]

The proposal was inspired. Not only might it offer Spain a way out, but it would remove the issue whether the United States could legitimately claim the islands by right of conquest. Instead, they would be purchased for good and valuable consideration, as in any business transaction.

European observers expected the Spanish commissioners eventually to yield to the United States's demands, although under protest. Nevertheless, the American position was not popular. As *Le Matin* suggested, the United States appeared to be acting on the basis of Bismarck's "brutal maxim" that "when you have your knees on a nation's neck you should make her cough out all you can."[38]

On November 21 the American peace commissioners submitted their "final proposition." As previously agreed, the United States would acquire Cuba, Puerto Rico, and Guam. It would also purchase the entire Philippine archipelago for $20 million, although for "a term of years Spanish ships and merchandise shall be admitted into the ports of the Philippine Islands on the same terms as American ships and merchandise." Claims for indemnity on both sides would be relinquished.[39]

═══◦)◦(◦═══

The November 21 London morning newspapers remarked on the generosity of the American willingness to pay a substantial amount for the Philippines, and agreed that Spain would be foolish to reject what was in substance an ultimatum. Their comment reflected widespread British support for the American position. To some extent this stemmed from concern that the alternative to American annexation was a German takeover of the islands. The English also hoped that an increasing American role in the Far East would lead to United States support for them in the Orient.

The apostle of empire, Rudyard Kipling, reflected the views of most of his fellow countryman when he wrote Roosevelt in September:

"Now go in and put all the weight of influence into hanging on permanently to the whole Philippines. America has gone and stuck a pickaxe into the foundations of a rotten house and she is morally bound to build the house over again from the foundations or have it fall about her ears."

In November, Kipling followed up this advice with a poem, "The White Man's Burden," that he wrote in order to influence the United States debate on the future of the Philippines. He immediately sent it to Roosevelt, who passed it on to Lodge, describing it as "rather poor poetry, but good sense from the expansionist viewpoint." It would be published in February on the day before the Senate vote on the treaty.[40]

On November 25 the American peace commissioners telegraphed to Hay the Spanish response to the "final" United States proposal. Spain would accept any one of three alternative propositions:

1. It would give up Cuba, Puerto Rico, Guam, the Ladrones and all the Philippines for $100 million.

2. Generally the same as the first alternative, except that Spain would retain the southern islands of Mindanao and Sulu "which have never formed a part of the Philippine Islands archipelago proper." The United States would pay $50 million.

3. The same as the first alternative, except that Spain would retain the Ladrones. Its cession of all the islands except for Cuba would be "gratuitous." However, the two countries "will submit to an arbitration tribunal what are the debts and obligations of a colonial character which should pass with the islands the sovereignty over which Spain relinquishes and cedes," i.e., what debts the United States must assume.[41]

The American commissioners were not unanimous as to the response they should make. Commissioners Day, Davis, and Reid believed that they should not modify their previously presented "final" position. Frye and Gray favored the second alternative, provided the United States paid only $20 million. Indeed, Day would have supported this response if "it were an original proposition", but believed that the United States must maintain a "consistent course."[42] Hay's response later the same day reflected this view. "The president," he telegraphed, "finds no reason for departing from his instructions and your proposal thereunder."[43]

On a dark, cloudy Monday, November 28, the Spaniards reluctantly agreed to the American demands:

"Seeing that an acceptance of the proposals is a necessary condition to a continuation of negotiations, and seeing that the resources of Spain are not such as to enable her to re-enter upon war, she is prepared, in her desire to avoid bloodshed and from considerations of humanity and patriotism, to submit to the conditions of the conquering nation, however harsh they may be."[44]

When the reading of the Spanish response had been completed and the American commissioners were preparing to leave the room, the sun suddenly broke through the clouds and illuminated the table at which Senor Ojeda, the secretary of the Spanish delegation, was making notes. Whitelaw Reid, trying to be as sympathetic as possible under the circumstances, turned to Ojeda and expressed the hope that the sudden burst of sunlight was an omen of good fortune for both countries. Ojeda was too downhearted to admit the point: "No, everything is gloom around here."[45]

Although the major issues before the peace treaty negotiators had been settled, other less important questions remained open. These included the future status of Spaniards in the conquered territories and which country should pay the expense of shipping Spanish prisoners home. At first the American delegates listened patiently and with some admiration at the breadth and ingenuity of the reasons advanced by the Spanish commissioners for making no further concessions. Finally, on December 3, they had had enough, and in the most friendly manner Commissioner Day uttered a sentence which, a *New York Times* correspondent wrote, "epitomized...the history of the document which will certify the passing of the oldest colonial power and the advent of the newest...:"

"A peace treaty can contain anything which the victors put into it."

The Spanish commissioners took Day's remark in good spirit. From then on the negotiators made progress.[46]

Ever since Ferdinand De Lesseps had failed to complete a canal linking the Atlantic and Pacific, sentiment had been building for the United States to construct and control its own inter-ocean passage. Partly because of the French experience in Panama, the primary emphasis was on Nicaragua. In July, 1897, McKinley had appointed a commission to consider which route through that country would be most feasible.

The voyage of the *Oregon* around the southernmost tip of South America had dramatized the military importance of a rapid passage between the two oceans. So also did the recent American territorial expansion in the Pacific. Thus, on December 5 in his annual message to the reconvened Congress, which was largely devoted to a history of the war, the President stressed "the urgency of some definite action by the Congress at this session, if the labors of the past are to be utilized and the linking of the Atlantic and Pacific Oceans by a practical waterway is to be realized."[47]

Opponents of Philippine annexation did not wait for the peace treaty with Spain to be signed before commencing their attack on its ratification. One of the most active was Andrew Carnegie, whose vast wealth made him an especially formidable foe of administration policy.* Now that Spain had agreed to give up the Philippines, he was prepared to oppose the peace treaty through financial as well as vocal support.[48] On November 29 in a letter to Reid, the usually mild mannered Hay reflected the irritation that many imperialists felt toward the steel magnate:

"There is a wild and frantic attack now going on in the press against the whole Philippine transaction. Andrew Carnegie really seems to be off

---

* Carnegie once suggested, probably facetiously, that he, rather than the United States, buy the Philippines for $20 million.

his head. He writes me frantic letters signing them "Your Bitterest Opponent." He threatens the President, not only with the vengeance of the voters, but with powerful punishment at the hands of the mob...He does not seem to reflect that the Government is in a somewhat more robust condition even after shooting down several American citizens in his interest at Homestead."[49]

On December 6, the second day of the new Congressional session, Senator George Vest of Missouri introduced a resolution stating that

"...under the Constitution of the United States no power is given to the Federal Government to acquire territory to be held and governed permanently as colonies."

Any territory, he argued,

"...must be acquired and governed with the purpose of ultimately organizing such territory into States suitable for admission into the Union."[50]

Since it had never been contemplated that the former Spanish possessions would become states, the effect of the resolution was to deny their acquisition.

Perhaps because Vest was an accomplished lawyer, he supported his resolution by quoting a statement in the otherwise infamous *Dred Scott* decision in which the Supreme Court stated that the Constitution gave the Federal Government "no power...to establish or maintain colonies bordering on the United States or at a distance, to be ruled or governed at its own pleasure." "It is incredible," Vest argued, "that the men who fought for seven long years...against the proudest and strongest nation in the world, resisting the doctrine upon which the colonial system of Europe is based, should...deliberately put this doctrine in the written Constitution framed to govern them and their children."[51]

Under the Constitution, ratification of the treaty would require a two-thirds Senate vote. Since the Republicans held only a small majority, the Administration would need significant Democratic backing as well as solid Republican support. Unfortunately, one of the strongest critics of annexation was the seventy-two-year-old senior senator from Massachusetts, Republican George F. Hoar. Cantankerous and pugnacious by nature, he contended that colonialism was nothing less than the subjugation of an entire people to slavery. He believed that Cuba, Puerto

Rico, and the Philippines should be given their independence after a short period of American protection during which they would put their political houses in order. It was essential to the Administration that Hoar should not sway other Republican senators to his cause.[52]

At 8:45 P.M. on December 10 the peace treaty formally ending the Spanish-American War was signed in a large room at the French Foreign Ministry. Since its terms had already been agreed to, the event was largely ceremonial. The picture was impressive, with the black of the commissioners' clothing contrasting with what *The New York Times* correspondent referred to as "the brilliant green and scarlet of the upholstery," which "the jets from the crystal chandeliers ...magnified... into gaudiness."[53]

The ceremony commenced with a reading of the English version of the treaty followed by its Spanish text. Two copies were then passed around the large mahogany table at which the commissioners sat, and were signed by them in the order of their rank. The Americans were intent on securing for souvenirs as many as possible of the signature pens. When the official American interpreter asked Senior Montero Rios for his pen, the head of the Spanish delegation readily obliged. The Spaniards sat as if crushed by this national tragedy in which they were unwilling participants.[54]

William Jennings Bryan had been serving in the Army as a colonel. Now that the war was over, he decided to return to civilian life. As he said in his December 10 letter of resignation, "I can be of more service to my country as a civilian than as a soldier."[55]

The Adjutant General promptly accepted Bryan's resignation. The former colonel wasted no time, but immediately visited Washington to add his voice to the debate on McKinley's policy towards the Spanish overseas possessions. At a press conference in Savannah, Georgia before he left for the capital, he warned that the American people "must defend themselves and their country against a foreign idea—the colonial idea of European nations."[56]

As Bryan elaborated on his views after his arrival in Washington on December 16, the issue was not so simple. The United States would be justified in reserving harbors and coaling stations in Puerto Rico, the Philippines, and possibly even Cuba. Indeed, if the Puerto Rican people desired annexation, their wishes should be respected. The Philippines were a different matter; they were "too far away, and their people are too different from ours."[57] Nevertheless Bryan favored ratification of the peace treaty. It was better, he believed, temporarily to acquire the Philippines and grant them independence than to leave them isolated at the mercy of the other colonial powers. In this, he parted company from Carnegie, Hoar, and most other leading anti-imperialists. They were probably right. Difficult though it would be to keep the American camel's nose out of the Philippine tent, once in, it would be even harder to get it out.[58]

In a mournful ceremony on December 12, the ashes of Christopher Columbus were removed from Havana's Cathedral and in a solemn procession were borne to a waiting Spanish warship. It sailed that evening for Spain.[59] When Columbus's last remains arrived in Spain, they appropriately were placed in a magnificent tomb in the Cathedral of Seville, for many years the river port to which the vast riches of Spain's once all-powerful New World empire had been delivered.

The war with Spain had brought the North and South together. McKinley used the excuse of a Peace Jubilee to visit Atlanta on December 14 and address the Georgia Legislature. The President drew loud cheers as he said:

"Sectional feeling no longer holds back the love we bear each other... The Union is once more the common atlas of our love and loyalty, our devotion and sacrifice."

The response to this sentiment was nothing, however, compared to the emotion that was engendered when this former Union army major proposed that "the time has now come...when in the spirit of fraternity we should share with you in the care of the graves of the Confederate soldiers." There were wild cheers and yells, and Confederate veterans stood and waved their hats. According to *The New York Times*, "one old man...buried his head in his arms, and, while cheers rang out, cried like a little child."[60]

Republican Senator Orville H. Platt of Connecticut was an ardent imperialist and leading Administration spokesman. As a lawyer, the seventy-one-year-old Platt was able to respond in kind to the legal arguments of Vest and his allies. In a December 19 speech on the Senate floor, he denied

"...that there is any constitutional or moral obligation to fit the territory for statehood or to ever admit it as a State. To claim that there is is to deny the inherent sovereign right of this people, this nation, to do what any nation may do anywhere. To do it is to deny that our nation has the same rights that other sovereign nations have."[61]

Further, Platt noted, the Constitution specifically confers on Congress the power to make regulations respecting a United States territory.[*] This power, he contended "is full and plenary." It permits the United States to

"provide for the people of any territory that we may acquire the most liberal, just, and beneficent government which they may be capable of enjoying, always with reference to their development and welfare and in the hope that they may be finally fitted for independent self-government."[62]

The next day, Colorado's Henry Teller took the Senate floor. As the author of the resolution calling for Cuban independence, his views were awaited with special interest. Teller asserted that Cuba was different from Puerto Rico and the Philippines. In Cuba there had been a significant independence movement, while in the other islands there had been "no pretense at self-government."[63] A lawyer like Vest and Platt, he pooh-poohed the constitutional issue:

"The United States is a sovereign. Whatever any nation may do she may do."[64]

The real question, said Teller, was: "Who else can govern Cuba, Puerto Rico and the Philippine Islands but the United States?"[65] To him the answer was obvious: they must be placed under the American flag, where they would receive "that moral aid, that moral encouragement, which will enable them to take care of themselves." After a probationary period, the length of which Teller did not estimate, they would become either independent nations or integral parts of the United States.[66]

With Christmas fast approaching, Congress adjourned on December 21. It would return in January to act on the treaty. Three days later, the American peace commissioners landed in New York, and immediately went by train to Washington. At the White House, McKinley welcomed and thanked them for their successful negotiation. The President was in an optimistic mood, predicting: "I feel sure that I can assure you that the treaty will be ratified by the Senate."[67]

As the year closed, it was not only the military and naval power of the United States that was attracting world-wide notice. The December 25 *New York Times* carried a report from London which began:

"It is no exaggeration to assert that the foremost topic compelling attention in Europe in general and to Great Britain in particular, overshadowing the dreary broils of domestic politics, is the remarkable, aggressive, commercial prosperity which the United States is manifesting."

The *Times* quoted "the manager of one of the greatest London banks," who stated to an American banker "in an awestruck tone:"

"This is the first time in the history of finance that New York has been in a position to dictate money rates to London, Berlin, and Paris."[68]

Few readers of this report probably sensed the future ramifications of this observation.

Six days later the London *Times* summed up the events of the momentous year that was about to end:

"Of greater importance than the campaign on the Nile was the war which broke out in April between the United States and Spain; a war which ended in less than three months in the loss by the latter power of her once vast colonial empire, and—what is of far greater consequence to the world—in the apparently definitive adoption of an imperial and military policy by the United States."[69]

TWENTY

Into The New Century

O n Monday, February 6, 1899, the Senate ratified the peace treaty with Spain. Obtaining the necessary two-thirds vote had been much more difficult than McKinley had predicted. Shortly after the Senate reconvened in early January, Hoar delivered a passionate speech, arguing that the founding fathers had never anticipated that their descendants

"...might strut about in the cast-off clothing of pinchbeck emperors and pewter kings; that their descendants would be excited by the smell of gunpowder and the sound of the guns of a single victory as a small boy by a firecracker on some Fourth of July morning."[1]

Initially, other Republican senators shared Hoar's doubts. It took intensive lobbying, including offers of patronage and choice committee assignments, to bring some of them into line. Indeed, a populist Republican from Idaho angrily claimed that he had been offered a bribe, and temporarily joined the opposition. When the final votes were counted, however, only one other Republican added a "No" vote to Hoar's.[2]

Probably equally important were Bryan's efforts on the treaty's behalf. Stationing himself in a room at the rear of the Senate chamber, he tried to convince Democratic senators that the party needed the imperialism issue to win the 1900 Presidential election, and that the only way to preserve it was to ratify the treaty. Estimates of the number of senators that he influenced ranged from two to ten.[3] Until a few minutes before the vote at 3:00 P.M. on February 6, the outcome was still in doubt. As it was, the treaty squeaked through with only an extra vote to spare. In a letter to Roosevelt, Lodge called it "the closest, hardest fight I have ever known."[4]

Commencing in 1901, the Supreme Court effectively rejected a Constitutional challenge to the acquisition of the former Spanish colonies.[5] In 1900 the voters had already affirmed their annexation. Once more, Bryan was the Democratic Presidential nominee, with former Vice-

329

President Adlai E. Stevenson of Illinois* as his running mate. The platform stipulated "imperialism" as the campaign's paramount issue.[6]

As expected, McKinley was the Republican candidate. A boomlet for Admiral Dewey never materialized. The President's running mate, replacing the deceased Garrett Hobart, was Governor Theodore Roosevelt. Early in 1900, Roosevelt had successfully challenged Boss Platt's effort to reappoint Louis F. Payn as New York Superintendent of Insurance. Suggestions in the Governor's annual message for reforms such as the greater regulation of public utility companies also were not to Platt's liking. The boss's immediate response was to suggest publicly that Roosevelt "ought to take the vice presidency for both national and state reasons." Roosevelt's good friend Lodge had already actively been furthering his candidacy on the theory that as Vice-President he would be in a good position to receive the Presidential nomination in 1904. At first, Roosevelt rejected the idea on the basis that as Vice President he would have nothing to do. Gradually, however, he was persuaded that as a good Republican, he was obligated to accept the nomination should it come his way.[8]

Meanwhile, wholly apart from Platt's efforts to get Roosevelt out of New York, a countrywide boom for his nomination was developing. Here was an impeccably honest, certified war hero who appealed to all classes. By the time the Republican convention opened in June in Philadelphia, in Platt's words: "Roosevelt might as well stand under Niagara Falls and try to spit water back as to stop his nomination by this convention." The apoplectic Hanna exploded: "Don't any of you realize that there's only one life between this madman and the Presidency?" but by now the Ohio senator had lost much of his influence over McKinley. Thus, when the President left the nomination entirely to the convention, it chose Roosevelt with only one dissenting vote—his own.[9]

With McKinley conducting another "front-porch" campaign, Roosevelt took the Republican cause all over the country. By election day he had made 673 speeches in 567 different locations. The United States was prosperous, and the Republican emphasized the same gold standard issue that had won them the White House four years before. It worked again, and Bryan was defeated by even greater electoral and popular majorities.[10] As he left New York to attend the inaugural ceremonies, Platt joked, "We're all off to Washington to see Teddy take the veil."[11]

---

* The grandfather of the 1952 and 1956 Democratic Presidential candidate of the same name.

On September 6, 1901, at a public reception at a Pan-American Exposition in Buffalo, New York, McKinley was shot by an anarchist and died
eight days later. At forty-three, Roosevelt became the youngest President in the country's history. Imperialism was in the saddle, and under
Roosevelt's leadership the United States assumed its role as a world
power.

To the surprise of many observers, the United States honored the Teller
Amendment. After three years of sympathetic military government
under Leonard Wood, Cuba was given its independence. The United
States kept the right to intervene if necessary to preserve order, but this
reservation, which was invoked only once, was renounced in 1934. Thus,
when the communist insurgent Fidel Castro seized power in the late
1950s, the United States had no legal right to remove him. The abortive
1962 attempt of the Soviet Union to install missiles on the island led to a
confrontation that could well have resulted in a thermonuclear war.

Puerto Rico was a different story. Partly because there had never
been a strong independence movement, there was little pressure to free
it from United States rule. In 1917, its inhabitants were granted American citizenship, and in 1948 the island became a self-governing United
States commonwealth benefiting from American economic incentives.

The increased American role in both the Caribbean and the Pacific
made the construction of an isthmian canal a necessity. Its site, however,
would not be Nicaragua but Panama, which in 1903 with Roosevelt's
active participation broke off from Colombia and declared its independence. The new nation at once granted the United States a canal zone,
and the ensuing "path between the seas" was completed in 1914.

On the evening of February 4, 1899, an army sentry outside Manila fired
on an insurgent patrol that he thought was coming too close to the American lines. This led to a rebel attack, which was repulsed with significant losses on both sides.[12]

The full-scale revolt that followed lasted for more than three years.
Aguinaldo was captured on March 23, 1901, but still the fighting continued. By July 4, 1902, when President Theodore Roosevelt declared the
war's end, some 4,200 Americans and 20,000 insurgents had been killed.
Hostilities were finally terminated by separating the Filipino civilians
from the guerrillas. Ironically, the United States thereby had adopted a

policy which resembled the Spanish Cuban reconcentration that had so outraged the American public several years earlier.[13]

Over time, the government of the Philippines was gradually turned over to the Filipinos. In the mid-1930s, the United States agreed to grant the Islands' independence on July 4, 1946. Since American occupation of the Philippines would block a Japanese seizure of the rich resources of what is now Indonesia, the Islands were attacked at the same time as Pearl Harbor in December, 1941. After stubborn resistance, their American-Filipino defenders were defeated. In 1944 American forces reconquered the Islands. The Philippines received their independence on schedule in 1946, with the United States agreeing to provide long-term economic aid and reserving a 99-year guarantee of military and naval facilities.

Meanwhile, acquisition of the Philippines had permitted the United States to establish itself as a major force in the Western Pacific. In 1899 the other major powers agreed to Secretary Hay's Open Door proposal, under which China's territorial and administrative integrity would be respected. In 1905 Roosevelt called a peace conference at Portsmouth, New Hampshire, where he helped negotiate an end to the Russo-Japanese War.[*] Although Japan would later dispute their claim, many in the United States began to view the Western Pacific at least all the way to the Philippines as an American lake.

The friendly relations between the United States and England that had developed in 1898 continued into the twentieth century. In the past there had been strong American hostility to any efforts to quell independence movements in British colonies. In 1899, however, when England asserted its authority over the two South African Boer republics, the McKinley Administration kept silent. Queen Victoria's death, two years later, saw an unprecedented outpouring of sympathy throughout the United States. For the first time in history, the flag atop the White House was lowered to half-staff in respect for a deceased foreign sovereign.[14]

This good feeling was reciprocated on the other side of the Atlantic. As the need for an isthmian canal became more evident, the United States felt increasingly irritated that, under an 1850 treaty with England, any Central American canal was to be a joint British-American venture. After the Senate refused to ratify without amendment a treaty

---

[*] In 1906, Roosevelt was awarded the Nobel Peace Prize for his efforts.

negotiated by Hay and British Ambassador Pauncefote that gave the United States most but not all authority over a Nicaraguan or Panamanian canal, the English agreed to a renegotiation. The Hay-Pauncefote Treaty that the Senate ratified in December, 1901, provided the United States with rights similar to those Britain enjoyed over the Suez Canal.[15]

The next September, after Venezuela refused to pay debts owing to British and German nationals, the two European powers shelled two Venezuelan ports and blockaded the coast. When Roosevelt invoked the Monroe Doctrine and threatened to move an American naval force to the area, the British told the Germans that they were no longer siding with them. In this isolated posture, Germany backed down.[16] Roosevelt returned the favor in 1905-1906 when he subtly intervened to thwart German efforts to limit the Moroccan sphere of influence of England's emerging ally, France.[17]

As the old century was drawing to a close, Roosevelt wrote Spring-Rice that although the existing close relationship between the two countries "probably won't last quite in its present good shape, ...I am greatly mistaken if we ever slide back into the old condition of bickering and angry distrust."[18] Six years later, and now President, he wrote another English friend, Arthur Lee, then in the Foreign Office:

"You need not ever be troubled by the nightmare of a possible war between the two great English speaking peoples. In keeping ready for possible war I never even take into account a war with England. I treat it as out of the question."[19]

This developing friendship between the two major English-speaking peoples that began in 1898 formed the basis of the partnerships that triumphed in two world wars. It was a "special relationship" that profoundly affected the course of modern history.

As the nineteenth century was closing, it appeared as though England also was growing closer to Germany. The 1898 understanding on the Portuguese debt manifested an assumption that Germany would not interfere with British actions in South Africa, and Victoria and her ministers appreciated German neutrality in the Boer War. When his grandmother died in January 1901, the Kaiser made a "private" visit to England to attend the funeral, and won favorable comment by his sympathetic behavior.[20]

The previous fall, riding on the crest of popularity caused by the Boer War victory, the Conservatives were returned to power with a large parliamentary majority. The aging Lord Salisbury continued as Prime Minister, but turned over the Foreign Office to the fifty-five-year-old Lord Lansdowne, who had been War Secretary in the preceding government. The effect of this change and of Salisbury's worsening health was to increase Chamberlain's influence even further. As Churchill, whose book *The River War* had been a huge critical and popular success and who had won his first parliamentary seat after a dramatic escape from the Boers, later observed:

"Mr. Chamberlain was incomparably the most live, sparkling, insurgent, compulsive figure in British affairs. He it was who had solutions for social problems; who was ready to advance, sword in hand, if need be, upon the foes of Britain."[21]

Chamberlain at once raised again with Baron Eckardstein the possibility of a British association with Germany. With Salisbury's influence seemingly waning, a majority of the Cabinet apparently was willing to go along. Shortly thereafter, when the Kaiser was in England for Victoria's funeral, his personal reaction was to welcome the proposal. It was only with difficulty that Bülow and Holstein held him back on the basis that a British alliance would endanger German relations with Russia, which was still perceived as England's enemy.[22]

Nevertheless, apparently serious discussions continued for several months. Initially they involved a defensive alliance proposal, similar to that advanced by British Ambassador Lascelles in 1898, under which England or Germany would intervene only if the other was attacked by more than one power. While this suggestion was still on the table, the Germans replaced it with a proposal under which Britain would join the Triple Alliance as if it were a single power. At this point, Salisbury put his foot down. The German proposal, he pointed out, would require British intervention if Austria or Italy were attacked by France or Russia, even if Germany was not directly involved. Among other things, it would also make much less likely the successful conclusion of the current negotiations looking towards an end to France's colonial rivalry with England.[23]

Following Salisbury's intervention, there were no further alliance discussions. Matters did not rest there, however. In October, 1901, Chamberlain in an Edinburgh speech attacked the critics of the British treatment of the civilian population in the Boer War. The German press claimed that the attack was directed against Germany, and in the Reichstag Bülow demanded an apology. Chamberlain indignantly refused, and the British public strongly supported him. A few weeks later a Foreign Office official wrote of an "extraordinary" change in British feeling: "Everyone in the Office talks as if we had but one enemy in the world, and that is Germany. It is no good trying to assure us unofficially or officially that they are really our friends. No one believes it now."[24]

Several weeks later, the new King, Edward VII, described the altered state of play to Eckardstein. At the close of a state dinner for foreign ambassadors, the monarch invited the German to remain for a drink and frankly told him:

"For a long time at least, there can no more be any question of Great Britain and Germany working together in any conceivable matter. We are being urged more strongly than ever by France to come to an agreement with her in all colonial disputes and it will probably be best in the end to make such a settlement."[25]

By now, a second Navy Law had been enacted, providing for doubling the size of the German fleet from 19 battleships to 38. Although the buildup would take place only in stages over a seventeen-year period, it was nevertheless troubling to England, since it clearly was directed at her. The result was not only an offsetting naval expansion, but also an impetus for Britain to replace "splendid isolation" with a European alliance.[26]

Britain's new ally would be France. Since the Middle Ages, the two countries had been traditional enemies. However, from the time he became Foreign Minister in June, 1898, Delcassé's major goal was to establish closer relations with England. He realized that if France were to recover Alsace-Lorraine from Germany, it would need allies. The lack of Russian support during the Fashoda crisis, as well as the Tsar's unilateral call for an international disarmament conference, raised serious doubt as to that country's reliability. Finally, the naval superiority demonstrated by England in 1898 pointed up the folly of France's continuing the two countries' colonial rivalry.[27]

Delcassé's first step was to send the experienced diplomat Paul Cambon to London as the new French Ambassador. Cambon's initial charge was to negotiate an end to the Fashoda imbroglio. The agreement, signed on March 21, 1899, confirmed Britain's claim to all of the Bahr al-Ghazal and the basin of the White Nile. In return, France gained some recognition of its claims in northwest Africa.[28]

Here matters rested for more than two years. Especially in French right-wing circles, the Fashoda crisis's resolution had led to feelings of humiliation and hatred towards England. In addition, reports that the British were seeking an alliance with France's arch-enemy Germany made it unlikely that the Salisbury Government would be interested in serious discussions with France. Indeed, even after the signing of the March 21, 1899 agreement, Delcassé worried that England had not been satisfactorily appeased and might be planning to destroy the still-weak French fleet.[29]

By the spring of 1901 Britain had broken off alliance discussions with Germany and the anger and fears on the French side of the Channel had abated. Thus, Cambon felt able to suggest to Lansdowne that an overall understanding on colonial matters might be reached. The English Foreign Secretary was receptive, but did not pursue the matter further until after Chamberlain's angry reaction to Bülow's Reichstag speech. The Colonial Secretary continued to believe in the importance of a British alliance with a major European power and as an association with Germany was now out of the question, France was the logical alternative.[30]

By 1903, the move towards an entente escalated. In early May Edward VII made a historic official visit to Paris, where his evident admiration for France and things French captivated the populace. This was followed in July by a visit of the French President to London. By April 1904 Cambon and Lansdowne had negotiated a broad agreement on colonial spheres of influence which formally recognized Britain's position in Egypt and the Sudan and waived British objections to French involvement in the still independent Sultanate of Morocco.

Although this agreement covered only colonial issues, Delcassé hoped that it would lead to an alliance on other matters. His wish was granted the next year when the Kaiser visited Tangiers to demonstrate publicly German interest in Morocco. England, feeling threatened by the German naval buildup that had continued after 1898, supported France. In the crisis that followed, Delcassé was forced to resign, but Germany finally backed off short of war. During the next few years, the resulting Anglo-French alliance deepened until it was tested in 1914 and endured.

By then, many of 1898's major players had left the scene. On July 11, 1902, beset by worsening health, Salisbury resigned as Prime Minister. He died a year later. His successor was his nephew Arthur Balfour. In 1903, Chamberlain proposed import duties on food, from which produce from the colonies would be exempted. This led to a split with Conservative and Unionist free-trade advocates, of whom Winston Churchill was one. Balfour tried to hold the party together by waffling on the issue, but by early 1906 was forced to call a general election. The Liberals won in a landslide. By then Chamberlain had suffered a severe stroke and had to give up politics. The thirty-one-year-old Churchill, now a Liberal, was included in the new Government as a junior minister in the Colonial Office. He and his colleagues would stay in power until 1914 and beyond.

As England and France grew closer together, a series of French Governments thought it prudent to de-emphasize Fashoda. When Marchand returned to France in mid-1899 after a slow and difficult journey east through Ethiopia, he was initially greeted as a hero, but refused to be exploited by opponents of the Government. Almost at once he was sent on an unimportant mission to China. When he returned, the Army placed him on half pay until 1914, when he rendered distinguished war-time service. Otherwise, he was soon forgotten. So, too, was Fashoda. Its name was tactfully changed to Kodok, which is all that appears on today's maps.[31]

Testimony on the Dreyfus case continued to be taken until late 1899. Meanwhile French political unrest continued unabated. On February 16, 1899, President Faure, who had publicly touted his sexual prowess, died in its performance with his mistress in a private room in the Elysee Palace. When the Assembly elected as his successor Emile Loubet, the President of the Senate and apparently sympathetic to Dreyfus, the Right planned a coup. It fizzled, but emotions continued to run high.[32]

On June 3 the High Court of Appeal "repealed and annulled" the Dreyfus verdict, and ordered him to be retried before a court-martial in the northwestern French city of Rennes. Dreyfus was immediately brought back to France. On June 4 Zola ended his exile and returned to Paris. A few days later the charges against Picquart were dropped and he was freed after 384 days in prison.[33]

The court-martial opened on August 8, 1899. For a month, the public waited in almost unbearable suspense, while in closed session the military court heard testimony from witnesses on both sides of the case. On September 9, by a five-to-two vote Dreyfus was reconvicted, but with a finding of "extenuating circumstances."[34]

The reaction to the decision, especially abroad, was shock and outrage. But the court's finding of extenuating circumstances provided the Government a basis to pardon Dreyfus, which it did on September 19. The next June he was granted amnesty. Not content with this and still asserting his innocence, Dreyfus pursued a judicial appeal. Finally, on July 12, 1906, a court unanimously annulled the Rennes decision and declared Dreyfus innocent on all counts. The next day, the Chamber of Deputies restored Dreyfus and Picquart to the army with the respective ranks of major and of brigadier general. On July 20 Dreyfus was inducted into the Legion of Honor.[35]

Dreyfus retired from the Army in 1907. He returned as a lieutenant in 1914, surviving to die as a civilian in 1935. Prior to his death, the publication of the now-deceased von Schwarzkoppen's account of what had actually occurred confirmed his innocence.[36]

Zola was not alive to see this final victory in which his efforts had been so instrumental. At his funeral in 1902, he was eulogized as a man who "for a moment...was the conscience of mankind." In 1908, his ashes were moved to the Panthéon.

Clemenceau served as Prime Minister for three years beginning in 1906. In 1917, in the darkest days of World War I, he was returned to that office, and as the "Tiger of France," formed a coalition cabinet that brought the country through its ordeal to final victory.[39]

On becoming Premier in 1906, Clemenceau honored Picquart, by now a national hero for his uncompromising honesty, with the post of Minister of War. In 1914, refusing medical attention after being thrown from his horse, Picquart died the following day.

The outcome of the Dreyfus case was a blow to French anti-Semitism, but by no means a fatal one. After France's 1940 defeat by the German Wehrmacht, the Vichy Government pursued an active policy of confiscation of Jewish property and internment. It was as if the anti-Jewish sentiments that had been pent up since the conclusion of the case had suddenly been released. Eventually, Vichy assisted the Germans in deporting a quarter of France's Jewish population to their deaths in the East, most of them at Auschwitz.[37]

This figure is shocking, yet it is much smaller than the two-thirds of European Jewry who died in the Holocaust. The comparison is especially surprising in view of the active anti-Semitism practiced by the Vichy government. There are probably a number of reasons for the difference, but perhaps the most important is what one observer described as "the good sense...the profound humanity of the immense majority of the French people."[38] It was, perhaps, the same devotion to justice that animated Scheurer-Kestner, Picquart, and Zola, and that eventually led to Dreyfus's exoneration.

Captain Alfred Dreyfus at the 1899 Retrial

In May, 1899, with varying degrees of enthusiasm, the delegates of the major powers gathered in the Netherlands at the Dutch capital of The Hague for the conference proposed by the Tsar. Soon after the opening session on May 18, Nicholas II's birthday, it became apparent that it would be difficult for the delegates to agree on anything significant. They finally decided to establish a permanent arbitration tribunal to which it would be the "duty" of nations to submit disputes, only to meet objections from the Kaiser. He complained that he had let Germany participate in the conference "only that the Czar should not lose face before Europe," but "In practice however I shall rely on God and my sharp sword. And I shit on their decisions." Germany finally consented to the tribunal on the basis that the conference should show at least one accomplishment. So did the Americans, after being assured that the "duty" to arbitrate did not commit the United States to "intrude, mingle, or entangle" itself in European affairs.[40]

In 1907 The Hague hosted a second conference. If anything, it accomplished less than its predecessor. Even though the Tsar had called the first conference to reach an agreement on disarmament, the delegates at the second session decided at the outset that it would be fruitless to discuss that subject. They adopted a ninety-six article convention regarding the peaceful settlement of international disputes, but it did not provide for a permanent court of international justice, which was strongly advanced by the American delegates on the instruction of Secretary of State Elihu Root. Other provisions adopted by the delegates, including one relating to the use of wartime bombardment by air, proved totally ineffective in the worldwide conflagrations that followed. As the chief German delegate predicted in a remark that led the British Poet Laureate Alfred Austin to suggest that England should adopt military conscription, any laws of international conduct that the conferees adopted might well be rendered useless by "the laws of facts."[41]

On the basis that progress could be made only in slow stages, the delegates agreed that a third conference should be called eight years later in 1915.[42] One wonders whether they and the national leaders who sent them to The Hague would have adopted a more concerned posture toward issues of war and peace had they known what lay ahead. Given the twentieth century's experience with the League of Nations and even the United Nations, the answer might not have been positive. Yet, the fact remains that the Tsar's 1898 summons was the genesis of the multipower efforts to eliminate or limit the ravages of war which have shaped the twentieth century.

As the new century dawned, the editors of the London *Times*, among others, attempted to prophesy its course. In their leading editorial on January 1, 1901, after quoting an Australian poet's reference to "the fiery ordeal that tries the claim to Nationhood" they wrote:

"We have a reasonable trust that England and her sons will emerge triumphant from that ordeal at the end of the Twentieth Century, and that for then and for ages to come they will live and prosper one united and imperial people to be a 'bulwark for the cause of men.' "[43]

No one who lived through the darkest days of World War II can gainsay the accuracy of that forecast for the new century's first half. By mid-century, however, imperialist sentiment had been replaced by a worldwide anti-colonial movement, and the vaunted British Empire was fast becoming history.

Looking back from the vantage point of the twentieth century's closing years, a more farsighted prediction appeared in the call to action that Theodore Roosevelt gave in a speech at the 1900 Republican Convention:

"We stand on the threshold of a new century big with the fate of mighty nations. It rests with us now to decide whether in the opening years of that century we shall march forward to fresh triumphs or whether at the outset we shall cripple ourselves for the contest...The young giant of the West stands on a continent and clasps the crest of an ocean in either hand. Our nation, glorious in youth and strength, looks into the future with eager eyes and rejoices as a strong man to run a race..."[44]

If Roosevelt were alive today, he almost surely would boast that the United States has met his challenge. Throughout the century, with occasional setbacks, America's world power status expanded through two World Wars and as it finally prevailed in the Cold War that followed. Today, the United States bestrides the globe militarily, economically, and technologically to a much greater degree than even the British Empire at the peak of its power.[45] The events of 1898 were instrumental in setting it on that course.

Author's Note

AND

Acknowledgements

The idea for this book began germinating about fifty-five years ago in central Ohio when I started exploring the library of histories and biographies that my father and, earlier, my grandfather had been accumulating. During my secondary and college education, I was particularly stimulated by my courses in American and European history, and my three years as a reporter and then chairman of *The Daily Princetonian* provided a unique experience in factual investigation and reporting. Throughout my career as a New York City tax lawyer, these interests continued.

Thus, when two years ago I began seriously consider retirement, it seemed natural to try my hand at historical writing. The year 1898, with its approaching centennial, riveting personalities and major events with their long-range ramifications, seemed a ready-made subject.

In writing this book, I drew material from the Sarah Lawrence College Library, the New York Society Library, the New York Public Library, the London Library, the Library of the Bar Association of the City of New York, and the Bronxville, New York Public Library.

Although the research for this book and its writing have been entirely my own, no work of this kind can ever be published without the assistance of others. Thus, I want to thank Charles Davey for his invaluable services in the book's design and production. Bridget Santiago spent many hours in word-processing the manuscript and its revisions, and my office secretary, Terry Sanders, took time from an already busy schedule to help with correspondence and other daily details. Others whose aid and encouragement I gratefully acknowledge include

Robert Marshall Jr., Gerard McCauley, Richard Moe, Alfred Clapp, Robert Frehse, Briscoe Smith, John Spurdle and Robert Wein.

Finally, I want to thank my daughter Anne for her enthusiastic support, especially when the warm reaction that she received from her friends to whom she showed an early draft of the first chapter led me to continue a project that I otherwise might have abandoned. My sister, Catherine Blakemore, who is concurrently writing a book on charter schools, provided very helpful information and advice on publishing questions. And last, but far from least, my special appreciation goes to my wife Emily for not only the many helpful editorial comments and suggestions that she made throughout the book's writing, but also the loving encouragement she constantly provided, especially when from time to time my efforts were not working out as I had hoped. For that I shall always be grateful.

End Notes

CHAPTER ONE

1 Adams, 343.
2 Millis, 5-6.
3 Olcott, 350-361.
4 Hayes, James A. Garfield, McKinley, William Howard Taft, and Warren G. Harding. The two other Republican Presidents who served during this period, Chester A. Arthur and Theodore Roosevelt, both acceded to office as Vice Presidents upon the assassination of their predecessors.
5 Leech, 6-7.
6 Dulles, 109-110; Leech, 17-33.
7 Leech, 134.
8 Dulles, 110.
9 Morison, 799.
10 Leech, 100-101.
11 Dulles, 110.
12 *Ibid.*
13 Leech, 102.
14 O'Toole, 198.
15 Morris, 566.
16 Leech, 106.
17 Morris, 560.
18 Bemis, 29.
19 O'Toole, 90.
20 O'Toole, 92.
21 Morris, Chapter 21.
22 *Ibid.*, 525.
23 Dulles, 91-99.
24 Morris, 569-571.
25 *Ibid.*, 571.
26 White, 297-298.
27 Millis, 16.
28 *Ibid.*, 59.
29 O'Toole, 57-58. Subsequent studies cast doubt on this extreme conclusion. Millis, 76.
30 O'Toole, 76.
31 Millis, 41-43.
32 O'Toole, 82. Hearst denied making the statement.
33 Millis, 80-81.
34 O'Toole, 103.
35 Millis, 87.
36 Millis, 88.
37 Millis, 88-89.
38 O'Toole, 109-110; Morris, 584.
39 O'Toole, 113.
40 *Ibid.*, 114.
41 Ferrara, 97.
42 *The New York Times*, January 13; Millis, 94; O'Toole, 111.
43 Millis, 94.
44 O'Toole, 111.
45 *Ibid.*, 22.
46 *Ibid.*, 21; Millis, 96.
47 Morris, 594.
48 Morison, 759-763.
49 Morris, 595.
50 Morison, 758.
51 O'Toole, 117.
52 *Ibid.*, 116-117; Leech, 163-164.
53 O'Toole, 117; Leech, 164.
54 *The New York Times*, January 25.
55 *Ibid.*, January 26; Millis, 95-96.
56 343, 119.
57 *The New York Times*, January 26; Millis, 96.
58 Leech, 165.
59 O'Toole, 122.
60 *Ibid.*
61 Bemis, 69.
62 Foner, 233-234.
63 *Ibid.*, 234; Bemis, 69-70.
64 O'Toole, 123.
65 Beer, 195-197.
66 Shippee, 756; Dugdale, 499.
67 Sigsbee, 32-39, 41-42; O'Toole, 25-26.
68 Sigsbee, 69-71.
69 C. Brown, 116.
70 Epler, 287-288.
71 Sigsbee, 75-79.
72 *Ibid.*

73 O'Toole, 34.
74 Millis, 102.
75 C. Brown, 121.

CHAPTER TWO
1 Rudyard Kipling, *Recessional* (1897).
2 Kipling, *The White Man's Burden* (1899).
3 Massie, 208.
4 A.L. Kennedy, 61.
5 *Ibid.*, 268. The phrase derived from a January 21, 1896, speech by Joseph Chamberlain; Salisbury neither coined it nor generally used it.
6 Massie, 202.
7 Davis, 58; *see* O'Toole, 69.
8 O'Toole, 69.
9 James, 244.
10 A.L. Kennedy, 238; Massie, 190.
11 A.L. Kennedy, 238-239.
12 *Ibid.*, 240.
13 Massie, 204-5. *See also* G. Cecil, III, 8.
14 Massie, 202.
15 *Ibid.*, 203-204.
16 W. Churchill, *My Early Life*, 179.
17 *Ibid.*, 233.
18 Garvin I, 467.
19 *Ibid.* I, 392.
20 *Ibid.* II, 80.
21 *Ibid.* II, 480.
22 *Ibid.* II, 350.
23 Massie, 234.
24 W. Churchill, *Great Democracies*, 367-368.
25 Garvin III, 247.
26 Garvin III, 248-249.
27 Garvin III, 249.
28 Langer, 465.
29 *Ibid.*, 467.
30 Grenville, 135-136.
31 British Document I, No. 8.
32 *Ibid.*, No. 8.
33 *The New York Times*, February 3.
34 Garvin, 251-252.
35 *Ibid.*
36 *The New York Times*, February 4.
37 British Documents, 14.
38 Grenville, 141; British Documents, 22-23.
39 British Documents, 29-30.

40 Langer, 472-273.
41 A.L. Kennedy, 276.
42 *Ibid.*

CHAPTER THREE
1 W. Churchill, *River War II*, 307.
2 Lewis, *Fashoda* 3-4; Giffen, 3-5.
3 Moorhead, 202-205; Taylor, A.J.P., *Mastery in Europe*, 289-290; Maurois, *France*, 490.
4 Moorehead, 207.
5 Jenkins, 509-511.
6 *Ibid.*, 515-516.
7 Giffen, 13-14.
8 Taylor, *Mastery in Europe*, 352-353.
9 Lewis, *Fashoda* 7.
10 *Ibid.*, 5.
11 Pakenham, 466.
12 W. Churchill, *The Fashoda Incident.*
13 Giffen, 29.
14 Moorehead, 333.
15 Neillends, 170-171.
16 Moorehead, 335.
17 *Ibid.*
18 A.L. Kennedy, 280.
19 Lewis, *Fashoda* 109.
20 *Ibid.*, 110.
21 Pakenham, 514-515.
22 *Ibid.*, 506.
23 *Ibid.*, 525.
24 *Ibid.*, 526; Lewis, *Fashoda*, 94-95.
25 *Ibid.*, *Fashoda* 94-95.
26 *Ibid.*, 95; Pakenham, 526.
27 Lewis, *Fashoda* 96-97; Pakenham, 526-527.
28 *Ibid.*, 527-528.
29 Lewis, *Fashoda* 125-131.
30 *Ibid.*, 127.
31 *Ibid.*, 131 & 133.
32 *Ibid.*, 132.
33 *Ibid.*, 132-133.
34 *Ibid.*, 133; Pakenham, 529.
35 Lewis, *Fashoda* 134; Pakenham, 530.
36 Lewis, *Fashoda* 135, 209-210; Pakenham, 530.
37 Lewis, *Fashoda* 210-211; Pakenham, 530-531.
38 Lewis, *Fashoda* 210-211; Pakenham, 531.
39 Lewis, *Fashoda* 75-76.

40 *Ibid.*, 55.

41 *Ibid.*, 87.

42 *Ibid.*, 91.

43 *Ibid.*, 159-160.

44 *Ibid.*, 160-161.

45 J. Conrad, *Heart of Darkness*, (New York, Norton 1903) orig. pub. (1902) 34; quoted in Lewis, *Fashoda*, 172.

46 Lewis, *Fashoda* 174.

47 *Ibid.*, 172 & 174.

48 *Ibid.*, 179.

49 *Id.*

50 *Ibid.*, 180.

51 *Ibid.*, 180-181.

52 *Ibid.*, 183.

53 *Ibid.*, 183-184.

54 *Ibid.*, 184-185.

55 Giffen, 16.

56 *Ibid.*, 16-17; Bates, 87; Lewis, *Fashoda*, 185.

57 *Ibid.*, *Fashoda*, 213.

58 *Ibid.*, 88.

59 Parliamentary Papers, 1-2.

60 *Ibid.*, 2-3.

61 *The The New York Times*, January 16.

62 Arthur, 222-223; W. Churchill, *River War I*, 359-365; Royle, 219.

63 W. Churchill, *River War I*, 368.

64 *Ibid.*, 369.

65 *Ibid.*, 378.

66 *Ibid.*, 374-375.

67 *Ibid.*, 377.

68 *Ibid.*, 378.

69 Bates, 88-89.

70 *Ibid.*, 90.

71 *Ibid.*, 91.

72 *Ibid.*, 91.

73 *Ibid.*, 103-104.

74 *Ibid.*, 104.

75 *Ibid.*, 105-106.

76 Lewis, *Fashoda*, 121; Bates, 106.

77 W. Churchill, *River War I*, 374-376.

78 *Ibid.*, 381-382.

79 *Ibid.*, 376, 383-384.

80 Arthur, 224-225.

81 *Ibid.*; Magnus, 119-120.

82 Arthur, 225.

83 *Ibid.*; Magnus, 120.

84 Magnus, 120; Arthur, 225-226.

85 W. Churchill, *River War I*, 416-420; Arthur, 225.

86 W. Churchill, *River War I*, 416-420.

87 *Ibid.*, 421-422.

88 *Ibid.*, 427-428.

89 *Ibid.*, 429-432.

90 *Ibid.*, 434-435.

91 *Ibid.*, 447-448.

92 Magnus, 122; Royle, 122.

93 Magnus, 121.

94 *Ibid.*, 123.

95 R. Churchill, 352-353.

96 *Ibid.*, 353-354.

97 Manchester, *Visions of Glory*, 267; R. Churchill, 366-367.

98 R. Churchill, *Companion*, 930-931.

99 R. Churchill, 354.

100 *Ibid.*, 355-356.

101 *Ibid.*, 372-373.

102 *Ibid.*, 374-375.

CHAPTER FOUR

1 Maurois, *France*, 483; Tuchman, *Proud Tower*, 173.

2 Maurois, *France*, 491.

3 Tuchman, *Guns of August*, 40.

4 Massie, 115.

5 Tuchman, *Proud Tower*, 173.

6 Shirer, 45-46.

7 Maurois, *France*, 484-485.

8 *Ibid.*, 486.

9 Shirer, 49-55.

10 *Ibid.*, 87.

11 Tuchman, *Proud Tower*, 187.

12 Shirer, 59. Tuchman, *Proud Tower*, 188-189.

13 Bredin, 218-219.

14 *Ibid.*, 221-222.

15 *Ibid.*, 224.

16 All of this is discussed in Bredin, 224-231.

17 Tuchman, *Proud Tower*, 189.

18 As to Zola's career prior to the Dreyfus case *see, generally*, F. Brown. Also *see* Bredin, 245-246, and Tuchman, 194-195.

19 F. Brown, 725-726; Lewis, *Prisoner*, 188-189; Bredin, 246.

20 F. Brown, 726-727.

21 F. Brown, 727; Snyder 161-168.

22 Snyder, 168-169.

23 *Ibid.*, 173.
24 Bredin, 239-240; Lewis, *Prisoner*, 193-194.
25 *Ibid.*
26 Lewis, *Prisoner*, 195.
27 F. Brown, 734.
28 Lewis, *Prisoner*, 196.
29 Bredin, 247.
30 *Ibid.*
31 *Ibid.*
32 Snyder, 177.
33 *Ibid.*
34 *Ibid.*, 185-186.
35 Bredin, 252.
36 Snyder, 186-187.
37 F. Brown, 736-737; Lewis, *Prisoner*, 202.
38 *Ibid.*
39 Bredin, 252.
40 F. Brown, 737-738.
41 Bredin, 253; *The New York Times*, January 15.
42 Bredin, 253-254.
43 *Ibid.*, 254.
44 *Ibid.*, 285-299.
45 *Ibid.*, 285-289; *The New York Times*, January 18 and 19.
46 *The New York Times*, January 15; Tuchman, *Proud Tower*, 197.
47 Bredin, 255-256; *The New York Times*, January 23.
48 Lewis, *Prisoner*, 202-203; Snyder, 187-188; *The New York Times*, February 8.
49 Lewis, *Prisoner*, 202; Bredin, 259.
50 *Ibid.*, 259.
51 Lewis, *Prisoner*, 202.
52 Bredin, 258-254.
53 *Ibid.*, 259.
54 Lewis, *Prisoner*, 208.
55 Bredin, 263.
56 Lewis, *Prisoner*, 205.
57 Bredin, 264.
58 *Id.*
59 *Id.*
60 Snyder, 190; F. Brown, 739.
61 F. Brown, 740.
62 Bredin, 266; Snyder, 190.
63 F. Brown, 740.
64 Bredin, 266.
65 Lewis, *Prisoner*, 157-159.

66 Bredin, 267.
67 *Id.*
68 Bredin, 268.
69 Lewis, *Prisoner*, 207.
70 Bredin, 267.
71 Lewis, *Prisoner*, 207.
72 Bredin, 258.
73 Lewis, *Prisoner*, 208; *The New York Times*, February 19.
74 Lewis, *Prisoner*, 208.
75 *The New York Times*, February 19.
76 Bredin, 268.
77 F. Brown, 741; Bredin, 269-270; Lewis, *Prisoner*, 208-209.
78 Bredin, 270, *The New York Times*, February 24.
79 Bredin, 270-271; Snyder, 212.
80 Bredin, 271.
81 *Ibid.*, 272.
82 Lewis, *Prisoner*, 209.
83 *Ibid.*; *The New York Times*, February 25.
84 British Documents, 146.

CHAPTER FIVE
1 Massie, 99.
2 Taylor, *Bismarck*, 264
3 Massie, 135.
4 Bülow I, 5.
5 Maurois, *Edwardian Era*, 177.
6 *Ibid.*
7 Massie, 123.
8 Maurois, *Edwardian Era*, 177.
9 L. Cecil, 265-269.
10 *Ibid.*, 268.
11 *Ibid.*, 264-265.
12 Massie, 227-228.
13 *Ibid.*, 231.
14 L. Cecil, 289.
15 *Ibid.*; Massie, 251.
16 Paul Kennedy, 224.
17 Massie, 173.
18 Paul Kennedy, 225.
19 *Ibid.*, 226.
20 *Ibid.*, 227.
21 Steinberg, 172.
22 Massie, 174.
23 Tirpitz, 134; Massie, 174-175.
24 Steinberg, 160.
25 *Ibid.*, 161.
26 *Ibid.*, 172.

27 *Ibid.*, 173-174.

28 Langer, 421-424.

29 Steinberg, 180.

30 *Ibid.*, 181.

31 *Ibid.*, 183-184.

32 *Ibid.*, 184.

33 *Ibid.*, 184-185.

34 *Ibid.*, 185.

35 *Ibid.*, 190-191.

36 *Ibid.*, 191-192.

37 *Ibid.*, 192-193.

38 *Ibid.*, 193-195.

39 *Ibid.*, 198.

40 *Ibid.*, 195-196.

41 London *Times*, March 28.

42 Langer, 441-442.

43 London *Times*, March 20.

44 Langer, 442.

CHAPTER SIX

1 C. Brown, 120 and 122.

2 Olcott, 12-13.

3 Morison, 773.

4 *Ibid.*, 774-775.

5 Sigsbee, 100.

6 O'Toole, 126.

7 Millis, 106.

8 O'Toole, 125; *The New York Times*, February 17.

9 C. Brown, 124.

10 *Ibid.*

11 *Ibid.*, 123-124; Millis, 108.

12 *Ibid.*, 108.

13 Reuter, 68-69; London *Times*, February 17.

14 O'Toole, 128; Sigsbee, 115-119.

15 Millis, 109.

16 Morison, 779-781.

17 O'Toole, 129.

18 *Ibid.*, 131-133.

19 *Ibid.*, 129.

20 *Ibid.* 129-130; Sigsbee, 129-131.

21 *Ibid.*

22 Sigsbee, 135-136.

23 Millis, 113.

24 Cervera, 12-13; O'Toole 120-121.

25 Cervera, 12-13.

26 *Ibid.*, 109

27 O'Toole, 138-139; Leech, 171.

28 Leech, 169.

29 Bemis, 77.

30 *Ibid.*, 76-77.

31 *The New York Times*, March 4.

32 O'Toole, 140-141, Cervera, 31-33.

33 Millis, 119-120.

34 Busbey, 186-188

35 *Ibid.*, 188-189.

36 *Ibid.*, 190.

37 *Ibid.*, 191; Millis, 116; Leach, 169.

38 Millis, 117.

39 *The New York Times*, March 11; Reuter, 70.

40 Cong. Rec. 55th Cong., 2d Sess. 2632; 2620; *The New York Times*, March 9 and 10; Millis, 117.

41 Foreign Relations, 684

42 O'Toole, 142-143.

43 *Ibid.*, 143-144.

44 May, 203.

45 *Ibid.*, 203-204.

46 Reuter, 71-72.

47 *The New York Times*, March 13.

48 O'Toole, 137; Millis, 123.

49 The speech is printed in Cong. Rec. 55th Cong., 2d Sess. 2916-2919, and in *The New York Times*, March 18.

50 *Ibid.*

51 Leech, 172.

52 O'Toole, 147.

53 Rhodes, 52-53.

54 Dugdale, 500-501.

55 *Ibid.*

56 Buckle, 236-237.

57 Foreign Relations, 685-688.

58 *Ibid.*, 692.

59 Leech, 173.

60 O'Toole, 148.

61 *Ibid.*, 149-150; Foreign Relations, 697-701.

62 Bemis, 80; Foreign Relations, 703-704.

63 Leech, 173; *The New York Times*, March 22 and 23.

64 Leech, 174; *The New York Times*, March 25.

65 Leech, 174-175.

66 Millis, 126; Foreign Relations, 704.

67 *Ibid.*

68 Morris, 607-608.

69 Morison, 799.

70 Morris, 608 and n.76.

71 O'Toole, 162; Morris, 601, 604.

72 Morison, 801-803.

73 Bemis, 81.

74 O'Toole, 159.

75 *Ibid.*; Dugdale, 503-504.

76 Foreign Relations, 711-712.

77 Bemis, 82-83; Foreign Relations, 712-713.

CHAPTER SEVEN

1 *The New York Times*, March 28.

2 Leech, 177-178.

3 Weems, 125-126.

4 Collier, 119.

5 Reuter, 74.

6 *Ibid.*, 74-75.

7 O'Toole, 295.

8 May, 208.

9 *Ibid.*, 208-209.

10 Foreign Relations, 721.

11 Rhodes, 54-55.

12 Morison, 804.

13 *The New York Times*, March 30.

14 Bemis, 85; Millis, 151; Foreign Relations, 927.

15 *Ibid.*

16 Leech, 178-180.

17 Dugdale, 505.

18 *Ibid.*, 506.

19 *Ibid.*, 306.

20 Buckle, 239.

21 F. Davis, 88.

22 O'Toole, 165.

23 Foreign Relations, 732; Millis, 133.

24 Foreign Relations, 732-733; Millis, 133.

25 *The New York Times*, April 3; Millis, 134.

26 O'Toole, 165-166.

27 Perkins, 36.

28 Grenville, 203.

29 Olcott, 130.

30 Perkins, 36-37; Millis, 136.

31 Leech, 183.

32 *Ibid.*, 183-184.

33 *Ibid.*, 184-185.

34 Dugdale, 508.

35 Foreign Relations, 747; Millis, 137.

36 O'Toole, 168.

37 Dulles, 127.

38 Tuchman, *Proud Tower*, 150-151.

39 Dulles, 126.

40 O'Toole, 168.

41 *Ibid.*, 169; Dulles, 127.

42 Dulles, 126.

43 Leech, 186.

44 *Ibid.*, 186-187.

45 Foreign Relations, 750, 759-760; Millis, 138-140.

46 Foreign Relations, 760.

47 Millis, 140-141.

48 *The New York Times*, April 12; Foner, 265.

49 Cong. Rec. 55th Cong., 2d Sess., 3813-3818; Rhodes, 68-69.

50 Cong. Rec. 55th Cong., 2d Sess., 3819-3821;

51 May, 216; Perkins, 37; Dugdale, 508-510.

52 May, 216-217; Perkins, 37-38; F. Davis, 89-90.

53 Dugdale, 510; Reuter, 80; F. Davis, 89.

54 Dugdale, 510; F. Davis, 89.

55 May, 217.

56 *Ibid.*

57 Dugdale, 509.

58 May, 219.

59 F. Davis, 90, quoting Bigbie, *Mirrors of Downing Street.*

60 Perkins, 309.

61 F. Davis, 90.

62 Garvin, 299.

63 *Ibid.*

64 Perkins, 39-40; Dugdale, 510.

65 F. Davis, 91.

66 Perkins, 40.

67 Foner, 267.

68 *Ibid.*, 267-268.

69 *Ibid.*, 268; Leech, 187.

70 Cong. Rec. 55th Cong., 2d Sess. 3988; Foner, 270; Leech, 167-168.

71 Cong. Rec. 55th Cong., 2d Sess. 3988; Millis, 143.

72 Cong. Rec. 55th Cong., 2d Sess, 3879; Leech, 188.

73 Dulles, 128-129.

74 Cong. Rec. 55th Cong., 2d Sess., 4040, 4062; O'Toole, 171.

75 Leech, 188.

76 Millis, 143.

77 Leech, 190-191.

CHAPTER EIGHT

1 Spector, 40.
2 Morris, 577-578; O'Toole, 102; Leech, 159.
3 Morris, 586-588; O'Toole, 102-103; Leech 159-161; Millis, 85-86.
4 Morris, 576-577; O'Toole, 98-99.
5 Morris, 601-602.
6 *Ibid.*, 602.
7 *Ibid.*
8 Sargent, 10.
9 Morris, 603.
10 Beale, 63.
11 Morris, 603.
12 McDougal, 216-217.
13 Dulles, 64.
14 *Ibid.*, 64-68.
15 Millis, 21-22.
16 *Ibid.*, 20 and 24.
17 *Ibid.*, 55.
18 *Ibid.*, 122; Dulles, 112-113.
19 *Ibid.*, 113.
20 *Ibid.*
21 *Ibid.*; Millis, 123.
22 Dulles, 113.
23 Sargent, 14-16.
24 Chadwick I, 156.
25 Leech, 191-192.
26 Millis, 141.
27 Leech, 192.
28 Sargent, 21-22.
29 Millis, 181-183.
30 Bowers, 67-70.
31 Chadwick I, 166-168; O'Toole, 176-177.
32 Chadwick I, 167-168.
33 Sargent, 30-31.
34 *Ibid.*, 31-32; O'Toole, 178, 180-181.
35 Sargent, 32.
36 Chadwick I, 173.
37 *Ibid.*, 160-161.
38 *Ibid.*, 173-176.
39 *Ibid.*, 168.
40 *Ibid.*, 160, 168; O'Toole, 183.
41 Chadwick I, 169-170.
42 O'Toole, 183-184; Chadwick I, 176-177.
43 O'Toole, 184-186; Chadwick I, 178-179.
44 *Ibid.*, 177-178; O'Toole, 186.
45 *Ibid.*, 187

46 Sargent, 37-38.
47 *Ibid.*, 39.
48 Chadwick I, 183-190; O'Toole, 188.
49 *Ibid.*; Chadwick I, 200.
50 Chadwick I, 208-209.
51 *London Times*, May 2.
52 *Ibid.*, May 3.
53 O'Toole, 189.
54 *Ibid.*; Leech 204; *The New York Times*, May 2.
55 Leech, 210.
56 Collier, 123-124.
57 Tuchman, *Proud Tower*, 155.
58 *The New York Times*, May 4; Leech, 204-205; O'Toole, 189.
59 Chadwick I, 211-212.
60 Leech, 205-206; *The New York Times*, May 8.
61 Leech, 206-207.
62 Millis, 198.
63 Hendrick, 264-265.
64 Sargent, 51-52; Reuter, 131-133; Bailey, 60-61.
65 *Ibid.*
66 Reuter, 132-133; Bailey, 61-62.
67 Shippee, 764.
68 *Ibid.*, 764-765.
69 *Ibid.*, 765.

CHAPTER NINE

1 Grenville, 150-153; Langer, 495.
2 Garvin, 255-256.
3 *Ibid.*, 256-257.
4 *Ibid.*, 257.
5 Grenville, 152.
6 Rich, 569.
7 Garvin, 254-255.
8 *Ibid.*, 259-260.
9 Rich, 570.
10 *Ibid.*, 266-267.
11 Rich, 571.
12 Garvin, 267.
13 *Ibid.*; Grenville, 154-155.
14 Garvin, 263-266.
15 Rich, 572; Garvin, 268.
16 Rich, 572.
17 *Ibid.*, 572-573; Langer, 495.
18 Langer, 497.
19 Taylor, *Mastery*, 376-377.
20 Garvin, 269.
21 Rich, 571.

22 Langer, 499.

23 *Ibid.*, 500.

24 Dugdale, 260.

25 Rich, 574-575.

26 *Ibid.*, 575.

27 German Documents, 513.

28 *Ibid.*

29 Garvin, 271-272.

30 Grenville, 162.

31 Garvin, 273.

32 Rich, 577.

33 Garvin, 273-274.

34 Rich, 578.

35 Garvin, 275.

36 *Ibid.*

37 *Ibid.*, 276.

38 *Ibid.*, 277.

39 Rich, 578.

40 *Ibid.*, 579.

41 *Ibid.*

42 Garvin, 278-279.

43 *Ibid.*, 279.

44 *Ibid.*, 279-280.

45 London *Times*, May 5.

46 *Ibid.*

47 Manchester, *Alone*, 348.

48 London *Times*, May 7.

49 Grenville, 166.

50 *London Times*, May 5.

51 Grenville, 166-167.

52 *Ibid.*, 168.

53 Langer, 506. The complete text of
    the speech was printed in the
    London *Times*, May 14.

54 *Ibid.*, 507.

55 *Ibid.*, 507-508.

56 London *Times*, May 16; Garvin,
    284-285.

57 Quoted in London *Times*, May 17

58 *Ibid.*, May 16.

59 Reuter, 156; *The New York Times*,
    May 15 and 16.

60 Reuter, 155-156.

61 London *Times*, May 17.

62 Langer, 500-501.

63 *Ibid.*, 510.

64 *Ibid.*, 508; Grenville, 170-171.

65 Rich, 581.

66 *Ibid.*

67 *Ibid.*, 581-582.

68 British Documents, 84-85.

69 Rich, 583.

70 *Ibid.*

71 Garvin, 288-289; Rich, 582.

72 Garvin, 289.

73 Rich, 584-585.

74 Langer, 442.

75 Grenville, 182-183.

76 *Ibid.*

77 *Ibid.*, 188-191; British Document, 55.

78 British Documents, 56.

79 Grenville, 191; British Documents,
    58.

80 British Documents, 58-59.

81 A.L. Kennedy, *German World
    Policy*, 614.

82 Garvin, 290; Grenville, 173.

83 Grenville, 174.

84 *Ibid.*, 174-175; Langer, 527-528.

85 Grenville, 174-175; Rich, 589

86 *Ibid.*, 175-176; Rich, 589.

87 Grenville, 192-193; Langer, 527.

88 Grenville, 193-194.

89 British Documents, 71-75;
    Grenville, 194-195.

90 Garvin, 315.

91 Grenville, 196-198; Langer, 528-529.

92 Langer, 529.

93 Crankshaw, 413.

94 London *Times*, July 31.

95 Crankshaw, 413-414.

CHAPTER TEN

1. O'Toole, 197; Leech, 201; Millis, 132.

2 O'Toole, 173; *The New York Times*,
    April 23.

3 *The New York Times*, April 24.

4 *Ibid.*; O'Toole, 195-196.

5 Morris, 613-614.

6 *Ibid.*, 577, 613-614.

7 Morris, 612.

8 *Ibid.*

9 Morison, 816-818.

10 *Ibid.*

11 Leech, 191.

12 Thayer, II, 173.

13 Reuter, 151; *The New York Times*,
    April 21.

14 London *Times*, April 21; Reuter,
    87-88.

15 London *Times*, April 29.

16 Reuter, 151; Buckle, 244.

17 O'Toole, 196; Leech 229.
18 O'Toole, 196.
19 *The New York Times*, October 28; Morris, 614-615.
20 Millis, 162-163; *The New York Times*, October 26.
21 Millis, 161.
22 O'Toole, 197.
23 *Ibid.*, 192.
24 Millis, 167-170; O'Toole, 194.
25 Roosevelt, *Autobiography*, 220-221.
26 Morison, 825.
27 *Ibid.*, 822; Morris, 615.
28 Leech, 215-216.
29 *Ibid.*, 216.
30 Millis, 206; Morris, 626.
31 *Ibid.*, 200-201.
32 Leech, 196-197.
33 *Ibid.*
34 *Ibid.*, 197.
35 *Ibid.*, 197.
36 Chadwick I, 214-237; Millis, 204-206.
37 *Ibid.*, 206.
38 Chadwick I, 250-255.
39 *Ibid.*, 238-240.
40 Millis, 230-231; O'Toole, 212; Leech, 220.
41 Chadwick I, 258-261.
42 *Ibid.*
43 *Ibid.*
44 O'Toole, 207-209, 212-214.
45 *Ibid.*, 215-216; Chadwick I, 266-267.
46 Chadwick I, 268-269.
47 *Ibid.*, 271-272.
48 O'Toole, 219.
49 Chadwick I, 288; O'Toole, 219.
50 Chadwick I, 297-298.
51 *Ibid.*, 298.
52 O'Toole, 216-217.
53 Chadwick I, 311.
54 *Ibid.*, 312.
55 Morris, 618-620; Millis, 218-219; *The New York Times*, May 7.
56 Morris, 621-622.
57 Morison, 833.
58 Morris, 623.
59 Millis, 214-217.
60 O'Toole, 230; Morris, 626.
61 *Ibid.*, 230; Morris, 626.
62 Millis, 237.

63 *Ibid.*, 237-238.
64 *Ibid.*, 238.
65 Chadwick I, 303-307; O'Toole, 219-220.
66 Chadwick I, 314-317.
67 *Ibid.*, 327-328.
68 O'Toole, 220; Leech, 222.
69 Chadwick I, 333.
70 *Ibid.*, 333-335.
71 Leech, 222.
72 *Ibid.*, 238-239.
73 Millis, 238.
74 Morris, 624-625.
75 Chadwick II, 14-15; O'Toole, 229-230.
76 Chadwick II, 14-15.

CHAPTER ELEVEN
1 Chadwick I, 333-334.
2 *Ibid.*, 337-338; O'Toole, 223-225.
3 Chadwick I, 337-339; Hobson, 1-36; O'Toole, 224-225.
4 Chadwick I, 338-339.
5 Hobson, 88-93; O'Toole, 235-236; Chadwick I, 341.
6 Hobson, 94-112; O'Toole, 236-237; Chadwick I, 341-342.
7 Hobson, 115-123; O'Toole, 237.
8 Morris, 677.
9 Chadwick I, 351-352.
10 Millis, 246.
11 *Ibid.*
12 *Ibid.*, 246-247.
13 Morris, 629.
14 *Ibid.*
15 Millis, 248.
16 *Ibid.*; 249, O'Toole, 243; Chadwick I, 368-370.
17 *Ibid.*
18 *Ibid.*, 362-364.
19 *Ibid.*
20 *Ibid.*, 364-366.
21 Morison, 837.
22 Millis, 259.
23 Buckle, 258-259.
24 Garvin, 509; Langer, 302-303.
25 Morison, 840-843.
26 O'Toole, 244.
27 *Ibid.*, 244-245; Chadwick II, 19.
28 *Ibid.*, 19-20.
29 Millis, 258.

30 Morris, 634.
31 *Ibid.*
32 Millis, 258.
33 *Ibid.*, 260-261; O'Toole, 255-256.
34 *Ibid.*
35 Millis, 260-261; O'Toole, 264-265.
36 Millis, 262-265.
37 *Ibid.*, 263-266; Chadwick II, 28.
38 Millis, 266.
39 *Ibid.*, 267; Morris, 637-638.
40 Millis, 267; O'Toole, 268.
41 Millis, 269.
42 *Ibid.*, 270-271; O'Toole, 270-271; Morris, 638-639.
43 Morris, 640-641; O'Toole, 271-272.
44 Millis, 271-273; O'Toole, 272-275
45 Millis, 273-274; O'Toole, 275-279.
46 Morison, 846.
47 Morris, 645-646.
48 Chadwick II, 63-67.
49 Morris, 647.
50 Morison, 845.
51 O'Toole, 282-285, 288, 293.
52 Millis, 276-278.
53 Chadwick II, 67-68.
54 *Ibid.*, 69-71; O'Toole, 293-295; Morris, 648-649.
55 Chadwick II, 71-72.
56 O'Toole, 294-295.
57 *Ibid.*, 205; Morris, 649-650.
58 Morris, 650; O'Toole, 298-299.
59 O'Toole, 300-309; Chadwick II, 78-80.
60 O'Toole, 314-322; Chadwick II, 80-81.
61 O'Toole, 300-313; Chadwick II, 84-91.
62 O'Toole, 313-315; Millis, 287-289; Roosevelt, *Rough Riders*, 122.
63 Millis, 289-290; O'Toole, 318.
64 Quoted in O'Toole, 316.
65 O'Toole, 315-317; Morris, 655.
66 O'Toole, 318-319; Morris, 655.
67 O'Toole, 322; Morris, 656.
68 O'Toole, 324.
69 *Ibid.*, 324-325.
70 Morison, 846.
71 *Ibid.*, 327-328; Millis, 297.
72 O'Toole, 326; Millis, 304.
73 Millis, 303-304.
74 *Ibid.*, 304.

75 *Ibid.*, 304-305.
76 *Ibid.*, 301; O'Toole, 329-330.
77 Millis, 302; O'Toole, 331.
78 Millis, 306-307; O'Toole, 332.
79 Millis, 307-308; O'Toole, 333-334.
80 O'Toole, 333; Millis, 308.
81 Millis, 308-309.
82 O'Toole, 335-336.
83 *Ibid.*, 335-336.
84 Millis, 311.
85 O'Toole, 337; Millis, 119, 311-312.
86 O'Toole, 338.
87 Leech, 254; Millis, 314.
88 Leech, 252-254; Millis, 314-315.

CHAPTER TWELVE

1 Millis, 298; O'Toole, 343-344.
2 O'Toole, 345-346.
3 *Ibid.*, 346.
4 Leech, 266-268.
5 O'Toole, 349-350.
6 *Ibid.*, 350-351.
7 *Ibid.*, 350; Leech, 269.
8 Morison, 851-853.
9 O'Toole, 353.
10 Leech, 278.
11 Millis, 336; O'Toole, 353.
12 Leech, 279-280.
13 O'Toole, 357-355; Leech, 280.
14 *Ibid.*
15 Reuter, 154-160.
16 *Ibid.*, 160-161.
17 *Ibid.*, 161.
18 *Ibid.*, 162-163.
19 Millis, 340.
20 *Ibid.*, 337-338.
21 O'Toole, 355-356.
22 *Ibid.*, 358; Millis, 330.
23 O'Toole, 358-359; Mills, 330.
24 O'Toole, 359.
25 *Ibid.*, 360.
26 Morris, 660.
27 *Ibid.*; O'Toole, 361.
28 Millis, 351.
29 *Ibid.*, 353; O'Toole, 363; Leech, 307.
30 Morris, 664-665.
31 Leech, 307-308.
32 *Ibid.*, 308-309; O'Toole, 374-375.
33 Grenville, 216-217.
34 Olcott, 59-61.
35 O'Toole, 361.

36 Leech, 282; May, 250.
37 Leech, 282-283, 285-286.
38 *Ibid.*, 286; Olcott, 63.
39 Leech, 286-287.
40 *Ibid.*, 325, 328.
41 *Ibid.*, 287; Chadwick II, 435-436.
42 Chadwick II, 436.
43 *Ibid.*, 437-439; Leech, 288.
44 Chadwick II, 439.
45 *Ibid.*
46 *Ibid.*, 440.
47 Leech, 289-290.
48 *Ibid.*, 291.
49 Leech, 328-329.
50 Adams, 365.
51 *Ibid.*, 366.
52 Perkins, 57.
53 Thayer II, 221.
54 Adams, 362-363.
55 Millis, 370-373; Leech, 328-330;
    Pratt, 331-332.
56 Leech, 329-330.
57 *Ibid.*
58 *The New York Times*, September 16
59 Chadwick II, 450-451; Millis,
    373-374.

CHAPTER THIRTEEN

1 O'Toole, 222; Leech, 211; *The New
   York Times*, May 22.
2 Leech, 211.
3 *Ibid.*, 211-212; Millis, 221-223.
4 May, 246-247.
5 Dennett, 491.
6 "What Shall We Do With the
   Conquered Islands," *North American
   Review*, June, 1898, 641.
7 "Strategical Value of the Philippines,"
   North American Review, June, 1898,
   759.
8 Dulles, 167; Tuchman, *Proud Tower*,
   152.
9 Tuchman, *Proud Tower*, 152-53.
10 Millis, 253-254.
11 Tuchman, *Proud Tower*, 155-156.
12 *Ibid.*; Pratt, 521-522.
13 Millis, 252.
14 *Ibid.*, 254.
15 O'Toole, 222 and 251; Chadwick II,
    386.
16 O'Toole, 251.
17 Chadwick II, 388-389.
18 *Ibid.*, 389.
19 Reuter, 138.
20 Sargent, 68; O'Toole, 251.
21 Sargent, 68-69; O'Toole, 251.
22 Reuter, 139-140.
23 Chadwick II, 373-374; O'Toole, 252.
24 *Ibid.*, 254.
25 Healey, 220-221.
26 Beisner, 174-175.
27 Healey, 222; Pratt, 270-271.
28 *Ibid.*, 296-298.
29 *Ibid.*, 323-324.
30 Cong. Rec. 55th Cong., 2d Sess.,
    6483; Millis, 317.
31 Cong. Rec. 55th Cong., 2d Sess.,
    6157; Pratt, 324-325.
32 Cong. Rec. 55th Cong., 2d Sess.,
    6712; Millis, 317-319.
33 Shippee, 767.
34 London *Times*, July 4.
35 Shippee, 767-769.
36 *Ibid.*
37 *Ibid.*, 769-770.
38 London *Times*, July 14
39 Spector, 71-73.
40 Bailey, 67.
41 O'Toole, 365-366.
42 Bailey, 68; Sargent, 73.
43 Collier, 126; Hatzfeldt reported to
    the Foreign Ministry that Hay made
    no response; Shippee, 771 n.44
44 Collier, 126-127.
45 Shippee, 769-773.
46 *Ibid.*
47 May, 249-250.
48 Millis, 333-334.
49 *Ibid.*, 334-335.
50 *Ibid.*, 355.
51 *Ibid.*, 356; O'Toole, 368-369;
    Sargent, 78-79.
52 Chadwick II, 405-406.
53 Leech, 290.
54 Sargent, 83.
55 O'Toole, 370; Reuter, 146-147; S.E
    Morison, 805; Bailey, 75-77.
56 Millis, 357-360; O'Toole, 370-371.
57 *Ibid.*
58 Bailey, 78; Shippee, 775.
59 Bailey, 78-79; 81.
60 Shippee, 775-777; F. Davis, 100.

61 Iriye, 48-49.
62 *Ibid.*, 48-53
63 Wolff, 145-146.
64 Millis, 373; *The New York Times*,
     September 12
65 *Ibid.*, December 2.
66 Leech, 346.
67 Wolff, 175-176
68 Millis, 395; Leech, 350.
69 *The New York Times*, December 29.
70 Millis, 396.
71 *Ibid.*, 396-397.
72 Bemis, 127.

CHAPTER FOURTEEN

 1 Bredin, 271.
 2 *The New York Times*, March 6.
 3 Bredin, 275-279, Lewis, *Prisoner*,
     221.
 4 Bredin, 279.
 5 Lewis, *Prisoner*, 226-227.
 6 F. Brown, 745.
 7 *Ibid.*, 745-746.
 8 Bredin, 302-305; Lewis, *Prisoner*,
     228.
 9 Bredin, 306-307.
10 *Ibid.*, 306-308.
11 *Ibid.*
12 *Ibid.*, 308-309; Chapman, 311-312.
13 Bredin, 309; Chapman, 211-212.
14 Bredin, 309-310; Tuchman, *Proud
     Tower*, 208.
15 Bredin, 310-311; Tuchman, *Proud
     Tower*, 208.
16 Tuchman, *Proud Tower*, 209,
     420-421.
17 *Ibid.*, 208-209.
18 Bredin, 313-315.
19 *Ibid.*, 316.
20 *Ibid.*, 316-319.
21 *Ibid.*, 317.
22 *Ibid.*, 317-318.
23 Chapman, 218; Bredin, 319-320.
24 Chapman, 218-219.
25 F. Brown, 748-749; Bredin, 320-321.
26 F. Brown, 749-750.
27 *Ibid.*, 750-751.
28 *Ibid.*, 751-752.
29 *Ibid.*, 753-755.
30 Bredin, 322-323.
31 Chapman, 220-221.

32 Bredin, 325; Chapman, 221.
33 Bredin, 324.
34 *Ibid.*, 325.
35 *Ibid.*
36 Chapman, 222; Bredin, 325-326.
37 Chapman, 222-223; Bredin, 326-327.
38 Snyder, 217-220.
39 *Ibid.*, 221
40 Bredin, 328-329.
41 *Ibid.*, 330; Snyder, 222.
42 Bredin, 329.
43 Chapman, 225.
44 Bredin, 330-331.
45 Chapman, 226-227.
46 Bredin, 334; Tuchman, *Proud
     Tower*, 211.
47 Bredin, 335-336.
48 *Ibid.*, 336.
49 *Ibid.*, 337-338.
50 *Ibid.*, 338.
51 *Ibid.*, 336-337.
52 Chapman, 231.
53 *The New York Times*, September 18;
     Bredin, 339.
54 *The New York Times*, September 18;
     Bredin, 339.
55 *Ibid.*, 339-340; Chapman, 232.
56 Bredin, 339-340; Chapman, 232.
57 Bredin, 340.
58 *Ibid.*, 341; Lewis, *Prisoner*, 246.
59 *The New York Times*, October 3.
60 *Ibid.*, October 16.
61 Bredin, 342.
62 *Ibid.*, 342-343.
63 *Ibid.*; Chapman, 236-237.
64 *Ibid.*, 236-237; Bredin, 343-344.
65 Chapman, 237-238; Brisson,
     343-344.
66 Bredin, 344-345; Chapman, 236.
67 Bredin, 345-346; Chapman, 238.
68 Chapman, 238-239; Bredin, 359.
69 Bredin, 353-355.
70 *The New York Times*, November 13.
71 Bredin, 355; Chapman, 239.
72 Bredin, 359-360; Chapman,
     239-240.
73 Bredin, 361.
74 F. Brown, 763-764.
75 Bredin, 361-362; Chapman, 241-
     242.
76 Bredin, 362.

77 Chapman, 242; London *Times*, November 26.
78 Chapman, 242-243.
79 *Ibid.*, 243; Bredin, 363.
80 Bredin, 363-364.
81 *Ibid.*, 364; Chapman, 244.
82 London *Times*, November 28.
83 Bredin, 364-365
84 *Ibid.*
85 Bredin, 365
86 *The New York Times*, December 13.
87 *Ibid.*, December 11.
88 *Ibid.*, December 20
89 London *Times*, December 20.
90 F. Brown, 764.
91 *The New York Times*, December 25.
92 Bredin, 367-368.
93 *Ibid.*, 368-369.
94 Buckle, 823-824.

CHAPTER FIFTEEN

1 Bates 93; Lewis, *Fashoda*, 216-217.
2 Bates, 93-95; Lewis, *Fashoda*, 217-218; Pakenham, 532-533.
3 Bates, 95.
4 Pakenham, 533.
5 Bates, 96.
6 *Ibid.*, 96-97; Lewis, *Fashoda*, 218; Pakenham, 534.
7 Bates, 106-107; Lewis, *Fashoda*, 212.
8 Bates, 106-107; Lewis, *Fashoda*, 212.
9 Bates, 107; Lewis, *Fashoda*, 212; Pakenham, 532.
10 Bates, 97-98; Lewis, *Fashoda*, 218-219.
11 *Ibid.*, 219; Bates, 99.
12 Pakenham, 535; Bates, 113.
13 *Ibid.*, 112.
14 Magnus, 123-124.
15 Bates, 125-126.
16 Arthur, 229-230; Magnus, 125.
17 *Ibid.*
18 R. Churchill, 376.
19 *Ibid.*, 377; Manchester, *Visions of Glory*, 253-265.
20 W. Churchill, *A Roving Commission*, 153-155.
21 *Ibid.*
22 R. Churchill, 378-379.
23 *Ibid.*, 381-382.
24 *Ibid.*, 383.
25 *Ibid.*, 380-381; Manchester, *Visions of Glory*, 266-267.
26 *Ibid.*
27 Sanderson, 332; British Documents, 159.
28 Bates, 113; Pakenham, 535.
29 Lewis, *Fashoda*, 220.
30 Bates, 113-115.
31 *Ibid.*
32 *Ibid.*
33 *Ibid.*, 115-116.
34 R. Churchill, 383.
35 Neillands, 199.
36 W. Churchill, *River War II*, 34.
37 *Ibid.*, 34-35.
38 *Ibid.*, 35
39 *Ibid.*, 36-39.
40 *Ibid.*, 49.
41 R. Churchill, 391-392.
42 Bates, 116-117.
43 *Ibid.*, 117; Lewis, *Fashoda*, 221.
44 Bates, 117-118.
45 *Ibid.*, 118.
46 *Ibid.*, 118-119.
47 *Ibid.*, 119.
48 *Ibid.*, 119-120.
49 W. Churchill, *River War II*, 54-61.
50 *Ibid.*
51 Neillands, 201-202; W. Churchill, *River War II*, 62-63.
52 *Ibid.*, 68-79.
53 Magnus, 128-129.
54 W. Churchill, *River War II*, 78-79.
55 *Ibid.*, 90-94; Magnus, 125.
56 W. Churchill, *River War II*, 87.
57 W. Churchill, *Roving Commission*, 176-177.
58 W. Churchill, *River War II*, 99; Royle, 129; Magnus, 126.
59 W. Churchill, *River War II*, 119-121; Pakenham, 543-544.
60 W. Churchill, *River War II*, 127-128; Pakenham, 544.
61 W. Churchill, *River War II*, 119.
62 Pakenham, 544; Royle, 130.
63 *Ibid.*, 110.
64 W. Churchill, *River War II*, 136.
65 *Ibid.*, 138.
66 *Ibid.*, 138-139; Royle, 130.
67 R. Churchill, 404.
68 Magnus, 128-129; Pakenham, 545.

69 Royle, 130-131; Pakenham, 545-546.
70 Magnus, 130-131; Royle, 133.
71 Magnus, 131-132; Pakenham, 546.
72 Magnus, 132.
73 *Ibid.*, 133-136.
74 Royle, 135-137.
75 Gooch, 90-94; Taylor, *Mastery*, 380.
76 British Documents, 158.
77 *Ibid.*, 163.
78 Andrew, 92.
79 *Ibid.*, 97-98.
80 British Documents, 164.
81 Bates, 128-129.
82 Riker, 65-66.
83 Bates, 114-115, 134.
84 *Ibid.*, 122-123.
85 *Ibid.*, 123-124.
86 Grenville, 223; Bates, 129-130.
87 Grenville, 223; Bates, 129-130.
88 British Documents, 165.
89 *Ibid.*
90 Bates, 130; Sanderson, 334.
91 A.L. Kennedy, 286-287.
92 *Ibid.*, 287.
93 Smith-Dorrien, 69-70; Bates, 132-133.
94 Bates, 133-134.
95 *Ibid.*, 134.
96 *Ibid.*, 135.
97 Sanderson, 336-337.
98 W. Churchill, *Young Winston's Wars*, xvii-xviii, 69, 79, 152.
99 W. Churchill, *Roving Commission*, 197; R. Churchill, 401.
100 W. Churchill, *Roving Commission*, 197.

CHAPTER SIXTEEN
1 British Documents, 167-168.
2 *Ibid.*, 168.
3 Bates, 137-138; Sanderson, 338.
4 Parliamentary Papers, *Correspondence*, No. 18.
5 British Documents, 169-170; Bates, 153-154.
6 *Ibid.*, 170.
7 *Ibid.*, 170-171.
8 *Ibid.*, 171.
9 Bates, 152, 154.
10 London *Times*, September 28.
11 British Documents, 172.

12 Andrew, 98-99.
13 London *Times*, September 30.
14 Buckle, 289-290.
15 Sanderson, 344.
16 British Documents, 173-175.
17 Sanderson, 344-345.
18 Quoted in British Documents, 175.
19 *Ibid.*, 175-176.
20 *Ibid.*, 176.
21 *The New York Times*, October 10 The papers are titled *Correspondence with the French Government Regarding the Valley of the Upper Nile.*
22 British Documents, 178.
23 Bates, 146-147.
24 British Documents, 178-179.
25 London *Times*, October 11.
26 *Ibid.*, October 14.
27 Parliamentary Papers, *Further Correspondence*, No. 3; Bates, 155-157; Sanderson, 346-347.
28 British Documents, 180.
29 London *Times*, October 14.
30 *Ibid.*, October 20.
31 Bates, 154-155.
32 W. Churchill, *The Fashoda* Incident, 740.
33 London *Times*, October 21.
34 *Ibid.*; *The New York Times*, October 20.
35 British Documents, 181-182.
36 *Ibid.*, 181.
37 Giffen, 160-161.
38 Bates, 147-149.
39 *Ibid.*, 147-148.
40 *The New York Times*, October 23.
41 London *Times*, October 24.
42 Andrew, 100.
43 *Ibid.*, 101-102.
44 London *Times*, October 25. The papers are titled *Further Correspondence Respecting the Valley of the Upper Nile."*
45 *The New York Times*, October 25.
46 *Ibid.*
47 British Documents, 182.
48 *Ibid.*, 183; Marder, 327.
49 British Documents, 183; Marder, 327.
50 Bates, 149.
51 *Ibid.*, 151.

52 Sanderson, 350.
53 *Ibid.*, 350-351.
54 Lewis, *Fashoda*, 226.
55 *The New York Times*, October 29.
56 British Documents, 186.
57 *Ibid.*
58 *The New York Times*, October 30.
59 British Documents, 187.
60 Buckle, 305-306.
61 Bacon, Vol. I, 119-120; *The New York Times*, October 31.
62 Marder, 325-330.
63 Andrew, 101.
64 Sanderson, 353-354.
65 *Ibid.*, 354.
66 London *Times*, November 2.
67 British Documents, 188; Sanderson, 354.
68 London *Times*, November 4.
69 Sanderson, 354.
70 London *Times*, November 5.
71 Giffen, 76-77.
72 *Ibid.*, November 7.
73 London *Times*, November 7 and 8.
74 British Documents, 191-192.
75 *Ibid.*, 192.
76 Bates, 162-163.
77 Garvin, 283.
78 Buckle, 312.
79 Sanderson, 364.
80 London *Times*, November 24.
81 *Ibid.*, November 22.
82 R. Churchill, 413; Manchester, *Visions of Glory*, 286-287.
83 R. Churchill, 406-407.
84 *Ibid.*, 407-408.
85 Manchester, *Visions of Glory*, 285; R. Churchill, 411.
86 Bates, 163-166.
87 *Ibid.*, 166-167.
88 *Ibid.*, 167; Pakenham, 555.
89 Bates, 167.
90 Pakenham, 555.

CHAPTER SEVENTEEN
1 Carr, 1-3.
2 Chamberlin, 35-36.
3 *Ibid.*
4 Carr, 1-3.
5 *Ibid.*
6 *Ibid.*

7 See the general discussion in Tuchman, *Proud Tower*, Chapter 2; *The New York Times*, September 11.
8 Marek, 360-365.
9 *Ibid.*, 365-367; London *Times*, September 12.
10 Marek, 366-367.
11 *Ibid.*, 366-368.
12 *Ibid.*, 368-370.
13 *Ibid.*, 370-372; London *Times*, September 12.
14 *Ibid.*
15 Tuchman, *Proud Tower*, 235-236.
16 London *Times*, November 10, 1897.
17 C. Davis, 42-46; Tuchman, *Proud Tower*, 236-237.
18 Tuchman, *Proud Tower*, 229-230; C. Davis, 37.
19 London *Times*, August 30, 1898.
20 *Ibid.*
21 *Ibid.*, August 31, 1898
22 *Ibid.*, August 30, 1898.
23 Nowak, 237.
24 Novick, 205.
25 Tuchman, *Proud Tower*, 244-245.
26 *The New York Times*, December 18 and 19.

CHAPTER EIGHTEEN
1 Morris, 665-666; Harbaugh, 108.
2 Morris, 665-666.
3 *Ibid.*, 667-668.
4 *Ibid.*, 666-667.
5 Morris, 671-672; Leech, 311.
6 Morison, 872; Morris, 670.
7 Morison, 872; Morris, 673.
8 *The New York Times*, September 17.
9 *Ibid.*, September 18
10 *Ibid.*
11 Pringle, 202; *The New York Times*, October 1.
12 Morris, 675.
13 *The New York Times*, September 12
14 *Ibid.*, September 26; Morris, 177.
15 *The New York Times*, September 24; Pringle, 203-224; Morison, 879.
16 Platt, 371.
17 Jessup, 188-189.
18 *Ibid.*, 198.
19 *The New York Times*, September 28.
20 *Ibid.*

21 Jessup, 199-200; *The New York Times*, September 28.
22 Alexander, 309; Pringle, 304.
23 Morris, 680; Alexander, 314-317.
24 *The New York Times*, October 6.
25 Morris, 680-681.
26 *Ibid.*, 681.
27 *The New York Times*, October 11.
28 *Ibid.*, October 15.
29 Morris, 681-682.
30 *The New York Times*, October 15.
31 Alexander, 319-320; Morris, 682-683; Pringle, 207.
32 *The New York Times*, October 18.
33 *Ibid.*, October 19.
34 *Ibid.*, Morris, 682-684.
35 Morison, 885-886.
36 *Ibid.*, 884-885.
37 Alexander, 320.
38 *The New York Times*, October 23.
39 Pringle, 206.
40 *Lodge-Roosevelt Correspondence*, 360.
41 Pringle, 207.
42 Morris, 683.
43 *Ibid.*, 683-684.
44 *The New York Times*, November 2.
45 Alexander, 320-321.
46 *The New York Times*, November 6.
47 *Ibid.*
48 *Ibid.*
49 *Ibid.*
50 *Ibid.*, November 9.
51 *Ibid.*
52 Platt, 373.
53 Morison, 888.
54 *Ibid.*, 889.
55 Morris, 686-687.
56 *The New York Times*, January 1, 1899.

CHAPTER NINETEEN
1 Collier, 130.
2 Millis, 373.
3 Leech, 332-333.
4 Bowers, 73-75.
5 *Ibid.*, 74-75.
6 Dulles, 169-170.
7 Leech, 334.
8 *Ibid.*, 334-336.
9 *Ibid.*

10 *The New York Times*, October 2.
11 Millis, 376-377.
12 Chadwick II, 454.
13 *The New York Times*, October 1.
14 Leech, 339; Millis, 377.
15 Millis, 378; *The New York Times*, October 12.
16 Leech, 341.
17 *Ibid.*, 341-342.
18 Cortissoz, 236.
19 Millis, 381; Wolff, 168.
20 Leech, 327, 339-340; Wolff, 166-167.
21 *Ibid.*, 167-168.
22 *The New York Times*, October 18.
23 Millis, 379-380; Cortissoz, 242.
24 Chadwick, 459-460; Millis, 383.
25 Chadwick, 460-461.
26 *Ibid.*, 462.
27 Leech, 341-342.
28 Quoted in Millis, 383-384.
29 Chadwick II, 462-463.
30 *Ibid.*, 464.
31 *Ibid.*, 465.
32 *The New York Times*, November 5.
33 *Ibid.*, November 10.
34 London *Times*, November 10; Sanderson, 365; May, 225; A.L. Kennedy, 294.
35 London *Times*, November 11.
36 *The New York Times*, November 12.
37 Chadwick II, 465-467; Millis, 385-387.
38 *The New York Times*, November 18.
39 Chadwick II, 467-468.
40 Beale, 148; Renwick, xxvi.
41 Chadwick II, 468-469.
42 *Ibid.*
43 *Ibid.*, 470.
44 *The New York Times*, November 29.
45 Cortissoz, 250-251.
46 *The New York Times*, December 7.
47 *Ibid.*
48 Beisner, 165-185.
49 Thayer, 198-199.
50 Cong. Rec. 55th Cong., 3d Sess. p. 20.
51 *Ibid.*, p. 93.
52 Beisner, 139, 152-153.
53 *The New York Times*, December 11.
54 *Ibid.*
55 Koenig, 287-291.
56 *Ibid.*

57 *Ibid.*

58 *Ibid.*

59 *The New York Times*, December 13.

60 *Ibid.*, December 15.

61 Cong. Rec. 55th Cong., 3d Sess. p.296.

62 *Ibid.*, 295.

63 *Ibid*, 328.

64 *Ibid.*, 325.

65 *Ibid.*, 326.

66 *Ibid.*, 330.

67 London *Times*, December 25 and 26

68 *The New York Times*, December 25

69 London *Times*, December 31, 1898.

CHAPTER TWENTY

1 Pratt, 347.

2 For a general discussion of the ratification debate *see* Pratt, 345-360; Leech, 353-358; Millis, 398-403.

3 Koenig, 291-293.

4 Leech, 358.

5 Warren III, 430-433.

6 Koenig, 322-333.

7 Morris, 712-717.

8 *Ibid.*, 711, 717-721.

9 *Ibid.*, 719-729.

10 Leech, 554.

11 Morris, 734.

12 O'Toole, 388; Millis, 402

13 O'Toole, 391-392, 395.

14 Perkins, 89-90.

15 *Ibid.*, 173-183.

16 *Ibid.*, 188-193.

17 Harbaugh, 286-292. For a complete discussion, *see* Beale, 354-387.

18 Morison II, 1051.

19 Morison IV, 1092.

20 Massie, 274-275, 296-303.

21 W. Churchill, *Great Contemporaries*, 57.

22 Massie, 301-303.

23 British Documents II, 68; Massie, 305-306.

24 Amery IV, 173.

25 Massie, 309.

26 *Ibid.*, 180-185.

27 Andrew, 91; Langer, 576.

28 Bates, 177-181; Massie, 342.

29 Andrew, 118.

30 Massie, 343.

31 Bates, 173-175; 184-186; Grenville, 218.

32 Bredin, 372-376; Tuchman, *Proud Tower*, 216-219.

33 Bredin, 383, 387-389.

34 *Ibid.*, 400-429.

35 Lewis, *Prisoner*, 298-318.

36 Tuchman, *Proud Tower*, 226.

37 Lewis, *Prisoner*, 320-322.

38 Marrus and Paxton, 343-372; Zuccotti, 278-289.

39 Marrus and Paxton, 343-372; Zuccotti, 286 (quoting Leon Poliakov).

40 Tuchman, *Proud Tower*, 251-267; C. Davis, 37.

41 *Ibid.*, 282-288.

42 *Ibid.*, 288.

43 London *Times*, January 1, 1901.

44 Morris, 728-729.

45 *See* Friedman, "Dear Dr. Greenspan," *The New York Times*, February 9, 1997.

Bibliography

GOVERNMENT DOCUMENTS

British Documents on the Origins of the War, 1898–1994, ed. G.P. Gooch and Harold Temperley, London, His Majesty's Stationery Office, 1927–1928, Vol. 1

Congressional Record

Papers Relating to the Foreign Relations of the United States, 1898. Washington, U.S. Government Printing Office

German Diplomatic Documents 1871-1914, translated by E.T.S. Dugdale, London, Methuen, Vol. 2, 1928.

Parliamentary Papers entitled "*Correspondence with the French Government Concerning the Valley of the Upper Nile*" and "*Further Correspondence Respecting the Valley of the Upper Nile*," London, Her Majesty's Stationery Office, 1898

BOOKS

Adams, Henry. *The Education of Henry Adams*. New York, Modern Library, 1931

Alexander, DeAlva S. *A Political History of New York State*. Vol. 4 "Four Famous New Yorkers." New York, 1923.

Andrew, Christopher. *Theophile Delcassé and the Making of the Entente Cordiale*. London, Macmillan & St. Martin's Press, 1968.

Arthur, Sir George. *Life of Lord Kitchener*. London, Macmillan, Vol. 1, 1920.

Bacon, Admiral Sir Reginald, *The Life of Lord Fisher of Kilverstone*, London, Hodder & Stoughton, Vol. 1, 1929.

Bates, Darrell. *The Fashoda Incident: Encounter on the Nile*. Oxford, 1984.

Beale, Howard K. *Theodore Roosevelt and the Rise of America to World Power*. Johns Hopkins, 1956.

Beer, Thomas. *Hanna, Crane and the Mauve Decade*. Knopf, 1941.

Beisner, Robert L.. *Twelve Against Empire—The Anti-Imperialists*, 1898-1900. New York, McGraw-Hill, 1968.

Bemis, Samuel Flagg. *The American Secretaries of State and Their Diplomacy*, Cooper Square Publishers, 1963-1972.

Bowers, Claude G. *Beveridge and the Progressive Era*. Riverside Press, 1932.

Bredin, Jean-Denis. *The Affair—The Case of Alfred Dreyfus*. Translated by Jeffrey Mehlman. New York, Braziller, 1986.

Brown, Charles H. *The Correspondent's War*. New York, Scribners, 1967.

Brown, Frederick. *Zola: A Life*. New York, Farrar Straus, 1995.

Buckle, George F. *The Letters of Queen Victoria, 1886–1901*. New York, Longmans Green, Vol. III, 1932.

Bülow, Prince Bernhard von. *Memoirs*. Boston, Little, Brown, Vol. I, 1931–1932..

Busbey, L. White. *Uncle Joe Cannon*. New York, Henry Holt, 1927.

Carr, Edward Hallett. *The Russian Revolution, 1917–1923*. Macmillan, Vol. 1, 1931.

Cecil, Lady Gwendolen. *Life of Robert, Marquis of Salisbury*. London, Hodder & Stoughton, Vol. III, 1921-1932.

Cecil, Lamar. *Wilhelm II, Prince and Emperor—1859–1902*. University of North Carolina Press, Chapel Hill and London, 1987.

Cervera y Topete, Pascual. *The Spanish American War: A Collection of Documents Relative to the Squadron Operations in the West Indies*. Washington, U.S. Government Printing Office, 1899.

Chadwick, French Ensor. *The Relations of the United States and Spain: The Spanish American War*. New York, 1911.

Chamberlin, William Henry. *The Bolshevik Revolution*. Macmillan, Vol. 1, 1925.

Chapman, Guy. *The Dreyfus Case: A Reassessment*. New York, Reynal, 1955.

Churchill, Randolph. *Winston S. Churchill, Youth, 1874-1900*. Boston, Houghton Mifflin, 1966.

_____. *Companion Volume, Part 2 (1896–1900)*. Boston, Houghton Mifflin, 1966. ("Companion").

Churchill, Winston S. *Great Contemporaries*. New York, G.P. Putnam's Sons, 1937.

_____. *The Great Democracies*. New York, Dodd, Mead, 1958.

_____. *My Early Life*. New York, Scribners, 1930.

_____. *The River War*. Longmans Green, 1899.

_____. *A Roving Commission.* New York, Scribners, 1950.

_____. *Young Winston's Wars.* New York, Viking, 1973.

Collier, Kenton J. *John Hay: The Gentleman as Diplomat.* Ann Arbor, University of Michigan, 1975.

Cortissoz, Royal. *The Life of Whitelaw Reid.* Thornton & Butterworth, 1921.

Crankshaw, Edward. *Bismarck.* New York, Viking, 1981.

Davis, Calvin De Armond. *The United States and the First Hague Peace Conference.* Cornell, 1962.

Davis, Forest. *The Atlantic System.* New York, Reynal Hitchcock, 1941.

Dennett, Tyler. *John Hay—From Poetry to Politics.* New York, Dodd, Mead, 1933.

Dugdale, Blanche E.C. *Arthur James Balfour.* London, Hutchinson, Vol. I, 1939.

Dulles, Foster Rhea. *The Imperial Years.* New York, Crowell, 1956.

Epler, Percy H. *The Life of Clara Barton.* New York, Macmillan, 1930.

Ferrara, Orestes. *The Last Spanish War, Translated by William E. Shea.* New York, Paisley, 1937.

Foner, Philip S. *The Spanish Cuban-American War and the Birth of American Imperialism.* New York, Monthly Review Press, 1972.

Garvin, J.L. and Amery, Julian. *The Life of Joseph Chamberlain.* London, Macmillan, 1932–1851.

Giffen, Morrison A. *Fashoda—The Incident and Its Diplomatic Setting.* University of Chicago, 1930.

Gooch, G.P. *Before the War: Studies in Diplomacy.* London, Longmans Green, 1928.

Grenville, J.A.S. *Lord Salisbury and Foreign Policy: The Close of the Nineteenth Century.* Athlone Press, University London, 1964.

Harbaugh, William Henry. *Power and Responsibility: The Life and Times of Theodore Roosevelt.* New York, Farrar, Straus, 1961

Healey, David. *U.S. Expansionism—The Imperialist Urge in the 1890s.* University of Wisconsin, 1970.

Hendrick, Burton J. *The Training of an American: The Earlier Life and Letters of Walter H. Page, 1855-1913.* Boston and New York, Houghton Mifflin, 1928.

Hobson, Richmond Pearson. *The Sinking of the "Merrimac."* New York, 1899.

Iriye, Akira. *Pacific Estrangement: Japanese and American Expansion, 1879–1911.* Cambridge, Harvard University Press, 1973.

James, Henry. *Richard Olney and His Public Service.* New York, Houghton Mifflin, 1923.

Jenkins, Roy. *Gladstone.* London, Macmillan, 1995.

Jessup, Philip C. *Elihu Root.* New York, Dodd, Mead, Vol. I, 1938.

Kennedy, A.L. *Salisbury, 1830-1903.* London, John Murray, 1953.

Kennedy, Paul. *The Rise of the Anglo-German Antagonism.* London, Allen & Unwin, 1979.

Koenig, Louis P. *Bryan.* New York, Putnams, 1971.

Langer, William L. *The Diplomacy of Imperialism.* New York and London, Knopf, 1935.

Leech, Margaret. *In the Days of McKinley.* New York, Harper & Row, 1959.

Lewis, David Levering. *Prisoners of Honor—The Dreyfus Affair.* New York, Henry Holt, Owl Edition, 1994.

_____. *The Race to Fashoda.* New York, Henry Holt, Owl Edition, 1995.

Lodge, Henry Cabot. *Selections from the Correspondence of Theodore Roosevelt and Henry Cabot Lodge, 1884-1918.* New York, Scribners, Vol. 1, 1925.

Magnus, Philip. *Kitchener: Portrait of an Imperialist.* London, John Murray, 1958.

Manchester, William. *The Last Lion—Winston Spencer Churchill.* Boston, Little Brown.

_____. *Visions of Glory, 1874-1932,* 1983.

_____. *Alone, 1932-1940,* 1988.

Marder, Arthur J. *The Anatomy of British Seapower: A History of British Naval Policy in the Pre-Dreadnought Era, 1880–1905.* New York, Octagon Books, 1976.

Marek, George R. *The Eagles Die: Franz Joseph, Elizabeth, and Their Austria.* New York, Harper & Row, 1974.

Marrus, Michael D. and Paxton, Robert O. *Vichy France and the Jews.* Basic Books, 1988.

Massie, Robert K. *Dreadnought: Britain, Germany and the Coming of the Great War.* New York, Random House, 1991.

Maurois, Andre. *The Edwardian Era.* New York, Appleton-Century, 1933.

_____. *A History of France.* New York, Farrar, Straus, 1956.

May, Ernest R. *Imperial Diplomacy.* New York, Harcourt, Brace, 1961.

McDougal, Walter A. *Let the Sea Make a Loud Noise . . . A History of the North Pacific from Magellan to MacArthur.* Basic Books. 1993.

Millis, Walter. *The Martial Spirit.* Chicago, Dee, Elephant Paperbacks, 1989.

Moorhead, Alan. *The White Nile.* New York, Harper & Row, 1960.

Morison, Samuel Eliot. *The Oxford History of the American People.* New York, Oxford, 1965.

Morris, Edmund. *The Rise of Theodore Roosevelt.* New York, Coward, McCann & Geoghegan, 1979.

Morrison, Elting E. and Blum, John, eds. *The Letters of Theodore Roosevelt.* Harvard, Vols 1 and 2, 1951. (Sequential paging).

Neillands, Robin. *The Dervish Wars: Gordon & Kitchener in the Sudan 1880–1898.* London, John Murray, 1996.

Novick, Sheldon M. *Honorable Justice: The Life of Oliver Wendell Holmes.* Boston, Little Brown, 1989.

Nowak, Karl Friedrich. *Germany's Road to Ruin.* New York, Macmillan, 1932.

Olcott, Charles S. *The Life of William McKinley.* Boston, Houghton Mifflin, 1916.

O'Toole, G. J. A. *The Spanish War: An American Epic 1898.* New York, Norton, 1984.

O'Toole, Patricia. *The Five of Hearts: An Intimate Portrait of Henry Adams and His Friends 1880–1918.* New York, Clarkson Potter, 1990 ("P. O'Toole").

Pakenham, Thomas. *The Scramble for Africa, 1876–1912.* London, Weidenfeld & Nicolson, 1991.

Perkins, Bradford. *The Great Rapprochement.* New York, Athenaeum, 1968.

Pratt, Julius W. *The Expansionists of 1898.* Baltimore, Johns Hopkins, 1936.

Pringle, Henry F. *Theodore Roosevelt.* New York, Harcourt, Brace, 1931.

Renwick, Sir Rolin. *Fighting with Allies: America and Britain in Peace and War.* New York, Times Books, 1996.

Reuter, Bertha Ann. *Anglo-American Relations During the Spanish-American War.* New York, Macmillan, 1924.

Rhodes, James Ford. *The McKinley and Roosevelt Administrations, 1897–1909.* New York, Macmillan, 1922.

Rich, Norman. *Friedrich von Holstein: Politics and Diplomacy in the Era of Bismarck and Wilhelm II.* Cambridge University Press, Vol. 1, 1965.

Roosevelt, Theodore. *An Autobiography.* New York, 1913.

_____. *The Rough Riders.* New York, 1899.

Royle, Trevor. *The Kitchener Enigma.* London, Michael Joseph, 1985.

Sanderson, G.N. *England, Europe and the Upper Nile.* Edinburgh, 1965.

Sargent, Nathan. *Admiral Dewey and the Manila Campaign.* Naval Historical Foundation, 1947.

Shirer, William L. *The Collapse of the Third Republic: An Inquiry into the Fall of France in 1940.* New York, Simon & Schuster, 1969.

Sigsbee, Charles D. *The Maine.* New York, 1899.

Smith-Dorrien, Sir Horace Lockwood. *Memoirs of Forty-Eight Years Service.* London, John Murray, 1925.

Snyder, Louis L. *The Dreyfus Case—A Documentary History.* New Brunswick, Rutgers University Press, 1973.

Spector, Ronald. *Admiral of the New Empire.* Baton Rouge, Louisiana State University Press, 1974

Steinberg, Jonathan. *Yesterday's Deterrent: Tirpitz and the Birth of the German Battle Fleet.* New York, Macmillan, 1965.

Taylor, A.J.P. *The Struggle For Mastery In Europe, 1848–1918.* Oxford, 1954.

_____. *Bismarck: The Man and the Statesman.* New York, Knopf, 1961.

Thayer, William Roscoe. *The Life of John Hay.* Boston, Houghton Mifflin, Vol. II., 1915,

Tirpitz, Grand Admiral Alfred von. *My Memoirs.* New York, Dodd, Mead, Vol. 1., 1919.

Tuchman, Barbara. *The Guns of August.* New York, Macmillan, 1962.

_____. *The Proud Tower: A Portrayal of the World before the War, 1890–1914.* New York, Macmillan, 1966.

Warren, Charles. *The Supreme Court in United States History.* Boston, Little, Brown, 1923.

Weems, John Edward. *The Fate of the Maine.* New York, Henry Holt, 1958.

White, William Allen. *Autobiography.* Macmillan, 1946.

Wolff, Leon. *Little Brown Brother*. New York, Doubleday, 1961.

Zuccotti, Susan. *The Holocaust, The French and The Jews*. Basic Books, 1973.

ARTICLES

Bailey, Thomas A. *Dewey and the Germans at Manila Bay*. American Historical Review, October, 1959.

Beale, Truston, *Strategical Value of the Philippines*. North American Review, June, 1898.

Churchill, Winston S. *The Fashoda Incident*. North American Review, December, 1898.

Kennedy, Paul M. *German World Policy and the Alliance Negotiations with England, 1897–1900*. Journal of Modern History, December, 1973.

Morgan, John T. *What Shall We Do with the Conquered Islands?* North American Review, June, 1898.

Riker T.W. *A Survey of British Policy in the Fashoda Crisis*. Political Science Quarterly, Vol. XXIV, No. 1.

Shippee, Lester Burrell. *Germany and the Spanish-American War*. American Historical Review, July, 1925.

NEWSPAPERS

London *Times*

The New York Times

Index

367